PRAISE FOR *Social Justice Isn't What You Think It Is*

I have read this book with real delight. Clear, profound, inspiring, and brilliant.—ROCCO BUTTIGLIONE, Italian Chamber of Deputies

Novak and Adams write with compelling clarity and force. They make a rich contribution to our understanding of social justice and the policy implications that flow from it.—CHARLES J. CHAPUT, O.F.M. CAP., Archbishop of Philadelphia

A profound treatise on a topic dear to the heart of political progressives and social work professionals. Those who have never given the meaning of social justice a second thought will be greatly rewarded with reflective insights and a new understanding. Those who think they know the meaning of social justice will be challenged to think again—and more deeply.—NEIL GILBERT, Chernin Professor of Social Welfare, University of California, Berkeley

Elegantly, winsomely, and with telling examples, Novak and Adams show how Catholic social thought challenges conventional "liberal" and "conservative" approaches to social issues. This is a terrific book for anyone who is prepared to look anew at the dilemmas facing a society that aspires to be both free and compassionate.—MARY ANN GLENDON, Professor of Law, Harvard University

A distinctively *caritas* and catholic take on the concept of social justice that is rich in its originality, provocative, thoughtful in exposition, challenging us to transform our approach to social policy.—JOHN BRAITHWAITE, Distinguished Professor, Australian National University

This book presents an innovative vision of social justice as a preeminent, creative, and outgoing virtue deeply rooted in genuine Catholic social thought. It provides an indispensable guide for advancing the common good in a contemporary landscape plagued by a pervasive secularism and an extreme moral relativism.—WILLIAM C. BRENNAN, Professor, School of Social Work, Saint Louis University

The challenge of writing about Catholic social thought is that doing so expertly requires prodigious learning in not only the Catholic tradition, but also in so many contiguous fields—such as economics, politics, law, theology, philosophy. Thankfully, our authors are masters of their craft. And they have produced a marvelous restatement, and interpretation, of this important body of Church teaching.—GERARD V. BRADLEY, Professor of Law, University of Notre Dame

Before reading this book, I was suspicious of the phrase social justice. In Latin America, politicians and policy makers who use the social justice banner have committed many injustices. Acting supposedly on behalf of the general interest, the common good, or the poor, government programs essentially concentrate power, bloat bureaucracies, and often promote corruption. Novak and Adams surprised me when they distilled, from Catholic social thought and other sources, a definition centered on free individuals, as opposed to the Leviathan state. The Novak seal is evident because the definition emphasizes innovation, creativity, and human flourishing. Here, social justice, like plain justice, is a virtue "that empowers individual persons to act for themselves, to exercise their inborn social creativity." How much will societies improve when they embrace this paradigm of social justice instead of the statist conception?—CARROLL RIOS DE RODRIGUEZ, Professor of Economics, Francisco Marroquín University, Guatemala

Social Justice Isn't What You Think It Is by Michael Novak and Paul Adams is a thoughtfully iconoclastic analysis and exposition of social justice as a virtue through the lens of Catholic social teaching—rejecting both individualism and collectivism and emphasizing the role of mediating social structures. Paul Adams, in particular, explores the application of social justice for Christians in professional social work. This book is an important resource for everyone interested in social justice and Christian practice. —DAVID A. SHERWOOD, Editor-in-Chief, *Social Work & Christianity*

No concept in ethical and political philosophy is more in need of clarification and critical analysis than that of "social justice." This term is a relatively late arrival in Catholic vocabulary. Novak and Adams provide a careful, thorough analysis of the term and the ideas and approach that make it useful. They also explain the ease with which the term can be misused. This is a very welcome book, not to be missed by anyone at all concerned with public order and understanding.—JAMES V. SCHALL, S.J., Professor Emeritus, Georgetown University

Michael Novak and Paul Adams's new book places the important discussion of social justice squarely within the best scholarship of the Catholic intellectual tradition. By transcending ideological biases, reading and interpreting the pertinent encyclicals impartially, and avoiding all political agendas, this thought-provoking new book should be welcomed by both the left and the right because of its fair, balanced, and reasoned approach. —JOHN G. TRAPANI, JR., Professor of Philosophy, Walsh University

The difficult and risky underground publication of Novak's *The Spirit of Democratic Capitalism* in 1985 was widely circulated among the Polish democratic opposition and inspired many debates about how to shape the free Poland for which we fought. This new book will remind Poles of the breathtaking appearance of *SDC* 30 years ago. When small groups discussed with John Paul II Novak's ideas, including those on social justice and others in the present volume, the pope several times said he considered Novak one of his best lay friends in the West. On those occasions when Novak was present, the pope listened with great attention.—MACIEJ ZIEBA, O.P., author of *Papal Economics: The Catholic Church on Democratic Capitalism, from* Rerum Novarum *to* Caritas in Veritate

Novak and Adams take on the hard task of defining social justice, which they identify as a personal virtue of a special modern type. Novak is unusually aware of abuses of the term by statists in former socialist lands like Slovakia, the country of his ancestors. Adams is especially good on the connection between charity and justice, and on the relation of marriage to both. Here in Europe, this book does a great and original service.—JURAJ KOHUTIAR, emeritus Director of International Affairs, Slovak Christian-Democratic Party, former anticommunist dissident and "Underground Church" activist

I lived half of my life in Argentina, where the overwhelming majority adopted as a guiding policy principle a statist concept of social justice. I lived my other half in the United States, where many have practiced social justice as explained by Adams and Novak, building the institutions of a free and charitable society. Argentina was destroyed; the United States still has a chance. This immensely valuable book provides rich foundations for those who love liberty, justice, and a social environment conducive to human flourishing. —ALEJANDRO CHAFUEN, President, Atlas Network, and 2014 winner of the Walter Judd Freedom Award

SOCIAL JUSTICE
Isn't What You Think It Is

MICHAEL NOVAK & PAUL ADAMS

with ELIZABETH SHAW

ENCOUNTER BOOKS

New York   London

First American edition published in 2015 by Encounter Books,
an activity of Encounter for Culture and Education, Inc.,
a nonprofit, tax exempt corporation.
Encounter Books website address: www.encounterbooks.com

Manufactured in the United States and printed on
acid-free paper. The paper used in this publication meets
the minimum requirements of ANSI/NISO Z39.48–1992
(R 1997) (*Permanence of Paper*).

FIRST AMERICAN EDITION

LIBRARY OF CONGRESS CATALOGING-IN-PUBLICATION DATA
Novak, Michael.
Social justice isn't what you think it is /
Michael Novak, Paul Adams with Elizabeth Shaw.
pages cm
Includes bibliographical references and index.
ISBN 978-1-59403-827-3 (hardback) — ISBN 978-1-59403-828-0 (ebook)
1. Social justice—Religious aspects—Catholic Church. 2. Christian sociology—
Catholic Church. I. Adams, Paul, 1943– II. Title.
BX1795.J87N68 2015
261.8—dc23
2015017129

Dedicated to

Kelli Steele Adams in love and gratitude

and to

Karen Laub Novak (1937–2009)
for the energy that flows from her still.

MATERIAL ADAPTED AND USED WITH PERMISSION

Chapters 1 and 2: "Defining Social Justice," *First Things* (December 2000); "Three Precisions: Social Justice," *First Things* (December 1, 2010).

Chapters 3 and 4: "Hayek: Practitioner of Social Justice," in *Three in One: Essays on Democratic Capitalism, 1976–2000*, ed. Edward Younkins (Lanham, Md.: Rowman & Littlefield Publishers, 2001).

Chapter 9: "Social Justice Redefined: Pius XI," in *The Catholic Ethic and the Spirit of Capitalism* (New York: Free Press, 1993).

Chapter 10: "The Fire of Invention, the Fuel of Interest," in *The Fire of Invention: Civil Society and the Future of the Corporation* (Lanham, Md.: Rowman & Littlefield Publishers, 1997).

Chapters 10 and 11: "Capitalism Rightly Understood," in *The Catholic Ethic and the Spirit of Capitalism* (New York: The Free Press, 1993).

Chapter 12: "Pope Benedict XVI's *Caritas*," *First Things* (August 17, 2009).

Chapter 13: "Agreeing with Pope Francis," *National Review Online* (December 7, 2013).

CONTENTS

Acknowledgments, vii

Introduction *by Paul Adams*, 1

$$\left[\quad \text{PART ONE} \quad \text{The Theory} \quad \right]$$
by Michael Novak

DEFINITIONS, CONTEXT

1 Social Justice Isn't What You Think It Is, 15

2 Six Secular Uses of "Social Justice," 29

3 A Mirage? 37

4 Friedrich Hayek, Practitioner of Social Justice, 49

5 Sixteen Principles of Catholic Social Thought:
The Five Cs, 55

6 The Five Rs, 65

7 The Six Ss, 78

THE POPES ON SOCIAL JUSTICE

8 Leo XIII's *Rerum Novarum*, 89

9 Forty Years Later: Pius XI, 106

10 American Realities and Catholic Social Thought, 121

11 *Centesimus Annus*: Capitalism, No and Yes, 139

12 Benedict XVI and *Caritas in Veritate*, 156

13 Pope Francis on Unreformed Capitalism, 161

FURTHER CHALLENGES

14 A New Theological Specialty: The Scout, 172

15 Needed: A Sharper Sense of Sin, 180

$$\left[\begin{array}{l} \text{PART TWO} \quad \text{In Practice} \\ \qquad \text{by Paul Adams} \end{array} \right]$$

Introduction Getting beyond Dichotomies, 200

16 Conscience and Social Justice, 202

17 Marriage as a Social Justice Issue, 220

18 Practicing Social Justice, 237

19 From Charity to Justice? 252

20 Charity Needs *Caritas*—So Does Social Justice, 265

Epilogue Social Justice: In the Vast Social Space between the Person and the State *by Paul Adams and Michael Novak*, 273

Notes, 287

Index, 313

ACKNOWLEDGMENTS

ONE PERSON WITHOUT WHOM THIS BOOK WOULD NOT EXIST IS Elizabeth Shaw, who managed the master text of a multitude of drafts and redrafts, as we labored on our separate parts of the book. She also incorporated all the suggestions and corrections offered by other readers over several years and from several locations. In addition, she made countless creative suggestions of her own.

Two friends with long experience in Rome, Rocco Buttiglione and Andreas Widmer, were especially helpful in offering corrections and suggestions in several key chapters.

Many other close readers caught errors, raised pointed questions about ambiguities, and caused us to do much rewriting. Among these were Paul's colleagues Gerald Gillmore of the University of Washington and Gale Burford of the University of Vermont, as well as five especially impressive students at Ave Maria University: Sarah Blanchard, Angela Winkels, Catherine Glaser, Peter Atkinson, and Monica Bushling. Nor can we forget the insights and suggestions of Mitch Boersma of the American Enterprise Institute.

Finally, our thanks go out to Roger Kimball and his team at Encounter Books, most notably Katherine Wong and Heather Ohle.

As Tiny Tim said, "God bless you, every one!"

Introduction

Paul Adams

THE DEFINITION OF SOCIAL JUSTICE HAS RECEIVED LITTLE serious attention for two related reasons. From one perspective, developed by Friedrich Hayek in the most compelling critique of the term to date, social justice is a mirage.[1] It is meaningless, ideological, incoherent, vacuous, a cliché.[2] The term should be avoided, abandoned, and allowed to die a natural death, or else killed off in a few paragraphs, but it does not merit a book-length critique. Hayek himself did not follow this logic; he wrote a sustained critique of the concept rather than dismissing it out of hand, and, we suggest, he was an exemplar of the virtue in his own public life.

From another perspective, the political and ideological force of "social justice" may be seen—by critics as well as some calculating proponents—as useful in its functional vagueness. Sometimes a term is helpful in politics precisely because it is vague. For example, "maximum feasible participation" became an important part of the War on Poverty because it was unclear and no one could agree on what it actually meant.[3] Social justice is a term that can be used as an all-purpose justification for any progressive-sounding government program or newly discovered or invented right. The term survives because it benefits its champions. It brands opponents as supporters of social injustice, and so as enemies of humankind, without the trouble of making an argument or considering their views. As an ideological marker, "social justice" works best when it is not too sharply defined.[4]

So why attempt a level of precision in defining and using the concept when such a project is, according to one view, unachievable and, according to another, politically unhelpful to those who use it most?

ONE RECENT EXCEPTION to the lack of serious consideration of social justice that is neither partisan nor dismissive is Brandon Vogt's book, *Saints and Social Justice*.[5] Vogt expounds Catholic social teaching by describing the lives of exemplary saints who dedicated themselves to God and to the common good through works of mercy and efforts to improve the lot of the poor and oppressed.

Michael Novak and I also emphasize social justice as virtue and aim to recover it as a useful and indeed necessary concept in understanding how people ought to live and order their lives together. We seek to clarify the term's definition and proper use in the context of Catholic social teaching. We discuss its application in the context of democratic capitalism, in which, we argue, social justice takes on a new importance as a distinctively modern virtue required for and developed by participation with others in civil society.

On this last point we believe Vogt falls short. He sees social justice as a universal category independent of time and place. The popes after Leo XIII treat "social justice" as a *new* virtue, necessary for dealing with a new era in social history, and for countering the dread threat of secular, atheistic, and collectivist social movements such as "Socialism" as they understood it. In the twentieth century, as Leo XIII feared, those movements overran huge stretches of the world. They rode roughshod over the transcendent dimension of the human person. They also violated many basic human rights, such as the right to personal economic initiative, to property, to association, to personal creativity, and the liberty to speak openly and honestly, to worship publicly, and to maintain the integrity of the family against the state.

This larger *social struggle* evoked the call for a new social virtue, at first called "social charity" and then, with more permanence, "social justice." Thus the concept social justice is far larger and more sharply focused than the evangelical Beatitudes and their admirable expression in the lives of the saints. In a sense, the virtues of the saints did take root in individual persons and flower in their beautiful lives; and, indeed, they also contributed to the common good, whether at local or at wider levels. But the depth of the modern social crisis requires a nontraditional—a "new"— response to new and unprecedented ruptures with the agrarian, more personal world of the past. National states became vastly larger, more powerful, and far more intrusive (abetted by new modern technologies) than any traditional authorities of the past. "Citizens" gained greater responsibilities than the "subjects" of the kings and emperors of the past. As Leo XIII and Pius XI grasped—and later popes elaborated, extended, and revised—the new "social justice" required modes of analysis, reflection, and action never possible before.

I CAME UPON the issue over many years as a social-work educator, helping prepare students to practice in a profession that defined social justice as a core value. Social work's accrediting body holds all bachelors and masters social-work programs accountable for incorporating social justice into their mission and goals and for assuring that students achieve competency in this area.[6] So, in this field at least, "social justice" calls out for clarification and cannot be so easily dismissed as it might be by economists.

My own search for coherence and precision in a "core value" that could also guide practice aimed at the common good led me to the work of Michael Novak. Here was the Catholic philosopher, theologian, and social critic who had given the most serious public attention to the concept of social justice. Throughout his career, Novak had sought to discern how we should order our lives together so that the most poor, oppressed, and vulnerable could thrive. He sought to "promote human and community well-being,"[7] in the language of social work's accreditation standards, though, like me, he had been led by an overwhelming weight of evidence and experience to reconsider what actually furthers this purpose.[8]

Novak sought to rescue social justice from its ideological uses and to define and use the concept in a way that met four criteria. First, it should be consistent with Catholic tradition and the social encyclicals. Second, it should take account of the new things of the modern age, both the breakdown of traditional patterns of work and family and the American experience of democratic capitalism. Third, it needed to withstand the criticisms of those who considered the concept to be irretrievably incoherent. Fourth, it must be nonpartisan, and recognize both left and right (and other) uses of the specific habits and practices that constitute social justice rightly understood, namely, skills in forming associations to improve the common good of local communities, nations, and indeed the international community. Both left and right may compete to see who better accomplishes the common good in specific areas.

It was my immense privilege and joy to find in Michael Novak a new neighbor when my family moved to Ave Maria, Florida, where a new university was springing up as a center of Catholic learning and culture. I conceived the project of gathering the various pieces he had written on social justice over the years, some chapters in books on Catholic social thought and democratic capitalism, and some occasional articles or pieces for invited lectures or speeches at award dinners. I urged him to pull this work together into a full and current statement of his argument addressed to a wider audience interested in social justice than might have discovered these disparate pieces produced over four decades.

He agreed, and as we worked together over the next two years, it became apparent that these pieces could not simply be collected with some light editing into a book of essays. There was too much overlap—the story of Novak's family history as Slovak serfs and the new economic, political, and cultural freedoms they encountered in the New World, although compelling, could be told only once in the projected book.

More importantly, there was a need to expand the existing work into a comprehensive vision that situates social justice in a context of Catholic teaching, especially its social teaching as a whole, and also in the context of democratic capitalism and the American experience. This last point was especially important to understanding the profound contributions to Catholic social doctrine of Pius XI and John Paul II, who lived much of their lives and most of their reigns under the shadow of European fascism and communism. Catholic social teaching prior to John Paul II tended to be Eurocentric, ignoring or misunderstanding the American experience of economic, political, and cultural freedom, even in official documents. The American experiment was the first to lift a large majority of its poor (largely immigrants) out of poverty within a generation, and to keep on doing so. The United States was, as it were, the laboratory for how undeveloped peoples break through the chains of centuries of poverty. It was the first developing nation.

A WORD IS NECESSARY about the nature of Catholic social teaching itself, which is subject to two key distortions. The first is the problem Novak identified in a different but related context: namely, the tendency among the opponents of reform in the Second Vatican Council toward what he called "nonhistorical orthodoxy." This tendency neglects history and contingency, as if Catholic social teaching constitutes a single and unchanging body of doctrine, in no need of development or adaptation to new circumstances.

This is not the way the popes themselves have read and interpreted the Church's social teaching. Leo XIII initiated the series of papal social encyclicals by both affirming permanent principles and providing an analysis "of the new things" (Rerum Novarum) of his day. In commemorating Leo's encyclical forty years after its publication, Pius XI, in Quadragesimo Anno (1931), both reaffirmed core principles of Catholic social teaching and offered his analysis of how conditions had changed. He reiterated the evil of socialism in all its forms, but now in the context of actual experience of Communism in Russia and the rise of National Socialism in Germany and Fascism in Italy.

Commemorating the centennial of Rerum Novarum in 1991, John Paul II faced an even larger task of interpreting the signs of the times in light of the large historical changes wrought by the hypertrophy of the state under Nazism and Communism and the collapse of both. He had lived his entire adult life under the shadow of National Socialism or Communism, and he now faced the task of considering the alternatives, a question often asked of him by other survivors or former admirers of the Communist system. Answering them required a careful distinction between what is a permanent part of the Magisterium, the principles of Catholic social teaching that all popes have upheld, and what constitutes the fruits of a particular pope's pastoral responsibility in his own time and place.

In his great encyclical Centesimus Annus (1991), John Paul II proposes a rereading of Rerum Novarum—a looking back, a looking around, and a looking forward. He reiterates those principles enunciated by Leo XIII which belong to the Church's doctrinal patrimony, but he distinguishes his own analysis of recent events "in order to discern the new requirements of evangelization," without passing definitive judgments, since doing so does not fall within his authority.

Insisting on this distinction between principles and their application in a specific historical context, John Paul follows the Council Fathers of Vatican II, who had emphasized the responsibility of the informed laity. The popes and the Church have no specific expertise in matters of economic or social policy but call on lay members who do to contribute to the discussion.

Treating Catholic social teaching as a "nonhistorical orthodoxy," a body of doctrine independent of time and place, not subject to doctrinal development or rereading in the light of the "new things" of the time, can lead to a peculiar kind of clericalist rigidity. In place of serious and open discussion in light of core principles, too often it shuts down discussion, dismissing opponents as ignorant of the texts or heretical, and resorts to "proof-texting" by citing quotations from the papal documents out of context. Catholic scholar and blogger Andrew M. Haines offers an implicit rebuke of this tendency:

> Simply put, the Church's social teaching is valuable because it offers examples of how to think through the types of problems associated with making good social decisions. It is not valuable because it provides all the answers to every particular social question ever raised. Nor is it valuable because it instructs on the inviolable dignity of all human life. (Once again, that's another kind of doctrine.) Instead, I venture, Catholic social teaching is a sort of praxis rather than simply a set of theories—a very public praxis, conducted by those whose teaching authority is well established. Certainly it is not a set of absolute propositions that hold true always and everywhere. This is the case even for strongly worded and oft-repeated themes, since the significance of terms—especially politico-economic ones—is wont to shift almost overnight.[9]

Novak and I approach Catholic social teaching and the light it casts on social justice in this same spirit. It is always a work in progress, not one in which basic principles are up for grabs or that helps score points in partisan battles of the day. Instead it challenges us to think through the problems we face and how this rich body of teaching—based on firm Christian principles and developed over millennia in light of the new things that have come and gone—may guide us in responding to the urgent social needs of our time.

The second, related distortion that bedevils much discussion of Catholic social teaching is the tendency to use it in a partisan way to support specific policies or programs that are under debate at a given moment. One constant of Christian teaching from the time of Christ on earth to the present is concern for the poor. All those who write on Catholic social teaching give this concern a central place. But the principle does not warrant a moral mandate to support any particular policy or party line on how best to help the poor.

Some writers on social justice, especially on the left, are particularly prone to this error. If the issue of the day is, say, raising the minimum wage or rejecting proposed cuts in Food Stamps (neither of which existed until the last century and neither of which is common even in the most generous welfare states today), it is not enough to express concern for the poor and then draw a direct line to the policy you favor. It is necessary to show that the favored policy actually helps the poor—as opposed to increasing unemployment, or undermining incentives to work of those with low incomes, or easing consciences while immorally burdening future generations with a mountain of debt. On all these and many other areas of policy debate related to social justice, faithful Catholics can and do disagree.

SINCE POLITICAL CATEGORIES often take on different and changing meanings in the United States, Michael Novak is sometimes mistaken for a libertarian or economic liberal (in the nineteenth-century, laissez-faire sense), or individualist (where the contrast is with collectivist or statist liberals). Together, we think it is worth clarifying our stance on these issues, at the outset.

Social justice, as we define it, represents a decisive rejection of individualism and liberalism. The social encyclicals denounce the ideology of the atomistic, unencumbered, autonomous self, the freely choosing individual detached from culture, family, church, and community. That liberal or individualist view of the self and its expression in economic and social life rests on a relatively recent anthropology of the person that opposes centuries of classical and Catholic understanding from Aristotle to Aquinas. In this older tradition, accepted by all the popes, is a view of the person as irreducibly social, man as a political or social animal, reciprocally indebted from before birth and at every stage of life, even when some humans pridefully imagine they are nakedly independent. Indeed, our flourishing as humans depends on our developing certain social virtues and recognizing our dependence on and duty to others in our continued vulnerability.

Catholic social teaching and any understanding of social justice compatible with it reject the individualism in economics as well as in personal and sexual life that, say, Ayn Rand embraced. It is telling that John Paul II cited in both his *Theology of the Body* and *Centesimus Annus* that crucial passage from Vatican II's pastoral constitution on the Church in the modern world, *Gaudium et Spes*, in which the Council Fathers affirm that God created man for his own good and that he "cannot fully find himself except through a sincere gift of himself."[10] Mutual gifting plays an indispensable social role in human life.

There are Catholic writers of the left and right who cite such considerations as evidence that the Church, and Catholic social teaching in particular, is unalterably and consistently opposed to capitalism. But the Church is committed to the defense of private property, as well as to the fundamental duty of Catholics as individuals and as a body to help the poor. Moreover, it is a significant fact that, beset as it is with cronyism and corruption, capitalism is the greatest tool of social advance and economic development ever known. In the last few decades alone, it has lifted hundreds of millions out of dire poverty.[11]

In John Paul II's hands, this immense benefit to humanity is not simply a utilitarian or materialistic matter. The social dislocations and harsh conditions for workers and families that accompanied industrial development were a central concern of Leo XIII and subsequent Catholic social teaching. These social failures needed to be criticized in strong terms; they were never seen as an acceptable trade-off for economic growth.

Moreover, like the other popes, John Paul II rejects capitalism wherever the liberty and full development of the human person is impeded or injured:

> If by "capitalism" is meant a system in which freedom in the economic sector is not circumscribed within a strong juridical framework which places it at the service of human freedom in its totality and which sees it as a particular aspect of that freedom, the core of which is ethical and religious, then the reply is certainly negative.[12]

Exploring these issues here, we distinguish capitalism as an economic system from the ideology that attached to it from its beginnings—what Patrick Deneen, for example, calls the "radical individualistic presuppositions of capitalism."[13] This individualist-liberal ideology, to the extent it finds practical expression in selfish behavior, ignores the needs of others and acts as if the individual lived, or could live, in splendid isolation from family and community, law and custom, tradition and culture. But this ideology is, we suggest, incompatible not only with human flourishing but also with a flourishing capitalist economy. Capitalism as an economic system cannot thrive when it is unbridled, unfettered, uncircumscribed by a strong juridical framework that is at its core ethical and religious. As an economic system, capitalism or the inventive economy requires and builds up the social virtues, and languishes in their absence. It presupposes in practice the moral norms, networks, institutions, and relationships that Robert Putnam defined as social capital.[14] It requires freedom and order in the political and cultural spheres, not just the economic. It depends on trust, reciprocity, and the rule of law.[15] In practice, the institutions of capitalism are social through and through—not individualistic.

Our book, then, is not a defense of unfettered capitalism or individualism against statism or collectivism in its various forms. Patrick Burke, working from a strong libertarian perspective, has written a thoroughgoing critique of the term social justice as commonly used.[16] Like us, he sees social justice, rightly understood, as a personal virtue. But unlike us, he places blame for the term's socialistic misuse squarely on the popes from Pius XI on. In the name of justice, Burke's book makes a decisive break with Catholic social teaching, whereas ours is consistent with it. In common with the Catholic tradition that emphasizes the mediating structures or voluntary associations that comprise the "rich social life" of the associations,[17] we reject any interpretive framework that understands political or policy choices or tendencies solely in terms of individualism or collectivism. The autonomous, unencumbered individual and the all-encompassing state are not mutually exclusive alternatives, but reinforce each other, to the detriment of the common good of all.

The first and most substantial part of this book, by Michael Novak, examines these issues in three sections. The first deals with definitions and contexts, reviewing the range of uses of the concept of social justice and its place within the larger context of Catholic social teaching. The second examines the contributions of five popes with regard to social justice: Leo XIII, Pius XI, John Paul II, Benedict XVI, and Francis. The third section of Novak's part addresses both the special function of the theologian as social scout and explorer of new social terrain, and also some challenges to social justice, such as the role of sin in an adequate understanding of social justice.

We judged that if social justice is better understood as a virtue than a state of affairs, then it is necessary to show what that virtue looks like in practice and how seeing social justice this way casts light on how we should think about helping others. This is the subject of Part Two of the book. I had the task, as a lifelong social-work educator, of developing this aspect of the argument, and in my chapters I reflect on the following themes.

Conscience and the rights of conscience, held in the highest regard by the American founders, progressives, and people of faith, have come under increasing attack by today's liberal elites. Those, including social workers, who once championed conscience and conscience rights as a defense against the overweening state, have now abandoned not only the protection of conscience but also any coherent understanding of the concept.

Marriage also needs consideration as an issue of social justice. Why? Because its disintegration and redefinition (above all among the poorest parts of the population but increasingly among the middle class, too) are linked to almost every social problem that social workers are called to address. Neither individuals nor the state can make marriage as attainable to many as it once was.

Another practical consideration stems from the fact that social justice is officially a core value of social work. But social work has become tied to the state, in funding and the strings attached to it and in the legal mandates it follows in areas like child welfare. How does the coercive power of the state that lies behind child protection square with the helping and empowering self-image of the profession? What does it mean to practice the virtue of social justice in this setting?

Finally, I dwell on some issues that arise from the fact that social work evolved out of attempts in the nineteenth century to organize charity, to make it more responsive to the needs of the individuals and families it served. In spite of these origins, the profession has sought to distance itself from its own history ever since. What is the relation of social justice to charity? Notwithstanding the centrality of charity as a theological virtue (*caritas*) and as the daily practice of helping the poor, it remains in both senses something of an embarrassment for professional social work. Unlike "justice," charity appeals neither to social work's professional practices (treatment, psychotherapy) nor to its activist tendencies.

How then are we to understand the relation of charity to justice, and to social justice in particular? The last two chapters of Part Two try to disentangle the two senses of charity, and the relation of social justice to charity. Like all my chapters, they seek to address, however indirectly, the fundamental question at the heart of social work and all professional helping: What is the proper relation of formal to informal helping (or care and control), of the bureaucratic-professional state to the traditional ways long preceding the state, through which communities and families have addressed and resolved problems and conflicts? How do empowering and coercive aspects—common to all care and control, including the most informal parenting—relate to each other? How then do we understand social justice as the virtue of that large social space between individual and state, the flourishing of which is vital to the health of both?

Michael Novak and I have in mind as readers intelligent inquirers who are thoughtful citizens, often practitioners and not just scholars. Most will have some acquaintance with conventional uses of the concept of social justice, since the term has become ubiquitous in the political discussion of social and economic issues. We discuss these uses briefly, but hope to cast a brighter light on neglected aspects of these questions. The concept and the virtue of social justice have indispensable work to do.

PART ONE

The Theory

Michael Novak

CHAPTER 1

Social Justice Isn't What You Think It Is

"SOCIAL JUSTICE" IS ONE OF THE TERMS MOST OFTEN USED IN ethical and political discourse, but one will search in vain for definitions of it. Because of its fuzziness and warmth, everybody wants to share in it. There is a whole band of Catholics calling themselves "social justice Catholics." But they rarely give you a forthright definition of social justice, or an explanation of how their view differs from other views of social justice that are widely held.

It is true that Pope Leo XIII in 1891 was searching for a new virtue for "new times." Yet he didn't choose the term "social justice." He thought briefly about "social charity," then Pius XI in 1931 settled firmly on "social justice."

Today the term has slipped into being used so broadly that a fairly recent obituary in the diocesan paper of Wilmington, Delaware, reported that a dear Sister Maureen gave her entire life as a nun for "social justice." Sister Maureen was a missionary in Africa for forty-six years, cared for the sick, taught the young, and brought assistance to the suffering and the poor. Are we to gather that "social justice," then, is a synonym for the deeds we must do to "enter the kingdom of heaven," that is, care for the widows, the hungry, the poor, and those in prison?

Saint Matthew's gospel lays out the underlying principle of both the traditional and the new understandings of social justice in two meaty chapters (24 and 25). His account includes the warning that the Last Judgment will be, yes, quite "judgmental." It will also be sharply "non-inclusive." It will separate the sheep from the goats, and some indeed will be cast out:

> Then it will be their turn to ask, "Lord, when did we see you hungry or thirsty, a stranger or lacking clothes, sick or in prison, and did not come to your help?" Then he will answer, "In truth I tell you, in so far as you neglected to do this to one of the least of these, you neglected to do it to me." And they will go away to eternal punishment, and the upright to eternal life.[1]

As Professor Adams noted in his introduction, the modern papal concept of social justice seems to go rather far beyond the demands of the Beatitudes (which demand the contributions of all Christians, often in private and barely recognized ways) and the heroic efforts of the saints. The *new* virtue enunciated by Leo XIII and Pius XI invites new modes of analysis, for both strategic thinking and immediate practical thinking. It also invites new capacities for organization never before summoned into being.

I ONCE HEARD a young professor at the Catholic University of Ružomberok, Slovakia, say that he thinks of social justice as "an ideal arrangement of society, in which justice and charity are fully served." This description appealed to me, and yet I found something troubling in the fact that it pictures social justice as an ideal arrangement toward which society should progressively strive.

The American Socialist Irving Howe wrote in *Dissent* in 1954: "Socialism is the name of our desire."[2] He meant a dream of justice and equality and democracy. Is social justice also the name of a dream, but not exactly the socialist dream?

In our search for a definition of the term, we may also ask: To which genus does social justice belong? Is it a vision of a perfectly just society? Is it an ideal set of government policies? Is it a theory? Is it a practice? . . . In sum, is it a virtue, that is, a habit embodied in individual persons, or is it a social arrangement?

On another plane entirely, we may ask: Is social justice a nonreligious concept? Many secular sociologists and political philosophers use it that way, trying to tie it as closely as possible to the term "equality"—in the arithmetical French sense of *égalité*. Like the equals sign.

Or is social justice a religious term, evangelical in inspiration?

Has social justice become an ideological marker, favoring progressives over conservatives, Democrats over Republicans, social workers over corporate executives? Is that the sort of favor "social justice Catholics" mete out?

———

To understand the meaning of this term, "social justice," we need to do two things: first, walk through the origin and early development of the term. To know where we are going, we must first know where we have been.

Second, we need to seek out a fresh statement of the definition of social justice—one that is true to the original understanding, ideologically neutral among political and economic partisans, and applicable to the circumstances of today.

Then, in chapters three and four, we shall confront one of the severest critics of the "mirage" of social justice, Friedrich Hayek, and the irony that he himself *practiced* social justice.

Social Justice—A Brief History

Let us begin with the *locus classicus* of the term "social justice," which was made canonical in the encyclical *Quadragesimo Anno* of Pius XI in 1931. This was at the height of the Great Depression, a time of crisis for the capitalist world. Hitler was gaining power in Germany. Mussolini had been ruling in Italy for nearly a decade. Stalin was about to stage the systematic starvation of millions of Ukrainians for clinging to their private property.

The occasion for Pius's encyclical was the fortieth anniversary of the first papal document on economic life. To begin, then, we must understand the eponymous "new things" in cultural and economic life at the turn of the nineteenth century, which prompted Leo XIII to write *Rerum Novarum* in 1891.

A quick aside: Popes are duty-bound to be concerned with the life of the spirit and with eternity. If humans do not work in the light of eternity, there will be an important dimension missing in their lives. This was Tocqueville's point when he said that religion is the first institution of democracy. Unless you understand that every human being has a transcendent importance beyond any pragmatic or utilitarian consideration, you cannot understand the meaning of human rights. That is the crucial frame of reference that religion supplies to democracy. For this reason, Tocqueville thought, in the United States, as distinguished from Europe, religion and liberty were lucky to have remained friends, because the doctrine of rights received its proper foundation in the Creator. As he wrote:

> I have already said enough to put Anglo-American civilization in its true light. It is the product (and this point of departure must always be kept in mind) of two perfectly distinct elements that elsewhere are often at odds. But in America, these two have been successfully blended, in a way, and marvelously combined. I mean the spirit of religion and the spirit of liberty. . . .
>
> Far from harming each other, these two tendencies, apparently so opposed, move in harmony and seem to offer mutual support.
>
> Religion sees in civil liberty a noble exercise of the faculties of man; in the political world, a field offered by the Creator to the efforts of intelligence. Free and powerful in its sphere, satisfied with the place reserved for it, religion knows that its dominion is that much better established because it rules only by its own strength and dominates hearts without other support.
>
> Liberty sees in religion the companion of its struggles and triumphs, the cradle of its early years, the divine source of its rights. Liberty considers religion as the safeguard of mores, mores as the guarantee of laws and the pledge of its own duration.[3]

In any case, with *Rerum Novarum* Leo XIII departed from the traditional papal consideration of eternal things to consider what was happening in the social economy of Europe. He did so because, as people began living longer, subsistence farms could no longer sustain growing families, and people were being driven from the countryside. When a father died, the eldest son inherited the farm; younger sons had to leave and find work elsewhere. They emigrated to North and South America and to the newly industrializing cities of Europe. These vast migrations to urban environments had devastating effects on traditional family life and, therefore, on the Christian faith. So, in the name of the family, Leo XIII decided to address the social crisis of the late nineteenth century.

In particular, Leo came to the defense of industrial workers. At any earlier time, he would have had to address an encyclical primarily to farmers because, for centuries, farming had been the occupation of 90 percent of the people on earth. In 1891, many of the world's leading philosophers and greatest minds thought that socialism would be the system of the future. To the contrary, Pope Leo listed a dozen reasons why socialism would prove to be not only evil, but also futile.

Flash forward to 1931 and *Quadragesimo Anno*. In this encyclical Pius XI pointed out the many successful reforms undertaken in capitalist economies since 1891. Still aware of the gathering storm, he urged the nations to address more seriously the social crisis still wracking Europe. On nine different occasions in the encyclical, he used the relatively new term "social justice" to designate his ideal. In other words, a sense of crisis and change was built into the term, or at least surrounded it.

The basic idea behind social justice has its roots in Aristotle and in medieval thought. The core of the ancient idea—then called "general justice"—may be adumbrated by the following: In times of war, occupation, and exile, it was hard for individuals to live sound moral lives. Order broke down; the rule of *homo homini lupus* ("man is a wolf to man") prevailed. The ethics of individuals, wise men observed, are much affected by the ethos of the city in which they live. Thus, the readiness to make sacrifices, to maintain the health and strength of the city, seemed to be good and virtuous, and needed a special name, beyond the simple "justice" that consists of giving each individual his due. This concept of general justice was not sharply developed until the twentieth century, but its roots were ancient. It pointed to a form of justice whose object was not just other individuals, but the community.

Nowadays, many people speak fervently of "social justice." Progressives everywhere speak of it; the Communists loved the term. Everybody has heard of it, but very few have defined it. Even in 1931, important commentators on Pius XI displayed considerable confusion. Allow me to quote the Jesuit priest who probably drafted the encyclical, a brilliant thinker who died at the age of 104, Oswald von Nell-Breuning. Nell-Breuning wrote:

> The encyclical *Quadragesimo Anno* has finally and definitively established, theologically canonized, so to speak, social justice. Now, it is our duty to study it, according to this strict requirement of scientific theology. And to give it its proper place in the structure of the Christian doctrine of virtue on the one hand and the doctrine of rights and justice on the other.[4]

Note the fateful ambiguity. We are left to wonder: Is social justice an abstract, regulative ideal? Some people who note a growing disparity of income in the United States say that such inequality is a sin against social justice. Is that the true meaning of the term? Or is social justice a virtue that individuals practice? Does the term refer to something inherent in society or to something inherent in individuals?

———

Here we must take an abbreviated tour through the terrain of virtue. In the ancient city of Athens in the time of Aristotle, there were roughly 300,000 inhabitants, most of them slaves. The consequence was that every Greek male citizen who was free and able to vote (about 30,000 men) needed to learn the arts of war. He needed to know how to handle a sword, a spear, and a horse and chariot. Such skills were crucial to defending the city, which was constantly in danger of being overrun by enemies far and near. In addition, the young men needed to learn the arts of peace. They needed to know how to persuade, how to make laws, and how to run an estate. By the time he was eighteen, a young Greek male was expected to be well-versed in these and other habits and skills.

That is what they meant by virtue: the kind of habit (or skill) you are not born with and do not always use, but which you develop and, when called upon, deploy. Virtue means those habits in particular that help a man to govern his passions and emotions so that he can act through reflection and choice. Virtues (and vices) are the habits that make you the distinctive kind of person you are. They define your character. A man who has prudence, for example, deliberates well and is reliable in action.

Until the 1930s, most education in America, especially in Sunday school, at the YMCA, and through the McGuffey Readers in the schools, concentrated on training in character, on bringing up Americans of sound habits. Why? Because if people do not know how to manage their passions and emotions when they make decisions, they cannot govern themselves. "Confirm thy soul in self-control," runs the old hymn; "Thy liberty in law." Citizens who cannot practice self-control cannot succeed at republican self-government. Without self-controlled citizens, the American experiment must fail.

To return to the main theme: Virtue is something you have to learn and master through practice. True, some people seem to be "naturals" at certain things and hardly have to learn them; virtues sometimes seem to be gifts some people are born with. For others, this or that virtue is a hard-earned self-modification. Once attained, however, it is an enduring and stable part of one's character. George Washington had a combustible temper when he was young, but by middle age he had disciplined it to achieve his legendary calm.

Now, is social justice such a virtue? As Friedrich Hayek points out, most of those who use the term today do not talk about what individuals can do. They talk about what government can do.[5] They talk about social justice as a characteristic of political states. Often they mean, in particular, situations of inequality, to be remedied by state-enforced redistribution. In most modern progressive usage, the cry for social justice is not a cry for greater virtue on the part of the citizenry. Indeed, the citizenry is deemed to lack sufficient virtue to such an extent that the state must intervene and effect by coercion the redistribution that individuals lack the virtue to effect on their own.

In brief, Hayek's challenge is the following: Either the modern term "social justice" refers to a virtue to be practiced by individuals, in which case it retains its claim to the traditional language of virtue, or else it refers to a state of affairs in society, in which case it is not about individuals or their habits at all. The problem, then, boils down to this: if social justice is not a virtue, its claim to moral standing falls flat.

Alas, I have not encountered a satisfying answer to Hayek's critique. We shall have to face this question more fully in chapter four.

The New Virtue of Association

So far ours has been a fairly broad search into what people today mean by social justice. Almost all current usages fall prey to ideology. A nonideological definition such as we are seeking is seldom encountered. But, in the words of Pope Leo XIII, new times demand a new response. So let us see if we can construct an approach to social justice for today's world that recovers its original understanding and does not fall prey to the current traps.

It is highly instructive to reread *Rerum Novarum* in the light of the events of 1989. Certainly, these events were fresh in the mind of John Paul II in 1991 as he repeated the century-old warnings against a growing socialist state:

According to *Rerum novarum* and the whole social doctrine of the Church, the social nature of man is not completely fulfilled in the State, but is realized in various intermediary groups, beginning with the family and including economic, social, political and cultural groups which stem from human nature itself and have their own autonomy, always with a view to the common good. This is what I have called the "subjectivity" of society which, together with the subjectivity of the individual, was cancelled out by "Real Socialism."[6]

I know from the experience of my own family over the past four generations, as many others must know, too, from their own families, how great the transformation has been. My family served as serfs on the large estate of the Hungarian Count Czaky, whose ancestor was a hero in turning back the Turks near Budapest in 1456. My ancestors were subjects of the Austro-Hungarian Empire, and as near as I can determine they were not able to own their own land until after World War I, in the 1920s. Prior to that time, the Czakys' cattle, sheep, goats, and other livestock were counted annually, for purposes of taxation—and in the same column with men, women, and children. All were the property of the Count.

My ancestors were taught to accept their lot. Their moral duties were fairly simple: PRAY, PAY, and OBEY. What they did and gained was pretty much determined by the Count and by settled customs. But beginning in about 1880, small farms could no longer sustain the growth in population that had begun. Almost 2 million people from the eastern counties of Slovakia began migrating to America (and elsewhere), one by one, along chains of connection established by families or fellow villagers. Usually the men left first and sent back for wives later.

Once in America, my grandparents were no longer subjects. They became citizens, which meant that if social arrangements were not right, they now had the duty (and liberty) to organize to change them. Now they were sovereign. Now they were free, but also saddled with personal responsibility for their own future. They needed to learn new virtues, to form new institutions, and to take responsibility for the institutions left to them by America's founding generations. All of this was called into being by a new form of political economy, a democratic republic and a capitalist economy, both of which positively cried out for grassroots action by people with initiative and new skills in forming associations of their own.

In this context the new term "social justice" can be defined with rather considerable precision. Social justice names a new virtue in the panoply of historical virtues, a set of new habits and abilities that need to be learned, perfected, and passed on to new generations—new virtues with very powerful social consequences.

This new virtue is called "social" for two reasons. First, its aim or purpose is to improve the common good of society at large, perhaps on a national scale or even an international scale, but certainly on a range of social institutions outside the home. A village or neighborhood may need a new well, or a new school, or even a church. Workers may need to form a union, and to unite with other unions. Since the cause of the wealth of nations is invention and intellect, new colleges and universities need to be founded. All these are social activities—the social activities of a free and responsible people.

In America, the new immigrants formed athletic clubs for the young; for men, social clubs to play checkers, cards, or horseshoes; for women, associations to tend to the needs of neighbors. In Catholic neighborhoods, they began Saturday night bingo games (how my mother enjoyed them!) to raise funds to pay off the church mortgage or to build a school. Immigrants formed insurance societies and other associations of mutual help to care for one another in case of injury or premature death.

But this new virtue is called "social" for a second reason. Not only is its end social, but so also are its constitutive practices. The practice of the virtue of social justice consists in learning three new skills: the art of forming associations, willingness to take leadership of small groups, and the habit and instinct of cooperation with others. All three are needed in order to accomplish ends that no one individual can achieve on his or her own. At one pole this new virtue is a social protection against atomistic individualism, while at the other pole it protects considerable civic space from the direct custodianship of the state.

In the absence of the art of association, the practice of modern citizenship is almost impossible. Without it, there is only the state, the Leviathan. Without it, civil society has no energy, the public square is empty, and citizens huddle in solitary privacy. Tocqueville observed this phenomenon in the prerevolutionary France of the *ancien régime* in the eighteenth century. Between the naked and solitary individual and *l'état* there were no mediating institutions. French citizens lacked the social protections and powers that networks of associations would have afforded them. At the time of the French Revolution, he opined, there were not ten men in France capable of starting an association.

Again, it should be noted that this new definition of social justice is practiced by both those on the left and those on the right. There is more than one way to imagine the future good of society. Humans of all persuasions do well to master the new social virtue that assists them in defining, and in working with others toward, their own vision of that good. Competition between left and right, and among factions of each, can be healthy.

Here we are seeking a completely open and nonideological definition of social justice. But not all who claim to be acting for social justice actually further the work of justice. Their motives may be suspect, and so may their grasp of important facts, their moral analysis, or their methods. We would not count "skinheads" or neo-Nazis as those doing the work of social justice. So it is with all claims to be practicing a virtue: Those claims must be examined in greater detail. In order to be just, an act must be correct in every aspect—manner, timing, motive, accuracy of perception, and all the other qualities of good actions. Otherwise, it is defective. Thus, to show someone that what he or she claims to be a virtue actually falls short of some of the demands of true virtue is to affirm the ideal of social justice as a standard of moral judgment.

Conclusion: Social Justice Is a Habit of the Heart

And so we arrive at this conclusion: Social justice is not what most people think it is, a building up of state bureaucracies which are impersonal, inefficient, and expensive far beyond their own original forecasts. True enough, government programs often do real good. But the programs very quickly reach a point of diminishing returns, and begin to suffer multitudes of new and unforeseen problems. If you add up all the money Congress has designated for the relief of the poor since 1965, the total money spent is far more than would be required simply to have given each poor family some $30,000 in cash per year.

But clearly, not every poor family in the United States is receiving that $30,000 per year. For that would put every poor family of four in America comfortably above the 2010 Federal Poverty Level of $22,350 per year, and poverty would have been eradicated, as a statistical matter, years ago.

Government bureaucracies consume most of the money, and relatively little of it passes through to the hands of the poor; in effect, the poor get the droppings.

By contrast, social justice is a virtue whose specific character is social in two ways: the skill in forming associations, and the aim of benefiting the human community, whether local, national, or international. Thus the virtue of forming associations, while turning to government as little as possible, is an immensely powerful way to build a better world. Without the practice of this truly effective social virtue, merely "feeling compassion" is ineffectual.

Dramatically important too: The practice of the virtue of social justice combats the widespread surrender to ever-larger governments. Big governments are too inefficient for their own humane intentions. They are too blind, too out-of-touch with the millions of individual wills at play in society, too domineering, too preachy. They waste too much money, stifle individual initiative, and starve out intermediate associations, hard work, and civic activities.

Of course, a strong government is necessary for a small number of important tasks, such as national defense, protecting the value of the national currency, and providing morally sound, not corrupted, public services such as waterways, airports, harbors, public roads and bridges, maintaining the legal framework required for a free economy, and other projects. Still, it is important to keep a tight grip on the growth of government. For when government grows too large, its people lose their freedoms. Checks and balances and vigilant oversight shrink in power, while coercive regulation knows fewer and fewer bounds. Gradually, too, the creative impulse atrophies.

To protect its own turf, big government tends to place obstacles in the way of individual initiatives; it wants no rivals in the field. By overregulation, insurance requirements, expensive licensing, and many other snares, it cripples free associations. Besides, human beings are always tempted to let others bear their expenses and do the heavy lifting, while exempting themselves from personal responsibility. Thus, in 2013 the U.S. Congress could not resist exempting itself from the rules of Obamacare that it legislated for ordinary people. Down the ages, humans have easily relaxed into soft living, free bread and circuses, and the "soft tyranny" of allowing higher powers to pay their way for them. The government is like the Greyhound bus driver: Leave the driving to us!

Besides, experience shows more and more that in attempting to produce happy lives for the public—good housing, good health, safe neighborhoods, good pay, good jobs, long-term financial security, good dental care, and so on—government lacks the concrete and detailed intelligence to manage all possible contingencies, personal failings, and fluctuating economic conditions. Big government is too gigantesque to be an adequate nanny. It cannot even pay its own debts. It can seldom be honest with those who must pay for its largesse. In due course, it runs out of money before it fulfills all its ever-expanding list of promises. Many who claim to be pursuing "social justice" (spending more government money) are not paying for their vaunted generosity out of their own money; they are spending the money of generations yet to come. Some generosity! Some social justice!

Worse still, big government and big business are tremendously encouraged to collude in going outside the law in order to profit both. It is a major disgrace to business that there exists such a thing as "crony capitalism," or "crapitalism." This thing may look like capitalism on the surface, and it certainly includes real (and even some famous) businesses. But it is really corruption and abuse of the system. Government officials—presidents, governors, and legislators—want at least some powerful allies in the business world to support their major initiatives, and they also want political contributions for their campaigns. Some companies want competitive advantages for themselves; some, exceptions in the law; some, special protections or shields against costs (taxes owed or otherwise). So some political leaders and some business leaders buy each other off; they trade advantages; they scratch each other's backs. Such conduct is against the rules and violates the fundamental commitments of each—principles of both government and business. It violates the rules of the separation of systems, and also the checks and balances of the American founding. It even violates the rules of the free market (which Adam Smith noted that business people are often prone to do, when it is to their advantage, and when they are not checked by competition). To call this "crony capitalism" is not damning enough.

To correct such abuses, in which government is also involved, the fundamental democratic remedy has always been for citizens to organize themselves, protest, and campaign for a change in the laws. In this way, the virtue of social justice is prior to actual change in the law. Put otherwise, behind every change in the laws lies the practice of social justice among many individuals. Rightly understood, social justice is a social virtue learned in painstaking practice by individuals—a social virtue both in its method and in its purposes. It is a noble habit truly worthy of the name "virtue." It is the living energy of the practice of democracy in America. It stands among the "habits of the heart" that Tocqueville so highly praised. It is, in fact, the habit that Tocqueville singles out as the "first law of democracy": the habit of forming associations in order to attend to the public needs of a democratic people.[7] It is a distinctly new and modern habit, made possible—and made frequent in daily practice—only by the new institutions of liberty in politics and economics.

This new political economy aims at creating wealth in every part of the population. Adam Smith defined its goal as "universal opulence."[8] It also creates political space for the widespread practice of virtues of association, invention, cooperative work, and personal creativity. Mobs drift together as lonely and unconnected individuals, Tocqueville pointed out. Their habits are not reasoned, ordered, or cooperative. Their passions easily and often turn destructive. It is through habits of association, Tocqueville shrewdly noted, that a "mob" is shaped into "a people." The habits and practices of social justice transform unattached individuals into community-minded individuals. Social justice so understood fuels the human dynamism of a creative economy, a thriving civil society, and the inner form of a democratic republic.

Since a numerical majority left to itself is easily stirred into a mob, one of the gravest dangers to a peaceful democratic republic is the tyranny of a majority. To constrain such tyranny by the rule of law, and to check and balance the factions latent in a majority, the form of government the American founders sought is better described as a "republic" than as a (purely majoritarian) "democracy."[9] A republic embodies checks against the majoritarian rule of an irrational mob. The principle of association is thus essential to the new political economy, both to its political part and to its economic part. The American founders had the conceit to think of their new system as a model never seen before on earth, a new form of political economy bound to be imitated around the world, properly thought of as the "new order of the ages," the *Novus Ordo Seclorum*. This was a huge conceit on the part of the founders of a fragile nation of fewer than 4 million citizens. For the next fourteen years, the Americans were barely able to hold their new nation together, and barely able to pay its debts. What chutzpah they showed in calling theirs a "model [without precedent] on the face of the globe."[10]

It took more than a hundred years before the Holy See began to take notice of the new lessons being taught to Europe by the American experiment. Leo XIII was delighted to study an ornamented copy of the

U.S. Constitution presented him by Cardinal Gibbons of Baltimore, and Pius XII, in the face of the dire circumstances of Europe at Christmas of 1944, commended the practice of democracy as the best check on tyranny and best protector of human rights.[11] In *Centesimus Annus* and elsewhere, John Paul II made abundant use of concepts such as the consent of the governed, checks and balances, the separation of powers, free associations, the cause of the wealth of nations as knowledge or know-how, and other forms of human capital. More than once—in Denver, in Baltimore, and at his reception of a U.S. ambassador to the Holy See—John Paul II stated the moral purposes and achievements of the American republic in eloquent terms.[12] Benedict XVI urged Europeans to study the model of religious liberty achieved by the United States, in contrast to the increasing secularization of European society.[13]

IT IS IN THE CONTEXT of the twenty-first century, both for the Catholic Church universal and for the United States, that Paul Adams and I begin our inquiry. We begin with a peek at how the secular elites who run our media, our universities, and our courts use the term "social justice" nowadays. Then we lay out the case put by the severest critic of the term "social justice," Nobel Prize winner Friedrich Hayek. After that, in chapter four, we add an ironic observation: At first, Hayek had derided "social justice" wrongly understood, but then he turned around and put into practice what might be called "social justice rightly understood." A delicious irony in intellectual history!

From there, we turn to the sixteen principles articulated by Catholic social thought in the teachings of the preceding 125 years of social-justice popes.

CHAPTER 2

Six Secular Uses of "Social Justice"

SO NOW LET US EXAMINE THE TERM "SOCIAL JUSTICE" AS IT IS currently used in the contemporary secular academy and media. I count at least six different connotations or meanings, while recognizing that each spills over into the others in greater or lesser degree.

It is striking how little reference is made to the Catholic role in introducing "social justice" into contemporary economic debates. It is also striking that little attention is paid to the question of why a secular-atheistic world, born of chance and moral insignificance, should care about the poor and the vulnerable (at least some of the most vulnerable) in the first place. And why it should imagine that a moral scheme such as "equality" has some structural and ethical bearing on human affairs. The notion that humans are in some respects "equal in the eyes of God" cannot be a tenable secular argument. History surely does not afford many (if any) examples of equality among peoples on earth. So whence comes that ideal?

Among secular thinkers, Bertrand Russell, Richard Rorty, and Jürgen Habermas have had the intellectual honesty to note that the idea of equality (as well as the idea of compassion for the poor) entered the world through the teachings of Jesus Christ and his Jewish predecessors, not through Aristotle, Plato, or any earlier moral teacher. These secular thinkers, and others like them, took their moral leads where they found them, and if in Socrates or Goethe, why not in any other master poet or teacher? It is striking to note that contemporary secular thinkers simply employ the criteria for social justice, without grounding them philosophically or theologically. Herewith, in any case, the meanings attached to "social justice" among such thinkers.

Distribution. Most people's sense of social justice is generic, amounting to little more than what we find in an internet search of the term "social justice": "The fair distribution of advantages and disadvantages in society." Now, notice that this standard definition introduces a new key term, not "virtue," but "distribution." This newly added term also suggests that some extra-human force, some very visible hand, that is, some powerful agency—the state—should do the distribution. And do it fairly. But I, for one, do not trust politicians to neglect their own self-interest ("Where will I pick up the most votes?") in their considerations of distribution.

Equality. Furthermore, the expression "advantages and disadvantages" supposes a norm of "equality" by which to measure. Consider this professorial definition:

> Although it is difficult to agree on the precise meaning of 'social justice' I take it that to most of us it implies, among other things, equality of the burdens, the advantages, and the opportunities of citizenship. Indeed, I take [it] that social justice is intimately related to the concept of equality, and that the violation of it is intimately related to the concept of inequality.[1]

This sense of the term expresses a whole ideology: "Equality" is good and ought to be enforced. But also note what has happened here to the word "equality." In English, equality can be taken to suggest fairness, equity, or what is equitable. But what is equitable often requires that each receive not exactly the same portions but rather what is proportionate to each, given different efforts and different needs. In many recent writings on social justice, however, equality is taken to mean something more like equality-as-uniformity. That conception of equality calls for some great power to sweep in and enforce on a society its strict measure of equality, and to restrict freedom accordingly. To maintain strict equality, such a great power must measure out by its own judgment the freedom and initiative allowed all individuals, families, associations, and communities.

God did not make individuals equal in talents or in the will to succeed. Nor did he force all families into the same mold of family traditions, disciplines, and inner character. Given the way any free world works, it is highly unlikely that all individuals and families would attain the same levels in human skills, ambition, and daily habits. Egalitarians scarcely attend to this reality, which is immediately observable in daily life (among students, for example, and even among one's own siblings and children). The radical and undeniable human inequality, as we shall see, was very important to Pope Leo XIII. Not grasping its reality was a major pitfall for what he called "liberalism."

Common Good. Social justice is typically associated with some notion of the "common good," a wonderful term that goes back to Aristotle. The Catholic tradition is very fond of this term, but does not mean by it exactly what the American founders meant by the "public good" or the "public interest." The precise meaning given to the "common good" by the Second Vatican Council was this: "the sum of those conditions of social life which allow social groups and their individual members relatively thorough and ready access to their own fulfillment."[2] As one can see, this definition avoids speaking of "equality of condition" or "collective equality," in favor of emphasizing the opportunity for each unique individual to develop his or her talents to their full potential. In any case, the common good is an important master concept among Catholic social principles, one that tries to do justice to both the communitarian nature of humans and their unique personal endowments. We shall see in chapters five and seven that the common good and social justice are intimately related concepts of Catholic social teaching.

Here it must be pointed out first that, in practice, the use of the term "common good" often hinges on a prior question: "In this particular situation, who decides what the common good is?" In ancient societies, often the wisest and strongest person was the ruler, and it was he who made the important decisions, such as where to camp at night or near which source of water to build the village. The person with the greatest strategic and tactical sense of what was safe, and the greatest ecological sense for which site would make for better community life, would make these decisions.

But in more recent times, that responsibility gradually shifted (under the influence of democracy) to all citizens. Over time, though, as government slipped from the ideal of "limited government," democracy got tied down like Gulliver in the wire cords of the bureaucratic state. Decisions have been made more and more by extensive staffs and committees, and sometimes by committees of committees. Very seldom today is one person (like the leader of old) held accountable for these decisions. And the beautiful notion of the common good is tied down like Gulliver, too.

For example, a fundamental misuse of the term "common good" came clear to me for the first time when, at the Helsinki Commission in Bern in 1985, I was prodding the Soviet delegation to recognize the right of spouses from different nations to share residence in whichever spouse's nation they chose. The Soviets stoutly resisted. The Soviet Union, they insisted, had invested much effort and great sums of money in giving an education to each Soviet citizen. The common good, they said, demands that these citizens now make commensurate pay-back. Therefore, the Soviet partner could not emigrate. Individual aspirations must bow to the common good of all. This is the opposite of the Vatican II definition.

The common good was the excuse on which communist totalitarianism was built. Also, in the United States these days, the "common good" is often used as a battle cry for more state spending. "Do not cut spending for the poor! Current disparities of income are unjust. More state money for the poor!" A clear translation of this slogan is: "Let Uncle Sam pay for it! And with other people's money, not mine." In this rhetorical field, the "common good" is often yoked to "social justice," essentially to furnish an excuse for more government power, spending, and domination—at the expense of anyone but the activists shouting the slogans.

It is the natural tendency of political power to expand and grow, and of progressives in power to become ever more skillful at making decisions for formerly free citizens. They do this under the delusion that those citizens do not know what is good for them, but that government officials, who are not only more knowledgeable but more moral, do know, and should intervene for the good of the people. In *God in the Dock* (1948), C. S. Lewis described this delusion quite deliciously:

> Of all tyrannies, a tyranny sincerely exercised for the good of its victims may be the most oppressive. It would be better to live under robber barons than under omnipotent moral busybodies. The robber baron's cruelty may sometimes sleep, his cupidity may at some point be satiated,

but those who torment us for our own good will torment us without end for they do so with the approval of their own conscience. They may be more likely to go to Heaven, yet at the same time likelier to make a Hell of earth. This very kindness stings with intolerable insult. To be cured against one's will and cured of states which we may not regard as disease is to be put on a level of those who have not yet reached the age of reason or those who never will; to be classed with infants, imbeciles, and domestic animals.[3]

Many steps announced as necessary for the common good are on a downward slope to serfdom.

Old timers in America have often warned new immigrants from their own ethnic background: "Stay away from the *welfare honey trap*." The honey trap gives you the sweet taste of cost-free benefits. But you must give up your own adult responsibility, your sound habits from the old country, the daily exercise of your own abilities. You will lose your self-respect. You will lose the happiness that flows from personal achievement. You will live more like a domestic animal than like a man.

As a result, there are many occasions today when one must argue sternly for individual rights and against the so-called common good. This is especially true when the eyes of many are blinded by the mere sound of the words. When people hear the "common good," many think of something noble and shiny and good, something motherly. But they do not think carefully enough about who is determining what the common good is, whether they are speaking truly, empirically, and whether they have a good track record of success. We should ask ourselves: *Who decides what the common good is, and who enforces this common good?* And what does it do to those who receive it, to their skills and their sense of accomplishment and personal happiness?

The Progressive Agenda. In America, many of our elites describe themselves as progressives. But what do they mean? Watch what they do, what they advocate for, and you will most often see that these are activists on behalf of larger government and more spending for their favorite causes: the poor, Planned Parenthood, solar and wind power, restrictions on the use of fossil fuels, and two of their most passionately held causes, abortion and gay marriage. Such progressives are not necessarily anticapitalist. Many of those funding progressive causes are, in fact, very wealthy capitalists themselves, or their heirs and foundations. George Soros, Warren Buffett, and Bill Gates are household names. But many other lesser known people with very deep pockets have much social and political influence, people like software entrepreneur Tim Gill, retired hedge-fund executive Tom Steyer, and green-technology investor David Gelbaum.[4]

Many progressives talk and act as though the trouble with the American people is that they do not know what is good for them. They have to be told, herded, regulated, fined, and forced into the right course of action. Nanny, nanny, everywhere the nanny state. Progressives now play the role that Puritans used to play in saying no. No smoking, no ozone, no gun-ownership, no this, that, and the other thing. Some of these may be admirable ideas; it is the relentless nagging in the progressive character that is new and troubling.

More than progressives recognize in themselves, they suffer from an inner passion for bossing other people around. They desire to do this for the good of the ones bossed. One of the more humble, but often annoying, of these impositions was the automatic safety belt that used to be in many cars, which closed around you whether you wanted it to or not. One of the more outrageous is the automatic cancellation of the health-insurance policy you have long experience with, chose for yourself, and like, in order to be fitted into a government plan you don't like or want.

Almost always, the rationale offered for coercing you into something you don't want is that it's for your own good. It is surprising how often the terms "social justice" and "common good" are pounded into our heads to make us do something we wouldn't otherwise choose to do. And that is probably why progressives turn to big government. Otherwise, they could not coerce us into seeing things their way.

New "Civil Rights": Gender, Sex, Reproduction. When I first went to the United Nations Human Rights Commission meetings in Geneva in 1981, two different delegates from opposite sides of the world (Norway and India) told me that the most hopeful signs they had seen in their lifetimes was the much delayed shift in the United States in favor of institutional support for the rights of black Americans. To change habits of mind so inveterate and so entrenched gives hope to the rest of humanity, they said. The calling of the Second Vatican Council by the old Pope John XXIII and the election of the handsome young President John F. Kennedy and his "New Frontiersmen" gave hope that the old thick ice was breaking up.

It is no wonder that nearly every new impulse and new social movement in the United States (and elsewhere) since that time has styled itself
in the image of that first great civil-rights movement of American blacks
and their allies.

In recent decades, for instance, a brand new element of the progressive
agenda has taken shape under the rubric of social justice: "reproductive
rights." As one writer puts it:

> The privileged in this world, for the most part, have unfettered
> access to the reproductive health and education services to decide for
> themselves when and whether to bear or raise a child. The poor and
> disadvantaged do not. Thus, the struggle for reproductive justice is
> inextricably bound up with the effort to secure a more just society.
>
> Accordingly, those who would labor to achieve economic and social
> justice are called upon to join in the effort to achieve reproductive
> justice and, thereby, help realize the sacred vision of a truly just society
> for all.[5]

This is how the thinking goes: The privileged of this world have a
chance to control the number of children they have, but the poor don't
have this chance, and that's not fair. So, in the name of the poor, progressives introduced a concept of reproductive rights, by which they primarily
mean the right to abortion. It's not so hard to get birth control anywhere
in the world; that transformation has by and large already happened.
What the issue really comes down to is abortion: How can you be for
social justice and against reproductive rights?

The situation is the same in the case of gay rights, another element of
the progressive agenda promoted as a matter of social justice. Consider
the following statement from an administrator of the Anglican Church
in New Zealand: "How can the Church be taken seriously or receive any
respect for its views on the far more important issues of poverty, violence
and social justice, when the public keep being reminded of this blot on its
integrity, the continued discrimination against gays?"[6]

Compassion. All these newly invented demands increasingly fly under the
flag of "social justice." And there is one more new word (or honorable old
word, used in a new way) by which to understand many today who talk
about social justice. There used to be a Tammany Hall saying: "Th' fella'
what said that patriotism is th' last refuge of scoundrels, underestimated

th' possibilities of compassion." In addition to equality and the common good, another term that came to be used in association with social justice is "compassion."

That Tammany Hall saying wittily reminds us of the contemporary sins committed in the name of compassion. We must never again allow that beautiful term "compassion" to become a blinding light, in whose name totalitarians seize power for "the people," and then practice the utmost cruelty. Abortion, for instance, the daily use of scissors to slice spinal cords and other medical tools to crush little skulls—this is compassion for women? It is a ruse to cover this with the name "choice." The question is: What is the choice, and how much do you want to look at it with your own eyes, in order to take full responsibility for it?

Compassion comes in true forms and in false forms. The American War on Poverty unintentionally ushered in a period of rapidly rising numbers of births out of wedlock and the relative decline in the number of married couples among the poor. This dramatic change in family composition was accompanied by a sharp increase in poverty among never-married women with children. By 1986, the fastest growing segment of the poor was found in this cohort of never-married women with children.[7]

To be fair, the War on Poverty did work very well for the elderly in the United States, whose condition in 1985 was far better than it had been in 1965. It was still better in 2005.

But here too we are up against the law of unintended consequences. The original premise of Social Security arrangements was that there would be seven workers for every receiver of benefits. Today, however, we are no longer having the numbers of children required to support such a program. We're getting to the point where by 2030 there will be only *two* workers for every retiree. It is therefore already clear that we are not going to be able to meet the obligations that we have assumed. That sword of Damocles hangs by an even more frayed thread over social-democratic Europe.

[CHAPTER 3]

A Mirage?

FOR MOST OF HIS LIFE, FRIEDRICH HAYEK SEEMED CONTENT
to be known as an economist, and in 1974 the Nobel Prize was awarded him
for his originality in economics. At crucial points, however, the principles
in whose light Hayek proceeded included extra-economic principles; for
instance, principles of law and representation on the one side, and on the
other, principles of morality, truth, and justice. Thus, although he is most
widely known for his originality in rediscovering and creatively advancing
the theory of the free economy, some of his most important work regards
the *constitution* of liberty and matters of *law* and *legislation*.[1] Beyond that,
having fought manfully in the war of ideas across most of the breadth of
the human experience, in history, philosophy, religion, and social thought,
Hayek was also a fierce warrior in the realm of *cultural* liberty.

Although born in a deeply Catholic culture and ever sympathetic to
the religious impulse in human nature, Hayek reluctantly called himself
an atheist. He wished he had an "ear" for God, he said, as most people do
for music; but he didn't. He felt it as a lack in himself.

In the heavily ideological post–World War II era, Hayek was keenly
aware of the urgent need all around the world to bring together the two
parties of liberty, secular and religious. No one party, he thought, could
plausibly win the intellectual battle for liberty by itself. Liberty suffered not

by too many supporters, but by too few. Hayek correctly foresaw the crucial role religion would play in the defeat of Communism many years later.

Hayek is famous for his sustained and animated criticism of most of the usages of "social justice" to be found in public speech during the middle of the twentieth century. He ripped to tatters the concept as it is usually deployed.[2] Indeed, he stressed its fundamental contradiction: Most authors claim to use the term to designate a *virtue* (a moral virtue, by their account). But, then, most of the descriptions they attach to it appertain to impersonal states of affairs: "High unemployment," they say, for instance, or "inequality of incomes" or "lack of a living wage," is a "social injustice." They expect the economic system to attain every utopian goal, as though all such goals are easily within reach and mutually compatible. They imagine that all social systems are under the command of identifiable persons, or should be, and they intend to find those persons and hold them responsible for outcomes of which they do not approve. Their main concern is to indict an entire *system* and its central institutions.[3] For decades many of them seemed to hold that socialism was a superior economic system, toward which history was moving. Their diagnosis, methods, and remedies belong to diverse intellectual traditions: socialist, social democratic, or Catholic.[4] They seem not to analyze the failures of the systems they prefer.

Hayek's critique laid out a multitude of objections to then-prevailing modes of thought. But his main thrust went to the heart of the matter: *Social justice is either a virtue or it is not.* Most of those who use the term do not ascribe it to individual virtue but to states of affairs, as when they assert that this or that state of affairs—unemployment, low wages, deplorable working conditions—is "socially unjust." Social-justice advocates seldom attempt to change minds and hearts one by one. Instead, they use political muscle to change the laws and to coerce mass compliance. In this respect, they are using the term "social justice" as a regulative principle of order, not a virtue, and by their own lights this is an illegitimate use. They are not appealing to "virtue" but to coercion. Thus "social justice" is a term used to incite political action for the sake of gaining political power. In Hayek's words:

> What I hope to have made clear is that the phrase "social justice" is not, as most people probably feel, an innocent expression of good will towards the less fortunate, but it has become a dishonest insinuation

that one ought to agree to a demand of some special interest which can give no real reason for it. If political discussion is to become honest it is necessary that people should recognize that the term is intellectually disreputable, the mark of demagogy or cheap journalism which responsible thinkers ought to be ashamed to use because, once the vacuity is recognized, its use is dishonest.[5]

Social justice! How many sufferings have been heaped on the world's poor under that banner! How malevolently it rolled off the presses of Lenin, Stalin, Mussolini, and Hitler. It is no wonder Hayek loathed it so.

Hayek alludes to a second defect of twentieth-century theories of social justice. Whole books and treatises have been written about social justice without ever offering a definition thereof.[6] The term is allowed to float in the air as if everyone will recognize an instance when he sees it. This vagueness seems both studied and indispensable. For the minute one begins to define social justice—as a virtue, for instance, related to the classical Aristotelian virtue of justice—one runs into embarrassing intellectual difficulties. For most of those who use the term do not intend to raise the worldwide quotient of virtue. They employ "social justice" as a term of art, whose operational meaning is "we need a law against that." They employ it, that is, as an instrument of ideological intimidation, for the purpose of gaining the power of legal coercion.

BEFORE CONTINUING, I must note two ironies in what I am undertaking. First, Hayek's demolition of false understandings of social justice was necessary before a better concept could come to light, a concept he himself lived out in practice before it could be thematized. (Hayek would have enjoyed this primacy of practice to theory.)

Second, Hayek's love of *theory qua theory* more than once led him to make bold claims which seemed at the time wildly at variance with observable phenomena, and for which he was often mocked and made fun of. Let me mention but two: first, that socialism was epistemically blind and, therefore, could not possibly produce rational outcomes on a consistent basis and must eventually falter on its own ignorance.[7] (For how could state bureaucrats, obliged each day to make up thousands of prices, possibly know how badly multitudes of individuals might want x or y, or how much sweat and effort they would be willing to expend to purchase it?) Again, Hayek argued that the power and permanence of the nation state in the twentieth century were greatly overestimated, and that (for instance) the state's power to control money would eventually slip out of its grasp. Hayek predicted, when it seemed farfetched, that at some future time private entities in an open market, not governments, would become more reliable guardians of the value of currencies, and that the monopoly power of governments over money would in this way be broken. Today's internet markets seem to be confirming his point, for through them today's profligate governments are being disciplined by freely acting individual agents, who emigrate and move their investments elsewhere, learning from many forms of international media what is going on elsewhere and choosing accordingly. New regional institutions broke down isolated nation-state control of unlinked economies, too, such as the Euro and Eurozone, Mercosud, and other unifying creations. As information moved more and more freely, so did freedom of choice.

Hayek made many predictions based upon purely theoretical findings that were later vindicated. I believe, therefore, that he himself would have enjoyed the claim that under a theory of social justice clearer than any he had found in the literature, he himself might be said to have been a practitioner of social justice. That claim will stand, however, only if we first seize the root of Hayek's objections to the most common construals of social justice that he found around him.

Social Justice Wrongly Understood

Hayek began by noting an anthropomorphic tendency in human thought, an itch to understand all processes, however different in kind, in terms of human agency.[8] Consider the human animation and psychology given in all ages to animal life, from Aesop's fables and Grimm's fairy tales, to Mickey Mouse and Bugs Bunny, to the Three Little Pigs and the Big Bad Wolf. Consider, too, the tendency of humans to understand the general rules by which societies are run in light of individual psychology and individual ethics. Even today many project onto the politics and economics of modern complex societies the same expectations as their ancestors who lived in simple tribes; they personify all outcomes, as if some all-powerful individual *chose* them or could alter them at will. Initially, Hayek hypothesizes, the term "social justice" was invented to make sense of the complex networks of causation in modern societies.[9]

John Stuart Mill gave this anthropomorphic approach to social questions almost canonical status for modern thinkers in 1861 in *Utilitarianism*:

Society should treat all equally well who have *deserved* equally well of it, that is, who have deserved equally well absolutely. This is the highest abstract standard of social and distributive justice; towards which *all institutions*, and the efforts of all virtuous citizens, *should be made in the utmost degree to converge*.[10]

At the head of his chapter on social justice, Hayek sets quotations from Immanuel Kant and David Hume, who had been much shrewder on the relation between "desert" and reward than Mill. Both saw that "merit" cannot be defined by general rules. Hume's is particularly sharp: "So great is the uncertainty of merit, both from its natural obscurity, and from the self-conceit of each individual, that no determinate rule of conduct could ever follow from it."[11] In other words, what Mill construes as a heavy moral obligation ("should be made in the utmost degree to converge"), Hume construes as an irrational pretension. Mill makes "merit" and "desert" sound clear and easy; Hume sees them as highly individual, obscure, and subject to self-centered bias. Mill makes "reason" seem luminous, dispassionate, objective; Hume sees reason as distorted and darkened by passion, ignorance, and bias.

Religious thinkers will here be reminded of Reinhold Niebuhr's sketch of significant differences between the ethics of individuals and the ethics of groups, as in *Moral Man and Immoral Society*.[12] Both Niebuhr and Hume thought certain conceits about reason could be fatal. And so, of course, did Hayek, whose last book was called *The Fatal Conceit*.[13]

Hayek argued that justice is the indispensable foundation and limitation of all law. (He had no difficulty speaking of legal discrimination, segregation, or apartheid and the like as "unjust," and in that sense he might employ the term "an unjust society.") But he argued, in the same vein, that the reigning conception of social justice—in part codified by Mill—is an abuse of the term justice, and is rooted in a naive anthropomorphic tendency. The abuse consists in taking the term justice out of the realm in which it properly applies to the acts and habits of individuals and using it, illicitly, to name an abstract standard of *distribution* which authorities ought to enforce—as when Mill speaks of "the highest abstract standards of social and distributive justice, towards which the efforts of all institutions, and the efforts of all virtuous citizens, should be made in the utmost degree to converge."

Mill here imagines that societies can be virtuous in the same way that individuals can be. Perhaps in highly personalized societies of the ancient type—under kings, tyrants, or tribal chiefs—such a usage might make sense; in such societies, one person made all crucial social decisions. Curiously, however, the demand for the term "social justice" did not arise in earlier societies, in which it might have seemed appropriate, but only in modern times, when more complex societies operate by impersonal rules applied with equal force to all under "the rule of law."

In ancient societies, however, even kings often made appeal to "reasons of state" to justify behaviors that by the rules of individual ethics would be blameworthy. Still, to the king one could assign personal responsibility. In the sprawling bureaucratic states, however, decisions are beclouded in internal turf wars, intramural tests of will, and decisions made by political horse trading. This is the point Niebuhr had in mind contrasting the possibilities of "moral man" with "amoral society."

How, then, shall we judge "impersonal mechanisms" and "market forces" that leave some individuals and groups in situations that evoke pity and a sense of moral outrage? We protest against the "injustices" of nature. Do not storms, plagues, wars, and natural calamities of all sorts sometimes punish the just and unjust equally, often unfairly and even unaccountably? From biblical times, such arguments have been advanced against God himself by Job, the Psalmist, and others who saw the just suffer and the unjust prosper. Does God himself lack respect for social justice? Such is our reaction to the ordinary course of nature. It seems only "natural" to extend these feelings to the disappointments and unfair fates we see in the social order. There is a great need in the human breast, Hayek notes, to hold someone accountable, even when in another part of ourselves we recognize that such a protest is absurd:

> Yet we do cry out against injustice when a succession of calamities befalls one family while another steadily prospers, when a meritorious effort is frustrated by some unforeseeable accident, and particularly if of many people whose efforts seem equally great, some succeed brilliantly while others utterly fail. It is certainly tragic to see the failure of the most meritorious efforts of parents to bring up their children, of young men to build a career, or of an explorer or scientist pursuing

a brilliant idea. And we will protest against such a fate although we do not know anyone who is to blame for it, or any way in which such disappointments can be prevented.[14]

The birth of the concept of social justice 150 years ago coincided with two other shifts in human consciousness: the "death" of God and the rise of the ideal of the command economy. "Man," Aristotle wrote, "is political by nature." When God "died," men began to trust a conceit of reason and its inflated ambition to do what God had not deigned to do: construct a just social order. This divinization of reason met its mate in the ideal of the command economy; reason (that is, science) would command, and humankind would collectively follow. The death of God, the rise of science, and the command economy yielded "scientific socialism." Where this sort of reason would rule, the intellectuals would rule (or so some thought). Actually, the lovers of power would rule.

From this line of reasoning it follows that "social justice" is given an adequate meaning only in a directed or so-called command economy (such as in an army) in which the individuals are ordered what to do, so that under "social justice" it will always be possible to identify those in charge and to hold them responsible.[15] For the notion presupposes that someone is accountable and that people are guided by specific external directions, not by internalized personal rules of just conduct. The notion further implies that no individual should be held responsible for his relative position. To assert that he *is* responsible would be blaming the victim and denying the relevance of considerations of "social justice." For it is precisely the function of "social justice" to blame somebody else, to blame *the system*, to blame those who (mythically) control it.

Some who think in terms of social justice seem unable to imagine a noncontrolled society, based on spontaneous behaviors, observing universal rules internalized by individuals and flowering in individual self-government. Society as they imagine it is always under command. If it is not under their command, they see it as under the command of powerful others, who by definition are foes of the party of social justice and, hence, oppressors. As Leszek Kołakowski writes in his magisterial history of Communism after many years of faithful service to that Party, the fundamental paradigm of Communist ideology is guaranteed to have wide appeal: *You suffer; your suffering is caused by powerful others; these oppressors must be destroyed.*[16]

We are not wrong in perceiving, Hayek concedes, that the effects of the individual choices and open processes of a free society on the fates of individuals are not distributed according to some recognizable principle of justice. The meritorious are sometimes tragically unlucky; the hardworking fail; good ideas don't pan out, and sometimes those who backed them, however noble their vision and their willingness to take risks, lose their shirts; some evil persons prosper; some of the just languish far below their goals; some receive much greater rewards than others for equal or less effort. The free society isn't beanbag. It may run on fairer rules and with more equal chances than any other regime known to the human race, but it does not and cannot guarantee equal outcomes.

Further, no one individual (no politburo or congressional committee or political party) has any possibility of designing rules that would or could treat each person according to that person's merit, desert, or even need. No one has sufficient knowledge of all relevant personal details. As Hume observed, such work is the work of Solomon, and no one is Solomon in his own case. It is work too obscure for humans. As Kant writes, no general rules have a grip fine enough to grab it.

Someone might object that criminal courts assess individual merit and desert all the time. But that objection strengthens Hayek's point. Systems of criminal justice take for granted that the agent is free in his choices, and that there are clear rules that must not be violated. Criminal courts underline the fact of personal responsibility. If an individual deliberately does violate the law, that is his choice, and it is contrary to the explicit will of the community. "The system made me do it" doesn't suffice as an excuse, since no one commands individuals or groups to violate the law (in fact, any system commands the opposite). Since the rule-abiding behavior of individuals is essential for its comity, a community can establish rules and pass judgment on violations of them. What it cannot do is imagine, mandate, or guarantee that all free choices of all free citizens, even when they obey all the rules and try hard, will issue in specific outcomes. No one knows all individual outcomes. Too many unforeseen contingencies and unique circumstances enter into each life.

If we wish to live within a system in which people are rewarded for how well they serve their fellow men, it follows that their fellows may not rank their services as high as we expect. Teachers, for example, may be "underpaid." The choices made by one's fellows are also free, and introduce a major contingency into the most strenuous efforts and best-laid plans.

Sometimes people who work hard and play by the rules are not as well rewarded as others, and sometimes their best efforts fail. For the system as a whole, failures by individuals are important, embodying significant negative feedback from which others may learn. A system that values both trial-and-error and free choice is in no position to guarantee outcomes in advance. Not every acorn becomes an oak; laws of probability work in the social order as well as in nature. No one predetermines or controls *who* will fail, but every law of probability says that some will. It is not unjust if some acorns fail to become oaks, and it is not unjust if some free acts fail of their intended outcomes.

> The attribute of justice may thus be predicated about the intended results of human action but not about circumstances which have not deliberately been brought about by men. Justice requires that in the 'treatment' of another person or persons, i.e. in the intentional actions affecting the well-being of other persons, certain uniform rules of conduct be observed. It clearly has no application to the manner in which the impersonal process of the market allocates command over goods and services to particular people: this can be neither just nor unjust, because the results are not intended nor foreseen, and depend on a multitude of circumstances not known in their totality to anybody. The conduct of individuals in that process may well be just or unjust; but since their wholly just actions will have consequences for others which were neither intended nor foreseen, these effects do not thereby become just or unjust.[17]

Moreover, it is indispensable to recognize that the term "market" refers to nothing other than the free choices of human beings in exchange: if I sell my house to you, our mutual choosing constitutes "a market." How these choices will work out for each of us cannot be controlled by either of us.[18]

Hayek's vision of the free society is nobler and higher than the vision of those who speak of "social justice."[19] They imagine something like a beehive or a herd or a flock, within which someone is responsible both for giving commands and for outcomes. Hayek thought that a free society has no other model in nature, but is wholly unique to the human species. Furthermore, it has been put into practice only during the past two centuries. Only in recent generations has the economic order been intellectually (and in practice) distinguished in its principles of operation from the political order, and both of them from a third, the moral and cultural order. The working of all three of them together is necessary, but the three orders each proceed according to different rules. Further, institutions and practices have arisen that allow individuals unprecedented scope for the actions proper to free persons, and in all three spheres.

Hayek held that free persons are self-governing, able to live by internalized rules (that is, good habits). For this reason, they need only a fair and open *system of rules* in order to act more creatively, intelligently, and productively than persons in any other form of society. While the free society will never be able to guarantee the outcomes desired by those who speak of "social justice," it does, Hayek observed, bring more rewards to all, on all reward levels, than any known system. It cannot and will not produce equal rewards for all, only higher rewards for all. Hayek summarizes this position as follows:

> We are of course not wrong in perceiving that the effects of the processes of a free society on the fates of the different individuals are not distributed according to some recognizable principle of justice. Where we go wrong is in concluding from this that they are unjust and that somebody is to blame for this. In a free society in which the position of the different individuals and groups is not the result of anybody's design . . . the differences in reward simply cannot be meaningfully described as just or unjust.[20]

Hayek observed that within any one trade or profession, the correspondence of reward to individual ability and effort is probably higher than is generally supposed. He surmised, however, that the relative position of those within one trade or profession to those in another is more often affected by circumstances beyond their control.[21] In certain fields of endeavor, too, for reasons not related solely to hard work or even ability, rewards are higher, even fantastically higher, than in other fields. Television hosts, movie stars, and professional athletes seem to some abnormally overpaid. He concedes that "systematic" considerations of this sort lead to accusations against the existing order rather than against the luck of circumstances of time and place. Technological change, changes in tastes and needs, and changes in relative value are also unpredictable, and in that larger sense spring not from the realm of choice but from the realm of luck.[22]

Throughout, Hayek makes a sharp distinction between those failures of justice that involve breaking agreed-upon rules of fairness and those that consist in results that no one designed, foresaw, or commanded.[23] The first earned his severe moral condemnation. No one should break the rules; freedom imposes high moral responsibilities. The second, insofar as they spring from no willful or deliberate act, seemed to him not a moral matter, but an inescapable feature of all societies and of nature itself. Insofar as labeling these results a "social injustice" leads to an attack upon the free society in order to move it toward a command society, he strenuously opposed the term for its enormous destructive potential. The historical records of the command economies of Nazism and Communism warranted his revulsion to that way of thinking.

Hayek recognized that at the end of the nineteenth century, when the term "social justice" came to prominence, it was first used as an appeal to the "ruling classes" (as they still were) to attend to the needs of the neglected new masses of uprooted peasants who had become urban workers. To this he had no objection. What he did object to was careless thinking and the coercion of free and creative societies by a remote conception of justice.[24] Careless thinkers forget that justice, in the nature of the case, *is* social. The addition of "social" to "justice" is like adding "social" to "language."[25] This move becomes especially destructive when the term "social" no longer describes the actual outcome of the virtuous actions of many individuals, but rather a utopian goal. Toward such utopian goals, as Mill put it, all institutions and all individuals are to "the utmost degree made to converge." In that case, the term "social" in "social justice" does not refer to something that emerges organically and spontaneously from the rule-abiding behavior of free individuals, but rather from an abstract ideal imposed from above.[26]

Behind Hayek's objections to the careless use of "social justice" lies his uniquely powerful insight into the nature of the free society. Hayek recognized that the nineteenth century's addition of the free economy to the eighteenth century's "new science of politics" had liberated women and men as never before. For instance, in lifting the proletariat into the middle class, as even the Marxist Antonio Gramsci had confessed in the 1930s, capitalism was far more successful than Marx and Lenin had predicted. Soon, he saw, there would be no more proletariat in Italy.[27] With great rapidity, in little more than a hundred years, Europe's impoverished, uprooted peasants (Victor Hugo's *les misérables*) had been lifted into the middle class and educated and were astonishing the world by their talent and creativity.

Hayek believed that the key to these successes of liberty was the rule of law and internalized, law-abiding, creative habits on the one hand, and on the other hand an economic system founded on rules that maximize free decisions, discovery procedures, and feedback mechanisms. Open to contingency, chance, and serendipity, such a system was already providing unparalleled universal opportunities. But it could not, and must not be expected to, guarantee outcomes. For any attempt to impose outcomes would force a new and foreign architectural principle upon the system; it would strangle the liberty from which invention and discovery bloomed. Recoiling from the dishonesty and destructiveness of the usual arguments for "social justice," Hayek writes: "I have come to feel strongly that the greatest service I can still render to my fellow men would be that I could make the speakers and writers among them thoroughly ashamed ever again to employ the term 'social justice.'"[28]

"Social justice" would end up harming most of those whom it putatively intended to help. Its chief beneficiaries would be the political and administrative classes. Ironically, it would by its own standards produce unjust societies. The legislators and their experts would be more equal than others and live by different rules from those they prescribed for the rest of society.

CHAPTER 4

Friedrich Hayek,
Practitioner of Social Justice

GIVEN THE STRENGTH OF HAYEK'S ARGUMENT AGAINST SOCIAL justice, it may seem grotesque even to hint, let alone to assert, that he himself was a practitioner of social justice—even if one adds, as one must, "social justice rightly understood." Still, in the sentence quoted at the end of the last chapter, Hayek does offer us a clue when he writes, "the greatest service I can still render my fellow men." This is not the only clue that Hayek saw his vocation as a thinker and writer as a service to his fellow men. He believed, further, that helping others to understand the intellectual keys to a good society, a free and creative society, is to render them a great benefaction. For the free society is an achievement of human wit and enterprise, daring and discovery; its secrets do not lie upon the surface of things, but must be painstakingly searched out through much trial and error, often at the cost of blood. How terrible to ill-treat these precious insights, then, or to lose sight of them, once gained. For this reason, it repulsed Hayek that the term "social justice" was commonly being used as a betrayal of the free society.

Ironically, then, Hayek's war against the misuse of "social justice" was itself a war fought on behalf of his fellow human beings, a service he wanted to render them, an act of considerable consequence for (if I may put it this way) the entire City of Man. Hayek's intellectual vocation imposed on him a duty to his fellow humans to defend the free society and to warn them of dangers against it. His intellectual work was, in this sense, a work of justice. It was also a work aimed at the long-run institutional welfare of the human race. Doing it well was not merely a matter of his own self-interest, narrowly considered, but of significance to the Human City as a whole. It was a work of justice in a plainly social dimension.

Social justice rightly understood, as I have argued above (chapter one), is a specific habit of justice that is "social" in two senses. First, the specific skills which it calls into exercise are those of inspiring, working with, and organizing others to accomplish together a work of justice. These are the elementary skills of civil society, the primary skills of citizens of free societies, through which they exercise self-government by "doing for themselves" (without turning to government) those things that need to be done. The second characteristic of social justice rightly understood is that it aims at the good of the City, not at the good of one agent only. Citizens may band together, as in pioneer days in Iowa, to put up a school or to raise roofs over one another's homes or to put a bridge over a stream or to build a church or an infirmary. They may get together in the modern city to hold a bake sale for some charitable purpose, to build or to repair a playground, to clean up the environment, or for a million other purposes to which the social imagination of individuals leads them. To recapitulate, social justice rightly understood is that specific habit of justice which entails two or more persons acting (1) *in association* and (2) *for the good of the City*.

Some Precisions

If I read Hayek correctly, he would make a much firmer practical stand on the libertarian side of welfare issues than I would, putting up strong resistance to the reasoning and practices of the welfare state. He would certainly do so for reasons of principle. But he might also do so for long-range practical reasons, holding that a premature withdrawal on that flank would result in a weakening all along the front and perhaps even a collapse of the center. In such circumstances, it would be more practical for him—a better service to others—to hold firm, even if he were to be accused of rigidity.

For myself, I believe that there is a strong argument for a modified version of the welfare state, certainly in a large, continental, and mobile society such as the United States. It would be wrong to argue that the welfare state is a desideratum of "social justice," for social justice (rightly understood) is an attribute of citizens, not of states. Social justice is a virtue that can be exercised solely by individuals. Still, one can in a secondary sense speak of a good society—Hayek himself does—and even a just society. By this one means that its laws and institutions respect the moral law governing individuals and do not systematically frustrate that law.

More than that, Judaism and Christianity have had a profound effect on Western humanists down the centuries, such that even secular, antibiblical thinkers like Bertrand Russell, John Dewey, and Richard Rorty freely admit to borrowing from Moses and from Jesus certain modern liberal principles that they did not learn from Socrates or even the Enlightenment: compassion for the weak and the vulnerable, solidarity, and the like. Most Christians, Jews, and secular humanists would not believe that a society that neglects the suffering of the poor and the vulnerable is a good society. They will no doubt argue long into the night about the means best suited to raising the welfare of the poor. Some libertarians would argue that the best means of raising up the poor—by far—is a strong, free, and growing economy. Others might note that this is not always enough, especially in certain hard circumstances: for instance, when people lack the insight or the habits to take advantage of opportunity.

For myself, the bright yellow line between a nurturing and a destructive welfare program must be drawn at those points at which welfare creates dependency in otherwise able-bodied and healthy adults, or in other ways corrupts their ability to make practical judgments for themselves and to bear responsibility for them. For instance, the Homestead Act that opened the American West gave hundreds of thousands of citizens a stake in property, on the condition that they would use their own practical intelligence and labor to develop it. This law did not create dependency; on the contrary, it helped families establish their independence.

Similarly, for older and more mature women, Aid for Families with Dependent Children (AFDC) did work for a while. Later, Temporary Assistance for Needy Families (TANF), created by the 1996 welfare reform, corrected for some of its burgeoning abuses. The majority, knocked off stride by a sudden and unforeseen misfortune, such as divorce or widowhood, use this program for one or two years, that is, until they regain their independence and then depart from it. But for younger, inexperienced women,

AFDC had on the whole been destructive to a very large proportion of their children, whose prognosis for the future is far bleaker than that of other children.[1]

Among young American blacks, it seems fair to say that this attempt to be of assistance went seriously wrong.[2] By 1993, out-of-wedlock births among whites and throughout the nation vaulted inexorably upward.[3] Even the reforms in TANF did not halt out-of-wedlock births from becoming a way of life for millions nationwide.[4]

This is not the place for an extended discussion of welfare programs, pro and con. My task has instead been to set forth a fresh concept of social justice, as a particular specification of the virtue of justice suited to free, democratic societies, and to defend it in such a way that every person who encounters this concept might see how this virtue can be (and is already being) practiced in his or her own life. In a few final words, let me show how I think it was practiced in Hayek's life.

Hayek's Practice

One of the great works of mercy is to give sight to the blind. For teachers and writers, this is a metaphor for what they try to do every day: to give understanding where there was darkness; that is, to precipitate those frequent light-bulb insights that give expression to the acute pleasure, "Now I get it!" No one who is reading through the corpus of Hayek's writings can doubt his tireless commitment to communicating the insights necessary to the health and preservation of the free and the good society. Few have worked so hard or tilled the soil so deeply, with as much originality and passionate instruction. Hayek committed his life to working for the free society—for the sake of all future human beings. He worked with as many others as possible to give this work diffusion. He worked for *the good of the Human City*, and he worked *with others*; that is, he fulfilled the two conditions that exemplify the habit of social justice.

Yet Hayek did more than write and teach. I have seen his portrait in institutions on practically every continent. He joined with Antony Fisher and others to launch a set of institutions committed to research and public debate on the foundations of the free society. Mr. Fisher chose a universal name for these institutes that embodied an appropriate metaphor, the Atlas Foundation, for it is ideas and moral commitments that hold high the free society. At considerable personal sacrifice, Hayek was unstinting in his willingness to help these and other institutions committed to liberty by travelling to them to give public lectures, making tapes, serving on boards, providing international contacts, even offering shrewd, concrete advice.

Hayek was an activist as well as a scholar. He was an intellectual *engagé*, as they said two generations ago—a public intellectual, as we say today. To work for the public good is also a work of social justice.

The most striking of Hayek's initiatives in this respect was his vision for and leadership of the Mont Pelerin Society, which he launched in 1947 as a prestigious international society of economists, political philosophers, legal scholars, statesmen, and others to probe and to discuss the contemporary crisis of the free society, so that after the horrors of World War II the world of intellect would not again rush pell-mell into ideas destructive of liberty.

One of Hayek's chief intentions was to draw religious thinkers into reflection on the desperate needs of the liberal society and to pull secular liberals back from unthinking antireligious prejudices. He believed that the friends of liberty were relatively few, and that those few must not work at cross-purposes. He believed, as well, that the "progressive" bias in favor of the free polity (democracy) *while cherishing disdain for the free economy* was a betrayal of the liberal intellectual tradition. That is why Hayek meant to recover the term "liberal" in its classical modern meaning. He at first proposed to call his new society, whose founding members were summoned by Hayek to a meeting in a village near Mont Pelerin, Switzerland, the Acton-Tocqueville Society. Whereupon a distinguished economist from the University of Chicago is reported to have announced: "I'll be damned if I'll belong to a society named for two Catholics!"[5] A compromise was struck: the name of the nearby mountain was chosen. The Society still prospers, with far more members than ever before.

I REST MY CASE. Despite his deep contempt for those concepts of social justice that do injury to the free society, Hayek overlooked a concept of social justice—social justice rightly understood—that put a name to the specific habit of justice of which he was an eminent practitioner. Moreover, if Tocqueville is right, that "the Principle of Association is the first law of democracy,"[6] then social justice understood in this way is the first virtue of democracy, for it is the habit of making the Principle of Association incarnate. This was for Hayek not just an empirical law; it also had moral consequences:

> It is one of the greatest weaknesses of our time that we lack the patience and faith to build up voluntary organizations for purposes which we value highly, and immediately ask the government to bring about by coercion (or with means raised by coercion) anything that appears as desirable to large numbers. Yet nothing can have a more deadening effect on real participation by the citizens than if government, instead of merely providing the essential framework of spontaneous growth, becomes monolithic and takes charge of the provision for all needs, which can be provided for only by the common effort of many.[7]

In brief, Hayek was something of a model for how a public intellectual ought to practice social justice: tirelessly, with wit, with civility, with gentleness, and with a very deep learning. As I have written elsewhere:

> [Hayek] did write deeply and systematically about ethics and society, about politics and the markets, and above all the kind of laws and institutions indispensable to human liberty. In the sense of working ardently to build a more humane society, he was a great practitioner of social justice.[8]

It might have killed him to say so, but he was in fact a model of the virtue of social justice rightly understood.

Looking Ahead

Until now, I have tried to be analytical, fair, clear, and terse. But the next three chapters are about the sixteen principles of Catholic social teaching, and they need to be elucidated in a rather more philosophical and theological language than in a language closer to social science, such as I have been using. Please note that in these three chapters I will not be laying out an argument or trying to persuade, but simply presenting the background principles from which I work. For readers who are not Catholic, some of these principles, rooted in experience, will carry plausibility, while those principles that derive from Catholic faith may not. Still, I hope such readers will find of some use an unvarnished statement of the Catholic view.

CHAPTER 5

Sixteen Principles of Catholic Social Thought: The Five Cs

SOCIAL JUSTICE IS A PIVOTAL PRINCIPLE IN CATHOLIC SOCIAL teaching today,[1] but it is not the only principle, nor the most important one. In fact, there are at least sixteen principles of Catholic social teaching. To grasp the concrete importance of social justice, it is best to see all sixteen principles arrayed together. Only in that way can one grasp the actual workings of social justice in their full context.

The sixteen principles of Catholic social teaching arise from an inner power infused in us by our Creator and Redeemer, which we try to knead as yeast into daily life. Catholic social teaching is constantly being informed by concrete experience, and as times change, new principles slowly gain clarity when new problems and new opportunities cast new light. As central governments grew swollen with new powers, the principle of subsidiarity—of limiting central power and respecting local powers—came more sharply into view. As each culture in the world became far more aware of all the others, even of distant cultures on the other side of the planet, the principle of human solidarity gained attention. As institutions of human rights were put to work (most unevenly) around the world, the salience of Church support for human rights in country after country gained international notice. Samuel Huntington of Harvard began to speak of the "Third Wave" of worldwide democracy as the "Catholic wave."[2]

1. The First C: *Caritas*

> Love of neighbor is thus shown to be possible in the way proclaimed by the Bible, by Jesus. It consists in the very fact that, in God and with God, I love even the person whom I do not like or even know. This can only take place on the basis of an intimate encounter with God, an encounter which has become a communion of will, even affecting my feelings. Then I learn to look on this other person not simply with my eyes and my feelings, but from the perspective of Jesus Christ.
>
> (Benedict XVI, *Deus Caritas Est*, §18.)

God is *caritas*, that is, the deepest and originating kind of love: God's own love,[3] the love (as Dante put it) that "moves the sun and all the stars." This is the poet's way of suggesting that all of creation, the whole known and unknown universe, was called into being at a point in time by a love so potent as to draw all things out of nothingness into existence, at their appointed times.

The Creator might have done otherwise. But in fact he chose to call into being a contingent, changing, evolving universe, whose inner laws operate mostly by emerging probabilities. Aristotle saw that most natural beings act by laws only "for the most part."[4] As modern science has discerned, most laws of nature work not by necessity but by probabilities. As some possibilities are made real, they change the probabilities of later evolution.

Schemes of probabilities—not fixed, rigid principles—seem a better model for the inner workings of our cosmos and most things in it. In that sense, the universe is imperfect, never flawless. It is this characteristic of the universe that favors the emergence at some point in time of fallible human agents, able to reflect and choose, armed with liberty to accept or to reject the path laid out by God for their own flourishing. As Thomas Jefferson once put it, "The god who gave us life gave us liberty at the same time."[5] It is this feature of the universe that allows humans to live free to act or not, to accept or to reject the friendship into which their Creator invited them. He did not have to do that. But he did.

The God who created us, according to the human story that both Judaism and Christianity have presented to us, plunged deep into our nature its most dynamic thrust: toward the free choice either to love God and our fellow humans or to reject such love. The first impulse (and law of our being) that the Creator placed into our hearts is to love God, who in his generosity gave us life, along with liberty and the responsibility for our own destiny. As Jacques Maritain wrote, "By its liberty, the human person transcends the stars and all the world of nature."[6] The second law God gave us is a call to love our neighbors as we love ourselves. These are very high targets for the human race. They are the ground of our unique dignity, and immortal beauty, among all other creatures.

It is true that very early in the Jewish/Christian drama of Creation, the first brother, Cain, slew his brother Abel. In the evolving world, then, the love of brothers is radically threatened by enmity and strife, and all manner of human fratricide and mass destruction. The human story— human history—is not a simple morality play in which good always triumphs, and love, justice, and peace prevail. Often the human project has for long, long periods spiraled downward in moral decline, not upward in moral improvement. The commandment of love is plainly not an empirical description of the way things are.

Christianity maintains that, nonetheless, each of us must love our enemies—we don't have to like them or enjoy their presence, but we must at least recognize that the Creator called them into his friendship, just as he called us. We must strive to see what the Creator loved in them. But that can seem too much to swallow and, frankly, utterly beyond our emotional inclination.

There are, of course, other narratives and story lines presented as models of how human history actually proceeds. There is the nihilist view: "Life is a tale told by an idiot, signifying nothing." There is also the narrative presented by those who call themselves secular humanists. Some of these present themselves as scientific humanists, others as humanists who love imagination and sympathy more deeply than science. (Compare the young A. J. Ayer's *Language, Truth, and Logic* with Albert Camus's *The Rebel*, or even more so, *The Plague*.)

Each human must question, reflect, and choose which narrative of human living comports better with his or her own experience of life and evidence, and which better serves the future of the human race. To do so is to exercise the radical freedom built into our nature.

It is in the nature of *caritas* to implant this liberty into our souls. In this implanting, many are led to see the potential images of *caritas* in themselves. That is the image of the civilization they try to build, the "City on the hill," the City of God. It is a world that requires radical spiritual liberty if it is to be fulfilled. *Caritas* is uncoerced or not at all.

Caritas is the propelling drive in which Catholic social doctrine begins, toward which it aims, and under whose searing judgment it falls short or, at times, does well. In the words of Saint Thomas Aquinas, "Charity is the form, mover, mother and root of all the virtues"; it is the inner fire of all the other habits infused in us by God.[7] It is the obscure magnetism that guides us through the dark night of the soul.

From this personal love that constitutes the inner being of God we can derive an acronym that ties all sixteen principles of Catholic social teaching together: CaRitaS—the five Cs, the five Rs, and the six Ss. It is fitting that the term *caritas* should tie together all sixteen principles, since the reality of *caritas* is their inner form.

2. The Common Good

Every day human interdependence grows more tightly drawn and spreads by degrees over the whole world. As a result the common good, that is, the sum of those conditions of social life which allow social groups and their individual members relatively thorough and ready access to their own fulfillment, today takes on an increasingly universal complexion and consequently involves rights and duties with respect to the whole human race. Every social group must take account of the needs and legitimate aspirations of other groups, and even of the general welfare of the entire human family.

(*Gaudium et Spes*, §26.)

The Good News brought by Christ is that the Creator of the universe is neither icily indifferent to us nor hostile. It is true that he chose to create a world of contingencies in which both heinous and holy acts could be chosen by men, and in which nature itself is full of hazards to all living creatures on earth. But the Creator asks us to trust him as a friend who walks with us. The Lord God Creator asks us to address him as "Our Father."

In the same spirit, he gives us to know that all the goods of this earth are intended by him for every single person on this earth. Intimate union with our Father is the highest common good of all who have ever lived or will yet live.

But even on an earthly level and within history itself, our Father willed a share of the earth to every single human being. Not an equal share. To some he gave more talents than others. Some he placed in more favorable climes and locations richer with natural resources than others. (He gave all the nations of the Middle East huge deposits of oil, but not Israel. He promised Israel a land of milk and honey, but he said nothing about oil.) The people of Israel he blessed in other ways. He taught them the secrets of the human spirit, the human law, and the habits of creativity and inquiry. He implanted in them the seed of the idea of progress, and the intimation that God's Kingdom to come was a place of truth, beauty, goodness, and compassion.

Human advance is not always upward, but often in a long period of decline and decadence. Human history, for Jews and Christians, gives reason to trust in human betterment and a common learning of wisdom, and a steady openness to the wisdom hidden even in humble, sometimes low-born, people. One must approach wisdom humbly.

All these teachings are more valuable than gold. Indeed, from them derive the methods that led to the discovery that black tar, oil, and shale have buried in them unsuspected riches, hidden for many ages. And even in the most humble, mean, and seemingly fruitless dry sand, there is silicon.

The Lord God Creator intended all the goods of the earth for all his human family. He has called all into friendship with him. We are reflective, choosing, creative persons, responsible for our own destiny. In other words, he made us free.

In this world, it is not so easy to pursue the common good. Except in the most abstract way, who knows what the common good actually is, in all its devilish detail? And how to make it work? And how to tame the sinfulness and self-destructiveness to which humans are demonstrably prone? Where is there a woman or a man so wise as to discern what the common good is? It is a very weak and dubious answer to say "political leaders" or "public authorities" or, weaker still, "politicians."

Yet it is an imperative given us by the Lord God Creator that we must move the whole commons forward, including every human being without exception, no one left behind. The historical problem is to figure out methods by which smaller human communities can build toward this goal, one small platoon at a time, then in larger coagulations, until a worldwide community can be served, and each part serve the other. Many wandering trials and errors attend that painful journey.

The common good is not for happy talk. Ways to get there are scarce and difficult to uncover, except by repeated efforts (or if I may use the distinctively American term, stick-to-itiveness). One must expect human duplicity, cruel manipulation, corruption, the naked will-to-power, and abundant self-destructiveness. We have already experienced all that. We have seen "the common good" used as a club against the personal dignity and personal liberty endowed in us by our Creator. In the Soviet Union, Soviet citizens who married foreign spouses were forbidden to join them, in the name of the common good; they owed their whole lives to socialism, and had a duty to serve it in return. The common good trumps individual choice. Such shortcuts to the common good end badly.

3. The Cause of Wealth

If incentives to ingenuity and skill in individual persons were to be abolished, the very fountains of wealth would necessarily dry up.

(Leo XIII, *Rerum Novarum*, §15.)

The source of wealth lies principally in the human spirit—its wit, its disciplines, its creativity, its reliable habits. The cause of wealth is a certain kind of humanism, a humanism that includes special virtues and trained inclinations, put into practice through institutions supportive of personal responsibility.

Many people ask the question: What are the causes of poverty? But that is a pointless question, a useless question, as one can instantly see by asking a follow-up question: What good would it do to learn the causes of poverty? Do we want to make more of it?

No, the fruitful question is this: What are the causes of wealth? Learning the answer to that question would set us upon a creative path toward generating more wealth in a systematic way, by designing the most practical incentives that inspire all humans to create new wealth and share its fruits.

For much of human history, agriculture was the main source of wealth, and wealth creation was dependent on good weather. Famines occurred in regular waves during long periods of drought (or flooding), under perduring freezes or relentlessly scorching summer days. Nature has not been overly friendly toward human beings. Through diseases and natural calamities (some of long duration) nature almost succeeded in making man extinct, as it did a very high proportion of all other formerly living species. Nature is not always a kindly presence.

But once humans learned that wealth could be created by human invention and enterprise, the prospect of a world of universal affluence came into view—and came to be desired. In earlier times, whole peoples were subject to suffering bitter want. Most were reduced to passivity and weary patience. Once the causes of wealth were mastered, the human race could begin removing poverty—and with accelerating speed it began doing so.

Once humans discerned a way to break the chains of poverty, a new moral obligation arose. Poverty shifted from being an irremediable condition to being steadily reducible. In more and more nations, majorities exited out of penury and poverty to better health, greater opportunity, and steadily higher education. Nations came to be labeled as "less developed," "developing," and "developed." In many, this progress was achieved within twenty years. China and India, for example, witnessed the fastest mass movement ever, raising more than 500 million of their citizens out of poverty between 1980 and 2000. The rise of Europe from the ruins of 1945 to measurable affluence in 1965 was also rapid. And so was the vault between 1945 and 1970 of the four "Asian Tigers": Hong Kong, Singapore, South Korea, and Taiwan.

In a word, the cause of wealth has been uncovered during the past 200 years. That cause lies primarily in the creative habits of the human mind, in invention, know-how, and disciplined work with others. That discovery has generated a new moral imperative: All the world's poor must be helped out of poverty. They must be helped in the most vital way: to make the discovery of the cause of wealth (their own human capital) in their own lives, so as to experience a freedom from penury never known before.

4. Creativity

The modern business economy has positive aspects. Its basis is human freedom exercised in the economic field, just as it is exercised in many other fields. Economic activity is indeed but one sector in a great variety of human activities, and like every other sector, it includes the right to freedom, as well as the duty of making responsible use of freedom. But it is important to note that there are specific differences between the trends of modern society and those of the past, even the recent past.

Whereas at one time the decisive factor of production was the land, and later capital—understood as a total complex of the instruments of production—today the decisive factor is increasingly man himself, that is, his knowledge, especially his scientific knowledge, his capacity for interrelated and compact organization, as well as his ability to perceive the needs of others and to satisfy them.

(John Paul II, *Centesimus Annus*, §32.)

The Jewish/Christian narrative of the human project casts humans as images of God the Creator. Humans create not only beauty in the arts and goodness (with its own beauty) in their moral lives, but also new, never-before-seen wealth in their working world.

Instead of following Marx's lead in seeing value solely in human labor, this narrative also proclaims the values to be found in the human mind, in its inventiveness and creativity. It is not always the man who labors with more arduous physical efforts who adds most value even to his own labor, but often the one whose labor is infused with the most originality, creativity, efficiency, and organizational skill. There are certain qualities in labor that spring from the subjectivity of the human person, that is, the laborer himself. He puts part of his own self into his work, his own originality, his own hopes, his own touch.

Another way of putting this is that the laborer who is creative adds a certain personal and human infusion from his own spirit into the work of his hands. To allow the fruit of his labor to rust outside in a yard—the iron girders fresh from his assigned furnace—is to injure something in him, his heart, his soul. He does not labor simply to produce useless waste, which nobody wants. He wants to contribute some good to the human community. A laborer is not simply an object, but also a subject, a being with imagination and creativity and zest of spirit.

This line of reflection, reportedly passed on to the pope by Mirosław Dzielski, the great Krakow journalist and thinker known as the "Polish Hayek," led Wojtyła to muse on the subjectivity of both labor and capital. Whereas in *Laborem Exercens* (1981) the pope spoke of capital as if it consisted just of material things, ten years later in *Centesimus Annus* he had come to grasp the human factor in capital. He saw the wealth enlocked in human capital, in the subjectivity of the laborer himself. The term "capital" is not well identified solely with things (iron, automobiles, even gold bars and bank accounts) but also points to treasures in the human mind and spirit (such as outstanding work habits, spiritedness, teamwork, education, expanded and refined tastes, and capacities for design).

The scientists who isolated quinine, and the one who first produced penicillin, may have reduced more human pain and probabilities of imminent death than all the previous humanitarian efforts in history. As Abraham Lincoln pointed out in Wisconsin in 1858, the person who discovers a new way to produce five grains of wheat instead of the previous expectation of one or two has more than doubled the output of the same amount of physical labor. Such an inventor contributes to doubling the agricultural wealth of peoples everywhere who use that method. John Locke made a similar observation about the new wealth produced by painstaking cultivation of a field of berries, compared with the low yields of uncultivated fields.[8]

There is in each human laborer the potential of generating creative human capital, that is, learned skills of mind, heart, and hand. And it is a great thing for each nation to invest a great deal in building up this human capital within its citizens. Thus, John Paul II wrote:

> Indeed, besides the earth, man's principal resource is man himself. His intelligence enables him to discover the earth's productive potential and the many different ways in which human needs can be satisfied. It is his disciplined work in close collaboration with others that makes possible the creation of ever more extensive working communities which can be relied upon to transform man's natural and human environments. Important virtues are involved in this process, such as diligence, industriousness, prudence in undertaking reasonable risks, reliability and fidelity in interpersonal relationships, as well as courage in carrying out decisions which are difficult and painful but necessary, both for the overall working of a business and in meeting possible set-backs.[9]

5. Community of Work

It is becoming clearer how a person's work is naturally interrelated with the work of others. More than ever, work is work with others and work for others: it is a matter of doing something for someone else. Work becomes ever more fruitful and productive to the extent that people become more knowledgeable of the productive potentialities of the earth and more profoundly cognisant of the needs of those for whom their work is done.

(John Paul II, Centesimus Annus, §31.)

If you lift from your desktop a bright yellow schoolboy pencil, with a bit of alloyed metal holding tight to a pink eraser, you may gain an insight into how the "universal workbench" of a global economy works. Do you know where the lightweight wood of that pencil comes from—from what country on earth? And the graphite that provides the mark of your writing on paper? And the bronze-colored alloy that holds the eraser? And the gum of the eraser itself? There are not many of us who know whence all those things derive, and what is the most efficient way to procure and to process them. And, by the way, someone needs to know how to produce and process the lacquer that makes the pencil shiny and prevents tiny paint chips from flecking off when schoolchildren put their pencils in their mouths.

No one person needs to know all the steps in finding, producing, and assembling these elements of the pencil. But some one person or small group does need to know where to find teams of people who know how to produce each element most efficiently and at high quality standards, and maybe another team to assemble them all together, and yet another team to market and to transport them to wholesalers and retailers. A simple yellow pencil may require a global workbench. The workers in Sri Lanka, Chile, and other nations who may have supplied one part or another will never get to speak with or even see the schoolchildren who end up using those pencils. Nonetheless, these workers serve those distant children well. If they do their work, providing good service to their fellow humans, this very ordinary form of love will accompany the pencils to the unknown, unseen hands that use them.

It is not a wasted idea for anyone who uses a pencil to say a word of thanks to the faraway people who produced it. In this way, there is not only a universal workbench, but also an invisible filament of mutual service racing around the earth, encircling the hearts of the whole world as one. Do not think that commerce means only a material bond. Do not think that globalization lacks all soul.

CHAPTER 6

The Five Rs

THE SECOND SET OF BASIC PRINCIPLES OF CATHOLIC SOCIAL doctrine can be remembered as the five Rs. These designate the five rights that Catholic social teaching has recognized throughout history, through close observation of necessities for human flourishing. Declarations of human rights long antedate the contemporary world.

1. The Right to Give to Caesar What Is Caesar's, But to God the Things That Are God's

"Tell us, then, what you think. Is it lawful to pay taxes to Caesar, or not?" But Jesus, aware of their malice, said, "Why put me to the test, you hypocrites? Show me the coin for the tax." And they brought him a denarius. And Jesus said to them, "Whose likeness and inscription is this?" They said, "Caesar's." Then he said to them, "Therefore render to Caesar the things that are Caesar's, and to God the things that are God's." When they heard it, they marveled. And they left him and went away.

(Matthew 22:17–22.)

The State may not impose religion, yet it must guarantee religious freedom and harmony between the followers of different religions. For her part, the Church, as the social expression of Christian faith, has a proper independence and is structured on the basis of her faith as a community which the State must recognize. The two spheres are distinct, yet always interrelated.

(Benedict XVI, *Deus Caritas Est*, §28.)

Natan Sharansky calls the principle about Caesar and God the "anti-totalitarian principle," for it lays out in such stark and simple terms the reality that some things do not belong to Caesar. No government has the right to claim total power. All government is limited, by right. One very large realm of human life (among others) from which Caesar is shut out is the life of the human spirit, the human mind, the human soul. The relentless questioning of science is by right free from the control of the state. So is the life of the arts. Even more so is the free inquiry and reporting of the press, both electronic and print. The same applies to the right to free public speech.

Yet more emphatic than any of these is the right of the human conscience to respond freely and without governmental restraint or burden to the internal calling of the Lord God Creator. It is self-evident that the difference in power, intellect, and love between the Creator and the conscious and reflective creature imposes a duty of awe, even a trace of what Kierkegaard called "fear and trembling," in the face-to-face of God and humans. Furthermore, the alert human feels, perhaps, a surge of gratitude. And if a duty toward the Creator is evident, then an individual has a right to respond unimpeded by any lesser power. The same freedom, based on an inalienable duty, has been felt by religious communities around the world throughout history. Most of the most important things in life do not come under the rule of Caesar.

That is why the freedom to exercise one's own religious conscience is the first freedom, from which all others descend. It is called the first freedom because it most brilliantly spotlights the transcendence of each human person. Each alone must choose to accept—or to reject—the friendship offered by the Lord God Creator. No other freedom goes so deep. No other freedom is so deeply inalienable.

Woe to the human who dares to block, or to meddle with, the interior personal encounter between the Creator and his free, responsible creature.

Atheists, too, share in this liberty. No human may be compelled either to believe in God or to consent to serve God. For atheists, the problem is to discover how to establish this right on atheist grounds. Tom Paine did not believe this could be done, and sailed to France to dissuade the leaders of the Revolution of 1789 from turning atheistic. He held that they would thus undermine the very argument that grounded their own rights. They would turn their rights into preferences, a reality of a very different order indeed. For if rights do not come from God, but only from human preference, what security shall believers find in "rights," and what security will atheists find in changeable and often fickle human preferences?

2. The Right to Worship God and Practice One's Faith

Also among man's rights is that of being able to worship God in accordance with the right dictates of his own conscience, and to profess his religion both in private and in public. According to the clear teaching of Lactantius, "this is the very condition of our birth, that we render to the God who made us that just homage which is His due; that we acknowledge Him alone as God, and follow Him. It is from this ligature of piety, which binds us and joins us to God, that religion derives its name."

(John XXIII, *Pacem in Terris*, §14.)

In all his activity a man is bound to follow his conscience in order that he may come to God, the end and purpose of life. It follows that he is not to be forced to act in a manner contrary to his conscience. Nor, on the other hand, is he to be restrained from acting in accordance with his conscience, especially in matters religious. The reason is that the exercise of religion, of its very nature, consists before all else in those internal, voluntary and free acts whereby man sets the course of his life directly toward God.

(*Dignitatis Humanae*, §3.)

Thank God, for us Americans this right is enshrined within our Constitution, in the most prominent place in the First Amendment. Among those who argued most forcefully for the state's public recognition of this right were Thomas Jefferson, James Madison, George Washington, George

Mason, and John Adams. Suffice it here simply to quote from James Madison, whose hand and political leadership were most responsible for achieving the final wording of the First Amendment, and then its ratification by the Congress and still later by the people:

> Because we hold it for a fundamental and undeniable truth, "that religion or the duty which we owe to our Creator and the manner of discharging it, can be directed only by reason and conviction, not by force or violence." The Religion then of every man must be left to the conviction and conscience of every man; and it is the right of every man to exercise it as these may dictate.[1]

From the beginning, then, Christianity has been a religion marked by its adherence to an inner life of conscience, in which God must be recognized in spirit and in truth, in a way no others of that time except Jews felt bound to act. When a Roman philosopher was asked to bow or burn incense before the gods, he felt no special inner conflict. All that was required of him was to go through the external motions; he did not have to believe a word of it. That option is not open to a Jew or a Christian, however. For a Jew or a Christian, what his body does, his soul must do likewise. He cannot in good conscience bow or burn incense before a false god. The First Commandment itself forbids that: "I am the Lord your God. Thou shalt not place false gods before me." And so it has been from that time to this. Deuteronomy tells us: "Worship your God in spirit and in truth."

Thus, the worship of God takes place in the spirit. But it is not confined to the spirit. It must be expressed in actions in the world where they will be seen, and it must at times be expressed in public. Religion is not solely a private affair, an affair of the heart. It is the inner and outward life, in the world at large, and in the eyes of other humans. Anything less would be hypocrisy. Some say, "My religion is my own private affair." Yes and no. More than that, religion is the inner and outward life of an entire people— a people larger and more universally placed than in any one state. For Jews and for Christians, true religion is both a conviction of heart and mind, and also a transformative inspirer of public practices, whole cultures, and a distinctive (but in principle universal, freely chosen) civilization.

The whole principle of freedom of conscience and worship is a child of Judaism and Christianity as it is of no other religion or secular community. As the historian of liberty Lord Acton (1834–1902) observed, more-over, the record shows that the history of liberty is coincident with the history of Judaism and Christianity. One need not be a Jew or Christian to benefit by this liberty, to live by it, and to adopt it as one's own. But Judaism and Christianity were the first and most enduring intellectual forces to recognize its necessity, to elucidate its grounds philosophically, and to think through the practical principles that would institutionalize it, not only in minds but also in polities.

While the principles of religious liberty are ancient, their institution-alization in the political world of the West is relatively recent. The practice of religious liberty is not yet universal. But the aspiration for it is univer-sal, and will increasingly become acute, if only because the immense suf-ferings now being inflicted upon humans for the choices of their religious conscience are unbearable. Religions that countenance such barbarity disgrace themselves. By the *via negativa* of unbearable suffering, the cause of freedom of conscience is being written indelibly in worldwide human experience.

3. The Right of Association

In all social matters, the companionship of others is of great advantage. "A brother that is helped by his brother is like a strong city," says Solomon (Prov. xviii. 19). "It is better, therefore, that two should be together than one: for they have the advantage of their society" (Eccles. iv. 9). . . . Again, any person who is competent to perform some special function *has a right* to be admitted to the society of those who are selected for the exercise of that function. For, an association means the union of men, gathered together for the accomplishment of some specific work.

(Aquinas, *Liber Contra Impugnantes Dei Cultum et Religionem*, ch. 2.)

Private societies, then, although they exist within the body politic, and are severally part of the commonwealth, cannot nevertheless be absolutely, and as such, prohibited by public authority. For, to enter into a "society" of this kind is the *natural right* of man; and the State has for its office to protect natural rights, not to destroy them.

(Leo XIII, *Rerum Novarum*, §51.)

In the middle of the thirteenth century, some of the faculties at the University of Paris became aware of the unusual brilliance and growing fame of the new bright lights of the orders of Franciscans and Dominicans who were flocking to teach there. The University of Paris was only then emerging on the world stage, becoming competitive with universities in Bologna (founded 1088), Oxford (1096), Cambridge (1209), and elsewhere. Alas, the secular faculties jealous of their new eminence tried to ban the Franciscans and Dominicans from the university. Naturally, these religious orders appealed their case to the pope. They thought it unjust that persons of talent could be barred from the university simply because they belonged to a religious association. Their protest, written by Thomas Aquinas, is one of the first known defenses of the natural right of association.

The argument was, as usual for Saint Thomas, brief, commonsensical, and logically set out. Human beings are not only rational animals but also social animals. For human flourishing, many associations are necessary and highly useful. For this reason, the law of association is deep in our nature. Even more praiseworthy are free associations which individuals join for common purposes. If individuals have rights, then for even better reasons do their free associations have rights, which well serve the common good. For evidence, examine the growing number of schools, clinics, and other service organizations staffed by the Franciscans, Dominicans, and others. Free associations of individuals are natural to humans; it is a natural right to form them and to work through them. Free associations are well fitted to contribute substantially to the common good. Q.E.D.

To put this in more contemporary terms: No man is an island unto himself. For human survival, prospering, and progress, we depend on others with whom we associate. This is true for progress in knowledge and beauty, in truth and goodness. But it is also clearly true in economic development and the building of cities and republics. Most important, the primary communities in which we associate are not states. Communities such as the family are much more deeply rooted in our nature than are states. Others of these primordial associations are our communities of worship, community building, and work. There are also our political associations, and our associations for mirth and play and cultural expression. Human life has always been thick with associations, but never with as many associations as in the days following the birth of democratic societies with free economies, bursting with new opportunities for social initiatives.

At the end of the nineteenth century, Leo XIII dreaded the rise of the omnipotent total state. He saw the first threat of it in the materialism promoted by Engels and Marx, which left no room for the life of the human spirit or for human transcendence and personal liberty. He could think of only one opposing force to throw against the gigantic state: the thicket of free associations of every sort, and in every department of human life. Social life in associations is prior to social life in states. It is prior in time and prior in right. Thus, Leo and later popes began to stress the creative and associative powers of free adults, their capacity for initiative and for responsibility, and their ability to better human life from the ground up. The free labor unions were just one group of these associations that were dear to Leo.

A century later, Pope John Paul II called the peoples of the world, beginning in Europe, to become subjects of their own destiny, not the objects of government will. Through their associations (such as Solidarity in Poland), human persons are capable of self-determination, taking responsibility for their own destiny, becoming provident for their own flourishing, generating immense energy for change from local communities, upward and outward, to circle the earth.

The popes' increasing reliance on associations led to their grasp of the importance of subsidiarity, and also the social need for freely willed solidarity in moral witness, concrete assistance, and mutual reliance on one another—in medical care (for example, Doctors Without Borders and the Red Cross) and in every other human sphere. The power of voluntary associations for bringing good into every corner of the world is immense. And those who participate in voluntary care worldwide have no problem in sharing love with all the others they meet, for it is love that moves them all.

Solidarity is a new name for *caritas* in a globalizing world of rapid air transport, electronic communications, and worldwide media. A massive explosion of nongovernmental associations has occurred in our time. This is what Leo XIII dreamed of.

4. The Right to Private Property

Property should be in a certain sense common, but, as a general rule, private; for, when every one has a distinct interest, men will not complain of one another, and they will make more progress, because every one will be attending to his own business.

(Aristotle, *Politics* 1263a25.)

Every man has by nature the right to possess property as his own. This is one of the chief points of distinction between man and the animal creation. . . . And on this very account—that man alone among the animal creation is endowed with reason—it must be within his right to possess things not merely for temporary and momentary use, as other living things do, but to have and to hold them in stable and permanent possession; he must have not only things that perish in the use, but those also which, though they have been reduced into use, continue for further use in after time.

(Leo XIII, Rerum Novarum, §6.)

When the 'sacredness of property' is talked of, it should always be remembered that any such sacredness does not belong in the same degree to landed property. No man made the land. It is the original inheritance of the whole species. Its appropriation is wholly a question of general expediency. When private property in land is not expedient, it is unjust. . . . Even in the case of cultivated land, a man whom, though only one among millions, the law permits to hold thousands of acres as his single share, is not entitled to think that all this is given to him to use and abuse, and deal with as if it concerned nobody but himself. . . . The rents or profits which he can obtain for it are at his sole disposal; but with regard to the land, in everything which he does with it, and everything which he abstains from doing, he is morally bound, and should, whenever the case admits, be legally compelled to make his interest and pleasure consistent with the public good.

(John Stuart Mill, Principles of Political Economy.)

Although it seems to many of today's progressives that the best way to create wealth and bring poor people out of poverty is socialism implemented through a network of government programs, human experience from ancient times until today has not borne this out. To the contrary, experience shows that personal responsibility for private property actually raises the common prosperity. It especially raises the well-being of the poor more reliably than collective ownership does. Experiments in socialism since the first winter at Plymouth in America have always come aground on the tendency of many to exert themselves no more than is necessary, especially when others exert themselves less. Socialism breeds free riders on the harder and smarter labor of others.

Testimonies to this human propensity go far back in recorded history (including the reports of Julius Caesar from Gaul and Germany), and in recent times have been refreshed by vast experience under socialist nations all around the world. Compare the prosperity of South Korea with the inertia of North Korea, West Germany with East Germany, socialist Cuba with capitalist Chile, precapitalist India and China with the rapid victories over poverty during the past twenty or so years. There are many other instances. Whatever socialist dreams may promise, human experience shows that collectivization retards economic progress. By vivid contrast, having all individuals in a nation take responsibility for their own property better raises the common good of all.

As we detail below in chapter eight, Leo XIII was particularly shrewd in his predictions in *Rerum Novarum* about what socialism would bring into the world, why it would cause evil, and why attempts to install it would be futile as well as destructive. Leo's perception holds up very well when compared with what preeminent Western thinkers (in this case, even Albert Einstein) hoped for from socialism:

> I am convinced there is only one way to eliminate these grave evils, namely through the establishment of a socialist economy, accompanied by an educational system which would be oriented toward social goals. In such an economy, the means of production are owned by society itself and are utilized in a planned fashion. A planned economy, which adjusts production to the needs of the community, would distribute the work to be done among all those able to work and would guarantee a livelihood to every man, woman, and child. The education of the individual, in addition to promoting his own innate abilities, would attempt to develop in him a sense of responsibility for his fellow-men in place of the glorification of power and success in our present society.[2]

John Paul II reaffirms Leo XIII, after a hundred years of experience following *Rerum Novarum*:

> Socialism considers the individual person simply as an element, a molecule within the social organism, so that the good of the individual is completely subordinated to the functioning of the socio-economic mechanism. Socialism likewise maintains that the good of the individual can be realized without reference to his free choice, to the unique and exclusive responsibility which he exercises in the face of good or

evil. Man is thus reduced to a series of social relationships, and the concept of the person as the autonomous subject of moral decision disappears, the very subject whose decisions build the social order. From this mistaken conception of the person there arise both a distortion of law, which defines the sphere of the exercise of freedom, and an opposition to private property. A person who is deprived of something he can call "his own," and of the possibility of earning a living through his own initiative, comes to depend on the social machine and on those who control it. This makes it much more difficult for him to recognize his dignity as a person, and hinders progress towards the building up of an authentic human community.[3]

The wonderful irony is that the common good suffers most under common property—and that a regime of private property produces a higher level of the common good more quickly and reliably than a statist regime.

5. The Right to a Living Wage

Equity therefore commands that public authority show proper concern for the worker so that from what he contributes to the common good he may receive what will enable him, housed, clothed, and secure, to live his life without hardship. Whence, it follows that all those measures ought to be favored which seem in any way capable of benefiting the condition of workers.

(Leo XIII, *Rerum Novarum*, §51.)

We therefore consider it our duty to reaffirm that the remuneration of work is not something that can be left to the laws of the marketplace; nor should it be a decision left to the will of the more powerful. It must be determined in accordance with justice and equity; which means that workers must be paid a wage which allows them to live a truly human life and to fulfill their family obligations in a worthy manner.

(John XXIII, *Mater et Magistra*, §71.)

The justice of a socioeconomic system and, in each case, its just functioning, deserve in the final analysis to be evaluated by the way in which man's work is properly remunerated in the system.

(John Paul II, *Laborem Exercens*, §19.)

In the agrarian age, the vast majority of workers were fed by their land and lived in ancestral homes. One did not have to be concerned about "wages" for landowners, only for day laborers. In contemporary times, however, most workers are not the owners of land sufficient to feed their families. They do depend on wages. More and more often, households have more than one income-earner. In the United States it turns out that families with higher income tend to be supported by three or four income-earners (often their teenage and twenty-something children earn wages), whereas the poorest households tend to have no workers—mostly because they are widows of advanced age or because they are unmarried females with young children and no husband present. For a very high percentage of the American poor, no one in the household is earning wages, or someone is working only part time for part of the year. Paying a living wage does not, then, solve the problem of poverty. At the lower end, most persons are not receiving any wage.

Addressing these circumstances, economists tend to fall into at least two camps. One side argues that the way to help is to raise the minimum wage, so that those who work at or near the minimum wage receive at least a marginally better income. The other side points out that the minimum wage is poorly targeted as an antipoverty measure, since many of its beneficiaries are middle-class students or secondary earners from affluent households. They also argue that raising the minimum wage results in the disappearance of more and more low-wage jobs. Beyond a certain price for wages, marginal businesses survive better with fewer employees. Besides, a regime of higher minimum wages is an incentive for developing labor-saving machines. At toll stops on the highways, at cash registers, on the floors of department stores, one sees today fewer and fewer human workers, more and more labor-saving devices. In addition, less and less is it true that a married man's income alone supports a household. Many millions of households are headed by single women. The greatest number of poor households tend to be exactly such households. Married-couple families are far less often poor. In more than half of those households, both husband and wife work.

In these new contexts, the definition of a living wage becomes far more complex than in earlier times. Moreover, the policies of governments have huge effects on business activity. For example, one may compare the condition of the working poor during the Carter administration (1976–80) with their condition under the Reagan administration during the next eight years. The policies of the Carter administration placed high tax rates on business and personal income, increased regulation on business activities, and failed to control both inflation and unemployment (the simultaneous occurrence of inflation and unemployment had before then been thought to be impossible). Its final record showed that, through inflation, about 30 percent of those on fixed incomes fell into poverty during the Carter years, and the numbers of the poor went up dramatically. An uncommonly low proportion of all Americans of working age could find work. Median incomes were declining. Mortgage rates for borrowing to buy a home went up to as high as 15 percent, even spiking to 20 percent; inflation soared along at 10 percent or more per year; and unemployment rose as high as 11 percent in some states. Even President Carter referred to this as a "malaise." Candidate Reagan referred to the combined figures for inflation, unemployment, and borrowing costs as the "misery index."

President Reagan reversed policies on almost every one of these fields. Employment soared so high that by the end of his term a larger proportion of Americans was gainfully employed than ever before in our history. The workforce expanded to accommodate millions of women, as more women found jobs than ever before. Labor shortages developed, and immigration expanded to relieve them. The numbers of the poor decreased, the median income of all the lower percentiles rose sharply. The employment rate of blacks and Hispanics and their average incomes rose to the highest levels in history. After Reagan, one cannot say that government policies have no effect on unemployment, income, labor participation, inflation, mortgage rates, an atmosphere of new job creation, enterprise, or even the launching of whole new industries, such as computers and electronics in manufacturing, cell phones, fiber optics, fax machines, genetic therapies, and countless more.

More people were receiving wages, and wages were higher (adjusting for inflation) than ever before. This record led many people to think differently about economics. It also forced a rethinking of the components of the living wage. John Paul II reflected some of these changes in his treatment of the living wage in *Centesimus Annus*, where he commented on the goals that need to be met in order to spare workers from being treated as commodities: "These objectives include a sufficient wage for the support of the family, social insurance for old age and unemployment, and adequate protection for the conditions of employment."[4]

For myself, I would reformulate an approach to the issue of the living wage in this way. First, a good and decent society ought to aim at improving the standard of living of the poor in each decade, so that one can see measurable and admirable economic progress for the poor in each. Second, pastors, theologians, and others who think through Catholic social teaching ought to study the factors that lead to median incomes that rise in each decade, and that show higher income levels for the lowest 10 percent (or even the lowest 20 percent) of income earners. Some government policies impede this growth. Others make it more likely.

It does seem, based on the record, that political policies that encourage business activities, new job formation, new inventions and discoveries, as well as personal habits of enterprise and economic creativity, help the poor mightily. These are what enable more and more of the poor to work in the first place. Further, political regimes that measure the well-being of the poor solely by government money spent on them overlook two things: first, the fact that they accrue immense public debts to be paid off not by those who feel compassion today, but by their children and grandchildren. (Some compassion! Some self-sacrifice!) Second, they overlook the fact that they condemn the poor to habits of dependency, lack of self-fulfillment, and low economic achievement. The costs to the sense of personal dignity in the lives of the poor are immense. Besides, by this path poverty is never overcome, only perpetuated.

CHAPTER 7

The Six Ss

BESIDES THE FIVE PRINCIPLES BEGINNING WITH C, AND THE
five beginning with R, there are also six principles beginning with S. What
unites these six principles is a generations-long effort to give sharper
attention to the *human person* in the context of community. Thus, the first
two Ss give new prominence to the subject of inner human actions and
the inner distinctiveness even of communities themselves. Even communities have their own inner character, their own subjectivity which sets
them apart from other communities. These two principles take advantage
of the method provided by phenomenology's turn to the subject.

The next two Ss attend to recent differentiations in the universal
human experiences of community. One deals with the relation of local
communities to much larger communities (such as the state). This relation is specified as "subsidiarity." The other side deals with the new
experience—through modern means of communication—of the universal
bond of sympathy and respect for mutual rights. This relation among the
entire human community is called "solidarity."

Finally, since the goods of the earth were created by God for the good
of all human beings without exception, because we are all children of the
same God, emphasis has properly fallen in our time on the imperative
of "social inclusion" of all human beings in one economic network of

interchange. Thus is realized the "social destination" of the goods of the earth. Paradoxically, experience shows that this social destination is more quickly and thoroughly realized through methods of private ownership, personal initiative, and open and inclusive trade than by political command and management from above.

Analogously, the principle of social justice highlights the virtues learned and exercised by responsible persons—working through their creative associations—to build up the common good of local communities, as well as national and international communities.

In brief, the six Ss specify the new differentiations in modern societies that have brought these six new aspects of the relations among human persons and their communities into high definition.

1. The Subjectivity of the Human Person

In today's world, among other rights, the right of economic initiative is often suppressed. Yet it is a right which is important not only for the individual but also for the common good. Experience shows us that the denial of this right, or its limitation in the name of an alleged "equality" of everyone in society, diminishes, or in practice absolutely destroys the spirit of initiative, that is to say the creative subjectivity of the citizen.

(John Paul II, *Sollicitudo Rei Socialis*, §15.)

In *Rerum Novarum*, Leo XIII listed all the ways in which socialism was evil, futile, and bound to fail. John Paul II lived through all those failures.

Central to Pope John Paul II's thought is the question: What is a person? A person is an agent able to reflect on options and to choose among them, and to commit his entire self to another. In these potentialities he is made in the image of God. Even though he was not bound to do so, God made each person free, and provident over his or her own destiny. Therein lies the exceptional dignity of the human being among other creatures of God.

The human person is a self-starter, a creator of her own destiny, gifted with the right to personal initiative, someone who infuses every aspect of his actions and his work with his own personality. Denial of that truth is the fundamental error in socialism, the young Bishop Wojtyła bravely announced. Socialism saw only the material side of human life, he observed, and barely distinguished persons from things. It treated workers as objects of government decisions, not as subjects who produced human and personal things—who infused even steel girders with their own intelligence, hopes, craft, skill, and creativity. Socialism did not really respect "labor." It did not see laborers as persons. Socialism regarded human beings as factors of production, as cogs in a machine: quantifiable, interchangeable, and replaceable. For socialism, only numbers mattered: numbers of steel beams produced, often piling up in the mill yards only to rust, unfit for anybody to buy. How this waste of their work hurt the pride of workers. Yet socialist functionaries cared little for whether steel beams actually served the needs of others. Their job was to produce, not to serve needs. What mattered is that they had a production quota and it was met. They seemed incapable of seeing that this attitude toward the products of labor destroyed something in the worker's soul, deadened his whole outlook on life.

Even deeper, behind the socialist treatment of laborers as material factors in production lay a deliberate and ruthless atheism. Socialism could not see that every single human is a conscious, deliberating, choosing subject, who is entitled to take initiative in creating his own self-image and life path, as his own free conscience empowered him to do. It could not see the Creator in the creature.[1]

2. The Subjectivity of Society

According to *Rerum novarum* and the whole social doctrine of the Church, the social nature of man is not completely fulfilled in the State, but is realized in various intermediary groups, beginning with the family and including economic, social, political and cultural groups which stem from human nature itself and have their own autonomy, always with a view to the common good. This is what I have called the "subjectivity" of society.

(John Paul II, *Centesimus Annus*, §13.)

It is not only each person who is a subject and originator of actions, but also each people. For, as we know, no man is an island. Each of us has been plunged into a culture and a language, a set of founding sagas and poems, a particular historical dream to realize, and a matrix of loves and rivalries. Under the jackboots of marching totalitarians, whole peoples in our time have been overrun, and their communal subjectivity suppressed.

Poles, in particular, so long occupied by foreign powers from the east and the west, and the north and the south, have long had a special sense of peoplehood. The name the Polish people give to this social subjectivity is *Polonia*, which is not so much a territory as a national soul, a way of being inspirited as a whole people, an inner sense of integrity and authenticity. Poles who are Christians tend to identify their people with the crucified Christ, having been overrun and put through so much suffering. As a people they are also quietly and determinedly defiant. They insist on being who they are, and not allowing anyone to rip away their soul.

In the twentieth century, Poland's Jews suffered doubly: first for being Polish (for which the Nazis had contempt), and second for being Jews, all of whom the Nazis wanted to eradicate from the earth. And in Poland they almost did.

No one who has experienced twentieth-century Poland can deny the reality of the subjectivity of societies. Not necessarily states, but civil societies: all those intermediary institutions that bind a people as one, with one history, one national character, and one set of communal aspirations.

It offended Karol Wojtyła mightily that the Soviets were determined to take away Poland's literature, drama, and culture, and to show contempt for their language and deep Catholic faith (and for the Hebrew language and faith). It offended him mightily that the Socialists tried to coerce everyone into the worldview, architecture, and general homogenization of international socialism. Against the Nazis from 1939 to 1945, and against the Soviets from 1948 to 1989, Poles had to struggle daily to keep their own social subjectivity alive. It was the doggedness of millions of gnarled peasants, workers, and homemakers who struggled, prayed, and prevailed—those vulgar crowds at Czestochowa, along with some few journalists, artists, professors, and other professionals, who prevailed over one of the greatest military powers and most extensive mind-controlling systems in human history.

There is power in the subjectivity of societies. In our time, we have witnessed it abundantly.

3. Subsidiarity

In the English-language encyclopedia of the Catholic Church, *Sacramentum Mundi*, prepared by some of the most eminent theological leaders of the Second Vatican Council, the entry on "subsidiarity" begins by quoting

Abraham Lincoln on the principle of federalism and other intermediary societies of civil society, to the effect that the higher powers of the state ought not to intervene in matters in which the subsidiary, smaller societies practiced their own competencies. The higher power—the state—should step in only (and cautiously) where problems are too large for subsidiary societies to handle on their own. The principle of subsidiarity protects those social arrangements in which smaller groups, closest to everyday experience, make the maximum number of decisions. The reason for this arrangement is that authorities far away from immediate experience are too removed from facts on the ground. Their ignorance makes them a danger to the common good. Too often high officials insist on what seems rational to them, but in local circumstances is wildly inefficient, expensive, and even destructive.

True, there are two poles in the definition of subsidiarity—the higher authorities and the lower. The Catholic bishops of the United States have at times put their emphasis on the role of the state, because it brings its power to help (*subsidium*) the smaller, local powers. John Paul II, however, usually placed emphasis on the opposite pole, the lower powers, and for good reason. Their rights, competencies, and closer connection with facts on the ground are more likely to lead to wise prudential judgments than judgments made from far away.

Catholics who call themselves progressives sometimes make the same argument against the Vatican. They want more liberties and powers given to local authorities (national and lower), rather than held in the hands of the Vatican. At the same time, ironically, they have a tendency, particularly in regard to the social programs of the secular state, to favor the higher power over the lower. For instance, in the United States, decisions on school busing for racial purposes, authority over political elections, and laws promoting affirmative action were for a time entrusted to federal rather than local authorities.

These examples show that sometimes the common good may be better served by exerting federal powers. Still, the general rule holds. Higher powers tend to be more ignorant of local realities. And higher powers tend toward self-aggrandizement and the arrogance of power. Costs tend to rise precipitously; rules set from afar play out irrationally and counterproductively on local ground; and the competencies of local authorities wane from disuse. In addition, the bureaucratization of social assistance greatly diminishes the scope for human sympathies and personal knowledge. Abraham Lincoln willingly helped his brother with a significant loan, but by painful experience learned how his brother misspent it, and in consequence he refused to contribute further to his brother's dissipation by making another loan. He wanted to see a change in his brother's behavior first.

Neighbors know these behavioral tendencies in a way that distant welfare bureaucrats don't. Under the latter, recipients of social assistance must be treated like clients, not like neighbors and loved ones. From such experiences comes section 48 of *Centesimus Annus*:

> Malfunctions and defects in the Social Assistance State are the result of an inadequate understanding of the tasks proper to the State. Here again the principle of subsidiarity must be respected: a community of a higher order should not interfere in the internal life of a community of a lower order, depriving the latter of its functions, but rather should support it in case of need and help to coordinate its activity with the activities of the rest of society, always with a view to the common good.[2]

Finally, there is a natural tendency for taxpayers to let government do it all and to stop caring for the poor on their own. The impersonal squeezes out the personal. From this, huge miscalculations are made about what works, and about the real consequences of social action, as distinct from good intentions.

4. Solidarity

> By means of his work man commits himself, not only for his own sake but also for others and with others. Each person collaborates in the work of others and for their good. Man works in order to provide for the needs of his family, his community, his nation, and ultimately all humanity. Moreover, he collaborates in the work of his fellow employees, as well as in the work of suppliers and in the customers' use of goods, in a progressively expanding chain of solidarity.
>
> (John Paul II, *Centesimus Annus*, §43.)

In Poland after 1987, "solidarity" was an unavoidable word—and virtue and good method for human progress—for it was the name given by the electrician from Gdansk, Lech Walesa, to the labor union he helped to found, and to the broad circle of people who leapt to its assistance. In the early days of the free labor unions (before the arrival of National Socialist unions and Communist Party unions), the cry "Solidarity forever!" reminded unionists that their chances of survival and success depended above all on their unity. Each unionist alone was hopelessly weak, but all men and women working together in unbreakable solidarity—and only through solidarity—could prevail.

In June 1979, after Pope John Paul II's "nine days that changed the world," his first official visit to his native land, in crowds estimated at places to be in the millions, Polish citizens who despised communism saw quite visibly that "there are millions more of us than there are of them." They began to develop confidence in their own power, provided they stuck together. In facing down the Communist machine, they now knew they had more power than they ever had before. While Pope John Paul II was there in Poland, the Polish government and its police and army were visibly helpless to intervene. The Polish people knew that the pope was de facto the greatest power in Poland; or, rather, they themselves were. The pope would protect them by drawing universal attention to the depredations committed by their Communist government.

Reflecting on these things, Pope John Paul II began to grasp of the immense social power in unity of soul. By this he did not mean mass hysteria, or the drunken feeling of a mob sensing its capacity for violence. No, he meant the power of God's own *caritas* to unite free persons into one human family. The human race is one.

For Pope John Paul II solidarity did not mean a virtue of bonding together blindly at all costs, in order to act as a mob hot to coerce others. Rather, it meant the self-sacrificing cooperation of free women and free men, recognizing their mutual love as sisters and brothers of one same Father. It meant reaching out globally to help one another. It meant a new commitment to mutual concern for one another.

In December 2012, I was invited to Poland by President Bronisław Komorowski to receive an award for working for the liberty of the Polish people three decades earlier, in the days when they felt in extremis, when martial law was declared in 1981. Army troops and police struck suddenly and trucked hundreds of Solidarity leaders into prison camps. In December of that year, President Ronald Reagan went on television to ask Americans to put lights in their front windows to support the liberty of the Polish people. He put such lights in the White House windows himself. Now, said the Polish president thirty-one years later, it is the turn of the

Polish people and other free peoples to put lights in their own windows on behalf of those in Ukraine and Belarus and other nations that do not yet enjoy basic freedoms. He invited me to accompany him downtown to light candles in front of the bronze statue of Ronald Reagan on a broad boulevard across from the U.S. embassy, to join in solidarity with Reagan's candle lighting thirty-one years earlier. He wanted to broadcast this humble ceremony on international television, to spread the candlelight of hope into the places around the world that still remained dark.

That evening was, I thought, a lovely visualization of the global virtue John Paul II so eloquently introduced into papal social thought in contemporary terms and symbols, following the model of Saint Augustine's City of God, Paul VI's "Civilization of Love," and other such longings—and actions—around the world. Solidarity. Yes, solidarity as an appeal for the freedom and dignity of all individuals everywhere.

5. The Social Destination of All Created Goods

The original source of all that is good is the very act of God, who created both the earth and man, and who gave the earth to man so that he might have dominion over it by his work and enjoy its fruits (Gen 1:28). God gave the earth to the whole human race for the sustenance of all its members, without excluding or favouring anyone. This is the foundation of the universal destination of the earth's goods.

(John Paul II, *Centesimus Annus*, §31.)

In chapter five above, in the section on the common good, I noted that the Lord God Creator intended all the goods of the earth for all his human family. Down through history, this same theorem has been embraced by philosophers in many countries and over many centuries. Closer to our own time, John Stuart Mill grounded the right to private property on the working condition that the temporary owner improve that property for the future inheritance of all. He noted that a field of strawberries put into attentive cultivation produced many times more strawberries than the same field left untended. In this way, private care improved the common inheritance of all. (He did not notice that the converse of this theorem was also verified in practice: fields left to collectivist cultivation kept falling in yield. Contrariwise, the 2 percent of Soviet fields left in private cultivation grew over 25 percent of all produce in all Soviet lands.[3])

The destination of the earth's goods is the well-being of all humankind, both now and in the future. But the means for reaching that goal, as history shows over and over, is attentive cultivation by private owners. The moral template is this: No one may be excluded from the social benefits. All must be included. In emergencies of famine, disease, disastrous storms, floods, and the like, people around the world properly prompt their governments to intervene with often massive assistance. Recent experience also shows that the greatest success in reducing poverty is achieved by including the poor within the circle of global trade; education in the arts of enterprise and personal initiative; transferring knowledge, know-how, and skills; and expert counseling on how to do more fruitfully things already being done. The cause of wealth is human capital. Raising the level of human skills, desire, and inventiveness heightens that capital. The universal improvement of human capital is the best route to spreading human goods universally. For the last 150 years, under the influence of Communism and Socialism, distribution has been tried. It does little for the improvement of human capital, and what do nations that follow that route have to show for it?

It is morally right that attentive and hardworking owners should be significantly rewarded for all the good they bring to others. Such incentives are a realistic spur to great efforts in each succeeding year, and to sound preparations for activities still to come, many decades (even generations) in the future.

6. Social Justice

The condition of the working classes is the pressing question of the hour, and nothing can be of higher interest to all classes of the State than that it should be rightly and reasonably settled. But it will be easy for Christian working men to solve it aright if they will form associations, choose wise guides, and follow on the path which with so much advantage to themselves and the common weal was trodden by their fathers before them. Prejudice, it is true, is mighty, and so is the greed of money; but if the sense of what is just and rightful be not deliberately stifled, their fellow citizens are sure to be won over to a kindly feeling towards men whom they see to be in earnest as regards their work and who prefer so unmistakably right dealing to mere lucre, and the sacredness of duty to every other consideration.

(Leo XIII, *Rerum Novarum*, §60.)

It is most necessary that economic life be again subjected to and governed by a true and effective directing principle. This function is one that the economic dictatorship which has recently displaced free competition can still less perform, since it is a headstrong power and a violent energy that, to benefit people, needs to be strongly curbed and wisely ruled. But it cannot curb and rule itself. Loftier and nobler principles—social justice and social charity—must, therefore, be sought whereby this dictatorship may be governed firmly and fully. Hence, the institutions themselves of peoples and, particularly those of all social life, ought to be penetrated with this justice, and it is most necessary that it be truly effective, that is, establish a juridical and social order which will, as it were, give form and shape to all economic life.

(Pius XI, *Quadragesimo Anno*, §88.)

Following the destruction caused by the war, we see in some countries and under certain aspects a positive effort to rebuild a democratic society inspired by social justice, so as to deprive Communism of the revolutionary potential represented by masses of people subjected to exploitation and oppression. In general, such attempts endeavour to preserve free market mechanisms, ensuring, by means of a stable currency and the harmony of social relations, the conditions for steady and healthy economic growth in which people through their own work can build a better future for themselves and their families. At the same time, these attempts try to avoid making market mechanisms the only point of reference for social life, and they tend to subject them to public control which upholds the principle of the common destination of material goods. In this context, an abundance of work opportunities, a solid system of social security and professional training, the freedom to join trade unions and the effective action of unions, the assistance provided in cases of unemployment, the opportunities for democratic participation in the life of society—all these are meant to deliver work from the mere condition of "a commodity," and to guarantee its dignity.

(John Paul II, *Centesimus Annus*, §19.)

These are some key founding insights of the concept of social justice. While it is important to note that social justice does not dominate the entire field of Catholic social teaching, it is, nonetheless, one of its central operating dynamisms. As we have done in these first seven chapters, so we will continue throughout this book to bring to light everything that social justice isn't, and what it is. In the Catholic tradition, social justice is a concept (a strategy, too) invented to block the domination of totalitarian states over all of civic life. The term is also a guide for inventing rival institutions, particularly a multiplicity of associations created by citizens of ingenuity, initiative, and leadership, to solve as many social problems as possible without falling into dependency on the state. It is, finally, a spur to a new humanism, based on assisting the development of human capital in all countries and within all sectors of those countries.

We will turn now to brief accounts of the crucial discoveries made by the three popes most prominent in sharpening the meaning of social justice: Leo XIII, Pius XI, and John Paul II, along with their successors Benedict XVI and Francis. From there, we conclude Part One of the book with two further considerations. The first concerns the new specialization in theological method introduced by the invention of the new theology of social justice, the specialization of the scout and the explorer. The second concerns the urgent need for a much more realistic and detailed account of the reality of human sin. For it is human sin that most undermines all efforts to build a genuine humanism among the world's many peoples.

CHAPTER 8

Leo XIII's *Rerum Novarum*

AS WE NOTED AT THE OUTSET, DESPITE THE IMPORTANCE OF social justice, precise statements about its nature are hard to find. The index of the famous post–Vatican II encyclopedia *Sacramentum Mundi* lists only one reference, a single paragraph alluding to the concept, but no specific entry.[1] Rodger Charles, S.J., in *The Christian Social Conscience* does not even mention the term, but relies on the classical distinctions among commutative, distributive, and legal justice.[2] The discussion in Johannes Messner's magisterial thousand-page text, *Social Ethics* (1949), is disappointingly brief; he treats the concept on only one page.[3]

Aside from Nell-Breuning's commentary (mentioned earlier, but treated more thoroughly in the next chapter), the best treatments I have discovered agree that the term "social justice" came into contemporary usage with an unusual lack of clarity. Two of these treatments offer a brief history of the term and, in the main, complement one another. One of these speaks of the term with considerable disparagement (Ernest Fortin), while the other (by Jean-Yves Calvez and Jacques Perrin) puts the term in the best light it can muster—but still lacking a clear definition.

The third treatment, by William Ferree, Marianist Father at the University of Dayton, offers a highly stimulating interpretation, quite novel and sadly neglected.[4] Indeed, from him I have learned my basic insight, namely, that social justice is in fact *a virtue of individual persons*. More recently, Patrick Burke has published a detailed study reinforcing this view.[5]

Fortin dryly spells out the confusion surrounding the term "social justice" in this brief description of the way most people speak of social justice—what might be called the "vulgar" view of social justice:

> As nearly as I can make out, social justice, in contradistinction to either legal or distributive justice, does not refer to any special disposition of the soul and hence cannot properly be regarded as a virtue. Its subject is not the individual human being but a mysterious "X" named society, which is said to be unintentionally responsible for the condition of its members and in particular for the lot of the poor among them.[6]

This concept makes sense, Fortin continues, "only within the context of the new political theories of the seventeenth century." These theories shifted attention away from virtue and moral character—where nearly all philosophies had directed attention until then—to newly imagined social structures that would guarantee the security and freedom of atomistic individuals. "As such, it is of a piece with the modern rights theory," writes Fortin. "On the one side, it departed from traditional theories of virtue. On the other, it used the language of modern natural rights theory, but then stepped quite outside it, in order 'to equalize social conditions.'" But equalizing conditions, of necessity, dramatically diminishes personal responsibility, virtue, merit, and character.

Like Calvez and Perrin, Fortin notes that the first author to use the term "social justice" was the Italian Jesuit Luigi Taparelli d'Azeglio, in his *Theoretical Essay on Natural Right from an Historical Standpoint* (1840–43). Fortin adds that the influence of this Catholic scholar on Leo XIII can be clearly traced. Taparelli attempted to import the Enlightenment term "natural rights" into Catholic social thought by linking it to a new concept, social justice.

However, according to Fortin, what really laid the groundwork for this new concept of social justice was Rousseau's view that society corrupts the pure individual. Rousseau (1712–78) reformulated virtually all human problems in terms of the distinction between nature and history, as opposed to the classical distinction between body and soul. Fortin summarizes the consequences:

If society and its accidental structures are the primary cause of the corruption of human beings and the evils attendant upon it, they must be changed. Social reform takes precedence over personal reform; it constitutes the first and perhaps the only moral imperative.

No doubt Fortin is correct about the woolly sloganeering to which social justice has been prey. Even the Communists found "social justice" useful for their propaganda, and socialists and social democrats still use it unabashedly as the generic name for their own program. Since Leo XIII wrote expressly against socialism and the growing state, as well as against the destructive force of "equalizing conditions," the left has wandered very far from his express intentions.

To rescue the term from ideological misuse is no easy task. The first step is to disentangle the term's complicated history.

In his careful study, Burke details how Taparelli, as a nineteenth-century "conservative" opponent of classical liberalism and supporter of the old feudal powers, including the Church, viewed social justice in terms of constitutional order and as having nothing to do with economics (on which he also wrote without ever mentioning social justice). Burke also notes the contemporaneous significance of Antonio Rosmini, who, in contrast to Taparelli's conservativism, developed in *The Constitution under Social Justice*[7] and other writings a Catholic "liberal" understanding of social justice that hinged on the constitutional organization of political life, with principal concern for property rights and, in turn, the condemnation of redistributive economic policies and practices.[8]

Decades later, in drafting the encyclical *Rerum Novarum*, Pope Leo XIII and Matteo Liberatore, S.J., both students of Taparelli, were faithful to Taparelli's concept of social justice, particularly in their development of the doctrine of inequality. But forty years after *Rerum Novarum*, Pope Pius XI's *Quadragesimo Anno*, drafted in large part by Oswald Nell-Breuning, who was a student of Liberatore, set aside Taparelli's views on social justice and inequality, and promoted social justice as economic doctrine. Nell-Breuning's line-by-line commentary, *The Reorganization of Social Economy*, treats social justice as both a virtue and a regulative principle. Later usage picks up on the social regulative principle, and ignores the virtue.

In the subsequent debate, where mention is made of "social justice," no single generally accepted definition has emerged. Messner, in his work mentioned above, explains with considerable mixing of terms that "'social justice' refers especially to the economic and social welfare of 'society,' in the sense of the *economically cooperating community of the state.*"[9] Cardinal Höffner, in *Christian Social Teaching*, adopts the position that social justice is the late-medieval "legal justice" which is related to the later German "general justice." He suggests calling it "common-good justice, a virtue that is exercised only by the state, territorial authorities, professional classes and the Church."[10] Calvez and Perrin, who narrow down the term a bit more than Charles, Messner, and Höffner, conclude that "social justice is general justice applied to the economic as distinct from the political society."[11]

A wonderful chapter in a dissertation produced at Boston College by Normand Joseph Paulhus analyzes the theological school that explored the terrain on which the developing concept of social justice would be built. This group in southern Germany, called the Fribourg Union, spurred the widespread discussion of key background issues in the period before *Rerum Novarum*. Paulhus draws our attention to at least three of them.[12]

At the beginning of the 1800s, the word "political" dominated discourse, while the word "social" appeared with comparatively less frequency. The slow turning from monarchical to republican forms of government ("democratic" forms in today's usage) brought more attention to concrete differentials among the *demos*, the people. Thinkers began to differentiate farmers from city folk: craftsmen, tradesmen, manufacturing workers, and so on. Marx and others supplied political analysis with new theories of class and class warfare. Attention elsewhere shifted to the many "factions" among democratic peoples. The success of the young United States in lifting so many of its in-streaming poor from poverty to property ownership and steady upward mobility created for Europe *das Sozialproblem*: why was Europe not lifting up its own *les misérables*? In some discussions, the word "social" began displacing the term "politics," and was made to seem analytically prior to "political."

Meanwhile, the analysis of the word "social" was also beginning to undergo a sea change of a different sort. For centuries after Aristotle, man was said to be a "political animal," and the main method for analyzing polities was to study their laws and their rational principles—the well-formed habits, perspectives, and rules that bound peoples as one. But after Machiavelli (1469–1527), the main method of analysis began to shift

away from laws and principles of reason to the will of individuals, a volun-
tarist energy, and an awareness of the nonrational forces at play in social
life: self-preservation, the hunger for power, pride, greed, self-interest, and
self-exultation. The "real world" of naked will versus "dreams of reason."

As the word "social" came into common use, that use increasingly
came to be steered down three different tracks. Down one track, "social"
became pitted against "individual." Down another track, "social" (as in
civil society and in various traditional and newly arising free associations)
was more and more pitted against "state." As Paul Adams pointed out
in his introduction to this volume, excessive attention to the individual
on the one side, and to the state on the other, crushed out the space in
between them both, the space of civil society and its freely forming associative life.

Down a third track, "social" came to be divided by its basic inspirations: reasoned and law-abiding social energies versus social energies
moved primarily (it was said) by passion, will, and self-interest. It was
"rationalists" versus "voluntarists," Aristotelian-Thomists versus Machiavelli and Hobbes.

It was into this complex vortex of contrary meanings and energies that
the term "social" came to be paired with "justice." No wonder "social justice" became hard to define.

Let us, then, take another cut at the history of social justice. During
the nineteenth century, among those driven to use the term "social," one
side favored the tradition of "legal justice" laid out first by Aristotle, and
developed more fully by Aquinas. This side gathered wind in its sails from
the Thomistic revival (or "scholastic revival") that gained strength from
about the 1830s until its powerful blessing and impulsion by Leo XIII in
Aeterni Patris (1879).

As a rival to it, the other side used "social justice" to call for more political activism—activism demanding state coercion, usually to enforce new
patterns of redistribution of income via taxation.

Pius XI in *Quadragesimo Anno* and theologians such as Nell-Breuning
seemingly combined both factions. On the one hand, they promoted the
rebirth of the Thomistic tradition, with its praise for thick associational
living (as in the guilds and city-states), reason, law, and the virtues guided
by practical wisdom. On the other hand, they also felt it necessary to call
upon the will of the state to enforce certain social outcomes, such as
wealth redistribution and state protections of the vulnerable and needy.

It is not clear that any one thinker in those days foresaw the danger of a growing state Leviathan, using humanitarian motives to justify massive new state powers, even the totalitarian state claiming to speak for "the people." No one, that is, except Alexis de Tocqueville, who foresaw (and dreaded) the soft despotism which lies always ready to rise up under the cover of false sentimental motives. Few directly will the dictatorial state. But many cherish the sweet comforting desires that feed its rise—and which it falsely promises to satisfy. Presciently, Tocqueville wrote:

> I think, then, that the species of oppression by which democratic nations are menaced is unlike anything that ever before existed in the world; our contemporaries will find no prototype of it in their memories. I seek in vain for an expression that will accurately convey the whole of the idea I have formed of it; the old words despotism and tyranny are inappropriate: the thing itself is new, and since I cannot name, I must attempt to define it. . . .
>
> Above this race of men stands an immense and tutelary power, which takes upon itself alone to secure their gratifications and to watch over their fate. That power is absolute, minute, regular, provident, and mild. It would be like the authority of a parent if, like that authority, its object was to prepare men for manhood; but it seeks, on the contrary, to keep them in perpetual childhood: it is well content that the people should rejoice, provided they think of nothing but rejoicing. For their happiness such a government willingly labors, but it chooses to be the sole agent and the only arbiter of that happiness; it provides for their security, foresees and supplies their necessities, facilitates their pleasures, manages their principal concerns, directs their industry, regulates the descent of property, and subdivides their inheritances: what remains, but to spare them all the care of thinking and all the trouble of living?
>
> Thus it every day renders the exercise of the free agency of man less useful and less frequent; it circumscribes the will within a narrower range and gradually robs a man of all the uses of himself. The principle of equality has prepared men for these things; it has predisposed men to endure them and often to look on them as benefits.
>
> After having thus successively taken each member of the community in its powerful grasp and fashioned him at will, the supreme power then extends its arm over the whole community. It covers the

surface of society with a network of small complicated rules, minute and uniform, through which the most original minds and the most energetic characters cannot penetrate, to rise above the crowd. The will of man is not shattered, but softened, bent, and guided; men are seldom forced by it to act, but they are constantly restrained from acting. Such a power does not destroy, but it prevents existence; it does not tyrannize, but it compresses, enervates, extinguishes, and stupefies a people, till each nation is reduced to nothing better than a flock of timid and industrious animals, of which the government is the shepherd.[13]

From "common good" uncritically employed to the false justification of a soft despotism is not so long a step. Similarly for the move from "social justice" to state coercion.

———

As we have already noted above, the context in which Leo XIII encountered the term "social justice" sprang from one of the most enormous social transformations in human history: the end of the agrarian age that had begun before the time of Christ, and its fairly abrupt entry into an era of invention, investment, factories, manufacturing, urban growth, and city services. No longer did families have an inherited roof over their heads and daily food from their own land. They were uprooted, and now dependent on city dwelling, the availability of jobs, and their own initiative. Traditional social networks were cut to shreds. Associations of a lifetime were torn asunder.

Moreover, two radically opposed social ideals were propagandized during the nineteenth century: on the one hand, the socialism of Marx and those of similar mind and, on the other hand, the apparently radical individualism of Bentham and Mill. (Actually, English life was not nearly as individualistic as the latter two's abstractions suggested. Among Europeans, the English showed the most striking mutual respect, politeness, and consideration for others, as seen in polite queuing up at bus stops and ticket windows. Theirs was the most genial orderliness.) On the whole, the Continent leaned toward the statist emphasis and away from the model of civil society and respect for the individual. Pope Leo XIII in *Rerum Novarum* made it his aim to trace a new pathway, closer to the English model of civil society, and veering away from the socialist model.

John Stuart Mill was a great champion of the liberal order (meaning individual liberty and relatively free markets, of the sort that encourage invention). But taking a cue from his wife, he also leaned toward the sort of democratic socialism that he thought would own the future. Mill was a classical liberal in his well-worked-out principles, but in his sympathies he was a social-democratic liberal.

Pope Leo understood that new times demanded a new response. The old social order was fading fast, a new one was swiftly arising—which shape it would take was not yet clear. Since the family, he noted, has always been the most central and intimate institution for handing down the faith, new fractures and stresses in the family demanded that the Church enter into the battle for the shape of the future. The English line of argument would not convince the French or Germans, nor the reverse.

Leo XIII saw that new institutions and new virtues among individuals would be required for new times. He feared the socialist state (for thirteen specific reasons he carefully spelled out). He feared the futile and false idea of equality. And he also feared the ideal of radical individualism, which would eventually, he predicted, drive the undefended individual into the eager arms of the state.

The Rise of a New Moral Imperative

The best way to grasp both the complexity and concreteness of Leo XIII's thought is to meditate slowly and first-hand on some of his key texts, especially those that spell out long in advance the ill effects that socialism would wreak on the human race. For instance, Leo's long list of reasons for opposing real existing socialism proved remarkably more accurate in their pessimism than were the rosy hopes of many intellectuals of his time and later.[14]

Most vividly and at great length Leo XIII diagnosed the evils of socialism. But then he also diagnosed the fatal flaws in the idea of "equality of conditions" that underlies socialism. We must take these up in turn. But it is first necessary to put ourselves into the dilemma of the nineteenth century.

Until that time, it was taken as normal that the vast majority of the world was very poor. "The poor ye shall always have with you." That brute fact generated no urgency that said that poverty must be overcome. Resignation and acceptance were taken to be the moral imperative. But then, rather abruptly, came the beginning of a new age; new wealth was being created, inventions and discoveries led to a rapid increase in manufacturing and the spread of (at first) small factories, the growth of urban areas, and a decline in the primacy of agriculture.

The agrarian age which had ruled for more than two millennia slowly yielded to a new age, based on invention (the pin machine observed by Adam Smith, for example), enterprise, industry, new sources of power (such as the steam engine) and transportation (the railroads), and a massive exodus from the land to swelling towns and burgeoning cities. Families were uprooting themselves; more and more men no longer worked on the fields adjacent to their homes and alongside their families, but in factories that separated them from their families for long hours at a time, at first as long as ten to twelve hours per day, six days a week. Since for centuries the family had been the nursery of the faith, Leo XIII saw that the future of the Church was also at stake, as well as the condition of the working man, and millions of at least partially abandoned women and children.

But Leo also saw, as no pope before him could, that new wealth was being created not on farms, but more and more in industry. Railroads were being built, night lamps lit city streets, new inventions kept arriving yearly. For the first time, poverty in Europe came now to be experienced as a disgrace. Marx had described it as a disgrace, precisely because it stood out in contrast to the unprecedented wealth created by capitalism, but he had overlooked the widespread movement out of poverty in America. Worse still, he had failed to grasp the genius by which new wealth is created from the bottom-up. The same must be said of Leo XIII, too. For the United States presented to the world not only a new model of a republican polity (it was not like the French Republic or the Republic of Venice). It also presented a new model of the dynamic economy. It displayed unparalleled upward mobility. Few in Europe grasped America's inspirations, methods, and practices.

But Leo did grasp, more generally, the moral obligation of providing material and external help for the poor:

> We have insisted, it is true, that since the end of society is to make men better, the chief good that society can possess is virtue. Nevertheless, it is the business of a well-constituted body politic to see to the provision of those material and external helps "the use of which is necessary to virtuous action."[15]

So Leo saw that poverty is no longer inevitable for the human race. It is socially, morally wrong. It must be alleviated. But through socialism?

Thirteen Reasons Why Socialism Is Evil and Will Fail

With no hesitation, Leo dismissed the promises of socialism as futile—doomed to embarrassing failure—and evil. He recognized plenty of inequities and wrongs in the economic world of 1891:

> To remedy these wrongs the socialists, working on the poor man's envy of the rich, are striving to do away with private property, and contend that individual possessions should become the common property of all, to be administered by the State or by municipal bodies. They hold that by thus transferring property from private individuals to the community, the present mischievous state of things will be set to rights, inasmuch as each citizen will then get his fair share of whatever there is to enjoy. But their contentions are so clearly powerless to end the controversy that were they carried into effect the working man himself would be among the first to suffer. They are, moreover, emphatically unjust, for they would rob the lawful possessor, distort the functions of the State, and create utter confusion in the community.[16]

Leo later returned to dwell on the evils socialism would bring in its train. His reflections were all the more remarkable, since at the time neither the Soviet Union nor any other example of modern socialism actually existed. Leo was arguing from principles about human nature that are repeatedly verified in human experience. Thus, based solely on principle and its historical verification, he confidently predicted that socialism would be proven not only unjust, but more than that, too:

> It is only too evident what an upset and disturbance there would be in all classes, and to how intolerable and hateful a slavery citizens would be subjected. The door would be thrown open to envy, to mutual invective, and to discord; the sources of wealth themselves would run dry, for no one would have any interest in exerting his talents or his industry; and that ideal equality about which they entertain pleasant dreams would be in reality the levelling down of all to a like condition of misery and degradation. Hence, it is clear that the main tenet of socialism, community of goods, must be utterly rejected, since it only

injures those whom it would seem meant to benefit, is directly contrary to the natural rights of mankind, and would introduce confusion and disorder into the commonweal. The first and most fundamental principle, therefore, if one would undertake to alleviate the condition of the masses, must be the inviolability of private property. This being established, we proceed to show where the remedy sought for must be found.[17]

In these two paragraphs, Leo listed six reasons why socialism is evil and doomed to failure. Let us number them plainly here. The first six problems with socialism are:

1. It works upon the poor man's envy of the rich.
2. It strives to do away with private property.
3. It contends that all property should become the property of the state.
4. It robs the lawful possessor of what is his natural right.
5. It expands without clear limits the functions of the state.
6. It causes confusion in the community.

But Leo does not stop here. He keeps stomping away:

7. The socialist project strikes at the interests of the wage-earner by depriving him of liberty to dispose of his own wages.
8. Still worse, socialism destroys the poor man's hope of bettering his condition in life:

Socialists, therefore, by endeavoring to transfer the possessions of individuals to the community at large, strike at the interests of every wage-earner, since they would deprive him of the liberty of disposing of his wages, and thereby of all hope and possibility of increasing his resources and of bettering his condition in life.[18]

9. Socialism places man on the level of the other animals, by denying him basic human rights and his use of his freedom to reason, choose, and act for himself, his family, and others:

What is of far greater moment, however, is the fact that the remedy [socialists] propose is manifestly against justice. For, every man has by nature the right to possess property as his own. This is one of the chief points of distinction between man and the animal creation, for the brute has no power of self direction, but is governed by two main instincts, which keep his powers on the alert, impel him to develop them in a fitting manner, and stimulate and determine him to action without any power of choice.... It is the mind, or reason, which is the predominant element in us who are human creatures; it is this which renders a human being human, and distinguishes him essentially from the brute. And on this very account—that man alone among the animal creation is endowed with reason—it must be within his right to possess things not merely for temporary and momentary use, as other living things do, but to have and to hold them in stable and permanent possession; he must have not only things that perish in the use, but those also which, though they have been reduced into use, continue for further use in after time.[19]

10. By placing the state first, socialism undermines the natural order of things, in which man precedes the state:

Man, fathoming by his faculty of reason matters without number, linking the future with the present, and being master of his own acts, guides his ways under the eternal law and the power of God, whose providence governs all things. Wherefore, it is in his power to exercise his choice not only as to matters that regard his present welfare, but also about those which he deems may be for his advantage in time yet to come. Hence, man not only should possess the fruits of the earth, but also the very soil, inasmuch as from the produce of the earth he has to lay by provision for the future. Man's needs do not die out, but forever recur; although satisfied today, they demand fresh supplies for tomorrow. Nature accordingly must have given to man a source that is stable and remaining always with him, from which he might look to draw continual supplies. And this stable condition of things he finds solely in the earth and its fruits. There is no need to bring in the State. Man precedes the State, and possesses, prior to the formation of any State, the right of providing for the substance of his body.[20]

11. Socialism commits injustice by ordering that one man's labor be enjoyed by another, without the laborer's consent:

Is it just that the fruit of a man's own sweat and labor should be possessed and enjoyed by any one else? As effects follow their cause, so is it just and right that the results of labor should belong to those who have bestowed their labor.[21]

12. The socialist state intrudes into family life and the household and thereby destroys the home:

> The contention, then, that the civil government should at its option intrude into and exercise intimate control over the family and the household is a great and pernicious error. . . . Paternal authority can be neither abolished nor absorbed by the State; for it has the same source as human life itself. "The child belongs to the father," and is, as it were, the continuation of the father's personality; and speaking strictly, the child takes its place in civil society, not of its own right, but in its quality as member of the family in which it is born. And for the very reason that "the child belongs to the father" it is, as St. Thomas Aquinas says, "before it attains the use of free will, under the power and the charge of its parents." The socialists, therefore, in setting aside the parent and setting up a State supervision, act against natural justice, and destroy the structure of the home.[22]

13. Finally, socialism propagandizes falsely and denies the necessary lot of humanity. Socialism necessarily advances by deluding. The truth is not in it:

> To suffer and to endure, therefore, is the lot of humanity; let them strive as they may, no strength and no artifice will ever succeed in banishing from human life the ills and troubles which beset it. If any there are who pretend differently—who hold out to a hard-pressed people the boon of freedom from pain and trouble, an undisturbed repose, and constant enjoyment—they delude the people and impose upon them, and their lying promises will one day bring forth only evils worse than the present. Nothing is more useful than to look upon the world as it really is, and at the same time to seek elsewhere, as We have said, for the solace to its troubles.[23]

In summary, socialism is not a livable system for humans, for it incites envy, the most evil of social passions.

I thought of this passage in 1991, when I arrived in what my ticket called Leningrad. When we landed, however, the name of that famous city had reverted to presocialist Saint Petersburg, the jewel of pre-Soviet Russia. The flags snapping in the wind were the blue, white, and red bars of the old Russia; gone were the hammer and sickle. That night, a Russian philosopher, flush with pride at how he and an entire crowd of his fellow citizens had faced down the Soviet tanks commanded to crush them, rejoiced now in his nation's new liberty. Now he was a freedom fighter, too. He pounded me on the chest. "Next time you want to start an experiment like socialism, try it on animals first. Humans it hurts too much." (I enjoyed the irony of him blaming me.) A little later, after a vodka or two, he again announced: "If you socialized the Sahara, within two years people would be standing in line for sand."

The Root of Evil in Socialism Is Forced Equality

Leo was not at all shy about calling a spade a spade. After noting how socialism would incite envy, encourage invective, and disturb creative order, Leo's next words were so strong one suspects him to be carried away like a preacher with hyperbole and brimstone. But what he predicted actually happened. Witness the deliberate starvation of millions of Ukrainians in the 1930s because they refused to give up their family lands.

> Most of all it is essential, where the passion of greed is so strong, to keep the populace within the line of duty; for, if all may justly strive to better their condition, neither justice nor the common good allows any individual to seize upon that which belongs to another, or, under the futile and shallow pretext of equality, to lay violent hands on other people's possessions.[24]

Moreover, Leo's unflinching eyes saw that a certain inequality is inherent in individual talent and behavior. And such inequality is a great advantage for human societies:

> It must be first of all recognized that the condition of things inherent in human affairs must be borne with, for it is impossible to reduce civil society to one dead level. Socialists may in that intent do their utmost, but all striving against nature is in vain. There naturally exist among mankind manifold differences of the most important kind; people differ in capacity, skill, health, strength; and unequal fortune is a necessary result of unequal condition. Such inequality is far from being disadvantageous either to individuals or to the community. Social and public life can only be maintained by means of various kinds of capacity for business and the playing of many parts; and each man, as a rule, chooses the part which suits his own peculiar domestic condition.[25]

Where then does this destructive dream of equality come from? That self-destructive metaphysics is built on conflict and enmity. Leo wrote:

> The great mistake... is to take up the notion that class is naturally hostile to class, and that the wealthy and the working men are intended by nature to live in mutual conflict. So irrational and so false is this view that the direct contrary is the truth. Just as the symmetry of the human frame is the result of the suitable arrangement of the different parts of the body, so in a State is it ordained by nature that these two classes should dwell in harmony and agreement, so as to maintain the balance of the body politic. Each needs the other: capital cannot do without labor, nor labor without capital. Mutual agreement results in the beauty of good order, while perpetual conflict necessarily produces confusion and savage barbarity.[26]

And for still another reason, God made human life an occasion for individual virtue and merit, as many parables of Jesus highlight:

> As for riches and the other things which men call good and desirable, whether we have them in abundance, or are lacking in them—so far as eternal happiness is concerned—it makes no difference; the only important thing is to use them aright. Jesus Christ, when He redeemed us with plentiful redemption, took not away the pains and sorrows which in such large proportion are woven together in the web of our mortal life. He transformed them into motives of virtue and occasions of merit; and no man can hope for eternal reward unless he follow in the blood-stained footprints of his Saviour.[27]

Still again, all must contribute to the common good. Each individual must do so according to his own talents and capacities, but not all in the same way. Social space in which individual commitments can be freely made is, therefore, necessary:

> But although all citizens, without exception, can and ought to contribute to that common good in which individuals share so advantageously to themselves, yet it should not be supposed that all can contribute in the like way and to the same extent. No matter what changes may occur in forms of government, there will ever be differences and inequalities of condition in the State. Society cannot exist or be conceived of without them.[28]

In other words, Leo predicted that great inequalities would persist under communism. And so they did.[29] Leo XIII's main task, however, was not to condemn socialism, but to specify the remedy for it. He saw in the material progress of the nineteenth century, including the steam engine, locomotives, gas lights, and (on the horizon) electricity, that poverty is not the necessary condition of the human race. More and more people could be freed from the shackles of poverty. "The poor ye shall always have with you" is no fateful imperative. If wealth could be created to raise the lot of many humans (of all nations) out of poverty, then poverty is not a necessary condition but a wrong. And what is the creative remedy? Not socialism.

If Not Socialism, What?

Leo XIII recommended that free and self-determining persons turn to their own distinctive strengths: social initiatives and the arts of association. They themselves should conceive of and build free labor unions and many other organizations seeking to better the life of all. And their aim should be to better life not only materially, but also in the pursuit of truth, beauty, and the interior love of God and love of neighbor. All humans need to learn to cooperate with one another for the good of all. They need to learn to focus not only on themselves.

To get to this point, Leo said quite forcefully that the "liberal" (that is, capitalist) nations would have to undertake serious reforms. He was not ready to condemn liberalism, but he was not ready to give it a clean bill of health, either. He held that both utilitarianism and Anglo-American individualism had too narrow a view of the importance of community. He feared that liberalism left the lonely individual too much at the tender mercies of the omnivorous state. Here I think Leo XIII shares a vision not unlike Tocqueville's in *Democracy in America*. Tocqueville noted new forms of community taking shape in America, which people on the Continent did not perceive. In America, Tocqueville noted how local associations were everywhere having beneficent effects. He praised the American emphasis on building small communities: villages, then towns, then counties, then states, and only in the end a united community of one nation. Further, Americans showed much more reverence for religion than Europeans, at least religions of the biblical type (Jewish and Christian) which highly valued both the person and the community.

Furthermore, as Pius XI later noted in *Quadragesimo Anno*, Leo XIII's distance from communism and capitalism was not symmetrical: He severely criticized capitalism and insisted on its revision, whereas he rejected socialism root and branch.[30]

Although Leo did not expressly linger on it here, the practices of the new habits he called for constituted in themselves a new school of virtue, suitable to free and democratic times, in which lay persons and their associations would have ever larger concerns for one another, and active and cooperative roles in changing the world. *Rerum Novarum* was preceded by the vision of *Novus Ordo Seclorum*: "of new things" and "the new order of the ages." Each of these visions had something to teach the other.

CHAPTER 9

Forty Years Later: Pius XI

DESPITE THE GREAT DEPRESSION THAT HAD SPREAD WORLD-wide since the Wall Street crash of 1929, the seasoned and tough-minded Pope Pius XI issued an encyclical in 1931 that noted the social and economic progress since 1891. The project of social reconstruction launched by Leo XIII still faced grave challenges. Much remained to be done. Still, in law and in fact, the situation of workers had clearly improved, and nearly all the advanced nations (the only ones with an industrial proletariat) had inaugurated programs of social legislation. Labor unions effected many beneficial changes in the lives of workers. The radio, the cinema, the telephone, the automobile all arrived; then, too, progress in agriculture, railroads, and the early beginnings of air transport; plus great advances in the prevention and cure of many common diseases, and also advances in vision and dental care. All these were transforming the conditions of daily life...until BOOM! The crash came, and tens of millions suffered.

On the negative side, especially in Germany, the aftermath of the First World War (1914–18) had encouraged the growth of great cartels, and banking in particular had become worrisomely concentrated. Pius XI denounced this dangerous economic centralization in no uncertain terms.

Yet Pius XI's longest-lasting contribution to Catholic social thought was that relatively new concept which he called "social justice." It lay behind the postwar term "social market economy," as well as behind European social democratic and reformist capitalist movements generally. But what did it mean to Pius XI? The person to interrogate first is the German Jesuit who played an important role in drafting *Quadragesimo Anno*.

In his eightieth year, Oswald von Nell-Breuning, S.J., wrote in the journal *Stimmen der Zeit* of the trepidation he had felt when, in 1931, at the age of forty, he had been given practically sole responsibility for the authorship of *Quadragesimo Anno*. In a nice touch, Nell-Breuning added that, regarding the very few paragraphs actually penned by Pius XI (90–96), he himself was given authority over whether they should be included and where. Later, Nell-Breuning came to regret having included those paragraphs, which seemed to approve of the "corporatist state," since in many minds that linked the encyclical too closely to Mussolini and his Fascist-party program.

Nonetheless, Nell-Breuning added in his commentary, what Pius XI intended was not the corporatist state ruled from the top down, but the rejuvenation of civil society by what Leo XIII had called the "principle of association." Still, the frank revelation by Nell-Breuning of his own role in drafting *Quadragesimo Anno* makes all the more valuable his line-by-line, book-length commentary on that encyclical, published in English as *The Reorganization of Social Economy*. Pius XI's encyclical, soon treated as the *locus classicus* of social justice, sets forth two roles of social justice: the role of virtue and the role of conceptual framework.

"Both social justice and social charity have been investigated but little by theology," writes Nell-Breuning in his commentary on *Quadragesimo Anno*. "Both are neither unknown nor new to it, even though the terms have been introduced but recently." Nell-Breuning is able to find, indeed, only one reference to social charity in papal documents before *Quadragesimo Anno*, and that in a personal but official letter of June 24, 1923, from Pius XI. Nell-Breuning follows this observation up with the remark: "To extend and deepen the doctrine of social justice and social charity will be an important task of theology."[1] This challenge has not in all respects been met even today, and as such is partly the motive behind the present volume.

———

During the nineteenth century, the term "legal justice" came to be used by German jurists in ways that brought that term into disrepute (for example, "the letter of the law," "state laws"). This German controversy over "legal justice" and the rise of the slogan "social justice" in the mid-nineteenth century led a number of interpreters to bind the two as one. This German controversy is important context for the use of the term "social justice" by Nell-Breuning, who expressly credited it to one of his teachers, Heinrich Pesch, S.J. (1854–1925).

Writing in the depth of the worldwide Depression (and an especially severe banking crisis in Germany, in which wheelbarrows full of paper money could barely pay for a loaf of bread), Nell-Breuning began drafting *Quadragesimo Anno*, poignantly aware of massive social instability. Stalin was beginning to starve millions of Ukrainian farmers; Hitler was on the rise in Germany; German banks were embroiled in scandals and inflation was staggering; Mussolini was arrogantly exercising a bullying dictatorship in Italy; and Japan's warlords were plotting their expeditions overseas.

Forty years earlier, Pope Leo XIII had spoken of the spirit of revolutionary change undercutting European institutions. By 1931, the widening dimensions of the "social question" had overflowed from politics and economics into the world of terrifying moral ideals such as Nazism, fascism, communism, and fashionable Western nihilism. The world faced a moral and religious crisis, deeper than the highly visible economic crisis. The deepening dimensions of this moral crisis, as well as the more visible political and economic crisis, was clearer in 1931 than it had been forty years earlier.

Pius XI grasped the moral challenge in the rumblings of impending ruin, and asked what justice demands from humans in unstable times. He made an intensive effort to recover the idea that Aristotle and Thomas Aquinas had intended by the name "general justice" and, placing this new term in the context of rapid social change, gave it a new name: "social justice." The big picture Aristotle and Aquinas had in mind is that while justice had long been defined in terms of the duties of individuals "to give to each his due," important historical moments showed that humans sometimes also felt a keen duty to give their lives for their city. The heroic stand of the 300 Spartans against the whole force of a million Persians at the narrow pass of Thermopylae set a brilliant marker in world history. It was said that the young Spartans gladly took up their duty to fight to the death in defense of their city (and civilization), fought nobly as Spartans ought to fight, and died happy "doing justice." There are forms of justice beyond individual to individual. They owed a debt to their city.

A few words about the personality and background of Pius XI may illuminate his efforts. Poland gave the modern papacy one of its own sons, John Paul II, in 1978; but in an odd way it also gave the world Pope Pius XI. Born Achille Ratti in 1857, in the little industrial town of Desio near Milan, the young Father Ratti (ordained in Rome in 1879) was a most unlikely candidate for the papacy. Quiet, studious, and reclusive, his first assignment (after receiving three doctorates in three years) was as an instructor in the Milanese seminary. So scholarly was he that he was assigned to pursue historical research, notably in paleography, at the Ambrosian Library in Milan for twenty-two years (1888–1910). After that, he spent another eight years as vice-prefect of the Vatican Library in Rome, where he continued writing and publishing historical monographs, several on the history of Milan and one on the modern history of the Church in Poland.

At the age of sixty, Ratti might have expected to continue such obscure scholarly work for the rest of his life; but the emergence of Poland as an independent country in 1918 presented a perplexity to the Vatican diplomatic corps, since the Vatican at that time had no expert on Poland. Someone recalled Father Ratti's monograph; he was speedily consecrated a bishop and sent to Poland as nuncio. In Warsaw from 1918 until mid-1921, he endured the Communist siege of the city, worked closely with Josef Pilsudsky, and, in a way, midwifed modern Polish Catholicism (a work that eventually changed the world under Pope John Paul II). The organizational abilities, leadership, and diplomatic astuteness of this sheltered scholar surprised many, but Pope Benedict XV took note and that June made Ratti the Cardinal Archbishop of Milan, Ratti's own beloved city. Barely had the new archbishop established a Catholic university there—soon to become famous around the world—than Benedict XV died, and Cardinal Ratti was elected to succeed him on January 22, 1922.

Ratti chose the name Pius as a name of peace. As if he could see what was coming, he dedicated his whole pontificate to peace, even secretly offering God his life for it. In the crowd in Saint Peter's Square, receiving the new pope's first blessing, stood Benito Mussolini, soon to assume dictatorial power in Italy, not without menace to the Vatican. The two would become fierce antagonists: Peter and Caesar locked in yet another historical struggle. Indeed, the stubborn resolve of the scholar-priest from Milan would soon be pitted not only against Mussolini in Italy, but also against Hitler in Germany and Stalin in the steadily expanding Soviet empire.

Taking as his motto "The Peace of Christ in the Kingdom of Christ," Pius XI, almost as if in defiance, established the universal feast day of Christ the King in 1925. He called for the Catholic laity to awaken, to organize themselves voluntarily, and to act for justice. In 1937, he warned the totalitarians (Hitler, in particular), "The day will come when the *Te Deum* of liberation will succeed to the premature hymns of the enemies of Christ."[2] Pius XI died on February 10, 1939, shortly after the German occupation of Czechoslovakia and annexation of Austria. His death came only months before the second outbreak in twenty years of full hostilities. He was eighty-two-years-old. Gloom covered Europe like a pall, and, at an unprecedented cost in human lives, the war he had tried to prevent soon overwhelmed Europe and also Asia.

When Pius XI wrote of social change, therefore, he knew the stakes. When he wrote of social justice, he sought an alternative to the mad principles on which Europe was then basing its social order. In large measure he blamed liberalism—not so much for its institutions as for its irreligious mores and ideology. In sweeping the house of Europe bare of the morals of its ancient and medieval past, liberalism in the Continental sense had invited into this "clean, well-lighted place" a nihilism inhabited by seven devils worse than the first (as the biblical parable puts it). From his earliest years as pope, he had hearkened back to Leo XIII's plea for a sounder reconstruction of Europe's morals and virtues—not in opposition to change, but in search of better directions for change to take.

"There is an instability from which no single thing can escape, for that, precisely, is the essence of created things," Pius XI had written in 1926, for the thirty-fifth anniversary of *Rerum Novarum*. "Precisely in those social elements which seem fundamental, and most exempt from change, such as property, capital, labor, a constant change is not only possible, but is real, and an accomplished fact."[3] He looked at each of these fundamental social elements in turn. Here is his discussion of labor:

> From the primitive work of the man of the stone age, to the great organization of production of our day, how many transitions, ascensions, and complications, diversities!...What an enormous difference! It is therefore necessary to take such changes into account, and to prepare oneself, by an enlightened foresight and with complete resignation, to this instability of things and of human institutions, which are not all perfect, but necessarily imperfect and susceptible of changes.[4]

This is the perspective in which, five years later, Pius XI took up the term "social justice" as his solution to the moral problems inherent in social change. The pope used this new term nine times in his encyclical "On the Reconstruction of the Social Order," as *Quadragesimo Anno* is also referred to in English. No single meaning is easy to derive from these nine texts.[5] But where there had been considerable confusion and vagueness about the three terms "legal justice," "general justice," and "social justice," Pius XI intended to establish a term for practical modern use. He thereby raised questions no one before him had asked with such clarity.

In most of the passages in which he uses "social justice" in *Quadragesimo Anno*, the pope begins with a concrete problem—in paragraph 71, for example, the fact that fathers of families are not receiving wages adequate to support their children. The pope had already noted that social systems are in flux and that social change is quite natural. What he now added is that free citizens have a responsibility to shape these changes in a moral way. If fathers are not receiving wages sufficient to support their families "under existing circumstances," he wrote, "social justice demands that changes be introduced into the system as soon as possible, whereby such a wage will be assured to every adult workingman."[6] A society that would allow children to starve and individual fathers to be helpless to improve their family's condition is, in his view, neither a good nor a stable nor a fully legitimate society. Humans must not simply wring their hands about this. They should "introduce changes into the system as soon as possible." He did not say "by route of the state." Though the means were not specified, to introduce such changes is the object of the virtue of social justice.

Three points are worth stressing here: personal responsibility, institutional change, and practicality. First, humans are required by the morality written into their own nature to accept responsibility for the shape of the institutions of their society. This is because it is their nature both to be responsible and to live in society. Second, they should fix their eyes on changes in the system—that is, in those institutions and organizations that in their ensemble constitute society. Third, they should be realistic, aiming for what is possible, not utopian dreams. These three characteristics help to clarify the nature of the new virtue that Pope Pius XI called on us to develop. During past ages, common people were relatively passive subjects rather than responsible citizens. In the new circumstances of 1931, they needed to exercise new responsibilities whose object and methods are social, and whose exercise requires prudence and practicality.

The way was open for *Quadragesimo Anno* to set forth a full theory of social justice as a virtue. Pius XI did not do that. While it is true that the concept of social justice has undergone many changes since 1931, *Quadragesimo Anno* remains the urtext to which all others refer. And according to Nell-Breuning's commentary:

> Social justice is a spiritual and intellectual guiding rule which does not act through itself, but assisted by a power. This power, according to Leo XIII and Pius XI, is the state. The right social and economic order is established by the supreme authority in society, which in turn is bound by the demands of social justice from which it draws all its legal authority to direct and to regulate. In a properly regulated community, social justice finds its material realization in public institutions, and acts through public authorities or their representatives.[7]

Thus in the view of Pius XI, Nell-Breuning writes, social justice (1) "is always an efficient principle in public authority." It looks (2) "first of all to social legislation." Its aim is (3) to "bring about a legal social order that will result in the proper economic order." Christian social philosophy (4) "seeks to restore order which would lead economics back into firm and regulated channels and would ultimately exert its beneficial influence upon property." In this sense, social justice is (5) "a spiritual and intellectual principle of the form of human society." Social justice (6) "becomes an institution in the constitution and laws of society." Further, social justice (7) "determines the structural form and shape as well as the functioning of society and economics."[8]

Let me summarize. Looked at in this way, social justice is plainly not a virtue. It is an institution in the constitution and laws of society. It determines the structural form and shape of society. It is a spiritual and intellectual guiding rule. It is an efficient principle in public authority. It gives the state its legal (moral) authority. It looks first to social legislation. It brings about a legal social order. It results in the proper moral order for a sound economy.

Thus, Pius XI's program of social justice was not at first glance easy to distinguish from a heavy-handed political order which plans and directs the economy, and which enforces the monistic cultural order enshrined in the corporatist states of socialism and fascism. But to see Pius XI's program in this way is a great mistake. To be sure, as Nell-Breuning admits, the pope did bend over backward not to antagonize Mussolini and to be fair to the aims of fascism. After a few tense years, after all, the pope and the dictator had only recently signed an accord turning most of Rome over to the Italian state, while guaranteeing the autonomy of certain narrowly drawn properties and spaces (not all of them contiguous) as the Vatican state. These were wholly surrounded by Mussolini's Italy, and his police quite thoroughly had jurisdiction over Vatican employees who did not live within the Vatican's walls.

Pius XI tried to distinguish his own program from Mussolini's by way of irony rather than by direct verbal confrontation. For instance, he was vehement in his denunciations of socialism; as his successor John XXIII wrote: "Pope Pius XI . . . emphasized the fundamental opposition between Communism and Christianity, and made it clear that no Catholic could subscribe even to moderate Socialism. The reason is that Socialism is founded on a doctrine of human society which is bounded by time and takes no account of any objective other than that of material well-being."[9] It was a slap in Mussolini's face, knowing full well that Mussolini's fascism expressly boasted of being a form of socialism.

But what exactly were the differences Pius XI saw between a Christian social order built around the guiding rule of social justice and a fascist/socialist order? Fascists and Nazis went out of their way to contrast their commitment to community, society, and the collective with Anglo-American individualism and decadence. In fact, the very symbol chosen for fascism was a bundle of wood tied tightly together—as if to represent the power of the collective against the easily scattered individuals of the Anglo-American world.

There are, above all, differences in the fundamental philosophy of each. "The Pope," Nell-Breuning writes, "contrasts this truly social idea [that is, social justice] with the mechanist-individualist reform plans of socialism and its followers."[10] Socialism may desire "a restoration of sound social order" over against liberal individualism, but "it accepts all the materialism and individualism of the liberal order."[11] Besides, socialists (even when they try to appear moderate) seek the abolition of private property, while Catholic teaching emphatically does not. And socialism maintains both a powerful animosity against religion and an anti-Christian morality. Socialism is a morality of free love which deliberately undermines the family. The only thing socialism and social justice appear to have in common is the above-mentioned drive "to restore order which could lead economics back into firm and regulated channels."[12] But their philosophy of the state, private property, the family, and morals are worlds apart.

There can be no mistaking the animosity of Pius XI and Nell-Breuning toward the liberalist illusion which, oddly to Anglo-American ears, they see as the starting point of socialism and communism. Nell-Breuning writes: "The Pope keenly attacks the erroneous belief that the market under competition regulates itself." But this is not a factual description. Equally, Pius XI rejects the theory "that the human mind is capable of directing economic developments according to a definite plan." "We must admit," Nell-Breuning confesses, "that human endeavors to regulate economics are subject to the danger of error and false judgment, and that, indeed, not all experiments have led to the desired result." The conclusion that Nell-Breuning draws from these mistakes is that it "is necessary to advance cautiously and to learn from our mistakes."[13] He emphasizes that economics is a social science, concerned with "the existence of economic society," and that society is "far more than a non-cooperative mass of individuals."[14] It is this, he writes, that obliges the pope to conclude in paragraph 88 that it is "very necessary that economic affairs be once more subjected to and governed by a true and effective guiding principle." The pope, in short, "looks for something that is above economic power, and can therefore direct it toward the right goal." Here, Nell-Breuning adds, he "conceives of two powers: Social justice and social charity." And in seeking how these can be "implanted into economic society as a regulating force," the pope "attaches first importance to governmental and social institutions."[15]

Pius XI, Nell-Breuning comments, was here thinking of large institutional matters: of "constitution and government administration, something that can be attained by properly formed legal and material institutions."[16] However, here the pope becomes cautious. He insists on the principle of subsidiarity—a principle that can be traced to Abraham Lincoln.[17] The state is not an unlimited or totalitarian power. It is limited. According to Nell-Breuning:

> [The pope] puts his greatest and highest expectations on the state—
> not a state that intends to take care of everything, but a state strictly
> following the principle of subsidiarity. Therefore, while demanding
> security and protection for proper social order based on social justice,

he also appeals to state authority to abstain from interference with all matters of minor importance, in order the better to solve the one great task which it is called to take care of.[18]

Nell-Breuning seems to mean by this "one great task" something like what the Preamble to the U.S. Constitution identifies as "to promote the General Welfare."

In these central passages on social justice in his commentary, it is painfully obvious that Nell-Breuning begins by speaking of social justice both as a virtue and as a principle, but ends by treating it almost solely as a principle. Thus, he falls neatly into what we saw is Hayek's trap (chapters three and four, above). If social justice is a regulative principle of social order, it is not a virtue. For if the subject of social justice is society, then it is not a person, and only persons can practice moral virtues. Social justice appears at best to be an institutional ideal—of indeterminate shape or location—against which concrete institutions are measured. Social justice seems to characterize no society that has yet been seen. Indeed, the use of the term is left slippery.

Free modern societies are so complex that no one authority can possibly control their manifold outcomes, whether regarding supply and demand, prices, the distribution of income, or changeable family needs. The failures of socialism (so visible after 1989) make all this plain. The downfall of state-run systems is systemic ignorance. By comparison, market systems constantly reflect immense stores of information. Take a simple example: Every day, each new automobile sold in the United States is recorded, so that almost instantly automakers know how many units are moving, where, and in which models and colors and other consumer preferences. They also know whether the pricing of particular models is building up buyer resistance, and whether some models are selling in unexpectedly high quantities. By tomorrow morning they can change their production plans in view of this information. Day by day decisions are guided by virtually real-time information. Decisions are less made by long-range planners than by monitors of up-to-date flows of information. Decisions can be made much closer to the field of actual buying.

No one brain or collection of brains has the necessary intelligence to grasp, let alone to put in order, all the changing needs of every family. The state does not have a large or detailed enough intelligence. A dinosaur, the joke goes, has a brain the size of a pea. So does the state. That is the essential flaw in the socialist concept of "order from above." Alas, even Pius XI, though he resisted mightily, showed a tendency to wish that an intelligent order could flow down from above. Certain national cultures seem reluctant to recognize how much information arises upward from the daily work of markets—and how much order results from decisions based on that information. There is no magic in market systems, only very useful information about what is being bought, how much people are willing to pay, how changes in price affect volume, in what geographical areas specific items are selling least, and where demand is greatest. The preferences of buyers change often, and suppliers need to detect such changes quickly in order to organize their next efforts in advance of going to market. Markets are very sensitive to movements of human insight and will.

Moreover, much of the actual order in human life arises from the convergence of the thoughts, feelings, and decisions of many different human beings acting for their own purposes. Men's efforts are generally more fruitful if they take account of the decisions and consequences of the actions of others. Fishermen in Bangladesh may now use cell phones to call a number of nearby locations in search of the best price for that day. Women in Milan may watch prices of various brands very closely, in order to time their major fashion purchases. Wisdom in the use of markets requires keen market intelligence, acquired by multitudes of individuals not through orders from above but by close attention to the fluctuations of markets. To use a different example, paths are worn by hikers up and down a mountain over hundreds of years, based on hundreds of thousands of individual decisions. Consequently, say Hayek and other objectors, a great deal of human order necessary to the common good comes not from above but from attending closely to the timing and substance of market behaviors.

Thus many of those who claim to be speaking from above for the "common good" or "social justice" often overlook vital social information. Often, they are not speaking for most people, much less most wise and good people. They are consulting only their own conceptions, their own preferences, their own practical (or impractical) sense of what is happening. No one knows enough to be certain what the common good is, only what she or he thinks it is. Those who claim to speak for social justice often misjudge arguments concerning means and ends by failing to take account of the multitudes of unintended consequences that commonly arise from crisscrossing social interactions. They fail to foresee the likely unintended consequences of the means and ends they favor. In brief, use of the term "social justice" can sometimes mask moral imperialism based on abstractions. One can argue that the common good is best defined by goals x, y, and z. But there can easily be many contrary yet plausible arguments in favor of a, b, and c—or even j, k, and l. Who is correct? And who knows the best concrete, practical steps to take next?

It does not seem that Nell-Breuning escapes these limitations. His commentary, written during the early 1930s, lacks sufficient conceptual equipment. His animus against "liberal individualism" blinds him to the actual cooperative, associational, communitarian texture of nations beyond those of continental Europe. Like many in central Europe (Germany and Italy included), Nell-Breuning and Pius XI express a negative bias against the market and competition, and the unmistakable sense of order markets produce, an order often much more steady and reliable than the sometimes capricious decisions of unchecked authorities.

Long ago, when I studied at the Gregorian University in Rome (from 1956 to 1958), I was quite surprised by the resentment expressed against Anglo-Saxon philosophical and economic cultures by a sizable number of the Mediterraneans and Latins. They had a wildly exaggerated view of Anglo-American "individualism"; they missed entirely the degree of associational and other-directed skills, even conformism. They missed the social orderliness of life in England (take, for example, manners in boarding a bus). The mote in their own eye was the extreme individualism of traffic patterns in Rome. Their images of "unfettered" markets seemed based on their own experience rather than on the internalized order and actual self-restraint of Anglo-American mores.

AT LEAST, THOUGH, we might notice three things. First, the market *is* a social institution, rule-bound and guided by very old norms. For centuries individuals and groups have come together in markets, even in primitive forms in town squares, to meet their personal needs in fair exchange. To be sure, *caveat emptor*, let the buyer beware. Still, a market does not exist to favor only some individuals, but to draw all into it by familiar conventions and practices of fairness. Without trust, markets repulse rather than attract. Everybody in every community needs them and benefits by them.

Second, the most successful way to break up dreaded monopolies (or cartels) is by increasing new entries into the markets, and by nourishing greater competition among them. Government does play a useful role in that encouragement, on behalf of both sellers and buyers, as the fruits of the U.S. Sherman Antitrust Act (made law the year before *Rerum Novarum* was promulgated) amply show.[19]

The influence of Weimar Germany is tangible on every page of Nell-Breuning's commentary, in his references to cartelizations and the unchecked power of central banks, and in his underlying conceptual imagery. Many of his key terms were forged in the German discussions led by the great Heinrich Pesch, S.J., and in several other key centers of German social economic thought, such as Freiburg, Munich, and the Fribourg Union.[20]

Still, if we go back to the need for social reorganization announced by Pius XI, an approach to social justice overlooked by Nell-Breuning becomes apparent. In free societies, citizens need to use their capacity for association to exercise responsibilities, and to act for social purposes. Suppose that we define social justice in this way: Social justice is a specific modern form of the ancient virtue of justice. Men and women exercise this specific social habit when they (a) join with others, in order (b) to change the institutions of society. The practice of social justice means activism, organizing, trying to make the system better. It does not necessarily mean enlarging the state; on the contrary, it means enlarging civil society. Father Ferree (whose work I have cited above and elsewhere) thinks that this is exactly Pius XI's intention. I am less certain of that, but Ferree's argument does seem plausible, given Pius XI's premises and express warnings against excessive state power.

In my own humble judgment, the pope laid down a few stripes on Mussolini's back, under which Mussolini did in fact smart. Still, Pius XI tried to be evenhanded in his criticism of liberalism and socialism, though there is no question that the pope's description of the tasks of the state as he desired them was more guarded, hesitant, and cautious than Mussolini's approach to government rule allowed. Alas, portions of his language later caused much confusion, allowing many to conflate social justice with state action, and to see social justice as a form of the socialist project. It is beyond doubt that Pius XI intended to advance Leo XIII's project of building civil societies and the power of associations. But the language cited above by Nell-Breuning did allow some room for a socialist and/or corporatist interpretation.[21]

Aristotle himself thought that politics is the architectonic science: Everything else is protected or threatened by what happens in politics.

The freedom to worship, the public availability of beauty, the freedom of and material support for science, the quality of education, economic dynamism, and much else depend on the workings of the polis. Aristotle also articulated that ethics is a branch of politics. In his youth he had experienced the conquest of a small city-state by a foreign culture, so he knew firsthand the immense pressure this conquest placed on individuals and families to change their mores, habits, and loyalties. Formerly honorable citizens were now obliged to follow new masters and new ways, often contrary to their own native ethic and moral ecology.

Pope Pius XI knew that. But now he added two things to Aristotle: first, an emphasis on *the citizen's responsibility* for shaping the polis; and, second, a call for voluntary organizations to empower individuals by bringing them out of isolation. The pope saw that free men and women in modern times can join together, organize, and make changes in the institutions in which they live. He witnessed this, for example, in the often quite heroic activities of Don Luigi Sturzo and his energetic *Partito Popolare*, a nascent political party in Italy and something new under the Italian sun: Catholic and lay and democratic. Fulfilling this social potential required of free persons vigilance, initiative, farsightedness, courage, realism, organizational skills, and perseverance. Without the exercise of such virtues, the principle of subsidiarity would have no power to check the state.

Since the uses of social justice are plural, its definition must necessarily be general. But the concept is far from empty. The easiest way to understand it is to encounter its opposite. Visit a housing project in East Saint Louis where the apathetic, alienated, anomic residents seem unable or unwilling to organize themselves to meet the many problems that besiege them. Visit a Bolivian or Sicilian village in which family is the only recognized social reality, and outside the family no one is trusted, committees do not form, few organizations function, and armed thugs have a virtual free run of society. One can expect to see a capacity for social initiative only when citizens have a certain inner strength, a basic trust in others, and the skills and willingness to join together for common purposes.

Certain spontaneous sentences indicate the presence of the virtue: "We've got to do something." "Let's do it." "Divide up the responsibilities." "Who'll volunteer?" We take such sentiments for granted in America, so we may not recognize a habit that many among us possess in abundance. Children in playgrounds spontaneously "choose up" sides, arrange bases, establish boundaries. The art of association, as Tocqueville wrote, *is* the first law of democracy.

———

After the horrific deaths of tens of millions in the Second World War, Pius XII (1939–58) led the Catholic Church, belatedly, to support the rebuilding of democracies as the best defense of human rights. Christian Democratic and Social Democratic parties rose up to defend those rights against communism. Leo XIII's pioneering effort to root concepts of human rights in Christian soil was capped by Pope John XXIII's proliferation of rights in *Pacem in Terris* (1963). Paul VI (1963–78), while avoiding the term "socialism," began to speak of a necessary process of "socialization," a euphemism that many interpreted as an endorsement of social democracy and the welfare state. Then, on October 16, 1978, the feast day of Saint Hedwig (patroness of reconciliation between neighboring states), the College of Cardinals electrified the world with the selection of the first non-Italian pope in more than four centuries, the Polish Cardinal Archbishop of Krakow, Karol Wojtyła, who chose the name John Paul II, and became famous for leading the world's huge "third wave" of building democracies and other institutions of human rights.

In 1931, Pius XI launched a world-changing movement indeed. Popes did not vanquish Stalin and his successors by armored divisions. They had a strong wind of the Spirit behind them, and inspired a new humanism of social virtue, brave persons, and resolute free communities focused on self-government, civil society, and the common good.

CHAPTER 10

American Realities and Catholic Social Thought

IN 1978, THE NEW POPE JOHN PAUL II—DRAMATIST, POET, athlete, polyglot—took as his mission the reconciliation not only of neighboring states but of the two great blocs, East and West, which from the first he insisted on calling "the two great branches of the one tree of Christian Europe." Until then, Saint Benedict (480–547) had been properly recognized as the patron saint of Europe, and his image graced the Medal of Europe awarded annually to the greatest contemporary artists, since so many European cities had grown up around early Benedictine monasteries with their cathedral schools, libraries of manuscripts and copyists, and patronage of music and the arts. The first Slavic pope added Cyril and Methodius as copatrons of Europe. These two brothers from Byzantium had translated the New Testament into the core Slavonic tongue a thousand years earlier. This translation took place at Nitra in Slovakia, at the very center of a larger Europe, well-described as comprising "the lands from the Atlantic to the Urals." Thus, both halves of Europe grew as branches from a single Christian trunk.

A philosopher by training, the vigorous John Paul II made clear early on that he wished to impart to the Catholic body a deep and original philosophic stamp. "Ordered liberty" is the key concept with which he chose to begin, a liberty practiced by the human person as a free and creative agent of his or her own destiny. The pope's emphasis on ordered liberty had special resonance behind the Iron Curtain, as well as among all those struggling under military dictatorships and national security states in the Third World. Having helped shape *Dignitatis Humanae* (1965), the Second Vatican Council's Declaration on Religious Liberty, John Paul II continued over the years to articulate his vision of religious liberty, the "first liberty." Gradually, he built up the foundations of a fresh theory of the "second liberty," economic liberty. Here he stressed the creative subjectivity of the free man and woman at work. This was fresh material, indeed—and to it we now must turn.

It is a curious matter that some of the key ideas which John Paul II was about to introduce into Catholic social teaching were voiced long before him, by a backwoodsman from Kentucky and Illinois, far out on the western American frontier during the 1830s, '40s, and '50s, right around the same time Father Taparelli in Italy was writing the first known book on social justice. Europeans may be unlikely to think immediately of Lincoln as a forebear of later developments in Catholic social thought, but the connection is natural for an American.

This link with Lincoln was reinforced in the post–Vatican II encyclopedia of Catholic thought, *Sacramentum Mundi*, which introduced its entry on "subsidiarity" by citing Lincoln.[1] In his effort to end the slavery that was legal in the southern states, Lincoln was quite prescient in laying out the principles of federalism on the one hand, and encouraging local communities based on almost-universal land ownership (see the Homestead Act, for example) on the other. Near-universal land ownership prevented the growth of the large plantations necessary for the practical use of slaves, and in addition bred in citizens a strong taste for liberty and a revulsion against slavery. On this social reconstruction, most new territories chose to live as free states and soon greatly outnumbered the older slave states.

Further, Lincoln was also among the first to highlight the dynamic role of knowledge and know-how (now often called "human capital") in the creation of new wealth, which undergirds the high spirits that drive free societies forward. For instance, on a cold winter day in February 1859, in Jacksonville, Illinois, Abraham Lincoln delivered a "Lecture on Discoveries and Inventions," in which he described, starting with the time of Adam, six great advances in the history of liberty. The last of these great steps, Lincoln held, is the law of copyrights and patents. His lecture gives the best account I have ever read of the reasons why the United States, in a brief Constitution of just 4,486 words, includes a clause guaranteeing the right of inventors and authors to royalties for patents and copyrights. In this clause is embedded the single mention of the term "right" in the entire body of the Constitution. Until I read Lincoln on this point, I had never encountered anyone who gave patents and copyrights such high importance.

On that cold February day on the Illinois prairie, you must imagine Lincoln, tall and gangling, gazing across the stove-heated room, with a sweep of his hand summoning up a vision of that first "old fogey," father Adam:

> There he stood, a very perfect physical man, as poets and painters inform us, but he must have been very ignorant, and simple in his habits. He had no sufficient time to learn much by observation, and he had no near neighbors to teach him anything. No part of his breakfast had been brought from the other side of the world, and it is quite probable, he had no conception of the world having any other side.[2]

By contrast with this naked but imposing Adam, able to speak (for he names the animals) but without anyone to talk to (for Eve "was still a bone in his side"), Young America, Lincoln noted, the America of 1859, was awash with knowledge and wealth. Whereas the first beautiful specimen of the species knew not how to read or write, nor any of the useful arts yet to be discovered, "Look around at Young America," Lincoln said in 1859. "Look at his apparel, and you shall see cotton fabrics from Manchester and Lowell, flax-linen from Ireland, wool-cloth from Spain, silk from France, furs from the Arctic regions, with a buffalo robe from the Rocky Mountains."[3] On Young America's table, one could find:

> Besides plain bread and meat made at home . . . sugar from Louisiana, coffee and fruits from the tropics, salt from Turk's Island, fish from New-foundland, tea from China, and spices from the Indies. The whale of the Pacific furnishes his candle-light, he has a diamond-ring from Brazil, a gold-watch from California, and a spanish cigar from Havanna.[4]

Not only did Young America have a sufficient, indeed more than sufficient, supply of these goods, but, Lincoln added, "thousands of hands are engaged in producing fresh supplies, and other thousands, in bringing them to him."[5]

Here, then, is the question Lincoln posed: How did the world get from the unlettered, untutored backwoodsman of the almost silent and primeval Garden of Eden to great cities, locomotives, telegraphs, and breakfast from across the seas? He discerned six crucial steps in this grand historical adventure.

The first step was God-given: the human ability to build a language.

The second step was the slow mastering of the art of discovery, through learning three crucial human habits—observation, reflection, and experiment—which Lincoln explained this way:

> It is quite certain that ever since water has been boiled in covered vessels, men have seen the lids of the vessels rise and fall a little, with a sort of fluttering motion, by force of the steam, but so long as this was not specially observed, and reflected and experimented upon, it came to nothing. At length however, after many thousand years, some man observes this long-known effect of hot water lifting a pot-lid, and begins a train of reflection upon it.[6]

Given how arduous it is to lift heavy objects, the attentive man is invited to experiment with the force lifting up the pot lid.

Thousands of years, however, were needed to develop the habit of observing, reflecting, and experimenting, and then to spread that art throughout society. Some societies developed that habit socially, and some did not. Why, Lincoln asked, when Indians and Mexicans trod over the gold of California for centuries without finding it, did Yankees almost instantly discover it? (The Indians had not failed to discover it in South America.) "Goldmines are not the only mines overlooked in the same way," Lincoln noted. Indeed, there are more "mines" to be found above the surface of the earth than below: "All nature—the whole world, material, moral, and intellectual—is a mine, and, in Adam's day, it was a wholly unexplored mine." And so "it was the destined work of Adam's race to develop, by discoveries, inventions, and improvements, the hidden treasures of this mine."[7]

The third great step was the invention of writing. By this great step, taken only in a few places, then spreading slowly, observations and reflections made in one century prompted reflection and experimentation in a later one.

The fourth great step was the printing press, which diffused records of observations, reflections, and experiments in ever-widening circles, far beyond the tiny handful of people who could afford handwritten parchment. Now such records could be made available to hundreds of thousands cheaply. Before printing, the great mass of humans

> were utterly unconscious, that their conditions, or their minds were capable of improvement. They not only looked upon the educated few as superior beings; but they supposed themselves to be naturally incapable of rising to equality. To immancipate [sic] the mind from this false and under estimate of itself, is the great task which printing came into the world to perform. It is difficult for us, now and here, to conceive how strong this slavery of the mind was; and how long it did, of necessity, take, to break it's [sic] shackles, and to get a habit of freedom of thought, established.[8]

Between the invention of writing and the invention of the printing press, almost 3,000 years had intervened. Between the invention of the printing press and the invention of a modern patent law (in Britain in 1624), fewer than 200 had passed.

The fifth great step was the discovery of America. In the new country, committed to liberty and equality, the human mind was emancipated as never before. Given a brand-new start, calling for new habits, "a new country is most favorable—almost necessary—to the immancipation [sic] of thought, and the consequent advancement of civilization and the arts." The discovery of America was "an event greatly facilitating useful discoveries and inventions."[9]

The sixth great step was the adoption of a Constitution, Article 1, section 8, clause 8 of which recognized a natural right of authors and inventors. Among the few express powers granted by the people to Congress, the framers inserted this one: "To promote the Progress of Science and useful Arts, by securing for limited Times to Authors and Inventors the exclusive Right to their respective Writings and Discoveries."

The effect of this regime was not lost upon the young inventor and future president. "Before then," Lincoln wrote, "any man might instantly use what another had invented, so that the inventor had no special advantage from his own invention." Lincoln cut to the essential point: "The patent system changed this, secured to the inventor, for a limited time, the exclusive use of his invention, and thereby added the fuel of interest to the fire of genius, in the discovery and production of new and useful things."[10]

"The fuel of interest added to the fire of genius!" Ever the realist, Lincoln knew what is in the human being: to be a genius is one thing, to be motivated is quite another, and then to be supported in this motivation by a wise regime is an unprecedented blessing. By contrast, a regime that does not secure natural rights depresses human energy. Natural rights are not mere legal puffs of air; they formalize capacities for action that in some societies lie dormant and in others are fueled into ignition.

The United States, Lincoln believed, ignited the practical genius of its people, among the high born and the low born alike, wherever God in his wisdom had implanted that genius. In the same year as his lecture, 1859, Lincoln himself won a U.S. patent (number 6469) for a "device to buoy vessels over shoals." That patent is not a bad metaphor for the effect of patents on inventions: to buoy them over difficulties.

The great effect of the patent and copyright clause on world history was a remarkable transformation of values. During most of human history, land had been the most important source of wealth; in America, intellect and know-how became the major source. The dynamism of the system ceased to be primarily material and became, so to speak, intellectual and spiritual, born of the creative mind. Lincoln's motive in favoring the Homestead Act and the patent clause (and both together) was to prevent the West from being dominated by large estates and great landowners, so that it might become a society of many freemen and many practical, inventive minds. And so it has. More than 6 million patents have been issued in the United States since the first patent law was passed in 1790.

Implicit in Lincoln's Jacksonville address are several assumptions about the nature and meaning of the universe. Lincoln saw history as a narrative of freedom. He believed devoutly that the fact that the Creator of all things had made human beings in his own image—every one of them, woman and man—was provident. History, he thought, is the record of how human beings have gradually come to recognize their true better nature and have striven to make it actual, both in their own lives and in the institutions of their republic.

Thomas Jefferson wrote that "the god who gave us life gave us liberty at the same time," and, while Lincoln did not actually say that our God wishes to be adored by men who are free, he sacrificed much, very much, so that this nation might have "a new birth of freedom." That horrifying bloody project, that new birth of freedom, cost some 40,000 dead and wounded in a single day, and multiples of that in the sum in many other bloody battles. All that, Lincoln said at Gettysburg, fell under the will of the Almighty:

> We can not dedicate—we can not consecrate—we can not hallow—this ground. The brave men, living and dead, who struggled here, have consecrated it, far above our poor power to add or detract. . . . It is for us the living, rather, to be here dedicated to the great task remaining before us—that from these honored dead we take increased devotion to that cause for which they gave the last full measure of devotion—that we here highly resolve that these dead shall not have died in vain—that this nation, under God, shall have a new birth of freedom—and that government of the people, by the people, for the people, shall not perish from the earth.[11]

The universe is so created that it positively calls forth human freedom. To that call, it is the sacred duty of humans to respond, even at enormous cost.

———

Some seven score and two years after Lincoln's address in Jacksonville, there came an international echo of his beliefs from an unlikely quarter, in a worldwide letter published by Pope John Paul II in Rome, on May 1, 1991: *Centesimus Annus*. No doubt John Paul II had few opportunities to encounter Lincoln's writings. What Lincoln and John Paul II did share was an ability to notice common, ordinary phenomena which other people tended to overlook. Lincoln's humble ruminations on how common things like covered pots behaved over a fire set a historical precedent for the pope's commonsensical reflections on the relation of land to wealth over so many centuries. Poland is a land of farm after farm, of great landholders and small. The pope recognized that the primary form of wealth had been land for a thousand years. But by 1991 the cause of wealth had changed: "In our time, in particular, there exists another form of ownership which is becoming no less important than land: the possession of know-how, technology and skill."[12] The wealth of the world's most economically advanced nations is based far more on this type of ownership than on natural resources. This is the same insight Lincoln had come to.

"Indeed, besides the earth," observed the pope, "man's principal resource is man himself. His intelligence enables him to discover the earth's productive potential and the many different ways in which human needs can be satisfied."[13] The pope's words seem cousin to Lincoln's words: "All nature—the whole world, material, moral, and intellectual—is a mine" echoes "the destiny of Adam's race" is "to develop, by discoveries, inventions, and improvements, the hidden treasures of this mine."

The pope goes on:

Whereas at one time the decisive factor of production was the land, and later capital—understood as a total complex of the instruments of production—today the decisive factor is increasingly *man himself*, that is, his knowledge, especially his scientific knowledge, his capacity for interrelated and compact organization, as well as his ability to perceive the needs of others and to satisfy them.[14]

Similarly, where Lincoln had written "but Adam had nothing to turn his attention to [but] work. If he should do anything in the way of invention, he had first to invent the art of invention," the pope writes:

At one time the natural fruitfulness of the earth appeared to be, and was in fact, the primary factor of wealth, while work was, as it were, the help and support for this fruitfulness. In our time ... work becomes ever more fruitful and productive to the extent that people become more knowledgeable about the productive potentialities of the earth and more profoundly cognizant of the needs of those for whom their work is done.[15]

Washington, Madison, and Lincoln held that the American regime, measured by "the Laws of Nature and Nature's God," would blaze a trail for other nations. Under John Paul II, important portions of America's "new science of politics," after much testing, have at last been ratified by what is now the most widely held body of social thought in the world. This practical intellectual influence may stand as an important contribution of American civilization to world history.

In this new era, observes Fred Warshofsky, a journalist-historian, "creativity, in the form of ideas, innovations, and inventions, has replaced gold, colonies, and raw materials as the new wealth of nations."[16] The remarkable "new technologies, new processes, and new products that constitute intellectual property now form the economic bedrock of international trade and national wealth."[17] As more and more nations take halting steps on the path of democracy and free markets, they will increasingly need the fire of invention, the fuel of interest.

Centesimus Annus hit Rome like a sonic boom on May 1, 1991. Even the first fleeting sight of John Paul II's new encyclical led commentators around the world to predict that it would lift the worldwide terms of debate on political economy to a new level. Immediately evoking praise from both the left and the right, this encyclical seemed, to some at least, to be the greatest in the series of which it is a part. In reply to questions raised about political economy and free social institutions by the events of 1989, it is a classic restatement of Christian anthropology.

Earlier in his career, the pope had done significant work in phenomenology, particularly in his book *The Acting Person*. The title of that book is a key to the nuanced approval that the pope later gave to capitalism rightly understood, rooted in the creative mind of the human person. It is such a capitalism, bounded by law, which he recommends to his native Poland, other formerly socialist nations, and the Third World. This approval surprised many commentators. The *London Financial Times*, probably basing its story on leaks from one faction among those preparing the document, had predicted the ringing endorsement of a socialism more advanced than that of European socialist leaders, such as Neil Kinnock, Willy Brandt, and Felipé Gonzalez. Pope John Paul II's Christian anthropology, plus his acute observation of the way the world works, led him to other conclusions.

The success of *Centesimus Annus* is due, in any case, to its philosophical profundity. From the beginning of his pontificate, the pope thought in a worldwide framework, appealing to the bond of human solidarity. But he also thought deeply, not only broadly. He rooted his social proposals in his anthropology of the acting person and creative subjectivity. This enabled him to criticize every existing ideology, including democratic capitalism. Of the three great ideologies that put their mark upon the twentieth century, National Socialism failed first, then Communist socialism. From Eastern Europe, from the Third World, many were asking the pope: What next?

John Paul II proposed a tripartite social structure composed of a free political system, a free economy, and a culture of liberty. After living through the great political debate of the twentieth century, he favored democracy; after living through the great economic debate, he favored capitalism rightly understood (that is, not all forms of capitalism). He was not satisfied with the way things were. He warned that a formidable struggle awaits us, in building a culture worthy of freedom. If we have the politics and the economics roughly (but only roughly) straight, how should we live? How should we shape our culture? These questions are now front and center.

Background Reflections

Soon after his election to the papacy in 1978, his Polish countrymen began to recognize that Karol Wojtyła was their international tribune. As long as a son of Poland sat on the chair of Peter, the Communist rulers of Poland found themselves in a glaring international spotlight. The Iron Curtain no longer hid their movements. Although they attempted to crush the labor movement Solidarity, they could not.

For the ten long years until 1989, a certain space for civic activity—intense, intellectual, practical—opened up within the bosom of the totalitarian society. Citizens in other Eastern European nations took heart. Poland was the first to nurture an independent people, spiritually free of communism, able to negotiate with the Communist leaders as equals—even better than equals. Once Solidarity broke the mask of totalitarian conformity, democratic movements began to grow in boldness throughout that empire which many finally dared to call evil.

In the days when he was the young Archbishop of Krakow, attending the Second Vatican Council in Rome, Wojtyła first came to international attention for a speech he gave before the Council on Religious Liberty. The American echoes in that speech were widely noted, for at the time a strong statement on religious liberty was high among the priorities of the American bishops. Then, from his first days as pope, John Paul II spoke often about liberty of conscience, going so far as to call it the "first liberty." Gradually, too, he came to understand that the American meaning of liberty—ordered liberty, as he came to call it (liberty under law, liberty under reason)—does not mean libertinism, laissez-faire, the devil take the hindmost. At least one American bishop played an important role in drawing the pope's attention to the vital difference in this respect between the American Revolution and the French Revolution.

In his many years as Archbishop of Krakow and professor at the Catholic University of Lublin, Karol Wojtyła provided intellectual leadership for the people who gave rise to Solidarity. When he became pope, but before the imposition of martial law in Poland in 1981, he announced to the world that all of Europe was a single tree with two branches, east and west. Europe's destiny, he said, is to be rejoined as one, drawing life from its common roots in Judaism and Christianity. As pope, he could on any day broadcast the pain of Poland and draw global attention to every Communist abuse. Perhaps unhappy with this role, someone sent one or more assassins to slay him on May 13, 1981. Although the pope nearly died, he recovered. Within a few days, he had planned to issue an encyclical celebrating the ninetieth anniversary of Leo XIII's *Rerum Novarum*; it had to be released nearly a year later, in early 1982, under the title *Laborem Exercens*. In this encyclical, John Paul II appealed to the anthropology implicit in the Creation story of Genesis as the single best starting place for religious inquiry into the nature and causes of the creation of wealth.

The underlying principles of John Paul II's anthropology are the creative subjectivity of the human person, together with the resulting subjectivity of society. From his earliest work onward, the pope had been struck by the human being's most arresting characteristic: the capacity to originate action; that is, to imagine and to conceive of new things and then do them. He found in creative acts the clue to human identity. Humans, he held, cannot take refuge from this responsibility by hiding behind society; for there, too, they are responsible for their acts. Being in society does not absolve them of the burdens of subjectivity. An unbeliever may achieve this insight with no benefit of religious belief. Karol Wojtyła approached it from two different directions: first in a philosophical way, and second in a Jewish-Christian way. For him, philosophy and theology meet in the anthropology of the real, existing human person. The philosopher sees *homo creator*; the theologian sees *imago Dei*. Man the creator (philosophy) is made in the image of the divine Creator (theology), and is endowed by him with an inalienable right to creative initiative.

From this principle John Paul II derived a corollary for social systems: It is an affront to human dignity for a social system to repress the human capacity to create, to invent, and to be enterprising. In human creative subjectivity, Wojtyła saw the principle of liberty, which naturally deploys itself in conscience, inquiry, and action. It would be fair to say that John Paul II was a philosopher of liberty. No end in itself, freedom must be for something and must be ordered by something. Deeper in his eyes than liberty, however, was creativity. Of the two notions, liberty is less satisfying; it raises further questions. Creativity is the deeper and more substantive notion. So it is more accurate to think of John Paul II as a philosopher of creativity.

From this starting point in creativity, the pope, over the years, slowly approached that much-disputed beast called capitalism.

At the beginning of his pontificate, John Paul II used the word "capitalism" in a pejorative sense—as it is often used in European countries, the more so wherever the Marxist tradition has been strong. In *Laborem Exercens*, he used "capital" to mean things, objects, or instruments of production. He reserved the word "labor" for all humane and virtuous attributes, including creative subjectivity.

Some years later, in *Sollicitudo Rei Socialis* (1987), the pope moved from the "acting person" and "creative subjectivity" to the fundamental human right "to religious freedom and also the right to freedom of economic initiative."[18] This was the strongest recognition of enterprise in Catholic social thought. He saw enterprise as a vocation, a virtue, and a right. By May of 1991, in *Centesimus Annus*, Wojtyła had moved further, to a theory of institutions as necessary for the flowering of this enterprise. From this he moved to a theory of the business firm and to a critique of the welfare state. At the heart of each of these positions lies his fundamental insight: Every woman and every man has been created in the image of the Creator, in order to help cocreate the future of the world.

The pope emphasized how noble it is, and how many complex talents are required, to gain insight into the economic needs of the human race, to organize available resources, to invent new resources and methods, and to lead a cooperative, voluntary community to achieve real results. In the whole of section 32, the pope was eloquent about the lessons of creativity and community found in a modern economy. By contrast, the fundamental flaw in socialism, he wrote, was its faulty anthropology. It misunderstood the active, creative nature of the individual; it misunderstood both human misery and human grandeur.

John Paul II rooted the capitalist ethos in the positive thrust of Judaism and Christianity, in their capacity for inspiring new visions and creative actions, rather than in the negative "this-worldly asceticism" that Max Weber found in the Protestant ethic. Common to the Jewish, Catholic, and Protestant views of the human economic agent is the "calling" or "vocation," which Weber erroneously thought to be distinctively Protestant. Every Jew and every Christian is called to be like God, since each is made in the image of God and called to be active and creative. Thence arises the visible dynamism of the Jewish and the Christian peoples in human history.

Outline of *Centesimus Annus*

Before plunging too far into the particulars, it may be well to fix in mind an outline of the six chapters of *Centesimus Annus*. First, John Paul II undertakes a rereading of *Rerum Novarum*, thus handing down an authoritative reinterpretation of that document, much as the U.S. Supreme Court includes in its decisions commentary on earlier decisions of that Court.

In chapter two, the pope takes up the "new things" that have happened since 1891 that still affect us today. He analyzes the shortcomings of socialist anthropology, and describes the reforms that transformed the real, existing capitalism of advanced countries from what it had been in 1891.

Next the pope lingers reflectively on the great events of "The Year 1989," one of the watershed years of human history. He lays out several reasons for the collapse of socialism, and a few lessons of worldwide importance to be drawn from it.

In chapter four, John Paul II addresses the classic Christian theme of the universal destination of material goods (which we also refer to above in chapter seven as the "social destination of all goods"). In this, the longest part of the encyclical, the pope examines existing political economies for their compatibility with the dignity of the human person. Here he develops his new approach to initiative, enterprise, profit, and capitalism itself. He severely criticizes abuses that still exist, particularly of the poor in the Third World, in whose name he eloquently urged inclusion in property ownership, the active worldwide market, and the spread of knowledge and skill.

Chapter five discusses the state and culture. Here the pope stresses the limited state, democratic checks and balances, human rights, and constraints upon the state regarding welfare rights. He criticizes rather harshly the present excesses of the welfare state in economically advanced countries. He turns as well to the moral and cultural sphere, which is too often ignored: "People lose sight of the fact that life in society has neither the market nor the state as its final purpose."[19] Here, too, are found the pope's comments on the formation of a "culture of peace."[20]

Chapter six, concluding on a theological note, looks to the future. We are, the pope thinks, "ever more aware that solving serious national or international problems is not just a matter of economic production or of juridical or social organization."[21] Rather, most problems call for "specific ethical and religious values as well as changes of mentality, behavior, and structures."[22] The most perfect structures will not function if citizens do not have the relevant attitudes, habits, and behaviors. Among these is the habit of effective concern for one's fellow human beings around the world (the habit of "solidarity," as the pope calls it—a new term for the old virtue of charity, calling attention to its international dimension).

In sum, *Centesimus Annus* calls for serious reform of the moral and cultural institutions of democratic and capitalist societies—including the institutions of the mass media, cinema, universities, and families—in order to make democracy and capitalism fulfill their best promises. The preservation of free political space achieved by democracy and the achievement of liberation from oppressive poverty wrought by capitalism are insufficient (alone or together) to meet the human desire for truth and justice.

A Christian Social Anthropology

This overview of the whole terrain fixed in our minds, it should now be easier to grasp the inner logic of *Centesimus Annus*. This logic begins with concrete inspection of the human being: "We are not dealing here with man in the 'abstract,' but with the real, 'concrete,' 'historical' man. We are dealing with each individual.... The horizon of the Church's whole wealth of doctrine is man in his concrete reality as sinful and righteous."[23]

When the young Wojtyła first wrestled with modern Western thinkers such as Scheler and Heidegger, he fully expected that he would be living the rest of his life under real, existing socialism. In that ideology, the individual counted for very little. In actual practice, socialist work was wholly oriented toward the piling-up of objects, products, things, with no real regard for the subjectivity of the worker. After toiling for days on the freezing seas at the risk of their lives, fishermen would discover that the refrigeration unit of the storehouse in which their catch had been deposited was defective and that the entire fruit of their labors had spoiled. Steelworkers would see the steel beams on which they had labored pile up in huge lots and rust, because distribution systems (such as they were) had broken down. Under the economic system developed in the name of Marxism, it was in no one's interest to see a product all the way through, from conception to execution to delivery to satisfying use. Every person felt like a cog in someone else's machine. A new type of alienation was experienced which John Paul II described in *Sollicitudo Rei Socialis*, precisely in contrast to a sense of personal action and initiative:

> In the place of creative initiative there appear passivity, dependence and submission to the bureaucratic apparatus which, as the only "ordering" and "decision-making" body—if not also the "owner"— of the entire totality of goods and the means of production, puts everyone in a position of almost absolute dependence, which is similar to the traditional dependence of the worker-proletarian in capitalism. This provokes a sense of frustration or desperation and predisposes people to opt out of national life, impelling many to emigrate and also favoring a form of "psychological" emigration.[24]

Amid such sour alienation, Wojtyła's emphasis on the acting person was entirely convincing. His emphasis on the creative subjectivity of the worker unsettled those Marxists who were assigned to do ideological battle with him. He turned the tables on them: He forced them to argue on Christian terrain. He accepted their emphasis upon work, but then asked about the meaning of work to the worker, obliging them to confront, on the one hand, the alienation inherent in socialist organizations, and, on the other, a deeper and richer humanism, Christian in lineage. While he was the Archbishop of Krakow, he had noted that the front between Catholicism and Marxism (or, more broadly, between humanism and socialism) had become a contestation over the meaning of man. In *Centesimus Annus*, he hit the mark exactly:

> The fundamental error of socialism is anthropological in nature. Socialism considers the individual person simply as an element, a molecule within the social organism, so that the good of the individual is completely subordinated to the functioning of the socio-economic mechanism. Socialism likewise maintains that the good of the individual can be realized without reference to his free choice, to the unique and exclusive responsibility he exercises in the face of good or evil. Man is thus reduced to a series of social relationships, and the concept of the person as the autonomous subject of moral decision disappears, the very subject whose decisions build the social order.[25]

"Reduced to a series of social relationships"—that was the fatal flaw: the loss of "the autonomous subject of moral decision." In other words, the loss of a healthy respect for the individual—the acting, deciding person—and the loss of society's subjectivity, too.

This direct confrontation with the erroneous anthropology of socialism allowed John Paul II to begin with the human individual and move to the larger context of social relations and social systems: "Today, the church's social doctrine focuses especially on man as he is involved in a complex network of relationships within modern societies."[26] The mere individual is not what is in focus; rather, the pope's emphasis on invention and choice obliges Western economists to deepen their understanding of work, the worker, and creativity in work.

The main lines of *Centesimus Annus* are clean and clear: The human is an acting, creative person, capable of initiative and responsibility, seeking institutions in the three main spheres of life (political, economic, and cultural) worthy of his or her capacities—institutions that do not stifle or distort human liberty. For God himself made human beings free:

> Not only is it wrong from the ethical point of view to disregard human nature, which is made for freedom, but also in practice it is impossible to do so. Where society is so organized as to reduce arbitrarily or even suppress the sphere in which freedom is legitimately exercised, the result is that the life of society becomes progressively disorganized and goes into decline.[27]

This is the lesson the pope draws from the self-destruction of socialism.

There is a further lesson about human capacities for evil. A good Calvinist joke roughly expresses the pope's views: "The man who said that man is totally depraved can't be all bad." Analogously, the pope: "Man tends toward good, but he is also capable of evil. He can transcend his immediate interest and still remain bound to it."[28]

Thus, respecting man's limited but genuine goodness, the pope urges us not to stress an opposition between "self-interest" and the "common good." He urges us, rather, to seek a "harmony" between "self-interest" and "the interests of society as a whole," wherever this may be possible: "The social order will be all the more stable, the more it takes this fact [man's two-sided nature] into account and does not place in opposition personal interest and the interests of society as a whole, but rather seeks ways to bring them into fruitful harmony."[29]

In *The Federalist*, James Madison and Alexander Hamilton caution against allowing the perfect to become the enemy of the good. They re-

sisted utopic theorists and appealed to a basic realism about human beings rooted in a sober consideration of historical experience. In a spirit
not altogether dissimilar, John Paul II recognized the claims of legitimate
self-interest:

> In fact, where self-interest is violently suppressed, it is replaced by a
> burdensome system of bureaucratic control which dries up the well-
> springs of initiative and creativity. When people think they possess the
> secret of a perfect social organization which makes evil impossible, they
> also think that they can use any means, including violence and deceit,
> in order to bring that organization into being. Politics then becomes a
> "secular religion" which operates under the illusion of creating para-
> dise in this world. But no political society—which possesses its own
> autonomy and laws—can ever be confused with the kingdom of God.[30]

In politics, Aristotle wrote, it is necessary to be satisfied with a "tinc-
ture of virtue." The pope displayed a similar sobriety. In this direct way,
Pope John Paul II grasped the horns of the contemporary problem of free
persons and the common good.

It was relatively easy to determine what the common good was when a
single chief was charged with pointing it out. It is far more difficult when
the freedom of each person to discern the common good is respected.
Moreover, many aspects of the good of a whole people are not achieved
in concert or by single-minded direction from above; on the contrary,
they are achieved by a large number of persons and groups independently
performing their own tasks with excellence. A sound family life is not
achieved in a society by dictate from above, for example, but by each pair
of parents independently doing their best. And individual small businesses do not await commands from planning boards, but achieve their
purposes within their own markets and in their own particular niches in
their own various ways. Thus, in asserting the principle that the coinci-
dence of private interest and public good, as often as it can occur, achieves
an outcome not at all bad for society, John Paul II was being more than
world-wise. He was not only taking account of both the good in humans
and its ordinary limits; he was also assuming a more subtle view of the
common good than was possible in the less pluralistic past.

There is a difficulty here, of course. Many societies today are entrenched
in "culture wars." Large and important factions hold radically different
views about which way the society as a whole ought to go. What one fac-

tion finds good, another finds evil. In the last chapter of *Centesimus Annus*, the pope pointed out that cultural issues are the most important of all—and perhaps the most neglected by thinkers and doers. So much energy has gone into earlier conflicts over which political and economic order is most suited to human nature that for more than two centuries, the West has been living off of cultural capital. Concern over the physical climate has not yet been matched by concern over the moral climate. The ecology of liberty needs as much attention as the ecology of air, water, and sea.

Since personal action always entails risk, fault, and possible failure, the universe of freedom must be open, indeterminate, contingent. Some new things appear in it; some old things disappear. Pope John Paul II regularly stressed the new things that happen, such as the new ideas that emerged in the years before *Rerum Novarum* and the many changes that occurred in the world between 1891 and 1991. For him, history was a realm of trial and error, of costly mistakes and lessons hard-earned. Moreover, the human person seldom experiences societies worthy of his or her capacities for freedom, for love, for truth, for justice—and these are the things that the human race seeks.

Here John Paul II is not focusing solely on the individual. He is pointing out that the fully developed person is social, collaborative, and sharply aware of what she owes to others—and of how, in some ways, all depend on all. He is at once the pope of the person *and* of solidarity. Would there have been a *Solidarność* with a lesser person than Lech Walesa to lead it? Would Walesa be the person he now is—the historical person—if he had not acted in and through *Solidarność*? Person and community are mutually defining. Neither is wholly developed apart from the other.

For human progress in history, moreover, new free associations need to be formed continually from the creative acts of some few individuals. Collaborating together, even just a few individuals can become an arrowhead of advance for their whole society, even the whole world. Could there have been contemporary Poland—free and prosperous and more virtuous (more responsible and cooperative than ever before)—without the small band that persevered in that new free association called Solidarity? Could there be a united Europe if Solidarity had not cut a path through the Iron Curtain, and in the aftermath brought down that barbarous Berlin Wall? Both individual persons—hugely brave and admirable persons—and the communions they formed were necessary to the task. John Paul II told both: "Do not be afraid!"

CHAPTER 11

Centesimus Annus:
Capitalism, No and Yes

PAPAL SOCIAL THOUGHT WAS ONCE SAID TO LACK SOPHISTICATION
in the social sciences and to be too focused on the individual. *Centesimus Annus* intends to expand its analytic apparatus broadly enough to contrast not just ideologies, but actual systems of political economy such as real, existing examples of socialism and real, existing examples of democracy and capitalism.

With some sophistication, the pope distinguished the sphere of the social from that of the state, and drew a line between civil society and government. He emphasized the importance of free labor unions, citizens' initiatives, and free associations. In a passage reminiscent of Tocqueville's worries about the "new soft despotism" of democracies, the pope launched a systemic critique of "the social assistance state," contrasting local, "neighborly" work among the poor with the sterility of bureaucratic relationships.[1] Whereas for centuries the Catholic tradition had maintained a positive view of the role of the state in social life, John Paul II was especially careful and detailed in setting limits to the overly ambitious states of the late twentieth century.

There had never been any question in John Paul II's mind that democratic institutions, whatever their faults, are the best available protection for human rights. He now added that capitalist virtues and institutions, whatever their faults, are the best available protection for democracy. To be sure, it was the famous section 42 of *Centesimus Annus* that drew most of the attention in the world's press. Until that point in the encyclical, the pope had been dealing with the events that had changed the world since 1891, and especially the events of 1989, as background for his practical advice for the present. Then in section 42 the pope was at last ready to return to the underlying question being pressed upon him from Poland, Czechoslovakia, Hungary, the Third World, and many other quarters: After the collapse of socialism, what do you propose? It is worth giving his answer in full, since the only sensible answer to the question requires some care with the highly disputed term "capitalism."

> Returning now [for the third time] to the initial question: Can it perhaps be said that after the failure of communism capitalism is the victorious social system and that capitalism should be the goal of the countries now making efforts to rebuild their economy and society? Is this the model which ought to be proposed to the countries of the Third World, which are searching for the path to true economic and civil progress?
>
> The answer is obviously complex. If by "capitalism" is meant an economic system which recognizes the fundamental and positive role of business, the market, private property and the resulting responsibility for the means of production as well as free human creativity in the economic sector, then the answer is certainly in the affirmative even though it would perhaps be more appropriate to speak of a "business economy," "market economy" or simply "free economy." But if by "capitalism" is meant a system in which freedom in the economic sector is not circumscribed within a strong juridical framework which places it at the service of human freedom in its totality and which sees it as a particular aspect of that freedom, the core of which is ethical and religious, then the reply is certainly negative.[2]

Point by point, this reply reflects the experience of those nations that since World War II have experienced both political liberty and economic prosperity. For example, recovering from the experience of Nazism, Germany after World War II had to undergo a major transformation which was not only economic, but also political and moral. In many of the formerly communist nations, the situation today is similar. In Anglo-

American nations, a structure of law has evolved over centuries, from which slowly emerged the political, economic, and cultural institutions that together frame "the free society." In fact, such neoliberal thinkers as Friedrich Hayek in *The Constitution of Liberty* and Bruno Leoni in *Freedom and Law* particularly stress these noneconomic factors. In *The Spirit of Democratic Capitalism* (1982), I called the resulting Gestalt a "tripartite system." Democratic capitalism is not a "free enterprise system" alone. It cannot thrive apart from the moral culture that nourishes the virtues and values on which its existence depends. It cannot thrive apart from a democratic polity committed, on the one hand, to limited government and, on the other hand, to many legitimate activities without which a prosperous economy is impossible. The inarticulate practical wisdom embedded in the political system and in the moral-cultural system has profoundly affected the workings of the economic system. Both political decisions and the moral climate encouraged this economic development. At various times in American history, both the political system and the moral-cultural system have seriously intervened, positively and negatively, in the economic system. Each of the three systems has modified the others.

In the second part of section 42, cited above, Pope John Paul II carefully ordered the roles of all three systems—economic, juridical, and moral. As one part of the tripartite structure, capitalism rightly understood flows from the pope's anthropology: "Man's principal resource is man himself. His intelligence enables him to discover the earth's productive potential and the many different ways in which human needs can be satisfied."[3] "Man," he wrote again, "discovers his capacity to transform and in a certain sense create the world through his own work . . . carrying out his role as cooperator with God in the work of creation."[4] And yet again, "Man fulfills himself by using his intelligence and freedom. In so doing he utilizes the things of this world as objects and instruments and makes them his own. The foundation of the right of private initiative and ownership is to be found in this activity."[5]

Moreover, the expression of personal creativity through work entails a social dimension: "By means of his work man commits himself not only for his own sake, but also for others and with others. Each person collaborates in the work of others and for their own good. Man works in order to provide for the needs of his family, his community, his nation, and ultimately all humanity."[6]

In these texts we see the elemental form of the pope's logic, from the image of the Creator in each person, to the work that flows from that source. Likewise, from the fecund mind of the creative God, to the exercise of human intelligence and choice in invention, initiative, and enterprise. Already in *Sollicitudo Rei Socialis*, the pope had seen that the right to personal economic initiative is a fundamental human right, second only to the right to religious liberty. Like religious freedom, economic initiative also flows from the "creative subjectivity" of the human person. This line of thought led the pope to discern the role of enterprise in economic activity.

John Paul II saw creativity at work in such acts of discovery and discernment. He even saw in them a new form of "capital." As pastor and theologian, of course, he went beyond a purely economic evaluation of innovation to make ethical judgments about its impact on individual persons and the common good. Although the origins of the word "capital" lie in a more primitive economic era, when capita referred to heads of cattle and the major form of economic capital lay in the ownership of land, the same word also suggests the Latin *caput* (head), the human seat of that very creativity, invention, and initiative the pope sees in "creative subjectivity." Indeed, the pope himself alluded to the crucial shift from the primitive meaning of capital as land to its modern meaning as human capital, as we must now examine.

The pope's thinking on this point again parallels that of Abraham Lincoln. In *Laborem Exercens*, the pope asserted "the principle of the priority of labor over capital."[7] Similarly, in his First Annual Message to Congress on December 3, 1861, rephrasing some of the words he had used at the Wisconsin State Fair in 1859, Lincoln wrote:

> Labor is prior to, and independent of, capital. Capital is only the fruit of labor, and could never have existed if labor had not first existed. Labor is the superior of capital, and deserves much the higher consideration. Capital has its rights, which are as worthy of protection as any other rights. Nor is it denied that there is, and probably always will be, a relation between labor and capital, producing mutual benefits. The error is in assuming that the whole labor of community exists within that relation.[8]

Yet Lincoln also saw that the great cause of wealth is human wit, and grew quite eloquent in praising the role of invention in drawing wealth from the hidden bounty of creation. Similarly, he saw in the Patent and Copyright Clause of the U.S. Constitution a remarkable incentive for inventors and creators (and thus one of history's great boons to human freedom), since the prospect of the temporary ownership of ideas (as property) "added the fuel of interest to the fire of genius." In a similar spirit John Paul II wrote:

> The earth, by reason of its fruitfulness and its capacity to satisfy human needs, is God's first gift for the sustenance of human life. But the earth does not yield its fruits without a particular human response to God's gift, that is to say, without work. It is through work that man, using his intelligence and exercising his freedom, succeeds in dominating the earth and making it a fitting home. In history, these two factors—work and the land—are to be found at the beginning of every human society. However, they do not always stand in the same relationship to each other. At one time the natural fruitfulness of the earth appeared to be and was in fact the primary factor of wealth, while work was, as it were, the help and support for this fruitfulness. In our time, the role of human work is becoming increasingly important as the productive factor both of non-material and of material wealth. Work becomes ever more fruitful and productive to the extent that people become more knowledgeable of the productive potentialities of the earth and more profoundly cognizant of the needs of those for whom their work is done.[9]

In a way different from that of Ludwig von Mises and Friedrich Hayek, but with an analogous concern, the pope saw work as building up the tacit, experiential, evolving network of a good society: "It is becoming clearer how a person's work is naturally interrelated with the work of others. More than ever, work is work with others and work for others: It is a matter of doing something for someone else."[10]

In an odd way, then, modern capitalism centers more and more attention on *caput*, on factors such as knowledge, insight, discovery, enterprise, and inquiry. "Human capital" becomes the major cause of the wealth of nations, more important even than natural resources. A country without natural resources can in fact become wealthy; another country quite rich in natural resources can remain very poor. The reader can think of his or her own examples, but for me—all due complexities added—Japan and

Brazil offer a potent contrast. Such considerations led the pope to a new meaning of "capital." In our time in particular there exists another form of ownership which is becoming no less important than land: the possession of know-how, technology, and skill. The wealth of industrialized nations is based much more on this kind of ownership than on natural resources.

The pope's emphasis on the "community of work" also led him to appreciate "entrepreneurial ability." It is not so easy, he saw, to discern just how to match human needs and human resources in a productive and efficient way. In many nations today, economic failure, not success, seems to be the rule. The pope discovered that a kind of social foresight is key to avoiding failure:

> A person who produces something other than for his own use generally does so in order that others may use it after they have paid a just price mutually agreed upon through free bargaining. It is precisely the ability to *foresee* both the needs of others and the combinations of productive factors most adapted to satisfying those needs that constitutes another important source of wealth in modern society.[11]

In particular, the pope stressed the social aspects of entrepreneurship. A free economic system is nothing if not a social system of exchange, based upon voluntary agreement. The pope followed this logic closely:

> Many goods cannot be adequately produced through the work of an isolated individual; they require the cooperation of many people in working toward a common goal. Organizing such a productive effort, planning its duration in time, making sure that it corresponds in a positive way to the demands which it must satisfy and taking the necessary risks—all this too is a source of wealth in today's society. In this way the role of disciplined and creative human work and, as an essential part of that work, initiative and entrepreneurial ability becomes increasingly evident and decisive.[12]

At this point, everything that the pope had heretofore written about the acting person, about creative subjectivity, and about the fundamental right to personal economic initiative falls into place. He was in a position to render a systemic judgment: "This [modern economic] process, which throws practical light on a truth about the person which Christianity has constantly affirmed, should be viewed carefully and favorably."[13]

This is an astonishing statement. The pope suggested that the free and cooperative economy sheds light on Christian teaching in a new way. And he did not neglect the virtues required to accomplish this task:

> Important virtues are involved in this process such as diligence, industriousness, prudence in undertaking reasonable risks, reliability and fidelity in interpersonal relationships as well as courage in carrying out decisions which are difficult and painful, but necessary both for the overall working of a business and in meeting possible setbacks.[14]

The basis of the modern business economy, the pope wrote, "is human freedom exercised in the economic field."[15] This is a very important recognition. To papal approval for the free political life of democracy, it adds approval for a free economic life; and in both cases freedom implies accountability.

The pope even found it useful to say a good word for profit as "a regulator of the life of a business":[16] "The Church acknowledges the legitimate role of profit as an indication that a business is functioning well. When a firm makes a profit, this means that productive factors have been properly employed and corresponding human needs have been satisfied."[17] Like many good business writers today, the pope also stressed that profit is not the only regulator of the life of a business: "Human and moral factors must also be considered, which in the long term are at least equally important for the life of a business."[18] Business writers such as the late Peter Drucker have stressed the crucial role of various types of human relations within firms; the pope spoke of a firm as "a community of persons . . . who form a particular group at the service of the whole of society."[19]

The Limits of Capitalism

Nevertheless, Pope John Paul II did not forget the costs of modern capitalism, based upon human creativity, whose other face is necessarily what Joseph A. Schumpeter called "creative destruction." The pope wrote that "the constant transformation of the methods of production and consumption devalues certain acquired skills and professional expertise, and thus requires a continual effort of retraining and updating."[20] He particularly worried about the elderly, the young who cannot find jobs, and "in general those who are weakest."[21] He referred to the vulnerable in advanced societies as the "Fourth World."[22]

Meeting their needs is the unfinished work of *Rerum Novarum*, including "a sufficient wage for the support of the family, social insurance for old age and unemployment, and adequate protections for the conditions of employment."[23] All such deficiencies of a market system need to be redressed with practical wisdom. In some cases government will have to take a leading role; in other cases various sectors of civil society will. The pope was no libertarian—but neither was he a statist.

Christian ends leave a great deal of room within these boundaries for rival approaches to means, programs, and policies. The pope was also eager to distinguish capitalism rightly understood from the "primitive" or "early" type of capitalism of which he did not approve. The latter is characterized by (1) systems of "domination of things over people"; (2) systems "in which the rules of the earliest period of capitalism still flourish in conditions of 'ruthlessness' in no way inferior to the darkest moments of the first phase of industrialization"; and (3) systems in which "land is still the central element in the economic process, while those who cultivate it are excluded from ownership and are reduced to a state of quasi-servitude."[24] In the Third World (quite visibly in parts of Latin America), landless multitudes suffer cruelly and stream toward the nearest megalopolis where pitifully little work (or housing) is available to them. Like Hernando de Soto, the pope saw that such propertylessness and exclusion characterize the conditions in which "the great majority of the people in the Third World still live."[25]

By contrast, the pope approved of "a society of free work, of enterprise, and of participation."[26] He added: "Such a society is not directed against the market, but demands that the market be appropriately controlled by the forces of society and by the state so as to guarantee that the basic needs of the whole of society are satisfied."[27] The words "appropriately controlled" exclude a pure version of laissez-faire, but are in line with the concept of the tripartite society envisaged in section 42. "Society" is distinguished from "state"; the moral and cultural institutions of civil society are distinguished from the political organs of the government. Both the society and the state check, balance, and regulate the economy. That the pope did not intend a socialist method of "control" is obvious from the preceding sentence, wherein the pope was crystal clear: "What is being proposed as an alternative is not the socialist system."[28]

In the same spirit, the pope repeated three times that "it is unacceptable to say that the defeat of so-called 'real socialism' leaves capitalism as the only model of economic organization."[29] But here as elsewhere his cure for unbridled capitalism was capitalism of a more balanced, well-ordered kind. For he immediately proposed as a remedy:

> It is necessary to break down the barriers and monopolies which leave so many countries on the margins of development and to provide all individuals and nations with the basic conditions which will enable them to share in development. This goal calls for programmed and responsible efforts on the part of the entire international community. Stronger nations must offer weaker ones opportunities for taking their place in international life, and the latter must learn how to use these opportunities by making the necessary efforts and sacrifices and by ensuring political and economic stability, the certainty of better prospects for the future, the improvement of workers' skills and the training of competent business leaders who are conscious of their responsibilities.[30]

Similarly, in section 42, after having introduced capitalism rightly understood, the pope attacked "a radical capitalistic ideology":

> Vast multitudes are still living in conditions of great material and moral poverty. The collapse of the communist system in so many countries certainly removes an obstacle to facing these problems in an appropriate and realistic way, but it is not enough to bring about their solution. Indeed, there is a risk that a radical capitalistic ideology could spread which refuses even to consider these problems in the a priori belief that any attempt to solve them is doomed to failure, and which blindly entrusts their solution to the free development of market forces.[31]

By "radical capitalistic ideology," the pope seemed to mean total reliance on market mechanisms and economic reasoning alone. In the United States, we usually call such a view "libertarianism"; it is the view of a small (but influential) minority. American libertarians do not "refuse to consider" the poverty of multitudes; they offer their own sustained analyses and practical remedies, and with some success. The economy of Chile has become one of the leading economies of Latin America, in part through the sustained advice of libertarians from "the Chicago school," who were once much maligned.

Ironically, nonetheless, the pope preferred to call the capitalism of which he approves the "business economy," "market economy," or simply "free economy." This is probably because of European emotional resistance to the word "capitalism." My own reasoning in preferring to speak of "democratic capitalism," rather than the "market economy," is to avoid sounding libertarian—that is, narrowly focused on the economic system alone. For in reality, in advanced societies the institutions of both the juridical order and the cultural order do impinge greatly on, modify, and "control" the economic system. Indeed, any religious leftist or traditionalist who still believes that the United States is an example of unrestrained capitalism has not inspected the whole thirty-foot-long shelf of volumes containing the Federal Register of legally binding commercial regulations. One might more plausibly argue that the economies of capitalist nations today are too heavily (and unwisely) regulated than too lightly.

In the real world of fact, the business economy is restrained by law, custom, moral codes, and public opinion, as anyone can see who counts the socially imposed costs they are obliged to meet—and the number of employees they must hire (lawyers, affirmative-action officers, public-affairs officers, inspectors, community-relations specialists, pension-plan supervisors, health-plan specialists, child-care custodians, and so on). The term "democratic capitalism" is an attempt to capture these political and cultural restraints that limit any humane economic system. It is defined in a way broad enough to include political parties from the conservative to the social democratic, and systems as diverse as those of Sweden and the United States.

In a similar vein, John Paul II noted three clear moral limits to the writ of the free market: (1) Many human needs are not met by the market but lie beyond it. (2) Some goods "cannot and must not be bought or sold."[32] (3) Whole groups of people are without the resources to enter the market and need nonmarket assistance. The market principle is a good one, but it is neither universal in its competence nor perfectly unconditioned. It is not an idol.

In addition, the pope thought in terms of international solidarity. The whole world was his parish. The pope's frequent travels to the Third World were meant to dramatize the primary human (and Christian) responsibility to attend to the needs of the poor everywhere. Economic interdependence and the communications revolution have brought the Catholic people (and indeed all people) closer together than ever before. This fact brought to John Paul II's attention many moral and social imperatives surrounding and suffusing economic activities. For example: Care must be taken not to injure the environment.[33] States and societies need to establish a framework favorable to creativity, full employment, a decent family wage, and social insurance for various contingencies. The common good of all should be served, not violated by a few. Individuals should be treated as ends, not as means, and their dignity should be respected.

The tasks to be met by the good society are many. No system is as likely to achieve all these goods as a market system is; but in order to be counted as fully good, the market system must in fact achieve them. The pope explicitly commended the successes registered in these respects by mixed economies after World War II. But he also stressed how much still needs to be done. Finding good systems is a step forward, but after that comes the hard part.

Toward a More Civil Debate

Centesimus Annus is so balanced a document that, even while neoconservatives such as myself took it up with enthusiasm, many on the left also quickly embraced it. Quietly, some even pointed out that the left these days is in favor of markets, enterprise, economic growth, and personal initiative. The Latin American left and a few others reacted grudgingly, perhaps because of the intense emotional commitment of many to "liberation theology."

Even some on the North American Catholic left first responded to *Centesimus Annus* with shocked silence, followed less by an exposition of its themes than by an attack on neoconservatives for "hijacking" the encyclical. For example, a leading American Catholic progressive columnist, Father Richard P. McBrien, warned: "Neoconservatives who seem to exalt democratic capitalism as if it were the moral as well as the economic norm for the rest of the world cannot, on the basis of this encyclical, enlist the pope in their cause. Pope John Paul II is more cautious and more critical."[34] As evidence, McBrien cites section 42: "Is this [capitalism] the model which ought to be proposed to the countries of the Third World?" McBrien replies: "If I understand the neoconservatives' position correctly, their answer would be, 'obviously yes.' For John Paul II, the answer is 'obviously complex.'" This passage reveals that McBrien confuses neoconservatives with libertarians. In fact, it is neoconservatives who introduced the idea of political, moral, and cultural counterbalances to capitalism into Catholic social thought. That is why without hesitation or cavil they endorsed the precise words the pope used, as an echo of their own. Even the sentence: "The answer is complex."

The editors of the lay Catholic journal *Commonweal* also shared McBrien's confusions. As a counterpoise to the encyclical's "praise for the freedom and efficiency of market economies," they quoted another line from the encyclical: "Even the decision to invest in one place rather than another is always a moral and cultural choice." Then, they added in their own voice: "So much for the magic altruism of the Invisible Hand."[35] That is precisely the reason why some of us have long emphasized, with John Paul II, the legitimate roles of the political system and the moral-cultural system in supplementing and correcting the market economy: to go where the market alone cannot.

In the not-so-centrist *Center Focus*, the newsletter of the radical Center of Concern, Father Jim Hug, S.J., fastened on a sentence from section 56: "Western countries, in turn, run the risk of seeing this collapse [of Eastern European socialism] as a one-sided victory of their own economic system, and thereby failing to make corrections in that system."[36] He also liked section 34: "There are many human needs which find no place in the market. It is a strict duty of justice and truth not to allow fundamental human needs to remain unsatisfied, and not to allow those burdened by such needs to perish." (Such a sentiment, said Samuel Johnson, is the test of any good society.) Astutely, Father Hug concedes that "some of the language and emphasis of *Centesimus Annus* suggests that U.S. neoconservatives helped to shape its content." He urges the left to outdo the neocons next time: "We in the progressive segment of the Church justice community need to become 'wise as serpents' to the ways of influencing Vatican teaching."[37]

Most assuredly, *Centesimus Annus* is no libertarian document—and that, to many of us, is its beauty. Quite as the *Commonweal* article asserted, "What the encyclical grants to market mechanisms it does not take away from its witness to injustice or defense of the poor." It denounced conditions of "inhuman exploitation."[38] Quite truly, as Father Hug writes: "*Centesimus Annus* does not, then, anoint any existing system." The pope saw a great many faults in the economic, political, and moral-cultural systems of even the most highly developed societies. His conclusion was as pointed as the obelisk in the center of Saint Peter's Square. He made a nuanced, complex, but entirely forthright judgment about "which model ought to be proposed to the countries of the Third World, which are searching for the path to economic and civil progress." His considered judgment? The "business economy," "market economy," or simply "free economy."[39] But these too must be regulated by law and moral virtues. What could be plainer?

I want to stress that *Centesimus Annus* gives encouragement to social democrats and others of the moderate left, as well as to persons who share my own proclivities and those whose preferences are further to my right. It is not a party document. Part of its brilliance lies in its discernment of several constellations in the vast night sky of social goods. John Paul II saw, as it were, the stars that those on the reasonable left are following, but also the stars that attract those on the reasonable right. Some reasonable persons, if they are also partisans, tend to glance past the stars that others follow, to focus with passion on their own. John Paul II had the largeness of mind to keep all the stars in view, and with remarkable equanimity and balance. Indeed, I had the happy experience in London in April 1992 of hearing a leftist church worker describe *Centesimus Annus* as virtually a Labour Party manifesto, in the conference room of an institute sometimes described as a Thatcherite think-tank, among conservatives delighted with the fair play that *Centesimus Annus* had shown toward enterprise and with the nobility it saw in civil society. The Tories liked its praise of creative subjectivity and its criticism of the welfare state (see section 48), while the Labourites were pleased to note the limits it set to market principles and its various appeals to state assistance.

Nonetheless, it took nearly a whole year for a serious essay to be offered by the American Catholic left. Addressing "Christian Social Ethics After the Cold War," David Hollenbach, S.J., a specialist in religious ethics and figure of the Catholic left, gingerly requested room in the conversation for a chastened socialist vision from Latin America and the liberal agenda of the American bishops. Here is how that plea poignantly concludes:

> Those who have been led to believe that *Centesimus Annus* endorses "really existing capitalism" should take a hard look at the text. I hope that this modest "note" will encourage both such careful reading and subsequent talking in the spirit of solidarity and commitment to the common good that permeates the encyclical.[40]

Very nicely put. Hollenbach later quotes (but only in part) one of my favorite passages from *Centesimus Annus*, as follows:

The fact is that many people, perhaps the majority today, do not have the means which would enable them to take their place in an effective and humanly dignified way within a productive system in which work is truly central. . . . Thus, if not actually exploited, they are to a great extent marginalized; economic development takes place over their heads.[41]

But the two sentences that Hollenbach leaves out in his ellipsis are central to the pope's argument, since they put the stress on *human* capital:

They have no possibility of acquiring the basic knowledge which would enable them to express their creativity and develop their potential. They have no way of entering the network of knowledge and intercommunication which would enable them to see their qualities appreciated and utilized.[42]

In other words, the communication of knowledge and the opening of markets and trade are among the best services that advanced societies can offer to the poor of the Third World.

Further, John Paul II insisted that the poor of the Third World must be allowed to become more economically active. But this will require basic structural reform, including changes in the laws of those Third World nations (particularly in Latin America) that hold most enterprise by the common people to be illegal. Skipping this radical critique of precapitalist states, Hollenbach interprets the pope as merely restating the formulation used by the U.S. Catholic bishops, which seems to picture the people as passive: "Basic justice demands the establishment of minimum levels of participation in the life of the human community for all persons."[43] In the pope's view, by contrast, governments must support the fundamental right of all persons to personal economic initiative. The pope stressed the creativity and activism of the poor, and criticized the barriers (often imposed by states) to the full exercise of their potential.

In summarizing John Paul II's proposed remedy for Third World ills, Hollenbach cites its promarket beginning: "The chief problem [for poor countries] is that of gaining fair access to the international market. . . ." But he leaves off its even more significant ending: ". . . based not on the unilateral principle of the exploitation of the natural resources of these countries but on the proper use of human resources."[44] Here again the pope focused on human knowledge and creativity. These need to be developed to their full potential. These need proper institutional support. These are the source of wealth. Repressing them is a very great evil. Most Third World states cruelly punish or neglect the human creativity of their citizens. More strikingly still, the two sentences the pope supplies that lead into this passage are quite stunning:

> Even in recent years it was thought that the poorest countries would develop by isolating themselves from the world market and by depending only on their own resources. Recent experience has shown that countries which did this have suffered stagnation and recession, while the countries which experienced development were those which succeeded in taking part in the general interrelated economic activities at the international level.[45]

"In my judgment," Hollenbach writes, "the principles [of *Centesimus Annus*] call for major changes both in the domestic arrangements presently in place in the United States as well as in the global marketplace." On that point, Hollenbach and I read the encyclical the same way. On what those "major changes" should be, however, Hollenbach and I are in different camps. The pope systematically recommends changes that open up and extend the benefits of market systems and encourage the domestic development of human resources. But Hollenbach has nowhere considered the concrete steps necessary to bring about "the proper use of human resources" in the Third World, particularly in the institutions that make personal economic creativity possible. One needs to ask him: How does one improve the skills of ordinary people, their knowledge, know-how, and capacities for enterprise (that is, human capital)? What institutional changes are necessary in Bolivia, Brazil, Colombia—and south central Los Angeles?

Recall Michael Ignatieff's description of the moral flaw in the British Labour Party, as shown by the loss of four straight elections, including that of 1992: "Labour always tells people what it is going to do for them. It never encourages them to do it for themselves."[46] Far better is it to build up institutions of enterprise and creativity, the social supports for that personal exercise of creativity and self-determination of which human dignity consists.

This was John Paul II's point: A clear call for creative approaches to replace tired progressive remedies, while giving the latter due credit for what they did achieve. There was room in the pope's house for many arguments among different tendencies and parties. But it was also important for those who disagreed to include each other in the discussion, and to conduct that discussion forthrightly, openly, and civilly.

The Catholic left (in the United States, at least) has expressed substantive agreement with *Centesimus Annus* even while showing considerable annoyance that the neoconservatives like it more than they. The left sees the poor and the vulnerable as passive, awaiting the ministrations of the state. The right and the center see the poor as capable, creative, and active. The left clings to its appeals to action by the state; it has become conservative in rhetoric, looking backward. The center and the right long for a new beginning, and sound positively radical in their demand for civil society, rather than the state, as their main hope for the future. Those in the center and on the right tend to emphasize all the encyclical's appeals to civil society; those on the left (but not so much as before) tend to emphasize the state. This debate among left, center, and right—besides being unavoidably built into the tripartite system—is altogether healthy.

Paul Adams reminds me that since, though not necessarily because of, *Centesimus Annus*, there has been much emphasis in some fields of social work on "empowerment." This term points to the practice of demanding assistance from government when strictly necessary, yes, but also recognizing that it is better to enable people to tap into their own wisdom, creativity, and initiative. See, for example, the reaction against deficit and needs-focused approaches to community development that only do things *for* the poor. More often praised among practitioners nowadays is Asset-Based Community Development. From hard experience, social workers have come to recommend strategies that build up civil society and increase local initiative. They stress the danger of the "doing-for" approaches of state or private charities. Too often "help" from outside sets communities back by inducing dependency and passivity. How best to help the poor, in practice? The answer is obviously complex!

Having always resented such moral imperialism as Paul Tillich's "Every serious Christian must be a socialist," and the British left's "Christianity is the religion of which socialism is the practice," I would by no means support the sentiment, "Every serious Christian must be a democratic capitalist," or "Christianity is the religion of which democratic capitalism is the practice." As *Centesimus Annus* insists, the Catholic Church "has no models to present," and, indeed, has powerful reasons to criticize many abuses and wrongs in democratic capitalist societies.[47] The pope rightly insists that no worldly system can ever claim to be the Kingdom of God. What good would a Church be if it didn't constantly criticize the City of Man in the light of the City of God, *sub specie aeternitatis*? Indeed, as Thomas Pangle reports in his study of Tocqueville's *Democracy in America*, such an appeal to the viewpoint of immortality and eternal life is the indispensable contribution of religion to the democratic experiment.[48]

The dread menace of communism, which in the Soviet Union alone took and blighted millions of lives, has been defeated. The ideology of socialism (at least as an economic idea) has been discredited, except among those whose investment in it has been too heavy to surrender quickly. In the long run of history, socialist economics will appear to have been a distraction. Our descendants may well wonder how so many of us, at least for so long a part of our lives, could have been taken in by it. Why didn't we heed Leo XIII's predictions about its futility and its immense damage to humanity? The death of socialism gives us an opportunity to think in fresh ways and to begin again with a new burst of social creativity. To have established that perspective, and to have set before us the immense challenge to create something much better than anything now available, is the true achievement of *Centesimus Annus*.

CHAPTER 12

Benedict XVI
and *Caritas in Veritate*

IT SEEMS TO PAUL ADAMS AND ME THAT CATHOLIC SOCIAL
thought is ill served by the sort of proof-texting people do to show that it
is whatever they want it to be. The major theme of Catholic social thought
is the nexus of the human person, her initiative and creativity, as linked
(from Leo XIII on) to the central and vital role of associations and, more
broadly, all of civil society.

John Paul II wisely warns that Catholic social thought is a work in progress. To borrow Newman's metaphor, it is like a squad making its way up a
mountain on a trail that sometimes switchbacks left and then right, back
and forth, on its climb upward. This very yin and yang creates factions. For
example, some stress liberty, initiative, risk, creativity, and an experimen-
tal/empirical conviction. Others, distrusting free persons always to do the
right thing, tend to stress the need for government oversight and action.
They fear the abuses of personal liberty. These latter tend to see Anglo-
American "liberalism" and "individualism" as great evils. They trust only
a more European and Latin solidarity that relies heavily on the state.

Centesimus Annus is the most developed expression of Catholic social
thought so far, in one view, but others see *Caritas in Veritate* (2009) or
even *Populorum Progressio* (1967) as restoring a more familiar perspective.

I think it is best to recognize that Catholic social thought is not now—and maybe never should be—a fully coherent and consistent body of teaching, framed like a book of logic in "eternal" principles. True enough, in Catholic circles more than in secular or Protestant circles, enormous care is taken to agree (or at least be consistent) with papal predecessors. Moreover, different factions among Catholics tend to pick the starting place that best fits with the argument they want to make. It is perhaps inevitable that those on the left like to emphasize *Populorum Progressio*, whereas those less state-inclined tend to find *Centesimus Annus* much more empirically minded and, on the whole, wiser.

To some extent, Benedict XVI continued in the line of development begun by John Paul II, rooted in a new synthesis of Thomistic thought and contemporary phenomenological analysis. Phenomenology introduces a more carefully articulated vision of human subjectivity and interiority to Thomism, which enabled Wojtyła to add many profound insights into the human subject. Cardinal Ratzinger, manifestly, was always more Augustinian in his approach to theology than most theologians of the past century, who have tended more to follow Saint Thomas than Saint Augustine. One should not forget that the young Ratzinger's *Habilitationsschrift* was a study of Saint Bonaventure, the Franciscan student of Augustine, more a theologian of the heart and the human subject than Saint Thomas, who was a theologian preeminently (but not solely) of the mind, as is suggested in his sobriquet the Angelic Doctor.

In his encyclical *Caritas in Veritate*, Benedict XVI stressed that the Church should be understood neither as holding a particular ideology about political economy nor as imposing specific practical solutions on individual countries or regions. He did not intend to pronounce upon the disagreements about political economy among Catholics or others. On the contrary, his aim was to put questions of political economy in a larger theological and philosophical context, dealing with such questions as the role of *caritas* in theology, and in philosophy such questions as sound concepts of the common good, the human person, and human community.

Moreover, in his concrete discussions about current affairs, almost every time Benedict seemed to give a point to the left, rooted usually in *Populorum Progressio*, he took it back or qualified it by drawing on lessons learned between 1967 and 1991, as recorded in *Centesimus Annus*. His practice followed his intention. He lets both horses run and does not himself choose to side with either one.

In some ways, this openness seems baffling to many readers, making this particular piece of Benedict XVI's writing come across as uncharacteristically waffly and opaque. It often seems to go in two directions at once. Some sentences are almost impossible to parse in practical terms: What on earth does *that* mean in practice?

This refusal to indulge in ideology has a great strength that compensates for the above-mentioned weakness. Its strength is that it raises the mind to other dimensions of the truth, and avoids squabbles that belong more to the City of Man than to the City of God.

For instance, this higher perspective enables Benedict to link the gospel of life to the social gospel. That makes immense practical sense. For instance, in the United States more than 50 million children have been aborted since 1973. If those girls and boys had been allowed to live, millions of them would now be in the workforce, helping with their social security taxes to close the deficits in our programs for the elderly. Policies regarding the beginning of life profoundly affect the welfare state as the average age of the population rises. Besides, the elderly require the heaviest medical expenditures in any population. Not only do they require more medical care for more ailments, but the new technologies and pharmaceuticals steadily coming to market are ever more expensive—and aging tends to last for many more years now than it used to. Thus high abortion rates deeply set back the medical prospects of the elderly.

Even more swiftly than the United States, Europe, with its failure to keep population up to a level of even bare replacement, is condemning its welfare state to an accelerating implosion due to costs.

HERE IS ONE of my favorite practical passages in *Caritas in Veritate*, which reports some of the most important gains for Catholic social thought over the past 120 years. Sadly, though, its language unrolls as though it was written by a committee, and falls on the ear more like bureaucratic jargon than like Benedict's usually profound and warm style:

> By considering reciprocity as the heart of what it is to be a human
> being, subsidiarity is the most effective antidote against any form of all-
> encompassing welfare state. It is able to take account both of the mani-
> fold articulation of plans—and therefore of the plurality of subjects—as
> well as the coordination of those plans. Hence the principle of subsid-
> iarity is particularly well-suited to managing globalization and direct-
> ing it towards authentic human development. In order not to produce

a dangerous universal power of a tyrannical nature, *the governance of globalization must be marked by subsidiarity*, articulated into several layers and involving different levels that can work together. Globalization certainly requires authority, insofar as it poses the problem of a global common good that needs to be pursued. This authority, however, must be organized in a subsidiary and stratified way, if it is not to infringe upon freedom and if it is to yield effective results in practice.[1]

Within this section, and several other places in the encyclical, a pattern begins to emerge whereby Benedict XVI makes a point important to the political/economic center-left, and then qualifies it in terms important to the political/economic center-right.

For example, regarding his concern to help the poor, the pope first advises that "more economically developed nations should do all they can to allocate larger portions of their gross domestic product to development aid, thus respecting the obligations that the international community has undertaken in this regard." This recommendation will arouse students of the great British expert on foreign assistance, Lord Peter Bauer, who thoroughly documented the record of damage caused by foreign assistance. As if recognizing that objection, Benedict immediately puts his suggestion back within the limits of subsidiarity and personal accountability: "One way of doing so is by reviewing their internal social assistance and welfare policies, applying the principle of subsidiarity and creating better integrated welfare systems, with the active participation of private individuals and civil society."[2] Still, these are all steps that nations counting on foreign assistance are highly unlikely to take. Counting on foreign assistance is easier than self-reform.

As for global government, we see Benedict XVI again call for a world political authority:

> To manage the global economy; to revive economies hit by the crisis; to avoid any deterioration of the present crisis and the greater imbalances that would result; to bring about integral and timely disarmament, food security and peace; to guarantee the protection of the environment and to regulate migration: for all this, there is urgent need of a true world political authority, as my predecessor Blessed John XXIII indicated some years ago.

But he is quick to define this authority in terms of restraint and of adherence to the core principles of Catholic social thought:

Such an authority would need to be regulated by law, to observe consistently the principles of subsidiarity and solidarity, to seek to establish the common good, and to make a commitment to securing authentic integral human development inspired by the values of charity in truth.[3]

For myself, I love best Benedict's starting point in *caritas*. When I was a young man, I wanted to write a book about the centrality of God's unique form of love, called *caritas* (rather than the more common, down-to-earth *amor*) in the theology of Thomas Aquinas. I loved his little treatise on charity (the poor English translation of *caritas*) and often taught seminars on it.

I have been trying to steer Catholic social teaching in this direction—beginning with my own thinking—for a long time. So watching Benedict XVI write about *caritas* so beautifully has brought me immense satisfaction.

In all candor, however, if we hold each sentence of *Caritas in Veritate* up to analysis in the light of empirical truth about events in the field of political economy since 1967, we will find that it is not nearly so full in its *veritas* as in its *caritas*.

For instance, the benefits the poor gained through the spread of economic enterprise and markets ("capitalism" is for many too unpleasant a word to use) should be more resoundingly acknowledged. In 1970, for instance, the mortality age of men and women in Bangladesh was 44.6 years old, but by 2005 it had risen to 63. Think what joy and vigor such increased longevity means to individual families.

Similarly, the infant mortality rate (deaths per 1,000 live births) in Bangladesh in 1970 was 152, or 15.2 percent. By 2005 this average had been brought down to just 57.2, or a little less than 6 percent. Again, what pain this lifts from ordinary mothers and fathers, and what joy it brings. There is surely more to do to raise health standards for Bangladesh. But such progress in just thirty years is unprecedented in world history.

Anyone with experience knows that humans do not live by economics alone. The most successful people in business today are the first to tell you that business alone, despite its nobility and satisfactions, is not sufficient. They need time to smell the roses—they need leisure, quiet, contemplation, thought, and prayer. And they also want, mightily, to contribute to the well-being of others, especially the poor. They welcome well-informed practical guidance from their spiritual leaders, and have been getting far too little of it down the years. *Caritas in Veritate* gives reason to believe that Benedict XVI has known all this, and meant to rectify it.

[CHAPTER 13]

Pope Francis
on Unreformed Capitalism

READING THE ACTUAL TEXT OF THE 2014 APOSTOLIC EXHORTATION *Evangelii Gaudium* by Pope Francis, after reading the wildly misleading analyses of it by *The Guardian* and Reuters, I was at first dismayed by how seemingly partisan and empirically unfounded were five or six of its sentences.

Later, rereading the exhortation in full in its English translation, and attempting to see it through the eyes of the current professor-bishop-pope who grew up in Argentina, I began to have more sympathy for the phrases used by Pope Francis. For one thing, when it comes to the Third World and to South America in particular, the second poorest continent on earth, the pope knows whereof he speaks. For another, he is only picking up a noteworthy theme highlighted in John Paul II's *Centesimus Annus*. After distinguishing among good forms of capitalism and bad ones, John Paul II writes very severely about a bad form of capitalism still weighing down the poor in many countries of the world. He points to countries kept outside "the sphere of economic and human development"[1] in which the more fortunate forge ahead. The lack of trade and communication, and the obstacles to the transfer of knowledge and skills, bring about the marginalization of many millions outside the mainstream of development. I quote here at length John Paul II's poignant description of this reality:

The fact is that many people, perhaps the majority today, do not have the means which would enable them to take their place in an effective and humanly dignified way within a productive system in which work is truly central. They have no possibility of acquiring the basic knowledge which would enable them to express their creativity and develop their potential. They have no way of entering the network of knowledge and intercommunication which would enable them to see their qualities appreciated and utilized. Thus, if not actually exploited, they are to a great extent marginalized; economic development takes place over their heads, so to speak, when it does not actually reduce the already narrow scope of their old subsistence economies. They are unable to compete against the goods which are produced in ways which are new and which properly respond to needs, needs which they had previously been accustomed to meeting through traditional forms of organization. Allured by the dazzle of an opulence which is beyond their reach, and at the same time driven by necessity, these people crowd the cities of the Third World where they are often without cultural roots, and where they are exposed to situations of violent uncertainty, without the possibility of becoming integrated. Their dignity is not acknowledged in any real way, and sometimes there are even attempts to eliminate them from history through coercive forms of demographic control which are contrary to human dignity.

Many other people, while not completely marginalized, live in situations in which the struggle for a bare minimum is uppermost. These are situations in which the rules of the earliest period of capitalism still flourish in conditions of "ruthlessness" in no way inferior to the darkest moments of the first phase of industrialization. In other cases the land is still the central element in the economic process, but those who cultivate it are excluded from ownership and are reduced to a state of quasi-servitude. In these cases, it is still possible today, as in the days of *Rerum novarum*, to speak of inhuman exploitation. In spite of the great changes which have taken place in the more advanced societies, the human inadequacies of capitalism and the resulting domination of things over people are far from disappearing. In fact, for the poor, to the lack of material goods has been added a lack of knowledge and training which prevents them from escaping their state of humiliating subjection.[2]

In absorbing Francis's perspective, what is most painful to Argentinians is that Argentina a century ago ranked among the top fifteen industrial nations. Then a destructive economic ideology dramatically slowed Argentina's economic and political progress, and instability in the rule of law undermined economic creativity. Inflation blew upward to impossible heights. (In the early 1980s, I brought home from Argentina a note for a million Argentine pesos that had declined in worth to two pennies.)

For over three generations, very little of Argentina's rich natural endowment has been available to the bottom half of the population. Upward mobility from the bottom up has been surprisingly infrequent. Even today, upward progress for Argentina's poor is not yet in sight. The poor receive little personal instruction in how to improve their independent creativity. Few laws and few lending institutions support them in moving upward. Humiliation wells up in the poor as they see their lack of personal achievement and their dependency. This is what Pope Francis was painfully remembering as he wrote his exhortation, and it is exactly what the eyes of many other observers have seen.

Argentina is an exceptionally complex society. In Mendoza province, great Malbecs are wrested from the mountainous terrain, thanks to many generations of toil and loving attention. There one meets unusually determined entrepreneurs who are proud of what their ancestors have built by imagination, artistry, and hard work. In teeming cities to the south, amid depressing slums, some millions are either unemployed or underemployed. There is an immense amount of work to do to make neighborhoods habitable, let alone prosperous. There are electric poles and wires to put up, sewer pipes to lay, cement slabs to be laid as foundations for houses that would be sturdier than the rickety shanties covering the landscape. On the one hand, there are millions of unemployed. On the other, millions of hands are needed to build a new Argentina, an Argentina more hopeful for the poor. What will bring these two poles together, the unemployed with the immense work yet to be done?

What system works best for raising up the poor into a creative and ever-rising middle class? For creating beautiful neighborhoods, parks, schools, and thriving small businesses in every urban center? There is no doubt that the poor need a reconstruction of the social order. This chief question desperately needs an answer: *How do we get there? How can we raise today's miserably poor toward ever-improving life chances and inspiring environs?*

All around the world, such progress is happening, even in some sectors of Latin America. In Chile, Uruguay, Brazil, Colombia, and parts of Mexico, one sees economic vitality bubbling up. This creative ferment seems to happen wherever economic policies evoke the creative and inventive energies of citizens. In other areas of Latin America, by sharp contrast, nations are sliding backward, down deeper into poverty, disorder, and dislocation—Venezuela most visibly of all. In different countries, different ideas guide the fates of nations. Thus, the most urgent question for the poor must be: *What is the most secure and speediest way out of poverty and misery?*

Some experts used to say that the problem is overpopulation. This opinion imploded when more astute scholars noted conclusively that densely populated nations, such as Japan, Taiwan, Singapore, Hong Kong, and many others, even with very few natural resources, could double and redouble the standard of living of their poorest people in one generation. Thus, the crisis of the poorest ones to which Pope Francis directs our attention is not a hopeless, desolate desert. Great economic progress can be made swiftly, and is *being* made, all around the world. I first saw Warsaw, Poland, in 1978: dark, drab, depressed, rundown, unpainted, still heavily pockmarked by ruins left by World War II. To see the festival of light it had become by my last visit at Christmastime in 2012 was to have my breath taken away by the stark contrast: the Polish miracle, one wants to say. Except that we have seen the same miracle in scores of countries around the world since 1945, including the Four Asian Tigers between the 1960s and the 1990s, in Eastern Europe after the fall of Communism in 1991, and in China and India over the last twenty-five years—and, to repeat once again, in many, many sectors in South and Central America. Still, both Africa and Latin America lag far below their economic potential.

On Terminological Consistency

Often one finds persons in different parts of the world today attaching widely different meanings to such terms as "socialism," "social democracy," "liberalism," "neoliberalism," "capitalism," and even "mercantilism."

Consider the many different meanings attached to the word "capitalism," based on very different experiences in many different parts of the world. In many Latin countries, today's corporate leaders are often the grandsons of the great landholders of the past. Some of these sons are men of vision, invention, and personal initiative who have built up whole new firms—or have at least formed alliances overseas to bring European, North American, or Asian brands into Latin America. Still, they are perceived as part of a rich-versus-poor culture that stretches back to the 1500s.

I learned in Italy in the 1950s that "capitalism" there meant a sharply two-tiered division of classes. Some owners of great companies were members of the old landed aristocracy, with their old fortunes now invested in automobiles, rubber tires, petroleum, chemicals, radio and television sets, fine wines, and large manufacturers of all sorts. The difference was not only rich versus poor, but also between those very few who could get into worldwide businesses and those who had no opportunity. Opportunity seemed open only to a few.

True, there were in the 1950s plenty of shopkeepers and small businesses of generations' standing: producers of fine stationery, milliners, fine tailoring shops, and many others. But there were not many entrepreneurs, inventors, creative builders of new businesses, or founders of whole new lines of products. In Italy, "capitalism" was still used as a fairly nasty term, linked to privilege, inheritance, and the old stability. On the other hand, a new type of critic such as Aminatore Fanfani disagreed strongly with the British liberal writers of the nineteenth century, such as Bentham, Mill, and others. He thought of them as "Protestants," outside the old humanistic consensus. He thought of them as giving their blessing to an irrational and destructive lust for unlimited acquisition.

But this is only one description of capitalism in the European context. As Hayek describes in *The Counterrevolution of Science*, the Continental model of capitalism is quite different from the Anglo-American model.[3] The former was strongly influenced by the well-known socialist theorist Henri de Saint-Simon. A disciple of Saint-Simon was Napoleon III, who followed Saint-Simon's theories in his policy for the industrialization of France. Similar models were deployed elsewhere in Europe, including Germany and Italy. Saint-Simon's influence (and that of his disciple Auguste Comte) was also felt strongly in Latin America. Briefly put, their model assigns the state a commanding economic role. It parcels out rights to incorporate new businesses and demands long lists of regulations and requirements. It levies very high taxes, usually to pay for a large air/rail/auto transportation system and an expensive military.

Under such a model, the state daily awards large contracts to "capitalists" (typically friends of politicians or dummy corporations owned by politicians), who set up their industries with the benefit of large investments from major banks, with whom they are given "connections." These individuals have very little capital of their own and assume very little risk. Their main asset is their connection with political power, and they form a kind of exclusive club, barring the vast majority from access to economic initiative. This has also been the historical model in Argentina, but there, due to the importance of agriculture, the landowning class has also played a significant economic role.

My own experience of capitalism in the American context was out of tune with these other national experiences of capitalism. Born in a small town in Pennsylvania founded in the early 1800s by German farmers, I was brought up proud of the great steel mills and complex coal mines pioneered by sturdy inventors, mostly born poor, who came to Johnstown as immigrants from many nations. By the time of the Civil War (1861–65), the iron mills of Johnstown had become, through newly invented processes, the first large makers of steel, and builders of some of the largest steel mills in the country. (Birmingham, Alabama, was its southern counterpart.) Steel was far more useful than iron, and later enabled many new industrial developments, with railway ties, bridges, automobile bodies, and girders for skyscrapers. We in America, by and large, were very proud of our many inventors. We owed our rich employment opportunities to such men. Among us, "capitalist" was a good name, and in our public schools one did not see portraits of aristocrats and soldiers, as in Europe, but local inventors of industry.

We begrudged no one who became rich by invention. Scores of thousands of young men in America were experimenting at home in order to become inventors who could own intellectual property. Abraham Lincoln himself earned two patents. My wife's grandfather and his brother took out nearly fifty between them, some highly significant such as baling wire, a special lightning rod, the stump-puller "that cleared the West" (which won a gold medal citation from the Seattle World's Fair of 1909), and an early prototype of the extension ladder.

For such reasons, we associated capitalism not with privilege but with an open door for poor young men of no particular family connections, but with inventive minds, initiative, stick-to-itiveness, and a knack for practical problem solving to produce new goods and services which made everyone's lives a little better. We thought of such initiatives as serving the common good, and the more widely your product was used, the more wealthy you might justly become for producing something so useful to so many, and so soon. (Patents were and are valid only for a relatively short period of time.)

Another example of how differently the same word rings in different parts of the world: As of now, I suspect, most Americans cannot name a single household item invented by Argentines. Some Englishmen of the World War II era, however, would think immediately of the ballpoint pen (a novel invention then), which they call a *biro*, just as they call the vacuum cleaner a *hoover*. Láslό Biro invented the ballpoint pen in Budapest, but then emigrated to Argentina and perfected it there. He made large quantities for the Royal Air Force in World War II because ballpoints worked better at high altitudes than fountain pens.

True, in several new fields, creativity and invention are now growing rapidly in Latin America. The Brazilian Embraer jets (popular in the fleets of many U.S. carriers) are highly praised originals. But still the economic systems of too many Latin American countries are more like static and traditional market systems than they are "capitalist" in invention and enterprise.

Catholic Social Thought Is a Work-in-Progress

Anyone commenting on the economic themes of *Evangelii Gaudium* will note at the outset that the pope insists that this document is *not* a full expression of his views on political economy, which will come later, but only an expression of his pastoral heart. In paragraph 51 Francis writes:

> It is not the task of the Pope to offer a detailed and complete analysis of contemporary reality, but I do exhort all the communities to an "ever watchful scrutiny of the signs of the times". This is in fact a grave responsibility, since certain present realities, unless effectively dealt with, are capable of setting off processes of dehumanization which would then be hard to reverse. We need to distinguish clearly what might be a fruit of the kingdom from what runs counter to God's plan. This involves not only recognizing and discerning spirits, but also—and this is decisive—choosing movements of the spirit of good and rejecting those of the spirit of evil. I take for granted the different analyses which other documents of the universal magisterium have

offered, as well as those proposed by the regional and national conferences of bishops. In this Exhortation I claim only to consider briefly, and from a pastoral perspective, certain factors which can restrain or weaken the impulse of missionary renewal in the Church, either because they threaten the life and dignity of God's people or because they affect those who are directly involved in the Church's institutions and in her work of evangelization.

Those who favor capitalist techniques to raise the poor out of poverty observe that, traditionally, the poor in capitalist economies move upward, with higher employment rates, higher wages, measurable outbursts of personal initiative and new enterprises, and widespread homeownership. Immigrants move out of poverty often in just a few years, and the working-class "proletariat" become solid members of the middle class. (In a televised debate in Italy, my Marxist partner kindly offered me an argument he said he would use if he were I. Bowing to Gramsci, he pointed out that the problem Marxists in Italy then faced was that capitalism had succeeded in making workers part of the middle class, now more capitalist in their politics. And so, he smiled, Communists were reduced to recruiting new members from the class of journalists, radio and television and cinema workers, professors, and students.)

The history of the United States, as well as that of postwar Europe, and now large swathes of China, India, and much of the Third World, is heavily laden with such evidence. But in other portions of the world, *Evangelii Gaudium* warns against "a crude and naïve trust in the goodness of those wielding economic power and in the sacralized workings of the prevailing economic system."[4] In Argentina and other static systems with little or no upward mobility, this observation might sadly be true. In nations with generations of reliable upward mobility, however, it is not really true.

The upward movement promoted by certain capitalist systems is the real experience of a large majority of North Americans, yet in some places it may seem to be "a crude and naïve trust." Nor is "trickle-down" (another phrase in the English translation of the exhortation) an apt description of what has happened in the advanced world; rather, what has been experienced there is wealth "welling up from below." This is precisely what continues to attract millions of immigrants into advanced economies.

In addition, the English translation of *Evangelii Gaudium* insists that there are people who believe that economic growth will *inevitably* produce greater justice and inclusiveness (*equidad e inclusion sociál*). But the Spanish text does not use the word "inevitably." The more moderate (and accurate expression) in Spanish is *por si mismo*, or "by itself." Unlike the English translation, the original Spanish gets it right: It takes a lot more than economic growth to make a system "equitable." It takes the rule of law, the protection of natural rights, and the Jewish/Christian concern for the widow, the orphan, the hungry, the sick, the imprisoned. In short, it requires effective concern for all the vulnerable and needy.

Despite its glaring faults, especially in its entertainment sector—pop music, nudity, decadence—the American system seems to have been more "inclusive" of the poor than any other nation on earth.

In the End, a Positive Evaluation

There are two things I especially value in *Evangelii Gaudium*. First is its focus on *caritas*. The whole of the cosmos, and the whole of human life, are upward leaping flames from the inner life of the Creator, from *caritas*—that outward-moving, creative love that is God. As the erudite Benedict XVI showed in his first encyclical, *Deus Caritas Est* (2005), everything crucial to human life begins in God's *caritas*. When we think of this in our own lives, we can ask: Is not the love you have for your dear spouse, children, and close friends the most "divine" experience you know?

That is one reason why Catholic social thought begins in *caritas*. It is also why the poor are so close to the center of Christian concern, and so much at the heart of Christian worship.

The second point I most value is the focus *Evangelii Gaudium* places on the main practical task of our generation: breaking the last round of chains of ancient poverty. In 1776, there were not yet even 1 billion people on earth—only an estimated 750 million. The vast majority of them were poor (*les misérables* of Victor Hugo's France), and mostly living under tyrannies. Just over two centuries later, there are more than 7 billion human beings. Rapid medical discoveries and inventions have helped to double (and more) the average age of mortality, vastly reduce infant mortality, and provide relief for hundreds of diseases. Economic progress has allowed six-sevenths of the greatly extended human race to break free from poverty—over a billion of them just since 1950, and another billion since 1980. There are another billion more still in chains.[5] The Jewish, Christian, and secular humanist task is to break this remaining billion free.

Worship of God, in the Christian view, gains its credibility from what the worshipper actually *does* in daily life to help the poor. If one doesn't come to the aid of the poor, then in practice one does not love God.

"No one has ever seen God," Saint John writes in his first Letter, "but if we love one another, God lives in us and his love is made complete in us" (1 Jn 4:12). And Jesus instructed, "Whatever you did for one of the least of these brothers and sisters of mine, you did for me" (Mt 25:40).

In the future, Francis will unfold his fuller arguments about the practical policies that best help the poor to move out of poverty. No doubt, consultations preparing him for this task have already begun.

Note, for example, what John Paul II said about the need for capitalist peoples to be vigilant and to do still more than before:

> The Marxist solution has failed, but the realities of marginalization and exploitation remain in the world, especially the Third World, as does the reality of human alienation, especially in the more advanced countries. Against these phenomena the Church strongly raises her voice. Vast multitudes are still living in conditions of great material and moral poverty. The collapse of the Communist system in so many countries certainly removes an obstacle to facing these problems in an appropriate and realistic way, but it is not enough to bring about their solution. Indeed, there is a risk that a radical capitalistic ideology could spread which refuses even to consider these problems, in the a priori belief that any attempt to solve them is doomed to failure, and which blindly entrusts their solution to the free development of market forces.[6]

Although economic growth falls far short of being the only goal of free societies, its blessings for education, medical improvements, the prospering of freedom of conscience, and the private financing of civic life are not inessential to the common good. Fault it we must. But in all justice, such a system surely deserves gratitude for what it does better than all prior systems.

There are good versions of capitalism and bad ones. One test of the difference is how well and how rapidly the good system raises its poor out of poverty. On that, Pope Francis is on target.

It is all too true that market systems do not *alone* produce upward mobility, economic progress for all, and wide economic opportunity. Argentina has always had a market economy. So, too, almost all the peoples in human history. Market systems alone do not lift up the poor.

Jerusalem in the biblical period cherished private property ("Thou shalt not steal," "Thou shalt not covet thy neighbor's goods"), and it lived by a vital market (it was the commercial interface of three continents). But for 1,800 years after Christ lived, none of the world's markets—nor the aggregate thereof—produced much economic development. The world's economies remained relatively static as they faced a merciless cycle of "fat" years followed by "lean" ones. In nearly every generation, traditional market systems experienced famines and massive outbreaks of deadly diseases. No more.

Pope John Paul II came to see this historical reality. His insights are still in the treasury of Catholic social teaching, and naturally they will come to the attention of Pope Francis, who devotes a whole section of *Evangelii Gaudium* to the theme "Reality is more powerful than ideas."

[CHAPTER 14]

A New Theological Specialty:
The Scout

MY KIND AND SUPER-INTELLIGENT PROFESSOR IN ROME, Bernard Lonergan, S.J., published *Method in Theology* to call attention to the eight different methods deployed in theology—different functional specializations, he called them.[1] To this list I want to add a ninth, which is of particular moment in the study of Catholic social teaching.

Necessarily, Catholic social teaching lags behind the times by a generation, because at least that long is necessary to test new initiatives, to see whether they work, and to discover what their unintended consequences might be. The reason is that Catholic social teaching, more than any other specialization, depends on accurate judgments about highly contingent movements in history.

Some early experiences with republican government taught the Church to be highly suspicious, indeed bitterly negative, toward propositions praising democracies and republics. For instance, the first French Republic was so anticlerical and anti-Catholic in its bloodlust and destructiveness that it emptied seminaries and convents, gutted whole libraries of books, and took over Catholic colleges and schools to use as army barracks. It choked off Catholic intellect in France altogether for at least a century. The Italian Republic was not much gentler. It took some generations for the papacy to grasp (from its missionaries) the more favorable fruits of republican institutions in America.

Europe, though, was slower to learn. As Mussolini grew in power in Italy, Pius XI sent the founder of Italian democracy, Don Luigi Sturzo, into exile (in faraway America), and discouraged Catholics from embracing democracy. Then bitter experiences under Fascism in Italy and Nazism in Germany led Pius XII in his Christmas Message of 1942 to recommend democracy, even with all its many faults, as a necessary defense against torture, concentration camps, and other abuses of human rights. This choice was further reinforced by the reliance of Pius XII on the Christian Democratic parties after World War II to turn back the rising tide of Socialist and Communist parties in European politics.

Meanwhile, thinkers and leaders of stature were quickly building postwar political parties, both in their theory and in their practice: men such as France's Charles de Gaulle, Robert Schumann, and Jacques Maritain (in *Christianity and Democracy*[2]), and in Germany Wilhelm Röpke, the Das Ordnung circle, Konrad Adenauer, and others, along with up-and-coming political leaders such as Italy's Giulio Andreotti and Amintore Fanfani. The continuance of a free Europe depended on the electoral victories of such leaders over powerful communist parties in their nations.

Yet, as we have seen, another example of historical change is recounted in meaty detail by John Paul II in *Centesimus Annus*, in which he shows what Leo XIII accomplished, but also the realities that had changed dramatically since 1891.[3] Few documents make it clearer how contingent in its practice Catholic social teaching necessarily is.

For this reason, Catholic social teaching always needs scouts and explorers willing to go out ahead of the main body, persons who are reporters and analysts both. Such persons have to be skillful in applying the lessons of the past while also recognizing their own limits. They often need to make new distinctions, assemble new concepts and new strategies to propose for meeting ever-changing circumstances. Consider, for example, the very different world forces arrayed by these and other pivotal events of the twentieth century: World War I, the Communist revolution, World War II and the atomic bomb, the close of Vatican Council II, the fall of the Berlin Wall, and the collapse of the Soviet Union. And the political economies of the world did not stop changing in 1991.

For this task, a new specialization in theology has grown up. It is in very large measure a theology of economics. This new discipline has at least three tasks. The first is to clarify realities that occur under all systems of economic thought, such as scarcity, development, decline, taxes, the creation of wealth and its distribution, and the like.

The second is to compare today's rival systems: traditional market systems continuous from ancient history onward, compared with such variants as feudalism, mercantilism, capitalism, and socialism (democratic and totalitarian).

The third task is to take account of newly emerging, concrete patterns of economic reality, such as globalization (in its many meanings), the movement of large numbers out of poverty, economic decline, patterns of new business formation, employment, and changing distributions of wealth (with special attention to movements in the bottom and top quintiles).

In this three-pronged discipline, special attention needs to be given to the causes of the wealth of nations and to the effects of neglecting them in particular societies. But there is almost no limit to questions that must be asked about economic realities.

All these realities are why a ninth specialization has grown up among the traditional methods drawn upon in theology. The theology of economics is fundamentally concerned with how to improve the condition of the poorest peoples in the world—how to help them break the chains of poverty and gain a better life, both in income and in education. It is focused not solely on the economics of these questions but also, and mainly, on their significance for the gospels and for theology. It is so young a discipline that it still relies on explorers and scouts. Two of its very real achievements thus far are drawing intense attention both to creating wealth, not just distributing it, and to the reality of *human* capital.

Three Perspectives in Conflict

In approaching economic reality down through history, there appear to be three conflicting paradigms. The first is the traditional perspective of the largely agrarian societies that characterized all of human history until recent centuries. Here, humans were dramatically affected by years of plenty versus years of scarcity, good times versus bad times, and these variations were largely out of human control. Huge majorities were born poor and stayed poor. Gains in wealth often accrued by sending armies out to plunder the wealth of others. (This armed stealing is the backstory of the saying, "The root of evil is cupidity: *Radix malorum cupiditas.*") Very little new wealth was created; the existing wealth of others was plundered. To relieve the most desperate needs of the poor, Judaism and Christianity championed alms—and also the many works of mercy mentioned in the bible, Jewish and Christian.

The second paradigm is statist, the ideology and practice of turning the powers of the state toward helping the poor in one after another of their many economic needs, such as food, housing, income, social insurance of various types, employment, health care, and so on. The two most extreme species of statism are communism and socialism. A third form, tempered by democracy and allowing some scope to a free (but heavily regulated and highly taxed) economy, is social democracy, such as what is found in Western Europe today.

One pattern that runs through both of these paradigms, the ancient and traditional one and the statist one, is the power of those at the top to provide, to guide, and to rule. In older times, those at the top were kings and aristocrats; the new style uses political leaders (unelected or elected) and a huge administrative apparatus. The latter type has become aptly known as the administrative state.

The third paradigm is to promote personal initiative, creativity, enterprise, ownership, and cooperatives, together with a whole realm of voluntary associations (such as the Red Cross) and natural associations (the family). In this paradigm, the stress is placed on the responsibility and the creative capacity of individuals and their organizations and associations. Even before the modern state came into being, individuals pursued many of their goals through organizations and associations they themselves founded and ran: the newly dubbed "mediating structures" that protect individuals from full dependence on the state. The term devised to name the whole realm of these mediators is civil society or, in Vaclav Havel's term, the *civic forum*.

Catholic writers are fond of describing the United States as a land of (Protestant) "individualists," lonely cowboys, and atomistic individuals. But those who say this lack experience in Protestant communities, bible camps, and church outings. In fact, the Anglo-American way is quite communitarian. Church potlucks, quilt sales, and bake sales are routine events. The thrust of the whole American project was to build up early settlements, villages, cities, territories, and finally, the Union. A principal aim of American life, as the Preamble of the Constitution of the United States puts it, is "to promote the General Welfare." The best way to promote that welfare, the American experience shows, is not through a dominating state but through the initiatives of as many citizens as possible working through their multiple associations, organizations, and businesses, both unincorporated and incorporated.

It was distinctive of the American Experiment, as Alexis de Tocqueville pointed out, that citizens in their social needs should not turn to the monarch (as the French do), nor toward the aristocracy (as the English do), but toward free associations of their own design and for their own variegated purposes. In America as nowhere else, leading colleges and universities were put up and supported by individuals and associations, not the state. My wife's ancestors, pioneers who went by horse and wagon to Iowa from New York State in the late 1830s, left behind diaries that show how their daily lives on the frontier were characterized by communitarian activities—building one another's cabins, then one month putting up a church, another planning a school and throwing a bridge over the creek. The Americans were not rugged individualists, but rugged communitarians. Look around you and observe: They still are.

Abroad, the lie persists that Americans are—and always have been— lawless libertines. But the emphatic record of pioneer life shows that the moral code of early Americans was rather strict, ascetic, and biblical—not necessarily Puritan, but not falling far from that tree. Nevertheless, the places beyond the frontier where the gospel had not yet been preached were regarded as lawless places, the "badlands." But as the pioneers moved westward they built churches and schools and libraries and, in a rugged communal effort, civilized the West. (Do not underestimate the contributions of "Marian the librarian.") Building the United States was a thoroughly communal project.

Generation by generation, sadly, we have been unlearning the older disciplines. There is now reason to fear that our institutions will not long endure. As John Adams said, "Our Constitution was made only for a moral and religious people. It is wholly inadequate to the government of any other."[4] Many of our political elites today, with the collusion of our media elites in Hollywood and in print and television journalism, are busy uprooting the biblical force from our institutions and practices. They are likely to reap the whirlwind, when families cannot hold, when lawlessness increases in the cities and rural areas, and the internal policemen—the personal consciences of citizens—have faded helplessly away. Only deep moral capital civilizes peoples, and this moral capital has an ecology of its own. It cannot be taken for granted. Destroy it, and in less than two generations a civilization tends to collapse.

Liberation Theology versus Creation Theology

Meanwhile, in turning attention to the poor, two underlying narratives have been developed in Catholic theology. One is *liberation theology*, and the other *creation theology*. The first narrative proceeds on the assumption that poverty is imposed from outside, as a matter of oppression. People are poor because someone else holds them down. (This is the proposition that the greatest of all Polish Communists, Leszek Kołakowski, called the basic Marxist stencil, to be applied to disparate situations all over the world.) The cure for this condition is to liberate the poor from their oppressors.

The operative passion in liberation theology is to bring down oppressors, rather than to assure the well-being of the poor from the bottom up. In liberation theology, not much is written about how the poor, relieved of their oppressors, are actually going to raise themselves up out of poverty. The Marxist narrative openly suggests that someone else—that is, the state—will lift them up. This narrative does not demand much in terms of individual effort and responsibility. And it fails to specify which social actions promote the creation of new wealth and which do not.

The second narrative, introduced by John Paul II in *Sollicitudo Rei Socialis*, chooses as its master narrative not liberation (from oppressors) but creation. It stresses for the first time in papal documents "the right to personal economic initiative"—an important part of the "subjectivity of the person." Subjectivity means in this sense the ability of a person to become a conscious subject, an active agent, a creator.

In addition to this stress on the responsibility of the human person, *Sollicitudo* also stresses the right of societies to maintain their own unique character, the integrity of their own culture, and the historical source of their own spiritual unity; all these constitute the "subjectivity of society." Thus, two types of subjectivity are stressed by John Paul II: the subjectivity of the person and the subjectivity of a society. What is noteworthy is the designation of these two as *rights* of human subjects, both alone and in their communities.

Creativity, therefore, is not only about the individual. It is also about the union, about the people, about the nation. For instance, that spiritual *Polonia* which has always held the Polish people together in their own culture, even when the territory of Poland has been—as so often in history—overrun and ruled by outsiders. So also, the dynamism of overcoming poverty lies in the creative capacities—the human capital—of the human person and his communities.

John Paul II drives this point home in *Centesimus Annus*, when he stresses that the cause of the wealth of nations is knowledge, know-how, and invention—in other words, human capital, the old *caput*, the seat of creative practicality.[5] Here is where whole new industries are generated. Here is where scores of thousands (even millions) of new jobs come into being. Here is where multitudes of the poor become entrepreneurs in their own fields, shops, and enterprises, allowing for the development of a huge range of different talents never before so empowered in all of human history. The talents of the poor are immense. It is through creative theology and its novel institutions, practices, and habits of the heart that these come into flower.

It is not at all necessary that there should be poor people on this planet. The Creator of this world has made it abundantly fruitful for all, and has hidden within it huge resources for human wit to discover and put to use for all. To ask, "What causes poverty?" is an otiose question; for answering it would merely enable one to exclaim, "Oh, great! Now we can create more poverty." Poverty is the natural condition of man, the most enduring condition of man. Poverty is what you get when people don't know the causes of wealth. Poverty spreads in human systems that fail to ignite the cause of the wealth of nations—the creativity of every single human person.

I do not argue that creativity is the soul, heart, and end of Christian life. I argue only that it is the best means, probably the only means, of making the "preferential option for the poor" into a preference for the raising up of all the poor (by their own creativity) out of material poverty.

Higher than creativity lies the calling to live in a manner worthy of economic creativity and political liberty, by living lives of *caritas*—the love of our Creator, his own love infused in us, the love by which he calls each of us human beings to accept his invitation to become his friend. Union in friendship with our Creator and Redeemer is the common good of every person on earth. The elimination of acute material poverty on earth is only one tiny step toward human dignity, and the happy acceptance of his friendship, in mutual love, in concert with the universal love of all.

We cannot expect all humans to accept a Christian vision of *Caritapolis*, the city of *caritas*, a city in which all humans are united by and in the love of God, in which God's love sweeps over all of us and urges us toward mutual love and forgiveness of one another. Yet among those of good will, many hold to a secular vision of a united world in which all humans will cherish good will toward all, peace among all, forgiveness among all, friendship among all.

I do not myself see how that vision can be made real, can descend from the realm of mere wishfulness, without reference to its transcendent origin in our Creator, a point of unity beyond all nations, classes, races, or ideologies. But if Richard Rorty, Bertrand Russell, Albert Camus, or any person of secular vision can do so, we ought to welcome them into our comradeship. All those of good will—together—can go very far.

Yet here we must not fall into utopianism, the perennial temptation of the rationalist liberal and the pious Christian. Catholic social thought without an adequate and detailed map of the maze of human sinfulness would be too easily sucked in by false utopias. Against powerful pressures from human sinfulness, utopias are not simply innocent illusions but open gates to moral disaster. In 1913, Germany was perhaps the most civilized nation in the world, which had taken music, philosophy, and poetry to classical heights seldom reached. Who could have imagined that by 1943 it would sink to the stinking degradations and depravities of Dachau and the entire network of death camps, whose aim was to kill the soul as well as the bodies of their poor, helpless, pitiable inmates? No available theory of sin prepared Christian thinking for this hell.

That is why I predict that in the near future, theologians engaged in the work of Catholic social thought, at least the scouts and explorers, will be called upon to sharpen the realism of Catholic social teaching. They will be asked to make a tighter fit between the formal teaching and the actual, wretched humans it aims to teach. Consider this point, brought home to me forcibly by an Asian delegate at a meeting on human rights in Prague in 2013: "Just try to absorb," she said, "how many tens of thousands of men on earth still take pleasure in torture, even in inventing new and more terrifying tortures." Many, many prisons on this earth still give blood-curdling witness to human inhumanity.

If you wish to be sick in your stomach, simply contemplate all the barbarities you encounter in the daily news. Pause to let them soak in. Then face your powerlessness to stop them now.

The world's barbarity has not been nearly so tamed by the unspeakable horrors of the Second World War as we might wish.

CHAPTER 15

Needed: A Sharper Sense of Sin

When We Lose the Sense of Sin

A 2014 article in the *Huffington Post* reported that "Miss Kay," the matriarch of the family on the popular TV show "Duck Dynasty," had "forgiven" the Duck Dynasty patriarch, Phil Robertson, for the way he had treated her in the first years of their marriage nearly fifty years earlier. The story is a familiar one, at least for Christians: a story of sin, repentance, forgiveness, and conversion of life, a couple sticking it out through the process and very happy they did so.

Huffington Post told the story more or less straight, at least compared with other liberal postings of the "gotcha!" kind. But the hundreds of hateful comments that followed made up for Huffpo's restraint.

Representative responses:

Why is it that these Christian values fools that keep telling the rest of us that we are wrong for not believing in "their" ways & teachings time & time again are always the ones caught cheating & breaking their own code?

So I guess this makes him a hypocrite and she is another enabler. Typical Christian behavior!

Such hypocrites.

Not all comments were of this kind. The charge of hypocrisy was common, but some pointed out that to have sinned, repented, and changed your life to conform to what you consider God's will does not make you a hypocrite. As one reader says:

Just in case you don't know:

hyp·o·crite [hip-uh-krit]

1. a person who pretends to have virtues, moral or religious beliefs, principles, etc., that he or she does not actually possess, especially a person whose actions belie stated beliefs.

He WAS an alcoholic and he DID commit adultery. Past tense.

The gulf of incomprehension between the Christian and anti-Christian commenters is striking. The story of a sinful man repenting, being forgiven, converting his life to follow God is thousands of years old and repeated many times in Old and New Testaments, from David to Peter, Paul, and countless others.

And yet this Christian vision is incomprehensible to the gotcha crowd who relentlessly judge those they accuse of judging. None of the anti-Christian commenters offers a shred of evidence to show that either Miss Kay or her husband of nearly fifty years is "a person who pretends to have virtues, moral or religious beliefs, principles, etc., that he or she does not actually possess, especially a person whose actions belie stated beliefs."

It is said that saints—men and women of heroic virtue—are those most aware of their own sins. But any humble Christian who examines his conscience knows he sins. When asked to describe himself, Pope Francis—himself no drunk or adulterer—said simply, "I am a sinner." The sinner is the starting place of Christianity. Sin and repentance are elementary.

Of course, there are hypocrites among Christians who, like the Pharisees of old, puff themselves up with virtues they don't possess. But in this case that is not the charge of the gotcha crowd. The charge they make is that Phil Robertson once struggled with alcoholism and committed adultery. For this, they allow him no forgiveness, no repentance, no conversion of life. For them, those like Miss Kay who do forgive are "enablers" of behavior, even when such behavior, repented of and forgiven, has not actually recurred for decades.

So how do we understand people who acknowledge neither sin nor repentance nor forgiveness? La Rochefoucauld called hypocrisy "the homage that vice pays to virtue." Sure, hypocrites are liars, but the virtues hypocrites pretend to have are themselves good and worthy, qualities people *should* want to have. (That's why some pretend to them, even when they don't possess them.) But that's an unpalatable premise for relativists who are anti-Christian. They actually condemn the "Christian values fools" *not* for pretending now to hold values or possess virtues they once betrayed, but for picking up those values once again, this time trying never to betray them again. It's a little odd for relativists to fault Christians for their practices. On what moral ground do relativists judge others at all? If there are no objective moral grounds and all moral views are relative, why not let Christians be Christians, on equal footing with relativists? Haven't relativists given up any ground on which to judge others?

From a postmodern, relativist point of view, the trouble with Christians, of course, is that they insist there *are* objective moral grounds. To these they hold themselves accountable, and by them they dare to measure others. Relativists seem to suspect that Christians may be right about that, and can't stand the thought that they may be judged by an undeceivable God—or by anyone else. But if there really is no God, what do they have to fear? Why let silly Christians get under their skin?

Postmoderns seem not to honor the prodigal son for abandoning his sinful ways and adopting a life of virtue. First of all, they do not admit that there are such things as sinful ways. Second, they sense that, if the prodigal son repents of the sinful way of life he once indulged in, he may also be judging their way of life as sinful. And this is intolerable.

In other words, one part of the gotcha response seems to be hatred for those who try to live virtuously, and thereby seem to be condemning by their own lives the moral state of those with whom they once cavorted.

What, then, does it mean to cease sinning and to "repent"? Anti-Christians scarcely recognize that way of framing the problem. There's no place for sin in their philosophy. The whole idea of living virtuously implies that one holds oneself to standards outside oneself. Virtuous habits are acquired through practice, often with considerable difficulty, and they are lost through disuse. Most humans must work hard at practicing virtue but still, discouragingly, sometimes fall short of their own commitments. In short, the classical and Christian understanding implies that there is a moral truth about what is good and what is evil, and there is a higher good toward which it is human nature to aspire.

Yet what repels so many anti-Christians seems to be the very idea that there are grounds for discriminating between good and evil—grounds other than just calling good the life that they now find pleasure in. Like Hume, some seem to believe that reason is passion's slave, the rationalization of whatever one feels like doing. Some share a *boo!* versus *hooray!* method of ethical disagreement. They think morals do not come under the authority of reason but of feeling. They recognize no cognitive grounding for morality, only feelings. Morals, in their view, are not cognitive but emotive. When they hear what purport to be ethical arguments, reason is out of play, so the best they can do is cheer for some moral theories and boo others. For in their view, good is whatever I feel like doing; evil is you pretending to judge me by some so-called standard which not even you live up to.

Better, in the relativist view, to rationalize and justify what we actually choose than to try to aim higher, for that would risk failing. Even *aiming* for virtue seems like an intolerable judgment on those who do not succeed at it. The best way to escape the charge of hypocrisy is by declining to hold any beliefs or principles. One *cannot* fail to live up to standards, if those standards are set simply by how one is actually living now.

Relativism may at first seem pleasant. If one wishes one's conduct to be judged by *nobody*, and if one insists that there are no universal standards, that may at first seem to take a burden from one's back. But to that view there is a dark downside. From there, how and on what grounds would one protest against tyranny or torture? If there were no moral truth, who could "speak truth to power"? If someone were to insist that torture is wrong, the easy retort would be: "That's just your opinion." Under moral relativism, further, what could stand firm as "social justice"? And why should anyone care? That is why moral relativism (sometimes called "subjectivism") has often proved to be a sure path to tyranny.

Where did this drive toward relativism come from? Some say that Jean-Jacques Rousseau turned Aristotle's notion of nature on its head. Aristotle said that nature defined not only what man is but what he should be. Rousseau countered that nature is not an end—a *telos*—but a beginning. Man's end is his beginning. Allan Bloom encapsulated this view succinctly: "There are no ends, only possibilities."[1]

Like many proponents of the sexual revolution today, for instance, Rousseau had a particular hatred of the family, that most constraining of institutions. He called for the education of children to be taken from the family and given to the state. As Robert Reilly puts it, "Once society is atomized, once the family ceases to interpose itself between the individual and the state, the state is free to transform the isolated individual by force into whatever version of 'new man' the revolutionary visionaries espouse."[2]

Something like Rousseau's influence is everywhere today. Recall the Obama campaign ads featuring "Julia," who from cradle to grave was nothing more than a ward of the state, and in whose life the family is nowhere present, not even when she wants to have a baby. This cartoonish view of reality has long antecedents.

As Mary Eberstadt has discerned more clearly than anyone else, the slow strangulation of the family has brought about the death of God. The family did not decay because of the loss of God. God died once the family decayed and ceased to be bound by love and commitment. Without that bond between loving parents, children missed the look of unconditional love in the eyes of their mother, along with the constant love and close care of a watchful father. Without a representation of God in the family, God disappeared from daily view. How could one think of God as love and compassion if these were not overwhelming realities in one's daily life at home?

Once God had died, sin also died, and there now had to take place a transvaluation of values. In this sense, sin used to be not just the violation of a taboo, a crossing of a line that one should not cross, disobedience to a code written in stone, but a breaking with a friend, the end of a loving relationship, an affront, a tearing away, a rupture with a personal, warm world. Once God died, Nietzsche warned those who were too giddy at the prospect, reason also died. There was no longer one intelligence, personal or not, infusing intelligibility and meaning into every blade of grass, every grain of sand, every lily in the fields. All became alien, unconnected, impersonal. Opposite of human reason, there was no longer a far greater Logos, omniscient, comprehending (and loving, and filling with beauty) all things—as Socrates might have imagined, and Plato and Aristotle, and then Plotinus, and scores of other pagan sages, who wrote intelligently and beautifully of the divine. Now there was only the void. Emptiness of meaning. Alienation from nature and from each other. Consciousness without purpose and without companions.

The once-common ground of the Judeo-Christian ethic—the Ten Commandments supported by family, church and temple, the whole community, the whole education system (the McGuffey Reader), and the old-fashioned patriotic local newspaper—all these have given way to a new kind of inner isolation, the loss of the sacred, a sharp awareness (even by the very young) of the pointlessness of life. Rushing in to fill this emptiness is the sexual revolution, defined by Mary Eberstadt as "the ongoing destigmatization of all varieties of nonmarital sexual activity, accompanied by a sharp rise in such sexual activity, in diverse societies around the world (most notably in the most advanced)."[3] Delight in sexual life, once a driving force for family and life and the growth of the human population down the generations, has now become a driving force into relativism and nihilism.

The mediating structures of family, church, and community have virtually lost their role (at least for a time) in defining and shaping sexual morality. These prior institutions, which precede the state both in importance and in time, nowadays increasingly exist on the state's sufferance. Thus, today, it is the state that determines what marriage is, how many people and of which configurations it may involve, and what kinds of sexual activity outside marriage are not only permissible, but must be enabled by state-enforced morals and promoted among children in schools.

After experiencing Nazism and Communism, John Paul II warned of *"the risk of an alliance between democracy and ethical relativism, which would remove any sure moral reference point from political and social life, and on a deeper level make the acknowledgement of truth impossible."* Indeed, he says, if there is no ultimate truth to guide and direct political activity, then ideas and convictions can easily be manipulated by those few who hold power. "As history demonstrates, a democracy without values easily turns into open or thinly disguised totalitarianism."[4]

Under relativism, social justice loses all its meaning.

Learning from Reinhold Niebuhr

These confusions of today's secularists offer the perfect opportunity for Catholic social thinkers to prepare the way for the Church to present an updated overview and more sophisticated teaching on what we Christians mean by "sin." The first great step here is to make plain that we Christians see the world as *through-and-through a personal world*, a world uplifted by the most exalted of personal relationships, that between each person on earth and the Creator of all, who knew what he was doing when he created this vast universe, and loves what he has created, and invites all women and men into his friendship. Perhaps no group saw this more directly than the Society of Friends, the Quakers.

Our view of sin, then, lies in ordinary experience, as common as causing pain to those we love, as common as letting down a friend. In daily life we observe that each of us sometimes turns away from what we know is right—turns away from the light—and out of weakness or just plain willfulness chooses what we know (or heavily suspect) is wrong. This view of sin is not to be believed because it is a doctrine of the Church. To grasp it does not take faith. All it takes is a little introspection. Each of us knows times when we have not done what we know we should have done, and when we have done what we know we should not have done.

The founders of the United States knew this. That is why they divided governmental powers and organized a check against each of them. That is why they arranged that rival institutional interests would push back against each other, so that each would check each.

The greatest American Protestant ethicist of the twentieth century, who developed the most detailed handbooks on the ways of sin, saw more clearly and quickly than any other into the aims of Adolph Hitler and Nazism. His name was Reinhold Niebuhr (1892–1971). Born in the Middle West of both Lutheran and Evangelical heritage, he became the teacher of presidents and legions of secular journalists and historians. He laid out the reality of human sinfulness in plain language: Every man sometimes sins. *The capacity for virtue in human persons makes democracy possible; the human capacity for sin makes democracy necessary.* Without checks and balances, democracy cannot work. As the saying goes, "In God we trust; for everybody else there are checks and balances."

What some might want to denounce here as Jewish and Christian dogmatism, others describe as the lessons of ordinary human experience, sheer common sense. That is the way *The Federalist* describes human reality, many times over.[5]

Thus, the reality of sin belongs not to the category of obscure theological refinements but to daily experience. Our reason for turning to Reinhold Niebuhr is that no theologian of the twentieth century wrote more analytically about sin and applied his analysis week by week to practical events through journalistic commentary. No theologian has been more helpful to practical leaders in many fields. No Catholic theologian has done as well. And without speaking accurately of sin, how can one speak credibly of injustice or even justice?

FOR CATHOLIC SOCIAL thought, Niebuhr's work suggests six specific lines of inquiry to pursue: The *rejection of utopianism* and a preference for a Christian realism; the more complicated considerations in *group behavior* than in individual behavior; a clearheaded analysis of the *powers* and *interests* at stake in social confrontations; and the often stark differences between *distant ideals*, proximate concrete ideals, and *next immediate steps*. In addition, Niebuhr makes frequent use of ancient Greek perspectives on *irony* and *tragedy*. All six of these points should figure prominently in Catholic social thought, but at present do not.

(1) *The rejection of utopianism*: Utopianism is wishfulness that the world would be a nicer place than it is. A "no place," as Thomas More's Greek term expressed it. For instance, the utopian pictures a world without self-aggrandizing powers and deeply rooted interests that voraciously seek self-expansion, a world without irony and tragedy, a world without conflict, a world without sin. The Nazis and the Communists used dreamy images of a "Third Reich that will last a thousand years" and a "socialist paradise," in which selfishness and possessiveness and greed would be banished once and for all. Underneath this dreamy utopianism, with its rosy images and alluring sentiments, was a *hard* utopianism that required harsh methods for dealing with recalcitrant resisters. Sometimes in Catholic social thought there is an easy way of speaking of peace that is innocent of the lessons taught by Saint Augustine about the deep, deep roots of war, conflict, insurrection, and chaotic disorder—ineradicable roots in the human heart. Saint Augustine foresaw wars and rumors of new wars in every generation. In our world today, there are at least sixty wars in progress.

"Peace and justice" must not be allowed to sound utopian, hollow, pharisaical. Appeals for peace and justice must include a hard-edged awareness of the evils in the human heart and tested methods for checking them and turning their energies, despite themselves, in creative directions. Factions in societies, for instance, as James Madison set forth in *Federalist* 10, cannot be eliminated, but they can be turned to larger social good.

(2) The greater difficulties presented by impersonal political *groups*, as compared with the more private, personal circles of family and friends, also need attention by ethicists. In the bosom of the family and in gatherings of friends, one can look into familiar eyes, recall many chains of

shared experiences, and know how to read even small nuances of tone, smile, wink, and nod. When dealing with an antagonistic group, one will not have these human resources to draw upon at all, for it is typical of humans to envision social groups they have never met in caricature. Personal experience is narrow. Imagination is limited. Niebuhr was a pastor in Detroit during the severe labor strife of the 1920s and shrewdly noted that the auto executives (Henry Ford and others) tended to picture their workers as thuggish hooligans, while the workers pictured their bosses as cartoonish fat cats. Across group lines, failures of imagination are virtually assured.

Among family and friends, one knows the names and faces of children and grandchildren, spouses and in-laws. One knows their tones of voice, the qualities of their hearts, their points of touchiness. For those shaped by American habits of the heart, it is not easy to imagine the intimate circles and characteristic feelings of members of the Taliban, or Russian invaders of Ukraine, or Syrian supporters of Bashar Assad. Social groups, on account of the limits of human imagination, experience, and mental ability, nearly always deal with one another as cardboard cutouts. Of course, many of us sit down at the Thanksgiving table with family members whose political, economic, and social views we cannot abide, and we can barely speak together of such matters. Much worse is it when we don't even know the individuals on the other side of the issues. Note how the left in our country imagines the right, and the reverse. Cardboard cutouts. Greedy villains. Shallow souls incapable of learning from experience.

(3) There is a typical avoidance among Christian ethicists of an analysis of the *powers, interests,* and *temporal changes* that shift beneath matters of social justice and political relations.

(4) The difference between the ethical analysis of the end time and the ethical analysis of the "not yet." The difference between *political and social ideals* and the next *concrete, practical, prudent steps.* The difference between the abstract common good and practical discernment among competing attempts to describe and identify it most realistically, the necessity of choice among practical routes to get there, the vital lesson that courses of well-intentioned action often have evil consequences, and the surety that the common good now in view is time-bound and movable—and may be a deviation from the fruitful path toward human flourishing.

Niebuhr treats all these matters under the rubric of the commandment of Christian love, which he refers to as appearing in history as an urgent drive toward the "impossible possibility" of a civilization based on love. He insists that it is necessary to move forward and keep striving, even within the always incomplete, sinning, and faulty world that we inherit.

(5) The age-old persistence of *irony in human actions*. Since Catholic educators embrace the classics so much more than most of their secular counterparts, it is surprising that Catholic moralists have not made as fertile use of the classic concept of irony as Niebuhr has, say, in *The Irony of American History*, and in almost all his writings. For it is a matter of common experience that human actions nearly always have unintended consequences, which often sharply contrast with best intentions. Within the buzzing, blooming, chaotic field of contingency in which all humans act, humans walk less in light than as blind men. We cannot possibly foresee all contingencies, nor take account of them in our plan of action. Thus, with absolutely no intention of doing so, we often defeat our own purposes. Ironically, good intentions are no shield against self-destruction.

(6) *The tragic element in human actions*. Often in the Greek and Roman classics we are shown how the very virtues of a human agent often lead to his undoing. A man's oft-proved courage may on one occasion lead him to take a step too far, which ends in his fatal wounding. A woman's famous cunning and wit may suffuse her with a conceit that blinds her to a tiny detail that on this occasion betrays her into downfall. Tragically, human strengths often bring human defeats. The seemingly iron-clad law sometimes makes us feel—to use a classic expression—like playthings of the gods.

In brief, human moral action is far deeper and more complex than most moralists today portray it. Far too many, in the very moment they take pride in their exquisitely refined moral distinctions, utter false simplicities.

How is it that Catholic moralists, above all, so systematically overlook the power of irony and tragedy in moral reasoning and moral action? This is not the place to develop a whole schema of these elements in human action. The aim here is solely to stir others to deepen the sophistication of Catholic social thought on these points, grounded in the wisdom contained in long, humble, historical experience.

To end with one down-to-earth example: How is it that the most Catholic continent of all, South America, with an open field for continuously implementing Catholic social thought ever since 1891, should come into the twenty-first century with the second-largest population of truly poor persons on the planet? With so many structural deficiencies? For all its strengths, Catholic social thought carries within it far more false turns, inner irony, and even human tragedy than its partisans (ourselves included) typically address.

The Problem of "Structural Sin"

Saint Augustine warns that even after a human being has been, by the grace and mercy of God, healed of the consequences of a fall, a once-fallen soul is like a knee that has popped out of joint from a hard fall in sports. Even after it is healed, that knee remains acutely vulnerable to going lame again. For this reason, the human race needs institutional checks and balances against human weaknesses and repeated falls. At the same time, it also needs institutions that do not smother personal responsibility.

Modern progressive movements, including the Wilsonian progressivism of the early 1920s, shifted its focus away from the acts of individuals in order to lavish its attention on social structures. They turned morality inside out: forget the individual heart and individual action; judge morals by social activism and structural changes. The source of evil lies not in man's heart, progressives judged, but in the traditions that constrict his future and sometimes crush him. The most humane thing, they opined, is to break the hold of these oppressors and to replace them with perfectible human institutions. The most philosophical of progressives held that history itself—some forceful, predirected push—created a tide that irresistibly moved the world in a progressive direction. And "more progressive" here means stronger government, more scientifically managed bureaucracies, and more tightly regulated individuals. The progressive task is to be "on the right side of history," to hold the correct political and social opinions, to go with the flow.

In short, progressives were convinced: *History always flows in the progressive direction.* Historical determinism as a kind of religion. Ideologues who insist that their systems were protected by historical determinism— the Nazis and the Communists, most obviously—regularly slide down into disgrace.

But history is not predetermined. Free women and free men again and again redirect it. Christian realists detect no sinless structures in this sinful world—not in any culture, not in any state, not even in the Church; not in past history, not now, not in the future. Human life is not like that; nature is not like that; reality is not like that.

Nonetheless, the term "sinful structures" was first given prominence among liberation theologians in Latin America. No one denies that Latin America has for some generations been desperately in need of new institutions. Three systemic changes, for example, would be of immense practicality in raising up the poor of Latin America (and elsewhere). First is better education: In some Latin American states less than half the population has an education that goes beyond sixth grade. Further, this education normally does not emphasize invention, discovery, and enterprise, but rather passive acceptance. Perhaps as a consequence, Latin Americans have invented few products, medicines, or household appliances of their own, and instead must use many invented on other continents. Latins are only beginning to restructure their schools so as to promote invention and know-how and enterprise—as John Paul II wrote, the main causes of the wealth of their nations.[6] Latins are extremely good at creativity in the fields in which it is much supported: the novel, dance, music, and others.

Secondly, most poor people in Latin America (of whom there are large majorities in almost every nation) find it far too cumbersome—and expensive—to protect their own small business with legal incorporation. Hernando de Soto has found that it can take 6,000-plus hours of delays and visits to government offices, and handfuls of bribes and fees amounting to well over $8,000—five times the average worker's annual income— in order to gain legal incorporation.[7]

By contrast, in Hong Kong, it takes something like $30 and an application sent through the mail. The government is required to provide a timely response, within six weeks. After all, government does not *create* small businesses; it merely lists them on its official rolls as incorporated. That registration allows these small corporations to operate legally, to borrow money in the name of the corporation, and the like.

Thirdly, the poor need cheap and easy access to credit, that is, the opportunity to borrow money to launch a business, at a low, reasonable, stable, payable rate. Before a business can sell its products, it has many start-up and production costs. To pay these, it needs to borrow money. Borrowed money is the mother's milk of new businesses.

These three simple reforms alone would greatly improve the present and future prospects of the poor in Latin America. They correct three pervasive "sins" in the Latin American approach to political economy. No doubt, *these* are not the structural sins spoken of by the liberation theologians. But they are easy to grasp and do show how the term has some validity, even though the use of the term "sin" here is merely metaphorical.

In fact, the term "structural deficiency" seems more empirically accurate than "structural sin." Do structures go to hell or to heaven? Personal responsibility is required for sin, which is a reflective, deliberate personal act. Most people in the world today (and in all prior centuries) live under structures that do *not* protect human rights or honor human dignity. In the light of full human flourishing, virtually all social structures in history have been seriously deficient.

Can anyone think of a perfect social structure anywhere on earth?

A Still Deeper Difficulty

A far deeper difficulty with the concept of "sinful structures" is that it allows individuals to escape personal responsibility. If a structure "sins," which agents are responsible? Who repents? Who leads the way to better practices and outcomes? As then-Cardinal Ratzinger pointed out in 1986, in his *Instruction on Christian Freedom and Liberation*, "sin" is a category that is properly used only of persons, who knowingly and willingly choose to turn away from the will of the Lord and to violate his friendship and his laws. Ratzinger writes:

> The priority given to structures and technical organization over the person and the requirements of his dignity is the expression of a materialistic anthropology and is contrary to the construction of a just social order. On the other hand, the recognized priority of freedom and of conversion of heart in no way eliminates the need for unjust structures to be changed. . . . It remains true however that structures established for people's good are of themselves incapable of securing and guaranteeing that good. The corruption which in certain countries affects the leaders and the State bureaucracy, and which destroys all honest social life, is a proof of this. Moral integrity is a necessary condition for the health of society. It is therefore necessary to work simultaneously for the conversion of hearts and for the improvement of structures. For the sin which is at the root of unjust situations is, in a true and immediate sense, a voluntary act which has its source

in the freedom of individuals. Only in a derived and secondary sense is it applicable to structures, and only in this sense can one speak of "social sin."[8]

In his earlier *Instruction on Certain Aspects of the "Theology of Liberation"* (1984), Ratzinger had already clarified this point:

> To be sure, there are structures which are evil and which cause evil and which we must have the courage to change. Structures, whether they are good or bad, are the result of man's actions and so are consequences more than causes. The root of evil . . . lies in free and responsible persons who have to be converted by the grace of Jesus Christ in order to live and act as new creatures in the love of neighbor and in the effective search for justice, self-control, and the exercise of virtue.[9]

In other words, it is persons who must do penance, reform their conduct, and straighten out their lives. The structures that most impede personal responsibility and reform are those of the bloated state, whose sheer size crowds out the liberties and sources of creativity inherent in every able-bodied human person. Too enlarged a state sucks the oxygen out of personal responsibility.

———

Although it is clear that class structures, laws, or environment can have a significant influence on human behavior, it is not at all clear that they can be called "sins."[10] Here we can take a hint from John Paul II, who takes up the language of "structures of sin" in his Apostolic Exhortation *Reconciliation and Penance*. While he allows that some structures can institutionalize injustice, even promote further injustice, the pope clearly affirms that structures themselves, although they can abet it, are never the *cause* of social evil. In *Reconciliation and Penance*, John Paul II traces social evil back to its source, the sin or sins of individuals. There is always a human will behind the actions, and that human will is responsible for the evil: "A situation—or likewise an institution, a structure, society itself—is not in itself the subject of moral acts. Hence a situation cannot in itself be good or bad. . . . At the heart of every situation of sin are always to be found sinful people."[11]

John Paul II carefully separates the three senses in which "structures of sin" can be understood. First, every sin, no matter how personal, always spreads its effects and leads to societal evil: "To speak of social sin means in the first place to recognize that, by virtue of human solidarity which is as mysterious and intangible as it is real and concrete, each individual's sin in some way affects others."[12] The effect of one individual's personal sin can be so pervasive and strong that it damages the entire community.

The second sense of structural sin that John Paul II refers to those sins which are particularly against one's neighbor, and therefore always have an immediate and obvious impact on the community members:

> They are an offense against God because they are offenses against one's neighbor. These sins are usually called social sins, and this is the second meaning of the term. In this sense, social sin is an offence against love of one's neighbor, and in the law of Christ it is all the more serious in that it involves the Second Commandment, which is "like unto the first."[13]

These sins are always an infringement on the freedom of other individuals, and so not only harm them, but also take away the freedom which was given by God.

The third sense of social sin regards the relationship among the various human communities, and is a structure of sin only by analogy. The leaders who make decisions set processes in motion, without knowing in advance the total results. Small decisions can inadvertently lead to massive social structures, which become a force of their own: "The term social can be applied to sins of commission or omission on the part of political, economic or trade union leaders, who though in a position to do so, do not work diligently and wisely for the improvement and transformation of society according to the requirements and potential of the given historic moment."[14]

The large structures which are created by bureaucratic bodies play a significant role by their effect on individual lives, yet are not always traceable back to a distinct cause or person. Since it is not easy to identify the origin of these changes, the pope states that these structures can be called structures of sin only analogously. He adds that this does not remove the responsibility of transforming society with new structures: "However, to speak even analogically of social sins must not cause us to underestimate the responsibility of the individuals involved. It is meant to be an appeal to the consciences of all, so that each may shoulder his or her responsibility seriously and courageously in order to change those disastrous conditions and intolerable situations."[15] Both John Paul II and Cardinal Ratzinger acknowledged the weight, force, and influence of certain unjust structures within society, but strongly asserted that the true origin of the evil lies in personal moral choice. Ratzinger wrote:

> Being necessary in themselves, [structures] often tend to become fixed and fossilized as mechanisms relatively independent of the human will, thereby paralyzing or distorting social development and causing injustice. However, they always depend on the responsibility of man, who can alter them, and not upon an alleged determinism of history.[16]

The danger in theories that emphasize the role of structural or environmental factors in social evils is that they significantly lessen personal responsibility. This lessening can lead to the assumption of a kind of determinism, in which the environment is responsible for the acts of individuals.

John Paul II warned against speaking of structures in ways that ignore personal responsibility:

> One must add at once that there is one meaning sometimes given to social sin that is not legitimate or acceptable even though it is very common in certain quarters today. This usage contrasts social sin and personal sin, not without ambiguity, in a way that leads more or less unconsciously to the watering down and almost the abolition of personal sin, with the recognition only of social guilt and responsibilities.[17]

In sum, there is a valid way to speak of "sinful structures." But materialistic assumptions must not be smuggled into that term. There is no such thing as "on the wrong side of history." All-determining fate is an illusion. Personal liberty is the one fundamental reality on which the whole ethic of Christianity depends. The primacy of personal responsibility is central to human action, and thus also to the struggle for social justice. Catholic social teaching is personalist. It emphasizes the primacy of the person over structures. Even when structures were spoken of as "sinful" by liberation theologians, these theologians did not have to think like Marxists. That is a responsibility they unnecessarily took upon themselves.

Conclusion

The conviction of Catholic social thought that individual liberty trumps the "dialectic" of materialism is one more reason to hold that social justice is not a program for the Leviathan state—more spending and more regulation—but the virtue of personal responsibility for the common good, via the large and small associations formed by free men. As Leo XIII was the first to diagnose, the best alternative to impersonal materialistic socialism is the free person and his or her free associations and self-governed communities. Between the Leviathan state and the creative human person, Leo stood with the free person—not the free person alone, but in associations of many sorts with many others. It is in that space between the state and the individual that social justice must flourish—or fail. Social justice is a practice learned and lived by free persons in their associations large and small. Its practices spring from the habits of individual citizens, working in unison with many other free persons, sometimes in international associations that circle the entire world (the Catholic Church, the Red Cross, Doctors Without Borders).

In the Christian vision, while all are called to practice social justice, some are likely to turn away. That is the prerogative of free persons. The theological definition of sin (*deviatio a Deo*) actually is an act that turns away from the Light, from the Good, from Justice, from the Person of our Lord. In this context, social justice is the virtue of free persons in their free associations, achieving the common good together, in a higher measure than the Leviathan state alone can reach. Free associations are more likely to act more respectfully of the dignity of human persons than the secular state. For one thing, free associations can preach the gospel, pray with those they wish to help, teach virtuous behavior that leads to social flourishing, and in other ways enter into moral and religious dimensions of human action forbidden to the secular state.

Social justice is not inherently hostile to the state. In fact, its organizations and energies are often focused on stimulating the state into action on behalf of the public good. But social justice does include within itself deeper reservoirs of devotion, love, wisdom, and nimbleness than the Leviathan (the huge, blind dinosaur) is permitted to exercise. It would be a fatal mistake, Leo XIII warned, for the human race to entrust all aspects of its flourishing to the collectivist government, as socialists were at that time demanding. That is why he called for Christians to summon up the strength to develop a new virtue, appropriate for the new world of the *rerum novarum* of his time. The state is neither equipped for achieving the full common good, nor fully trustworthy in its methods of envisioning it. The state is a guardian of certain important goods, but it has limited vision and limited purposes. It is neither flexible enough nor virtuous enough to be entrusted with the full treasure of human flourishing.

A more complete, more complex, and more penetrating understanding of sin, worthy of our greatest playwrights, novelists, and poets, is a very important part of achieving social justice. For we are all sinners. No use designing a republic for saints. There are not enough saints to fill a republic. (And saints are difficult to live with.) Republics must be built for sinners. That's all there are.

That is why, as Charles Péguy wrote, "the sinner is at the very heart of Christianity."

———

We now turn to Paul Adams, without whose determination this book would not exist. After reading every essay I had ever written on social justice, Professor Adams insisted that they be rewritten as a book, everything thought through anew and written in proper order. He made a plan showing how this could be done. What fascinated him, he said, was how uncannily the theory of social justice I developed coincided so neatly with the "best practices" that had evolved in his own field of social work.

So now that we have seen the theory, it is time to consider the practice.

PART TWO

In Practice

Paul Adams

When I first encountered Michael Novak's work on social justice, I was immediately struck by two of its main characteristics. First, his mind seems always to proceed by the method of *both/and*. That is my own favorite method, too, as the reader is about to see in the next five chapters. That shared characteristic may be what most fueled our collaboration.

Second, I saw immediately how the concept of *social justice as a virtue, internalized by individuals*, brilliantly articulates a key, if often overlooked, insight in my own field of specialization, the theory and the practice of social work.

It is not enough, social workers have learned through long experience during this past century, to do things *for* people. One must also help them to *internalize* certain basic social habits and skills—that is, virtues—of their own, so that *they* become the chief agents of their own destiny. There is no real success in rendering them totally dependent—on social workers or anybody else. Such dependency is no cure for what ails them; it is the condition from which they suffer.

Thus, the profession of social work identifies social justice as a core value, central to its ethics and identity. Social work aims to translate social justice into practice at every level, among individuals, families, and communities. It even tries to think through and to promote reform in economic, social, and cultural structures. But too often thinking in our field falls into dichotomies. We see *conscience* pitted against *social justice*, *individualism* against *collectivism*, *charity* against *justice*, *informal associations* against *state-run programs*.

Often our terms are conceived of as mutually exclusive—we have to choose *either* A *or* B. For instance, *either* respect the rights of conscience *or* promote social justice. Conscience, the protection of which was once a foundational value, has today been reduced to mere personal preference, always to be trumped by the claims of "social justice." But conscience is itself a matter of social justice: irreducibly social in nature, a key bulwark of civil society against the Leviathan. Conscience always makes claims about what is actually true about a given situation—it is either just or unjust, and (at least in large part) an evil or a good. Conscience always involves judgment about the right course of action to take in these particular circumstances. Thus conscience, rightly understood and rightly formed, cannot stand in opposition to social justice.

Another false dichotomy, *individualism* versus *collectivism*, often lies disguised in debates about conscience. But as Catholic social teaching has consistently emphasized, these are twin evils. Individualism—whether the expressive individualism of the sexual revolution or the economic individualism of nineteenth-century "liberals" or contemporary libertarians—offers no alternative to statist collectivism, but actually depends on and foments it. Consider the state of contemporary marriage, an unprecedented collapse that has done immense harm to the poorest and most vulnerable.[1] Here the proper response to the dichotomy of individualism versus collectivism is also *both/and*: The "moral ecology" of the civic order must support the personal commitment of one person to another.

Subsidiarity and *solidarity* are another fraught pair, often seen as opposite poles between which some correct midpoint must be identified. Subsidiarity—the principle that higher bodies should not interfere with or substitute for lower ones when those are capable of fulfilling their functions—is sometimes understood as an expression of individualism and laissez-faire. Solidarity—the principle of love and our responsibility for one another—then becomes the collectivist pole, the duty of the state as agent of collective responsibility. But both subsidiarity and solidarity—both/and—are needed at every level: in the family, in the community, and in state and supranational bodies.

Last, but most important, we must resist the opposition between *charity* and *justice*—"justice, not charity," as one theorist puts it. The last two chapters of this section take up the question of how we understand both charity in its double sense (works of mercy and *caritas*) and social justice. Justice needs *caritas* and charity needs justice—both/and.

In the field of social work, the term "social justice" is probably used more often than in any other field. As Novak notes more generally, in this field, too, the term is hardly ever defined. But once we do define it as a *virtue* (a strength, a skill) internalized by individuals—and also a skill properly described as *social*—we gain a very useful and practical tool indeed. We cast quite brilliant light on what, without ever having defined it, we have actually been trying to do for some time. In this respect, Novak's contribution in Part One above is actually quite a boon to our own field of social work. That is what drew me into this collaboration.

[CHAPTER 16]

Conscience and Social Justice

No provision in our Constitution ought to be dearer to man
than that which protects the rights of conscience
against the enterprises of the civil authority.

—*Thomas Jefferson to New London Methodists, 1809*

AS THE GULF HAS GROWN IN RECENT DECADES BETWEEN
traditional Judeo-Christian orthodoxy and the secular state in matters of
life, death, sex, and marriage, the question of conscience protections and
exemptions in law has become pressing.[1] Livelihoods, careers, charitable
organizations and activities, and whole communities have been put at risk
in the interest of imposing measures that require many Christians and
others to violate their consciences. Such coercion by the state is sometimes justified in the name of social justice.[2]

Unfortunately, there is as much confusion about the concept of conscience as there is about the concept of social justice. Conscience is, no
less than social justice, inherently relational, rooted in community, and
directed beyond the self. It is moral belief applied to conduct, conveys a
claim to truth, implies accountability, restrains power, and is inseparable
from personal integrity.[3] Like social justice, it is key to a healthy republic
and civil society, to expanding and protecting the rich associational life
that occupies the social space between individual and state. Some identify
with social justice, while others emphasize conscience, as if the two were

in opposition. Both perspectives frame issues in terms of the rights of individuals and the role of the state, neglecting the intermediary groups and institutions of civil society. One sees the world in individualistic terms, the other collectivist, but both in relation to the state and each as opposed to the other. So it appears as if individualism stresses conscience at the expense of social justice, and collectivism does the reverse. On the contrary, rightly understood, conscience, and social justice illuminate and reinforce each other, and both are necessary to a democratic pluralist society.

The Threat to Liberty of Conscience

"Have progressives abandoned the liberty of conscience?" asks legal scholar Robert K. Vischer.[4] Noting that the American Civil Liberties Union had filed suit to block George W. Bush's conscience protection regulations from being implemented, and that other progressive groups that "trumpet their commitment to defending an individual's moral integrity against government incursions were curiously silent about President Obama's rollback" of those protections in 2011, Vischer observes:

> We've come a long way from the times when ringing defenses of conscience were provided by progressive heroes such as Jefferson, Thoreau, and Gandhi. The former Democratic governor of Wisconsin justified his veto of a conscience bill for health care providers on the ground that "you're moving into very dangerous precedent where doctors make moral decisions on what medical care they provide."[5]

Among those progressive associations that have switched in recent years from defending conscience rights and protections to casually dismissing them, the National Association of Social Workers (NASW) stands in the forefront.[6] Indeed, no other profession gives shorter shrift to conscience or has so little regard for the conscience rights and protections of its own members. The threats to conscience and religious freedom confronting Christian social workers and health professionals have become ever more pressing in the United States, Canada, and Europe in recent years. A flood of writing about the subject covers everything from individual legal cases involving students, employees, and businesses across the United States to the HHS mandate and the hundred-plus lawsuits challenging it.

Here I will limit myself to developments most directly linked to social work and related practice (such as counseling) and to the threat posed to conscience by the very way in which the social-work literature frames its discussion of conscience exemptions and conscientious objection. My primary but not exclusive focus will be on threats to liberty of conscience of individual practitioners rather than, as in the case of the HHS mandate, their employers. I want to suggest that the usual way of framing conscience issues in current debates, as matters of individual rights enforced or limited by the state, is inadequate, and I mean to propose a more complex but far from new way to think about the options and ethical obligations of professionals in contested areas, where expanding state coercion of conscience conflicts most sharply with moral conviction or religious faith.

Threats

Christians, Jews, and others in social work and related fields who adhere to the Judeo-Christian tradition in matters of life, death, sex, and marriage face threats to conscience at every level. As Robert George argues,[7] the secular-liberal orthodoxy in these areas aims not to foster tolerance of religious orthodoxy or pluralism, but to build a monopoly in the public square.

In 2009, Julea Ward was dismissed from her counseling program at Eastern Michigan University after she sought to refer rather than treat a potential client who was seeking counseling about a homosexual relationship. The university's insistence that Ward needed "remediation" to help her abandon her beliefs about homosexual behavior and act against her conscience led to her dismissal from the program and resulted in a series of university and judicial hearings and appeals. In January 2012, the U.S. Court of Appeals of the Sixth Circuit[8] ruled in Ward's favor, and in June 2012, the Michigan House passed Bill 5040, known as the Julea Ward Freedom of Conscience Act, prohibiting religious discrimination against college students studying counseling, social work, or psychology.

In its review of ten social-work education programs, the National Association of Scholars found many examples of the coercion of student consciences,[9] legitimated by a constrictive and unwarranted reading of the NASW Code of Ethics. The cases involved requiring students to advocate and lobby for positions to which they were opposed in principle and as a matter of conscience. Again and again, we find students coerced into a morally degrading performance that requires public avowal of beliefs contrary to their own convictions, conscience, and faith.

The issue of coercing the conscience of professionals in the health and helping professions has come to the fore in recent years as a result of the promulgation of new rights in matters of life and death, sex, marriage, and family. Behaviors that were illegal or socially stigmatized for millennia have been declared legal and have become rights, expanding the options for those who wish to engage in these behaviors. But what is optional behavior for clients or patients rapidly becomes mandatory for professionals who must endorse or otherwise cooperate in the newly permitted behavior. An argument for tolerating certain behaviors has become a case for intolerance—of those who refuse to be personally or professionally complicit in them.[10]

For more than two millennia, physicians have sworn by the Hippocratic Oath not to engage or collude in practices like abortion, euthanasia, or assisted suicide. In the wake of the egregious violations of the Hippocratic ethic by Nazi physicians, the World Medical Association's 1948 Physician's Oath affirmed, "I will maintain the utmost respect for human life from the time of conception, even under threat."[11] The legally binding UN Declaration of Human Rights and the 1959 UN Declaration of the Rights of the Child affirm the rights of the child before as well as after birth.[12]

With astonishing speed, legal protections of children before birth have been swept away in both letter and spirit. UN officials have been attempting to pressure sovereign member states to establish abortion as a legal right.[13]

Far from resisting these threats, professional associations have revised the Hippocratic and other oaths to eliminate the prohibitions on killing—whether through abortion, euthanasia, or assisted suicide. Professional ethics codes once forbidding abortion and other life-terminating measures now come close to making direct or indirect participation in them a requirement of professional practice.[14]

In recent years, the threat to conscience rights has widened beyond abortion and the duties and rights of physicians, nurses, and pharmacists to areas in which social workers are more directly and routinely involved. Among these are counseling, psychotherapy, foster care, and adoption, where practitioners and agencies are expected to affirm same-sex sexual relations and, across the United States, same-sex "marriage," as equivalent in moral status, social honor, and appropriateness as family environments for children, to conjugal relations between husband and wife.

One driver of these developments, Helen Alvaré argues,[15] is the vigorous promotion by the federal government of a new moral orthodoxy, an ideology she terms "sexualityism" or "sexual expressionism." Against what social science tells us about human happiness, "the government is promoting sexualityism—a commitment to uncommitted, unencumbered, inconsequential sex."

> The HHS mandate stands on this theory. In a world of easily available birth control and abortion, the only reason for a federal mandate for a "free" and universal supply is to send the sexualityism message. The White House has all but come out and said, "women of America, vote for the incumbent this presidential election year because he supports women's equality and freedom, which he understands to include at the very least nonmarital and nonprocreative sexual expression." Why else choose Sandra Fluke—an affluent, single, female law student, who demands a taxpayer-subsidized, 365-day supply of birth control as the price of female equality—as your spokeswoman?[16]

The HHS mandate requiring all employers, with narrow exceptions, to provide "insurance" coverage for abortifacients, contraceptives, and sterilization threatens the religious freedom of all Catholic and many other Christian employers.

In cases such as a small town built around a Catholic or Evangelical university that refuses, on grounds of conscience, to comply with the mandate, the very existence of the whole community is in jeopardy due to the fines imposed for noncompliance. This modern variant of Saint Benedict's solution—building centers of Christian fidelity, learning, and devotion, tilling and keeping our own garden in the face of a culture of barbarism outside—would be foreclosed. Such communities face something more analogous to Henry VIII's dissolution of English monasteries in the 1530s.

In general, either Catholic organizations will violate the Church's authoritative teaching and effectively cease to be Catholic, or they will be closed down, sold off, or fined out of existence. As Cardinal George of Chicago put it, "a governmental administrative decision now mean[s] the end of institutions that have been built up over several generations from small donations, often from immigrants, and through the services of religious women and men, and others who wanted to be part of the church's mission in healing and education."[17]

One result of the stripping of these health and social-service programs from the Church would be to deprive Catholic social workers of even the possibility of practicing their profession in a Catholic context, that is, as part of the Church's corporate response to the needs of the poor, sick, homeless, and oppressed—an organized activity and duty of the Church from the beginning. Again, these considerations apply also to other adherents of Judeo-Christian orthodoxy (in the broad sense distinguished by Robert George from the state-imposed secular-liberal orthodoxy[18]).

Conscience

Among the health and helping professions, social work stands out for its opposition to conscience exemptions for its own members. More than two-thirds of respondents in J. Sweifach's study[19] believed that laws protecting some health-care providers should not be extended to social workers. In contrast, and despite ongoing attacks on conscience exemptions within these professions, other fields give more weight to professional judgment and discretion in choosing whom to serve and how to serve them. The American Pharmacists Association recognizes an individual pharmacist's right to conscientious refusal.[20] The AMA's Code of Medical Ethics states that "[a] physician shall, in the provision of appropriate patient care, except in emergencies, be free to choose whom to serve."[21] According to the American Nurses Association,[22] nurses have a right to refuse to participate in a procedure, but the conscientious objection must apply to the procedure, not the patient. Lawyers also assert the right to refuse representation in cases they consider morally repugnant, though they seem not to have the right to exclude whole categories of clients, such as men in divorce cases.[23]

In social work, by contrast, the tendency is to address the conflict in ways similar to that of the Eastern Michigan counseling program—treat or exclude the practitioner. Tellingly, Sweifach cites the NASW code of ethics' insistence on the social worker's primary responsibility to promote the well-being of clients, as though the practitioner's judgment of that matter were necessarily subordinate to the client's: "Commentators explain that when clients' behaviors and practices conflict with a social worker's personal morals or religious beliefs, the social worker may be in need of peer support, supervision, or values clarification training to responsibly serve clients."[24] Conscience is thus reduced to "personal values," and the professional as moral agent to a cipher.

In part, the failure of professional organizations like NASW to protect the conscience rights of their members is justified by an implicit rejection of the very concept of conscience as traditionally understood. In its place we find a contrast of public (or professional) and personal "values." Here values have no intrinsic authority beyond being the subjective opinions of those who hold them. If this is so, then why should the personal opinions of a practitioner not be subordinated to those of the state that licenses and funds his or her professional work?

Much social-work literature on the subject frames issues of conscience in this way, as a conflict between personal and professional values. Sweifach gives several examples framing the issue of conscience and conscientious objection in those terms.[25] For instance, N. Linzer suggests that "in conflicts between personal values and professional values, the professional is duty-bound to uphold professional values. Upholding professional values represents ethical action."[26] According to this view, it is ethical, in these circumstances, to act against your own conscience.

As Christian social workers come under increasing pressure to cooperate with what they consider evil, in the name of professional duty, the question of conscience becomes correspondingly more urgent. Statements from NASW, its executive director,[27] and its Legal Defense Fund[28] make it clear that their professional organization will not defend the conscience rights of members when policies they support are involved.

Opponents of conscience exemptions give little or no weight to the gravity of requiring someone either (a) to act against their conscience or (b) to leave their profession or be denied admission to it and hence to its schools. But the choice to act against your conscience can never be right; it is to choose to do what you believe to be wrong, and in the case of abortion, gravely wrong. For a Christian, it means putting your immortal soul in jeopardy; for a Catholic Christian, it means excommunicating yourself from your Church and its sacraments.

In its hotly disputed Opinion #385, "The Limits of Conscientious Refusal in Reproductive Medicine," the Committee on Ethics of the American College of Obstetricians and Gynecologists takes the position that pro-life physicians must refer patients seeking an abortion to other providers, must tell patients in advance of their views without explaining or arguing for them, and must, in emergency cases involving the patient's physical or mental health, actually perform abortions. It treats conscience as but one value among others that can and should be overridden in the interest of other obligations. Not only the hospital or clinic, but also the individual physician, is called upon to override the physician's conscience.

A prevalent idea of conscience, implicit in this opinion and most of the social-work literature, minimizes its claims by treating it as only one thing among others that the practitioner must take into account in deciding how to act. Conscience becomes a matter of personal values that must be left at the office door when duty calls. Professional duty trumps personal conscience.

But this account trivializes the very concept of conscience and renders it incoherent. It runs counter to the traditional understanding of the term, according to which conscience is the supreme and final arbiter for an individual's actions precisely because it represents the agent's best ethical judgment, all things considered. Here "all things" must include considerations of what the agency or the state or professional codes of ethics tell us our duty is. It could never be right to act against one's own conscience. It is hard to see how a notion of conscience as one value among others from which a professional should choose could be other than incoherent. On what ethical basis could such a choice be made? What is to be counted after everything has been counted?

NOT ONLY HAS the Nietzschean term "values" become a rhetorical device for subjectivizing and relativizing moral discourse, but conscience itself has become "the ghostly inner voice telling an individual what he or she should or should not do."[29] Conceptualized as a faculty of the individual, conscience too readily becomes detached from judgments of practical reason about the right thing to do. Herbert McCabe draws the contrast with the older Catholic tradition: "Aquinas does use the word *conscientia*, but for him it is not a faculty or power which we exercise, nor a disposition of any power, nor an innate moral code, but simply the judgment that we may come to on a piece of our behavior in the light of various rational considerations."[30]

Conscience in this view is not subjective opinion but involves knowledge and judgment, and is thus open to rational inquiry. It is not a conversation stopper, like the subjective preference for vanilla over chocolate ice cream. As Moreland explains, "A person is said, then, to act in accord with a good conscience with truthful knowledge, which, in turn, habituates one into the cardinal virtues of justice, temperance, fortitude, and especially prudence."[31] For Aquinas and the Catholic tradition, conscience—applying the general principles of practical reasonableness to specific circumstances—is closely linked to the classical virtues (above all prudence) acquired by experience and habituation.

We thus ought to follow our conscience not because it is a uniquely authoritative and correct autonomous inner voice, but because it is, all things considered, our best practical judgment of right action. It is a necessary but not sufficient condition of acting well. As Elizabeth Anscombe puts it in her justly renowned critique of "Modern Moral Philosophy," "a man's conscience may tell him to do the vilest things."[32]

Karl Jaspers gave the example of a young German concentration-camp guard he met in a hospital at the end of World War II—the man's conscience tortured him still because he let a Jewish boy escape instead of doing his duty of rounding him up and sending him to the gas chamber.[33] Our conscience is our last defense against cooperating with evil in the name of duty, but conscience can itself be wrong and direct us to do evil. We must both follow our conscience in all matters and also form our conscience well by following reliable authorities and the advice and models of prudent persons. Anscombe—in unpublished notes for a lecture—argues the dilemma thus:

> If you act against your conscience you are doing wrong because you are doing what you think wrong, i.e., you are willing to do wrong. And if you act in accordance with your conscience you are doing whatever is the wrong thing that your conscience allows, or failing to carry out the obligation that your conscience says is none.
>
> There is a way out, but you have to know that you need one and it may take time. The way out is to find out that your conscience is a wrong one.[34]

We do wrong both when we act against our conscience and when we follow a badly formed conscience into evil actions or failures to act, thinking they are good or morally neutral. The wrong in the second case is not that we followed our conscience, but that we failed to form our conscience correctly. We are obliged, John Paul II writes in *Veritatis Splendor* (1993), both to inform our conscience and to follow it. We can be at fault at either stage.

Whether conscience is treated as one factor among several to be taken into consideration or as a subjective, nonrational inner guide or faculty, it appears reasonable to reject its claims in policy and law, even when a religious motivation is claimed. The logic is expressed, for example, by the late political philosopher Brian Barry, for whom conscientious objections based on religious belief are simply preferences.[35] Barry asks why some, namely religious, preferences should be privileged in law or policy over others. Why should the state bend over backward to accommodate the preferences of a minority? Why should laws be crafted so that no one will ever be unnecessarily coerced into violating conscience?

Melissa Moschella summarizes the argument advanced by the editors of the *New York Times* and many others:

> Opposition to the [HHS] mandate seems like an attempt to impose
> Catholic views about contraception on the rest of the society, or an
> unjustified request for special treatment. Why should a minority
> of Catholics ... determine public policy for the entire country? Yes,
> the government could provide free access to contraceptives without
> conscripting employers to do it for them through their health plans,
> but why should we bend over backwards to adapt our policies to the
> religious or moral sensibilities of a minority?[36]

No one claims that the conscience of a given individual or group always trumps other considerations in policy making. A conscience, even one that is shaped by binding religious obligation, may be badly formed and contrary to moral truth, as when a religion requires its adherents to offer human sacrifice or kill nonbelievers. In those cases, the common good requires that such believers be coerced into violating their consciences.

But the moral integrity of persons is itself constitutive of the common good. Absent an absolute necessity to coerce the consciences of some in order to protect public order and the rights of others, the common good also requires respecting the claims of conscience.

The blurring of the distinction between preferences and obligations is one aspect of the trivialization of conscience. As Moschella argues:

> There is a world of difference between a law that makes me do some-
> thing I don't want to do, and a law that makes me do something I have
> an obligation not to do. The former is an annoyance, the latter an

assault on my moral integrity. I may not want to follow the speed limit, but that doesn't give me a claim to be exempted from the law. On the other hand, if I believe that killing animals is morally wrong, no law should force me to serve meat in my business's cafeteria, or give my employees gift certificates to a steakhouse, even if encouraging people to eat more high-protein foods would promote public health.[37]

Here we might add that there is also an important difference between my deciding whether or not to meet my religious obligation to attend Mass on Sundays or to have my sons circumcised and the state's compelling me to do or not to do so.

As Moschella argues, "laws that forbid individuals to act in accordance with the dictates of their consciences place a burden on those individuals that differs not only in degree, but in kind, from the sort of burden involved in forbidding someone to act in accordance with mere preferences, however strong."[38] Such laws distribute the burdens and social benefits of social cooperation unequally. A difference in kind of burden is imposed, not merely one of degree.

We may see this by looking at the notorious precedent created by Antiochus IV Epiphanes in the second century B.C. The tyrant required his Jewish subjects to eat pork and food sacrificed to idols and prohibited them from performing circumcisions. Those who refused to violate their consciences in this way "were to be broken on the wheel and killed."[39] The edict imposed a radically different burden on observant Jews than on others. It was a gratuitous act of forced submission, a brutal assertion of secular power against a people of faith. As Michael Stokes Paulsen puts it, the story remains "a remarkable two-thousand-year-old parable about tyranny and conscience, about cram-downs, accommodations, deception, and adherence to principle."[40] Like the HHS mandate, it was an unnecessary case of a government insisting "on vindicating its authority and overriding religious conscience for its own sake—purely for the symbolism of power prevailing over conscience."

Redefining Religion

With the HHS mandate, the Obama administration reduces religious freedom to freedom of worship. The mandate promotes a false but prevalent idea of religion as a private and marginal activity, the practice of which involves only coreligionists. Thus the state takes it upon itself to redefine religion, and to do so in ways that exclude essential elements of Christianity and other universal religions.

From this perspective, put bluntly by the British Equality and Human Rights Commission Chief, Trevor Phillips, religious beliefs end "at the door of the temple." For Catholic Christianity, the duty to evangelize non-Christians and to serve the poor, sick, homeless, prisoners, widows, and orphans—both Christian and non-Christian—is not an optional add-on to the free exercise of religious faith. These duties have been a corporate responsibility of the Church, not just of individual members, from the very beginnings.

Conscience, Professional Duty, and Moral Agency

Conscience and Duty

The argument against conscience exemptions for health-care and social-service professionals (physicians, nurses, social workers) is typically framed as a conflict between an individual's or institution's right to decide what services or treatment it will provide and patients' rights to treatment.

The client's right to a full range of services may depend on professionals' willingness to provide them, especially in rural areas. As the chair of the ethics committee of the American College of Obstetrics and Gynecology put it, the "reproductive health needs" of women should trump the moral qualms of doctors.[41]

In this discourse, the personal is contrasted with the professional, the idea being that a professional has a duty to provide whatever services are legal and demanded by clients. The conscience of the professional is invariably given short shrift and subordinated to the supposed right of the client to treatment.[42] In a shift characteristic of contemporary rights discourse, a right to freedom from state interference (a "right to privacy") is transformed into a claim on public provision.[43]

One response to the conflict between conscience and the newly defined duties supported by the new moral orthodoxy is to say, "Fine, if you cannot in conscience meet the expectations and duties of the profession, leave it or choose a different line of work." This may indeed be the only option facing conscientious individuals where no accommodation is made.

The exclusion from their professions of physicians, nurses, social workers, and pharmacists who adhere to the traditional Judeo-Christian religious orthodoxy and the closing down of institutions that respect life and adhere to Hippocratic ethics have practical consequences. But my argument here against exclusion does not depend on the empirical reality that religious professionals and institutions—for example, Catholic and other Christian physicians, nurses, social workers, and pharmacists, as well as hospitals and clinics—play an important role in the American health-care system. Their exclusion would involve a tremendous loss of talent, knowledge, skill, aptitude, and dedication for the healing professions. It would also substantially reduce health care, child welfare, and social services of all kinds and therefore the access of patients and clients to such services. The point, rather, is that the coercion of conscience of professional health-care and social-work providers is morally corrupting for the professions and their practitioners and damaging to civil society.

There is a sharp difference between allowing and requiring professional participation in certain services or treatments. Requiring participation pressures some professionals into morally degrading choices to act on beliefs contrary to those they hold, as a condition of entering or remaining in their chosen profession. To require violation of conscience in this way corrupts the profession and those who submit to such requirements. A regrettable irony is that the moral integrity of persons, and so of associations and their members, is itself constitutive of "human and community well-being,"[44] which social work and the other helping professions claim is their purpose to promote.

The Moral Agency of the Practitioner

The idea that if an action is legally permissible and demanded by a client, the social worker (or other health professional) has the duty to provide or participate in providing the requested service itself represents a fundamental shift in the balance of rights and powers between professional and client. It strips the professional of her full moral responsibility and reduces her to a kind of machine to deliver what the customer demands. The professional's right and duty to use her judgment about what is required or indicated or morally permissible is nullified. A new form of client "empowerment" thus radically disempowers, even dehumanizes, the professional.

Opponents of conscience clauses and exemptions sometimes frame the matter in terms of religious professionals' desire to impose their personal views or morality on clients or patients. This is a misunderstanding.

The case for conscience exemptions has nothing to do with imposing my will on the client.

The client may find abortion morally permissible, and it is certainly legally permissible at present in the United States. I respect the client's right under law to decide to have an abortion and will not condemn, moralize, or argue with her. But this is not the issue at stake with respect to conscience exemptions.

My right not to participate in what I believe is grave wrongdoing does not imply or depend on a right to impose my belief on the client. "Conscientious objection," Edmund Pellegrino writes, "implies the physician's right not to participate in what she thinks morally wrong, even if the patient demands it. It does not presume the right to impose her will or conception of the good on the patient."[45]

The question of whether someone's right to engage in a behavior entails an obligation on anyone else's part to assist her in the process has important implications for all professionals, but especially those supposed to be helping or healing their clients. In many cases, such legally mandated obligations pose serious threats to conscience and, as such, to professionals' humanity as moral agents. The issue, which applies to lawyers and physicians no less than to social workers, is only in part whether a professional is obliged to serve anyone who seeks her services. Leora Harpaz, discussing the 1997 ruling of the Massachusetts Commission Against Discrimination that a woman lawyer could not refuse to represent men in divorce actions under the state's public accommodation statute, shows that the issue of compelled service is not simple or confined to the health and helping professions.[46]

For social workers and many other professionals, as for priests, it is common to serve clients whose behavior they find morally repugnant. The challenge to conscience arises not from the requirement to serve—or not to discriminate against—a particular kind of client, but from the expectation in certain cases that practitioners will act against their own judgment and collude or participate in what the practitioner determines is wrong or harmful, simply because the client demands it.

Whose conscience counts, the client's or the professional's? This is the wrong question. No one can be bound by someone else's conscience. The professional remains a moral agent, not a robot or vending machine, and so is responsible for following his or her own practical judgment about the right thing to do, all things (including the client's wishes) considered.

Licensing and Professionalism

A novel view of professional licensing also emerges to support opposition to conscience exemptions, one that further narrows the scope of civil society, the social space between individual and state. In this view, licensing, traditionally justified as protecting the public by ensuring the competence of practitioners, becomes a process whereby professionals are transformed into public officials. And when they become public officials, they become legally bound to act in certain ways, regardless of personal conscience. If the state decides to recognize same-sex marriage, for example, then its public officials who issue marriage licenses are legally bound to issue those licenses to whomever the state decides is now qualified under its rules. Period.

So licensing of professionals, insofar as it transforms the practitioner into a public official obliged to do the state's bidding, has the effect not of safeguarding professional discretion while protecting the public, but of deprofessionalization. Social workers, precisely because they are among the least secure in their professional status, are less inclined to defend the scope and legitimacy of their own professional judgment and discretion against tendencies to subordinate them to bureaucratic-state or client demands.

Analogously, by providing most of the funding of voluntary social-service agencies like Catholic Charities, the state turns these into its own agents. Far from being a strength of civil society which guards the space between state and individual, such agencies become vehicles for increasing the reach of the state. Rather than allowing for alternative visions of the common good in the associations that people with differing religious and moral commitments have built over generations, the state weakens civil society and becomes absolute sovereign of all.

Conscience, Subsidiarity, and the State

The coercion of Christian consciences is a threat not only to individual practitioners but also to the institutional pluralism that lies at the heart of subsidiarity, social justice, and American democracy. From this perspective, it is wrong to reduce matters of conscience to the state's protection of individual rights, whether of consumer against provider, or professional against employer. Conscience is not simply a matter of individual rights or individual autonomy vis-à-vis the state and civil society. It is inherently relational.

This case for the relational dimension of conscience, in contrast to an emphasis on individualist rights talk and on the autonomous self, is persuasively made by Robert Vischer, who seeks to recapture the concept of conscience as shared knowledge. He argues,

> There is a clear need to recapture the relational dimension of conscience—the notion that the dictates of conscience are defined, articulated, and lived out in relationship with others. Our consciences are shaped externally, our moral convictions have sources, and our sense of self comes into relief through interaction with others. By conveying my perception of reality's normative implications, my conscience makes truth claims that possess authority over conduct—both my own and the conduct of those who share, or come to share, my perception.[47]

This argument has at least two important implications. First, conscience is not simply an internal oracle like a preference in ice cream flavors. It implies shared knowledge and truth claims about right action. And it binds those who share that knowledge and accept those truth claims.

Second, shaping our consciences is a matter of neither the individual nor the state, but of the subsidiary associational life that mediates between them, especially church and family. These are sources of conscience formation, communities of discernment, and venues for expression. In Vischer's words: "When the state closes down avenues by which persons live out their core beliefs—and admittedly, some avenues must be closed if peaceful coexistence is to be possible—there is a cost to the continued vitality of conscience."[48]

Catholic social teaching offers a sharp contrast to the Hobbesian picture, in which "the sovereignty of Leviathan is absolute, so subsidiary units of the social order—churches, groups, smaller units of government—exist merely at the sufferance of the sovereign."[49]

Attacks on religious freedom and conscience relentlessly seek to impose a new orthodoxy and an attendant intolerance of dissent from subsidiary associations—even, in Canada, imposing the new sexual morality on the curricula of private religious schools and homeschooling families.

The issue of conscience, then, needs to be understood not only in terms of the rights of individuals, who must look to the state for relief or protection, but also and especially in terms of the scope for a rich associational life that subsists in tension with both individual and state. A commitment to freedom of conscience, properly understood, "should underlie our legal system's reluctance to restrict the independence of the myriad associations that make up the vast space between person and state."[50]

Driving Christian organizations and professionals out of health-care, education, and social services does great social harm on several levels. Most directly, it threatens a tremendous loss of talent, knowledge, skill, aptitude, and dedication for these professions. It would also substantially reduce health care and social services of all kinds, and therefore the access of patients and clients to such services. In addition, coercing the consciences of professionals is morally corrupting for both individuals and their professions. Christians are bound to follow their correctly formed conscience, even if it means loss of livelihood. Some will fail the test, however, in the name of what is now called leaving your personal values at the door. But a regime that requires such heroic sacrifice of its members—like that of Antiochus IV Epiphanes—is also corrupt, falling into what has been called a soft or liberal totalitarianism.

Individual or group conscience is not at odds with the common good but constitutive of it. The common good is not solely expressed or subsumed in the state, but requires a healthy institutional pluralism.

Some Conclusions

One kind of choice in social-welfare policy is often reduced to a dichotomy between individualism and collectivism. This reduction not only artificially narrows the range of possible policy options[51] but also misses the ways in which these ideologies in practice reinforce and depend on each other precisely by hollowing out the space between individual and state.

Pius XI made the same point in a surprising context, the publication of his social encyclical *Quadragesimo Anno* (1931), at a time when Communist, Fascist, and National Socialist totalitarianism were ascendant. Startlingly, Pius blames individualism for pushing the state in this direction:

> When we speak of the reform of institutions, the State comes chiefly
> to mind, not as if universal well-being were to be expected from its
> activity, but because things have come to such a pass through the
> evil of what we have termed "individualism" that, following upon the
> overthrow and near extinction of that rich social life which was once
> highly developed through associations of various kinds, there remain
> virtually only individuals and the State. This is to the great harm of

the State itself; for, with a structure of social governance lost, and with the taking over of all the burdens which the wrecked associations once bore, the State has been overwhelmed and crushed by almost infinite tasks and duties.[52]

Both Catholic social teaching and the social-work empowerment tradition reject the individualist hypertrophy of the autonomous unencumbered self no less than the hypertrophy of the state. The space—of civil society or mediating structures—between individual and state is the one in which conscience is shaped and the virtues on which it depends are developed through practice and habituation. The virtue of social justice also requires and develops that space in which citizens join together in pursuit of the common good.

[CHAPTER 17]

Marriage as a Social Justice Issue

MARRIAGE IS A SOCIAL JUSTICE ISSUE. INDEED, IT IS CENTRAL to the possibility of a just society. Historically and universally our most child-centered institution, marriage and the marriage-based family, reduce the risk of poverty, crime, mental and physical illness, poor educational outcomes, domestic or intimate-partner violence, and so on. The marriage gap between the more educated and affluent on one hand, and the poor and middle class, both black and white, on the other, is widening. That is both a reflection and a source of increasing inequality.[1] Paul R. Amato's 2005 study shows the profound impact on children of changes in family structure since 1970, when the sexual revolution took off.[2] The consequences associated with these changes include the explosion of divorce, an increase in nonmarital births, and rises in cohabitation and fatherless and blended families. The revolution's defining feature was the destigmatization and increased incidence of almost all kinds of sex inside and especially outside of marriage. If U.S. family structures were as strong today as they were in 1970, he calculates:

643,000 fewer children each year would fail a grade at school

1,040,000 fewer children each year would be suspended from school

531,000 fewer children each year would need psychotherapy

453,000 fewer children each year would be involved in violence

515,000 fewer children each year would be cigarette smokers

179,000 fewer children would consider suicide

71,000 fewer children each year would attempt suicide.

Children's experience of repeated family-structure change has a robust association with compromised development across the early life course. In a recent study published in the *Journal of Marriage and Family*, Paula Fomby and Stacey Bosick investigate the relation between family-structure instability during childhood and adolescence and children's transition to adulthood, up to age 24.[3] Using data from the National Longitudinal Study of Adolescent Health (N = 8,841), the researchers find evidence of associations between early and later family instability and low rates of college completion, early union formation and childbearing, and early entry into the labor force. The researchers find that these associations are explained by family structure, delinquency, and academic performance in adolescence.

Another study conducted by Michael Gähler and Anna Garriga, using longitudinal data from two waves (1968 and 2000) of the Swedish Level of Living Survey, finds that as alternative family forms have become more prevalent and accepted, the negative impact of parental divorce on children has not faded.[4] The evidence from Sweden suggests that the link between parental divorce in childhood and psychological distress in young adulthood remains as robust now as it was forty years ago. This link is strong, in spite of government policy to offset the negative effects of parental divorce on children and the social acceptance of divorce.

The considerable benefits of marriage, attested to now by decades of social-science research and recognized by scientists across the political spectrum, cannot be reduced to a selection effect. That is, it is not simply that healthier or more affluent people are more likely to get married in the first place, regardless of any independent effect of marriage itself. Of course marriage does involve this kind of selection. That's part of its purpose and function—as personified in the young woman's father who questions the young man about his prospects. But we know from longitudinal studies that follow subjects as they enter, leave, and reenter marriages, that marriage has benefits from the start that other kinds of relationship status lack. These benefits that distinguish marriage from other kinds of relationships begin even before the wedding, with the increase in earnings and decline in risk-taking behavior of young men when they get engaged.[5] The benefits for women and men and their children—in income, health, mental health, and so on—are lost with divorce and regained with remarriage (the more so the shorter the gap between marriages).[6]

So, given that marriage is a key protective factor, and as such of key importance for the lives of young people, what do we teach them? In particular, what do we teach students of social work and related fields, those who seek to help those negatively affected by marriage's decline? The Institute for American Values published a report under the direction of the late sociologist of the family, Norval Glenn, entitled "Closed Hearts, Closed Minds: The Textbook Story of Marriage."[7] Glenn analyzes twenty textbooks used in some 8,000 courses across the country to teach hundreds of thousands of young people. He explains: "The college instructors who are training the next generation of counselors, nurses, therapists, social workers, and teachers often rely on precisely these books for their own understanding of the scientific consensus on family matters."[8] But the books are riddled with errors. They show little interest in the effects of marital disruption or single parenting on children, devoting an average of only 3.5 pages to this topic. Three times as much space is devoted to adult relations, without regard to how they affect children. Current textbooks convey a pessimistic view of marriage. These books repeatedly suggest that marriage is more a problem than a solution. The potential costs of marriage to adults receive exaggerated treatment, while the benefits of marriage, both to individuals and society, are downplayed.

Mary Eberstadt, in *Adam and Eve after the Pill*, describes the widespread "will to disbelieve" the empirical evidence on the negative impact of the sexual revolution.[9] There is a similar reluctance to admit the benefits of marriage and monogamy for children and adults, including those in disadvantaged families. The blindness to evidence she describes perpetuated in classrooms and textbooks across the country a view of marriage that had long been disproved by research. A big gap opened up between research and researchers on one hand and textbooks and teachers on the other. It was the latter that shaped the ideology in which social workers and other helping professionals were trained for decades.

Among those living in poor communities, it is not the case that they no longer aspire to marriage. They do, but it has ceased to be the path to "settling down," devoting oneself to another and to the children who result from the union of husband and wife. Instead, marriage has become for them, not a path to achievement of such stability, but a reward. Marriage is viewed as a dream and a luxury. Children are seen as more important— and more attainable—than marriage and so precede it, even though the children themselves suffer from the instability and complexity of the new system. Given the disappearance of the "shotgun marriage"—marriage as an obligation and expectation for men who father children outside it— and the ubiquity of cohabitation, divorce, and single parenthood in poor communities, marriage is no longer the institution that structures and stabilizes relations between the sexes. Instead, it has become a practically unattainable ideal.[10]

For social workers, who deal with populations where marriage has largely fallen apart, the tendency rightly has been to focus on helping those who suffer most from the collapse. These include abandoned mothers and their children, "blended" families, single parents, children in chaotic homes living without emotional or economic security, and so on. But, as with welfare policy, this approach raises a dilemma. Do the policy interventions supported by social workers help promote marriage and prevent its breakdown? Do they support policies that incentivize marriage and encourage the virtues and norms on which its success depends? Or do they promote and reinforce the sexual revolution and its effects in the name of celebrating family diversity—or in the name of destigmatizing, or of being nonjudgmental, or of providing income to those in need?

A virtue-based understanding of social justice may help us toward a different, more empowering orientation that helps us build and sustain a culture of marriage, one that makes it easier for individuals to develop the virtues needed for marriage, even while helping those in problematic (to themselves) nonmarital situations.

Social Justice as a Virtue

J. Brian Benestad, in his outstanding introduction to Catholic social doctrine, says:

> The contemporary concern for social justice leads primarily to a stress on public-policy initiatives, to a reorganization of "the system," and to social reform. In addition, there is a tendency to regard social justice as a principle of rights against society rather than as a virtue inclining a

person to fulfill duties toward society. There is a stress on the demand for just treatment for others rather than the duty to act justly oneself.[11]

I do not discount the injustices resulting in a state of affairs in which marriage has largely collapsed for a large part of the population, or deny the need for public-policy initiatives. Instead, I want to suggest how a virtue-based understanding of social justice offers a fuller, more complete understanding of the challenge that social workers, other helping professionals, and we as a society currently face. An approach to social justice that looks primarily or exclusively to asserting claims on the state by or on behalf of others rests on an impoverished understanding of the human person, tends toward utopian statism and authoritarianism, and contradicts the best, most empowering traditions of social work.

Society will not be just unless individuals are virtuous. Political and economic structures in themselves cannot produce individual virtue. Nor can they provide the love and support that humans, as naturally social, "reciprocally indebted," "dependent rational animals" need and for which the human heart longs.[12] This is the claim of the whole of the central Christian tradition, from Augustine and Aquinas to the present. Its roots lie in the Christian understanding of human dignity as derived from our creation in the image and likeness of God. It draws on the ancient Greek understanding of the cardinal virtue of justice. In this classical Aristotelian-Thomist tradition, justice is rooted in natural law and what is objectively necessary for humans to flourish as they order their lives together.

In this tradition, justice and natural rights are, as Edward Feser says,

> Safeguards of our ability to fulfill our moral obligations and realize our natural end. It follows that anything which tends to frustrate our ability to fulfill those obligations and realize those ends violates our rights and amounts to an injustice.[13]

So justice is the cardinal virtue by which, as a matter of habit and will, we give others what is due them. Aquinas defines justice, following Aristotle and Cicero, as "the habit whereby an individual renders to each one his due (*ius*) by a constant and habitual will."[14] If we frustrate the ability of another to fulfill her moral obligations—say to worship God (which implies the right to religious freedom, as the American founders argued) or to preserve her life or that of her child—we act unjustly.

How do we get from this classical concept of the virtue of justice to social justice as a virtue? Feser continues:

> And if that which frustrates this ability [to fulfill our moral obligations] is not merely the actions of a particular individual or group of individuals, but something inherent in the very structure of a society—in its legal code, its cultural institutions, or the tenor of its public life—then what we have can meaningfully be described as a social injustice. In particular, any society whose legal framework fails to protect the lives of its weakest members, whose popular culture is shot through and through with a spirit of contempt for and ridicule of the demands of the natural law, or whose economic structure makes it effectively impossible for a worker to support himself and his family with his wages, is to that extent an unjust society, a socially unjust society.[15]

Social justice can be defined as the virtue that inclines individuals to work with others for the common good. It is justice in directing the virtues to giving others their due, and social, as Novak argues, in a double sense.[16] First, it aims at the common good rather than at what is due another individual (as in the commutative justice that inclines one to equitable exchanges between individuals). Second, it involves joining with others to achieve a common purpose that individuals cannot achieve on their own. It is the virtue of association, the virtue par excellence of civil society.

Marriage Does Not Just Happen

The collapse of marriage is perhaps the cardinal social injustice of our time. As we saw and as research clearly documents, most injustices that social workers confront in their daily work at any level hinge in some way on this one. What would it take to sustain an environment or ecosystem in which marriage and marriage-based families could thrive?

Philosopher Michael Pakaluk has offered what even those who disagree with his vision might consider as a thought experiment. In a brief essay, he offers an opportunity to open oneself, at least temporarily and with tentative sympathy, to a traditional view of marriage. He writes:

> Here is marriage, considered in context. A young man and woman remain chaste, and they have the virtue of "purity" (an old-fashioned word, but it is real). As a result, they have joy, and an ideal of the

complete gift of self is readily understandable to them. They fall in love but do not "date" so much as "court" with reverence, each viewing the other as an almost divine gift.

They don't have the baggage that comes with sleeping around. They don't cohabit. They don't think that oral sex is a sign of love, or even that it's sex.

The death to self and complete binding of each to the other which they gleefully accept on their wedding day makes it also easy for them to accept their complete and total binding to a child for life, who incarnates their love into a single being. That is to say, they are "open to life." They so cherish their bond that they have no private good except what comes through their union, and they place the safeguarding of that bond so high that it is a priority, for them, equivalent to faith, honor, religion, worship, and life itself.[17]

What Pakaluk describes here is not a utopian ideal made out of whole cloth in the imagination of a social reformer. It is, as he says, "in Shakespeare and other classical authors and, in Christendom, it used to be something like the ordinary experience of (how can I put it?) people who were well brought up. (Think: Song of Songs.)" It rests implicitly on an understanding of man's nature and destiny as the creature whom God, who is love, created out of love, for love, who "cannot fully find himself except through a sincere gift of himself."[18]

The point here is not to look back with nostalgia on an imagined golden age when there was no fornication, adultery, or other sexual vice. It is to remind us how completely the possibilities and understandings of marriage depicted by Shakespeare in *As You Like It* and *Much Ado About Nothing*, or in the novels of Jane Austen, have ceased to be socially available. What Pakaluk describes "is lived today, is even attainable, by only a handful of persons." Yet, he continues, "anyone who understands historic Christianity, and is well read, must hold (I think) that it would be desirable for culture once again to make such a way of life generally attainable."

What Pakaluk diagnoses is a grave social injustice in the sense defined by Feser, "something inherent in the very structure of society—in its legal code, its cultural institutions, or the tenor of its public life—that tends to frustrate our ability to fulfill our moral obligations and realize our natural end." The kind of life-affirming marriage and marriage-based family culture Pakaluk describes has been swept away, above all for the lower socioeconomic strata, by the cultural and legal changes of the past half-century.

So how is such a marriage, one consonant with our nature and destiny and corresponding to our deepest longings, possible today? Pakaluk goes on:

> But a culture cannot be created or sustained by a single person; it can barely be kept alive by a family; and it certainly cannot be created or transmitted without sound education. So, the immediate path forward for marriage, regardless of the Supreme Court, is the creation and fostering of institutions where modesty and purity are practiced with full confidence and self-knowledge.[19]

Is Marriage Possible?

There are two main responses to the current state of affairs. One is to normalize and even to celebrate the collapse of marriage in the name of diversity of family forms. We talk not of the family, but of families. The aim is to offset the negative effects of this social breakdown on children and women. This has been done both by the destigmatization of non-marital births, divorce, sex that is delinked from marriage and children, and also by using government programs to meet the needs of low-income women and children.

Another response is to seek, by policy incentives or personal influence, to change the behavior of "target populations." Welfare reform, with its marriage promotion measures and time limits, did this in 1996.

The first approach offers direct relief, but at the risk of legitimating behavior and situations that harm children, society, and the institution of marriage. It maintains the poor in their poverty and reinforces the very cultural forces in the structure of society that undermine marriage and the marriage-based family. These forces celebrate the unencumbered autonomous self and the claims of adults at the expense of their obligations to children.

The second approach runs the risk of dividing society into sinners and saints, those whose behavior needs to change and those who want to bring about the change... in others. One approach calls evil good and good evil (Is 5:20); the other inclines to moral superiority.

Is a both/and approach possible, one that recognizes the need for immediate help for those plunged into or maintained in poverty by the collapse of marriage, while at the same time strengthens and rebuilds a culture of marriage rather than assuming and even incentivizing its breakdown? In one way, this is the perennial problem of social policy and social work, and indeed helping in general—the problem that the English Poor Law reformers of the 1830s wrestled with. A social-justice perspective, with its emphasis on the personal virtues and on the associations or mediating structures of civil society, offers a different way of looking at the problem.

Social justice cannot be reduced either to redistribution or to reform of government policies or institutions, though it does not exclude either. It requires virtue on the part of each individual in society so that all can contribute to the common good. In joining with others in civil society, citizens can support the institution of marriage while remedying those social injustices in law, culture, and the tenor of public life that put a healthy marriage beyond reach for many.

A social-justice perspective takes sin seriously, seeing, as Solzhenitsyn put it, the dividing line between good and evil not as running between social groups or political parties, but as going through the human heart. It begins, not with priggish finger wagging, but with the recognition that we are all sinners and affected by sin, not least sins associated with the breakdown of marriage and its effects on children.

In his provocative and startling essay "The Moral Structure of Pedophilia," Anthony Esolen draws our attention to the moral harm caused by the shift away from a child-centered view of marriage and the marriage-based family.[20] In his view, marriage provides the optimum setting for bearing and raising children. In its place, our society upholds an adult-centered view of marriage as being about adult relationships, an intense form of friendship. Esolen shows how our failure to give children their due penetrates far more deeply and pervasively than the most obvious and appalling cases. The obvious cases are the ones in which the claims of children are subordinated to the desires of adults. We have failed children systemically in ways that permeate our cultural institutions, laws, and public life.

Esolen shows this failure by posing the question: How does pedophilia differ in our minds from other kinds of sexual expression? Its moral structure, he says, "is simply this: the welfare of children is subordinate to the sexual gratification of adults." Lack of consent cannot in itself be morally decisive when we compel children to do all kinds of things to which they do not consent:

> If we altered the question, and asked not how many people have done sexually abusive things with children, but how many people have done sexual things that redounded to the suffering of children, then we might confess that the only thing that separates millions of people from Jerry Sandusky is inclination. Everything that was once considered a sexual evil and that is now winked at or cheered, everything without exception, has served to hurt children, and badly.

Divorce is a case in point:

> Unless it is necessary to remove oneself and one's children from physical danger and moral corruption, the old wisdom regarding divorce should hold, if children themselves have anything to say about it. Parents will say, "My children can never be happy unless I am happy," but they should not lay that narcissistic unction to their souls. Children need parents who love them, not parents who are happy; they are too young to be asked to lay down their lives for someone else. It is not the job of the child to suffer for the parent, but the job of the parent to endure, to make the best of a poor situation, to swallow his pride, to bend her knees, for the sake of the child.

The same applies to births out of wedlock:

> The child has a right to enter more than a little nursery decorated with presents from a baby shower. He should enter a human world, a story, a people. He should be born of a mother and a father among uncles and aunts and cousins and grandparents, stretching into the distant past, with all their interrelated histories, with his very being reflected in all those mirrors of relation, not to mention his eyes and his hair, the talents in his fingers and the cleverness in his mind. This belonging to a big and dependable world can be secured only in the context of the permanent love of his mother and father, declared by a vow before the community and before the One in whom there is no shadow of alteration.

This neglect of the interests of children is endemic in our culture. Consider the way we talk, not only about marriage, but also about things like artificial reproductive technologies or surrogacy.[21]

What Is to Be Done?

What is to be done? Feser argues that the "duty of remedying such injustices rests, in accordance with the principle of subsidiarity, primarily with individuals, families, and private associations."[22] That principle also recognizes, as part of natural law, the state's duty to deal with those injustices that cannot effectively be remedied in this way. But when the state confirms in law "what was already the practice, trend, and effect of an alternative culture that had its immediate origin in the 1950s and '60s," then the task falls all the more heavily on the associations of civil society.[23]

As Sherif Girgis, Ryan Anderson, and Robert George reflected after two important Supreme Court decisions concerning the definition of marriage:

> If you believe, as we do, in the importance to children and to society of the marriage-based family, then of course you were hoping for different results in yesterday's marriage cases. But you probably also put your trust in the institutions of civil society—in that vast arena between man and state which is the real stage for human development. And in that case, you never expected a court of law to do our work for us, to rescue a marriage culture that has been wounded for decades by cohabitation, out-of-wedlock child-bearing, and misguided policies like no-fault divorce.[24]

Whatever one's opinion about the Supreme Court's decisions concerning marriage, or the scope for any legal measures to address the collapse of marriage, the task remains for social work what it was. In line with its historic emphasis since the Charity Organization Societies and the Settlement House movement, its task of empowerment is still to combat social injustice by strengthening families and communities. The challenge is to work out how to help rebuild a culture of marriage in civil society, especially in the poorer half of the population where the disintegration has been most complete and devastating in its effects.

Attempts to promote and strengthen marriage come in various forms. At the policy level, there are attempts to remove disincentives like the marriage tax penalty, and otherwise to incentivize marriage and make it easier for people to meet their moral obligations—of spouses to each other, to their children, and to society.

In 2004, a group of social scientists produced a list of policy proposals under the head, "Can Government Strengthen Marriage?"[25] They proposed a shift of emphasis from preventing teen pregnancy to preventing unwed pregnancy, since the data revealed no benefits to delaying nonmarital birth into the twenties, but considerable benefits to getting married before having children. They recommended support for marriage preparation education to reduce violence, conflict, and unnecessary divorce; lengthening the waiting period for no-fault divorce; removing perverse incentives to cohabit rather than marry; and evaluating and strengthening the pro-marriage aspects of the 1996 welfare reform (among other things). All these measures can be understood as promoting an ecology that fosters the virtues required for and developed by marriage.

Such efforts flew in the face of the sexual revolution and its increasing adoption as law and official government policy. As Alvaré argues, recent court rulings promoting a culture of "sexualityism" can only be understood as the government's systematic embrace of and commitment to sex without consequences.[26] Government, not least through its imposition of an HHS mandate that requires employers to enable access to contraceptive—even abortifacient—drugs, as well as to sterilization, is promoting the destruction of marriage by normalizing and promoting the delinking of sex from marriage and from both the bearing of children and their rearing by the two parents who made them.

Little wonder then, that supporters of marriage and marriage-based families put little faith in government and its capacity for interest in promoting a culture of marriage. I will leave aside further discussion of the kind of social policy measures that have been my bread and butter as a policy analyst. Instead, I will look at some approaches within civil society to promote and sustain the kind of culture that makes the vision of marriage described by Pakaluk attainable by those who want it. I will also look at what is involved in promoting the virtue of social justice in social workers themselves, as well as in the families and communities they work with.

Building an Alternative: *Reculer pour Mieux Sauter*

In the famous ending of his *After Virtue*, Alisdair MacIntyre recalls the example of Saint Benedict as he considers a way forward in our own dark ages: "What matters at this stage is the construction of local forms of community within which civility and the intellectual and moral life can be sustained through the new dark ages which are already upon us."[27] In our own dire times, "the barbarians are not waiting beyond the frontiers;

they have been governing us for quite some time."[28] "Benedict's greatness," MacIntyre explains, "lay in making possible a quite new kind of institution, that of the monastery of prayer, learning, and labor, in which and around which communities could not only survive, but flourish, in a period of social and cultural darkness."[29]

Our own times are very different from Benedict's, and a Benedict for our times would, as MacIntyre writes, doubtless be very different. Combined with MacIntyre's call for construction of local forms of community, the monastic example suggests the need—alongside local or parish-level initiatives to support marriage in a hostile environment—for distinctly Christian communities centered on faith and family.

MacIntyre's call to construct local forms of community, combined with the need in our time to rebuild an authentic culture of marriage and Benedict's example of a strong community of faith and learning, brings into focus the promise of a small, seriously Catholic Christian university and community like Ave Maria in Southwest Florida. To what extent is a modern day analog of sorts to the strategy of Saint Benedict possible? Can it build not only a center of learning, culture, and faith in contrast to the received wisdom of the contemporary Zeitgeist, but also specifically a culture of marriage closer to Pakaluk's vision? Can it serve both as a beacon to attract or guide others, keeping things alive that would otherwise be lost, and also as a training ground to prepare people to go out into the world and, in the current phrase, "evangelize the culture"?

To this combination of university and community, we may add the pathbreaking work of Mary Eberstadt on the profound impact of the pill as the technological base of the sexual revolution and on the relation between faith and family—*Adam and Eve after the Pill* (2012), and *How the West Really Lost God* (2013).[30] Eberstadt confirms the strong link between religious observance and high fertility rates, but she emphasizes the ways in which large families foster religious observance and not simply the other way around. Children drive their parents to church, as she puts it. She notes how Christianity in particular, with its Holy Family, its God the Father who loves, guides, and protects, with a Son who addresses God the Father as Abba (Daddy), and so forth, is near to unintelligible in communities where fathers who love and protect their families are rare. Christianity and the family, she argues and shows empirically, rise and fall together.

Ave Maria is a community of large families and strong faith, each reinforcing the other. A faithful Christian community and locus of Catholic learning and culture, it attracts many who live in isolation from these things but are drawn to them. It is home both to Pakaluk, chair of the university's philosophy department, and to Novak and me. The marriage Pakaluk describes could be that of his own daughters. The reference to Shakespeare recalls students' involvement in the plays, *As You Like It* and *Much Ado About Nothing*, that a class on Shakespeare in Performance presented in recent years, playing, as Michael Novak put it, "characters their own age, with the distinctively tender and fragile feelings, high excitements and crushing blows of that gloriously vulnerable time of life."[31] In the exhilaration of the performances, one could sense the identification over the centuries of a shared culture of marriage, a shared understanding of the sincere gift of self it involves—the gift of the couple to each other and to the children that may result from their comprehensive union, a union at once emotional, bodily, and a matter of will. Play and audience share an understanding of marriage as the institution through which each generation sacrifices itself for the next.

Patiently Explain: In Hostile Territory

Serious Catholics and other Christians, social workers not least, live and work amidst hostile liberal-secular media, academia, and legal, political, and professional elites. In this aggressively secular world, sexual expressionism, the ideology of the sexual revolution, is absolute dogma and state religion, dissent from which will not be tolerated. For this cultural elite, the Catholic Church's organized structure and presence in the public square are the main obstacle to their vision of the future, which they seek unrelentingly to impose everywhere, all talk of respecting other cultures notwithstanding.

Most families in Ave Maria chose to live in the Florida swampland, far from a major city or other centers of learning, because they had experience of a beige, accommodationist Catholicism in their former parishes and saw the erosion of faith and family around them. Ave Maria attracts many others too, even though they do not live there, as a beacon reflecting and keeping alive the light of faith amidst the powerful forces that seek to extinguish it as a public presence in their world. It does not substitute for other strategies for building a strong culture of marriage, faith, and family. But it helps. It is an example of the virtue of social justice practiced by members of a community, joining together in many groups and projects to further the common good, not least creating and fostering a culture of marriage that corresponds to the nature and destiny of the human person as *imago Dei*.

While Ave Maria as a community tends to attract intense hostility from comment box writers whenever it is mentioned, most faithful Christians who remain within the orthodox Judeo-Christian tradition in matters of life, death, sex, and marriage face hostility without such solid community support, as individuals or congregations, as employees, parents, or small entrepreneurs trying to make their way and retain their integrity, often condemned, in Justice Scalia's words describing the effect of the Supreme Court's DOMA decision, as *hostes humani generis*—enemies of the human race.[32]

Navigating this hostile terrain is a different challenge that has elicited many initiatives, mostly lay-led, at the parish or cross-parish level. The Stand With Children movement in California, with its Faith and Action Circles, offers one outstanding example of a grassroots effort.[33] In Norway, the government is rethinking its attitude toward divorce and encouraging "date nights" for couples to sustain marriages and reduce divorce rates.[34] For several reasons—a different view of the role of government and the present government's commitment to the sexual revolution among them—such a strategy is highly improbable in the United States. That is true, at least, for government, but not necessarily within parishes or other intermediary groups of civil society.

The people involved in these grassroots activities exercised the virtue of social justice by joining together for the common good, the good of marriage and marriage-based families. They did so in face of overwhelmingly powerful forces tending toward their dissolution. These forces include both political and cultural movements and the pressures of the sexual revolution on individual families. Among the effects are the normalizing and increased incidence of divorce, including the devastating impact of no-fault or unilateral divorce, pornography, sex before and outside of marriage presented as the norm by media and "enlightened opinion," cohabitation, and children raised without one or either of their parents. Unfortunately, social work has done much harm in promoting and normalizing some of these developments.

Social workers, indeed, have had little to do with the developments I have described that promote a positive culture of marriage. Despite our literature and tradition of empowerment-based practice, we have tended to think of social justice not as a virtue at all, not as rights derived from God or moral obligations or duties, but as claims on the state in the name of equality. Social justice becomes a series of demands on government aimed at a desired state of affairs, with no connection to personal character. This is at best a very partial understanding of social justice.

The Professional Challenge

Possibilities for practicing and promoting the virtue of social justice in oneself and one's clients vary for social workers according to employment and funding constraints. There is no straightforward answer to the question of what is to be done—the "practice implications." Here I want to discuss some of the challenges social workers face in trying to orient their own practice to the social justice of which I speak. What principles might guide us in meeting our own moral obligation to the common good and helping those we work with to meet theirs?

In Aristotle and Aquinas, justice is the virtue that orders all the virtues to the common good. Habitually giving others their due requires, in Benestad's words, "the laborious effort to prepare one's soul for action through the cultivation of the virtues and the acquisition of knowledge. . . . Some works of justice require very sophisticated knowledge and very great effort to control pride, anger, and fear as well as love of pleasure, money, honor, and power."[35] In the language of the virtues, we recognize the dual emphasis in social-work education on acquiring knowledge and on the qualities of character, like those of self-effacement, prudence, courage, and self-mastery, needed for the "professional use of self" in practice.

Marriage and its breakdown present particular challenges to social work. Marriage requires virtues on the part of the couple, their families, and the community. It requires a culture of marriage to support the gift of self that is comprehensive, permanent, and faithful. This gift and the culture that supports it assure any children that result from the spouses' union the emotional, financial, and legal support and the kin of the two parents who made them. Marriage doesn't just happen, and the cultural, political, and economic structures needed to support it, or even understand it, are in disarray.

These conditions for healthy marriage barely exist for most of the people social workers work with, or even, in many cases, for the workers themselves. I have found Master of Social Work (MSW) students incredulous at research that shows that cohabitation is not equivalent to marriage, that women are safer from intimate-partner violence in marriage than in other kinds of relationships, that children do better when they are raised by their own married mother and father, and so on. Part of the reason for their surprise, no doubt, is the ideological miseducation that students of marriage and family routinely receive as undergraduates. Part is that many of the MSW students sitting in the classroom themselves live with partners and/or children outside of marriage and marriage-based families. Their discernment of reality is blurred by cognitive dissonance, denial, or defensiveness.

Decades of promoting, normalizing, and celebrating alternatives to marriage have done immense damage to professional helpers as well as to those they aim to help. The task of social-work education today—in helping students acquire the knowledge, the virtues, and the habits of the heart they need to be effective—is formidable.

Three Principles

I conclude with three principles to guide a way forward.

1. We have to face the reality of marriage's disappearance as a socially available, attainable choice among much of the population. We need to acknowledge at a deep level the effects of that destruction in widening inequality, perpetuating poverty, and damaging mothers' and fathers' ability to meet their moral obligations to each other and their children. We need a sense of the sin through which we have corrupted marriage as an ideal and the social injustice perpetrated in particular against the poor and children.

2. We need a sense of the joy of marriage as understood in Christian tradition, as described by Pakaluk (and Shakespeare and the Song of Songs), as rooted in a chaste longing in the human heart. Marriage offers an opportunity for the sincere gift of self through which humans find fulfillment.

3. As Christians, we understand that God's mercy and forgiveness are greater than our sin, including social sin. As social workers or Christians or concerned citizens, we have to find ways to offer hope to and support for initiatives in civil society through which people exercise the virtue of social justice, joining with others to rebuild a culture of marriage.

CHAPTER 18

Practicing Social Justice

WE HAVE DISCUSSED HOW THE VIRTUE OF SOCIAL JUSTICE involves skills, knowledge, and habits required to join with others for the common good. Social justice is the virtue particularly required for and developed by participation in civil society. It concerns how people exercise their initiative and creativity in the associations and groups that fill the space between individual and state. Brandon Vogt has shown how saints, practitioners of heroic virtue, have worked to make common life better on predominantly national and local levels, generally doing so in the space between the lone individual and the Leviathan state. He draws lessons from these saints about how ordinary Christians today who are neither professionals nor agents of the state may practice social justice in their own lives.[1]

But what of the efforts of those who seek to help others as their primary occupation? Can professional helpers like social workers exercise and promote the virtue of social justice in the course of their practice? The question seems absurd since social workers regard social justice as a core value and combating social injustice as a professional obligation. We have used examples of social justice in practice in nonprofessional, nonstate cooperative efforts like bridge building or barn raising. We had in mind, too, activities such as organizing young adults who were born to sperm donors and whose voices and needs were neglected in prior discussions of artificial reproductive technology. Or those who campaign against gendercide, the selective abortion and infanticide of baby girls. Or workers who organize and press for a just wage that enables them to live decently and support their families.

Social workers engage in such activities, but usually from the outside, as helpers. They practice in poor neighborhoods where they do not live. They work with impoverished and oppressed people but are not poor or exploited themselves. They provide psychotherapy for those with mental illness, but as professionals to clients, not as fellow patients or family members.

Professional Helpers and Social Justice

The concluding chapters on charity take up some of the issues involved in this kind of helping relationship. Here I want to look at examples of how the virtue of social justice may guide the practice of professionals, even those employed by or working under contract for the state. In the first case, the outside helpers are economists or people with financial expertise, helping women in poor communities and financially fragile circumstances. The other two cases involve social workers in their most regulatory, coercive role on behalf of the state, intervening in families to protect children from abuse or neglect. What does exercising the virtue of social justice look like in these situations? All three cases illustrate how a program may require and develop, in both its organizers and clients, the virtue of social justice as the personal disposition and habit of joining with others to promote the common good.

Grameen Bank

Like the Franciscan friars of the fifteenth century and Archbishop McGrath, C.S.C., (1924–2000) of Panama City in the twentieth, the economist Muhammad Yunus saw the importance of providing small loans at low interest to poor people (primarily women) so that they could use their entrepreneurial creativity and energy to build small businesses. As loans were repaid, new loans could be made to other borrowers in the community. A key aspect of the Grameen Bank model is the forming of groups of women who repay their loans via frequent installments in a group setting.[2] Founded in 1976 as a research project in Bangladesh, the

Grameen Bank (literally the Bank of the Villages in Bengali) was authorized by the government as an independent bank in 1983. Since then it has flourished and now has more than 2,000 branches, inspiring imitations and variations in over forty countries. Repayment meetings provide clients opportunities they did not have before, including "walking across the village to attend the center meeting, sitting in conversation with a diverse set of women, handling money for the group and receiving personal address."[3]

When researchers compared the effects of the standard weekly meetings with an alternative of monthly meetings, they found that those in the former groups were 90 percent less likely to default on their loans and had substantially higher rates of interaction with each other and their families outside the meetings. The women held each other accountable and built community and democratic participation. The weekly meetings were important for both economic and social development.

The bank has grown to the point of having many thousands of employees, including loan officers and financial experts, and 3.5 million members. It has distributed more than $15 billion in loans. It is owned by its members, most of them poor women. The bank is an extraordinary example of people joining together—with outside help—to achieve a common purpose they could not have achieved on their own. The bank's microcredit programs have many secondary benefits in terms of empowering women, enabling their creativity, resourcefulness, and initiative, and ensuring the education of their children. (It is a condition of membership to send your children to school.)

If those in dire poverty are to be helped, they need, at least for the children, education that will enhance their human capital and tap into their creativity and capacity for innovation. They need secure property rights and a business environment in which it is easy to start even a very small business, a setting more like that of Hong Kong than Argentina—or than the Peru described by Peruvian economist Hernando de Soto, where excessive regulation, bureaucracy, bribery, and corruption made the cost of starting a business prohibitive for the poor.[4] And they need lines of credit at low and predictable rates. In Bangladesh, it is not government programs of redistribution or income maintenance but the Grameen Bank that provides most of these. An important role of the state is to get out of the way and not to hamper the economic and social development that wells up from below in civil society.

As wonderfully illustrated in the series of DVDs created by *Poverty-Cure*, Grameen Bank and its founder Muhammad Yunus have had an enormous impact in spreading these principles and the practice of microfinance in many forms through much of the developing world, where the lack of private property rights and the rule of law have kept the poor in poverty, stifling their creative energy and entrepreneurial spirit.[5]

Patch

"Patch" is an approach to delivering social services, including child protection and other forms of social care, that was developed in the United Kingdom and uses a locality-based integrated team of human-service workers.[6] In the 1990s I was involved in adapting this approach for a distressed neighborhood in Cedar Rapids, Iowa. The Iowa patch team continues to operate in expanded and modified form, and other patch teams have sprung up in various parts of the United States since.

In the United Kingdom, a patch team would usually involve a single agency, the local authority social-services department responsible for statutory child welfare, mental health, aging, and other services. The agency's social workers and other staff were redeployed from a central downtown office to a number of small, neighborhood-based teams and given responsibility for work within a locality of about 10,000 residents. The team contained specialists in various areas of practice but, as a team, offered integrated, comprehensive services.

In the context of a more fragmented American urban service system, the Iowa Patch Project integrated staff from five state or local programs—Iowa Human Services (four child-protection social workers), Juvenile Court Services (a probation officer), City Housing inspector, County Homemaker Services, and a community center—into a multiagency team located conveniently within the neighborhood. The idea was to take advantage of some decategorization of funding streams in order to offer more integrated and responsive services on the ground.

The team started with the recognition that most helping in communities is nonprofessional, involving extended family, friends and neighbors, churches and informal networks, schools and voluntary associations, beauty parlors and natural helping figures, and informal groups and systems. The task of social work, they concluded, was to identify who else was involved and close to the situation, to enable them to tap into their own knowledge of the situation and resources in order to interrupt problem-perpetuating patterns of relationship. Such an approach requires decentering both the service system and the professional-client relationship. It depends on teamwork among the patch members and the residents of the neighborhood.

The shift in practice—from case-by-case work to a shared workload, from crisis response to providing a little help when needed at an earlier stage, from professional responsibility for solutions to sharing responsibility among those involved and interweaving formal and informal helping— is best illustrated by an example. On visiting a house to inspect for code violations, the housing inspector (who despite her lack of any social-work education was one of the first to grasp the patch concept) found some frayed electrical wiring. In the past this would have been the extent of her professional concern. But she also noticed a single mother, new to the neighborhood, with several children and only one piece of furniture, a sofa. She reported this to the team, which sent out an MSW practicum student and a child-protective services (CPS) worker to talk to the woman. They put her in touch with a local church which set her up with needed furniture, and they invited her to join a moms' group that the team had initiated. Thanks to "a little help when needed," what might have become in a few months a formal case of child neglect never became an official case at all.[7]

Responding in this way depended on the role flexibility and shared work of the team members and their proactive approach. (Normally CPS would target only more serious cases where bruises were evident or a child had run away or committed a serious offense.) The team's response to this situation depended on their prior work in the neighborhood. They were able to involve the church because they had already built relationships with the churches in the neighborhood. The moms' group had developed out of a tae kwon do class offered free to local kids by the team's probation officer. Moms would hang around during the class and chat with each other despite their own isolation or shyness, and a regular moms' group formed naturally and continued under its own steam.

Family Group Conferencing

As an alternative to honor killings and vendettas between families, some form of restorative-justice practice seems to have been universal across time, place, and cultures prior to the development of the modern state, as a way of confronting and correcting injustices and making things right.[8] Of the many adaptations across the world in the context of a bureaucratic-professional state, I want to focus briefly on the use of the Family Group Conference (FGC) in New Zealand and Hawaii.

The Maori *whanau hui* and the Hawaiian *ho'oponopono* are surviving indigenous practices of family group meetings. In both New Zealand and Hawaii, the state's child-welfare system has drawn on (but not supplanted) this experience to develop a hybrid process that is traditional and modern, formal and informal, to address cases of child abuse and neglect among the whole population, indigenous and other. These processes are the FGC in New Zealand and the 'Ohana Conference in Hawaii. The professional practice in both cases is to plan for and conduct a meeting of the extended family group (*whanau*, *'ohana*) to address concerns about children's safety and to come up with a plan to ensure it. Meetings vary but typically include introductions, information sharing, private family time, and a decision about the plan, how to monitor it, follow up, and reconvene as needed. Professionals involved, such as conference coordinators, social workers, school counselors, and therapists, share their knowledge of the situation and answer questions. Then they leave the family alone to discuss the situation and formulate their own plan. That plan, which may involve extended family, community, and agency resources, is normally accepted after some clarification and negotiation. Families are usually far more creative in generating options and identifying family and community resources than social workers are.

The relation of family and community to state is one which John Braithwaite describes, by analogy to regulating business, as "responsive regulation," and which Susan Chandler and I call "state-enforced family self-regulation."[9] In either case, the state does not abdicate responsibility for the "bottom line" (child safety in this case) and retains its full coercive power in the background, while widening the circle of responsibility for finding and implementing solutions and aiming to keep family self-governance and empowerment in the foreground.

Building Community

These examples mark a shift in professional-client relationships. Both professionals and families bring knowledge and expertise to the task at hand. And rather than substituting for the more proximate knowledge of local people, the professional task involves restraining oneself from imposing plans, solutions, or ultimatums (do this if you want your children back!).

In these examples, outside helpers enable those directly involved in the situation to tap into their own wisdom, knowledge, resources, creativity, and initiative. They bring professional knowledge and expertise to bear, but at the same time rest on the assumption, as Gale Burford and Joe Hudson put it, that "lasting solutions to problems are ones that grow out of, or can fit with, the knowledge, experiences, and desires of the people most affected."[10]

These practices fundamentally alter the relationship of professionals to the families and communities they serve. They both de-emphasize that relationship and also widen the circle of responsibility and decision making to include those whose relationship to the families and community is based not on professionalism but on caring and kinship.

In the case of child protection, the state's statutory responsibility for child safety remains. The key shift in practice and legislation is from professional-dominated practice resting on a model of regulatory formalism to a process for decision making and planning that mobilizes and empowers children's kin and community. It does not replace the formal processes of the court system, but—and this is surely the advantage of this kind of social practice—it enables both formal and informal care and control to enrich and constrain each other.

All three cases involve two basic changes in ways of doing business. One is a change of relation between professional and client. The other is a widening of the circle of responsibility so that the professional-client relationship is no longer at the center of the helping process, but is instead a part (though still an indispensable part) of a larger system of both formal and informal elements.

In each case, the professional intervention meets particular needs and builds community. But these processes are generally understood without reference to the virtue of social justice as discussed in this book.

The Grameen Bank approach to microcredit is discussed in terms of social capital[11]—trust, norms of reciprocity, and networks—that is, in terms of the forms of social organization the program develops.[12]

The patch approach is often described in terms of the shift in practice it requires, to what has been called "partnership practice" or "empowerment practice," or in terms of the changes in service system, from crisis driven to prevention oriented, from fragmented to integrated.

FGC came to be viewed as part of the larger field of the theory and practice of restorative justice. It is about making things right, repairing harm, restoring community. It requires both restorative processes and restorative values. Braithwaite added the important element of responsive regulation, so as to incorporate the formal regulatory element into restorative practices when the state becomes involved. He drew on his experience in business regulation, where the response of the regulated business (a nursing home, say, or an insurance company or a nuclear power station), not the seriousness of the violation, defines the response of the regulatory body. Is the business both able and willing to come into compliance?

A similar approach prevails with accreditation of professional programs like those in social-work education. In areas like youth justice and child protection, the regulatory body (e.g., child-protective services) can see its task as closer to that of an accrediting body, helping the family meet standards and come into compliance, rather than that of a rescue operation or an emergency surgery, performing a "parentectomy" for the children. Except as a last resort, the aim is not the termination of parental rights (the equivalent to revocation of a license to do business or loss of accreditation). As with businesses and educational programs, the regulatory body requires that standards be met and that the family come into compliance. Seen from this perspective, the regulator does not dictate exactly how this must happen, becoming the boss of the family. Rather the government enforces the self-regulation of families, as it does of businesses.

In child protection, the coercive power of the state still lies in the background of even the most empowering or partnership-oriented professional practice. But coercion, which cannot be abdicated or wished away and of which parents are well aware, should remain as far in the background as possible. The empowerment of families and communities to protect their members by regulating themselves stays in the foreground as much as possible. Families are required to meet their responsibility to their children. The state's coercive power comes into play to the extent parents demonstrate their continued incapacity or unwillingness, notwithstanding the help of kin, community, and professional services, to regulate themselves and keep their children safe.

What Does Social Justice Add?

In these three examples, practitioners have developed practices with theories for what they were doing, but without explicit reference to the virtue of social justice. They refer to social capital, empowerment, restorative justice, or responsive regulation. But what does a social-justice perspective add? What new light does it cast on these practices?

In these examples, the aim is not to supplant the decision making, self-regulation, creativity, resourcefulness, or caring capacity of families, but to strengthen and support them. It is not to squeeze out the space between individual and state, but to make it more capacious and competent. In line with the principle of subsidiarity, higher-level institutions intervene (but only as necessary) to ensure the capacity of lower-level groups to carry out their moral obligations.

Resisting the bureaucratic-professional temptations to assert their control unnecessarily and to usurp the proper functions of subsidiary groups, practitioners act with social justice. They help individuals to join with networks of others to further the common good of their families and communities. In doing so, they mitigate those social injustices embedded in cultural patterns and social practices that weaken individuals' capacity to provide for and protect themselves and each other. Professionals' help strengthens subsidiary groups of civil society, not the state. This help requires and develops the virtue of social justice—the disposition, habits, skills, and knowledge for association and democracy—in those being helped as well as those helping.

These examples challenge the binary oppositions into which social-policy discussions tend to fall. Neither state provision nor leaving those in need bereft of help exhausts the alternatives. In Catholic social teaching, individualism and collectivism are seen not as alternatives but as twin evils, the one reinforcing the other as they squeeze the life out of civil society.[13] Providing professional help to people who are poor, weak, or oppressed does not have to create dependency and weaken personal responsibility. Professional help does not have to disempower, pace John McKnight, who shows in the famous example of a bereavement counselor how professional intervention isolates "clients" from circles of support provided by friends and neighbors who have nurtured the grieving for generations. In that example, the grief expert renders a competent community dependent on professional services.[14] My examples, on the other hand, show how professional help, even when it is legally mandated, can enable those served to join with others for the common good of family and community, tapping into and building their own cultural and personal resources.

A social-justice-as-virtue perspective also enables us to recover a focus on what used to be called, in social work, the professional use of self. The character of the social worker, not only her practice theories and methods of practice, shapes the quality of the client-practitioner relationship and so constitutes an important part of the helping process.[15]

The virtues work together, talk to, and require each other. Social justice orders the virtues to the common good. For the practitioner, acting with the virtue of social justice requires prudence, humility, courage, self-mastery (temperance), and other virtues that ensure "order in the soul." No amount of rules and regulations designed to constrain the bureaucratic-professional tendency to overreach can substitute for the practitioner's virtuous character, a formation of the heart.

The bureaucratic tendency to respond to crises and scandals—a child known to CPS who is left with his mother and subsequently is battered to death by a live-in boyfriend; a child removed from his family who is later abused in foster care—with tighter controls over practice carries a high price. It reduces the practitioner's room to maneuver, to exercise professional judgment, wisdom, and flexibility. Benestad reminds us of a neglected but consistent theme of all Catholic social teaching, namely, that a just society depends on virtuous citizens.[16] Rules and regulations are necessary in social work, for we are fallen, imperfect in character and judgment. But they cannot substitute for the virtues that good practice requires and develops. Social work is, in MacIntyre's use of the term, a virtue-driven profession.[17]

Similar considerations apply to those whom professional helpers aim to assist. Tighter control over families through rules, regulations, and ultimatums cannot adequately substitute for a culture and community that support and build in individuals the virtues they need to meet their moral obligations to their families.

Empowerment, Coercion, and the Regulatory Pyramid

FGC merits particular study because it addresses most directly the challenge of exercising social justice while carrying out a regulatory process that has a strong coercive aspect. At the apex of the regulatory process sits the prospect of the permanent removal of children from their parents and the termination of parental rights. The process recognizes the family's potential to be a site of tyranny but also sees the limits of even the most benevolent state's capacity to run families or rear children. Both formal and informal systems have advantages and dangers. The legally mandated court system can be rigid, emphasizing the harm done with less attention to setting things right and more to the retributive punishment of wrongdoing. On the other hand, the informal system of care and control can be disproportionate in its response and careless of the rights of due process.

The regulatory pyramid presented by Braithwaite in the context of restorative justice enables us to understand the relation of two apparently contradictory but essential elements of FGC (and much social work)—empowerment and the context of social control or state coercion. The pyramid shows how, in the complex field of child welfare, combining the empowering aspects of FGC with the coercive power of the state is not necessarily a limitation or contradiction. Rather, empowerment and control are different but necessary and mutually enriching aspects of a dynamic model of state regulation of families to protect children.

Braithwaite contends that "restorative justice, deterrence and incapacitation are all limited and flawed theories of compliance."[18] Each needs to be understood and applied in a model that includes all three. In his figure entitled "Toward an Integration of Restorative, Deterrent and Incapacitative Justice," Braithwaite hierarchically orders these concepts and places restorative justice at the base of the pyramid, filling up most of the space.

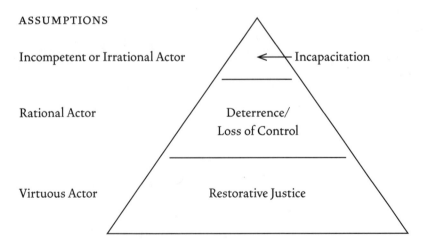

ASSUMPTIONS

Incompetent or Irrational Actor   ← Incapacitation

Rational Actor   Deterrence/ Loss of Control

Virtuous Actor   Restorative Justice

Figure 1. "Toward an Integration of Restorative, Deterrent and Incapacitative Justice" adapted from Braithwaite, *Restorative Justice*, 32.

This pyramid provides a dynamic model of governmental regulation (whether of a nursing home, a nuclear power station, an insurance company, or a family). By contrast, the formalist approach to regulation seeks to define in advance which problems or failures of compliance require what official responses, and then mandate them in regulations. In responsive regulation, however, there is a presumption, regardless of the seriousness of the offense or violation, in favor of starting official intervention at the base of the pyramid. Deterrence, in the middle of the pyramid, would mean for a business the threat of a fine, but for a family in the CPS system it would mean relative loss of control of their situation as the agency or court imposes solutions. Moving up the pyramid to deterrence and, ultimately, incapacitation, is a response not to the seriousness of the harm done but to the failure to elicit reform and repair at the base with restorative-justice processes. Of course, as with other violent crime—a shooting spree in progress, for example—an immediate move to incapacitation (at least temporary) may be necessary in cases of child abuse where there is imminent and continuing danger to the child.

The presumption in favor of starting at the base of the pyramid, Braithwaite argues, not only favors less coercive and costly state intervention where possible, but also makes more coercive measures more legitimate when escalation up the pyramid is necessary. This is important because "when regulation is seen as more legitimate, more procedurally fair, compliance with the law is more likely."[19]

By analogy, accreditation of a professional school, whether of law, medicine, nursing, or social work, is a process of required self-regulation through self-study and reform. The accrediting body—for example, the Council on Social Work Education in the case of U.S. baccalaureate and master of social work programs—has a range of escalating options to encourage schools to address concerns and come into compliance, culminating in the rarely used action of withdrawing or denying accredited status. This option is understood by all to be at the Council's disposal as a last resort, and site visitors and accreditation commissioners work in collegial partnership with schools with the shared aim of avoiding escalation up the regulatory pyramid.

Applying this model to a business such as a nursing home or insurance company, a regulator would begin to work with the firm's management at the base of the pyramid. Both management and regulator are aware that if the firm proves unable or unwilling to make the changes needed to come into compliance, the next level of regulation will be more coercive. The initial assumption is that the firm's management is a "virtuous actor," with the will and capacity to respond to the regulatory process by taking the steps needed to come into compliance. Regulator and regulated work together to prevent a more coercive regulatory response. At the next level, if management has no wish to cooperate with regulators, it is still assumed to be a "rational actor" who—faced with a fine or other penalty and the threat of being put out of business—will calculate that it is better to comply. At the highest level of the regulatory pyramid, management is assumed to be an "incompetent or irrational actor" who is unable or unwilling to comply and who therefore needs to be incapacitated by losing its license to operate.

Applying this model to FGC, we see conferencing as a restorative process at the base of the pyramid. FGC may be seen as a "process whereby all the parties with a stake in a particular offence come together to resolve collectively how to deal with the aftermath of the offence and its implications for the future."[20] Conferencing involves core values as well as processes that entail healing and setting right, moral learning, community and kin participation, respectful dialogue, responsibility, apology, and forgiveness. "So restorative justice is about restoring victims, restoring offenders, and restoring communities. . . . Stakeholder deliberation determines what restoration means in a specific context."[21]

The regulatory pyramid in the context of child welfare and FGC promotes social justice. It requires and develops in practitioners and family members the habits and skills of plural deliberation and working together to come up with solutions and to create, implement, and monitor plans to ensure children's safety.

The model assumes that the level of regulation, or the appropriate degree of participation and self-determination of the regulated entity, depends on the virtue of those managing it. As Figure 1 illustrates, at the base of the pyramid the actor (parent, management) is assumed to be virtuous, both able and wanting to come into compliance. At the next level, the actor is assumed to be rational, and so able to respond to the deterrent effects of penalties or loss of control of the situation to the state. At the apex of the pyramid, where incapacitation through license revocation or termination of parental rights is at issue, the actor is taken to be either irrational or incapable of compliance. The process itself responds to the virtues exercised by the subject of the regulation. As Braithwaite puts it in his essay "Families and the Republic":

> Responsive regulation is a way of thinking, not a definite list of prescriptions. Some pyramids may specify moving an adult out of the family rather than a child, for example, or moving an adult member of the extended family into the household to keep an eye out for the rights of the child. Indeed the superstructure of the pyramid can be redesigned by democratic deliberation at the base of the pyramid. So a family group conference might decide that there will be a trial period of a family member attending an anger management program. Further it might agree that if this fails and degrading tirades of anger persist, there will be an escalation of intervention that requires this person to move out and live with their uncle. Finally, if the tirades still come back to haunt the family and spill into violence, family members may resolve to escalate to lodging a formal assault complaint with the police. Signaling in advance that these escalations will occur if interventions at lower levels fail can be good protective practice. This is because it communicates to the actors who need to change their behavior that if change does not occur, this will not be tolerated. The pre-commitment to an escalated response can motivate change because of the message the pre-commitment gives that change is inexorable.
>
> Later, the conference may resolve that if the tirades have dissipated under the joint influence of the anger management program and living under the firm hand of the uncle, conditions may be set for a return to live with the family. Signaling a pre-commitment to de-escalate in advance can also be good practice because it offers a positive incentive for change. The idea of responsive regulation is that it is better to be at the base of the pyramid where democratic conversation does the regulatory work, but that if escalation is necessary the decision to escalate should always be open to revision, so de-escalation occurs.[22]

These models and processes depend on and promote the exercise of social justice both by professional actors and by adult family members. But underlying the whole pyramid discussed here is a much larger, less formal base in civil society. That is, FGC is itself a formal, legally mandated process resorted to when informal resources of care and control in families and neighborhoods, in the culture, helping networks, churches, and other intermediary groups and associations, are unable on their own to solve the problem or make things right. By far the bulk of care and control in society takes place beyond the direct reach of the state or professionals—above all in families, the basic building blocks of society, but also in the vast space of civil society that lies between individual and state. For social work and other fields involved professionally in care and control, it is a mistake to treat coercive and empowering aspects of practice as if they were incompatible or mutually exclusive. The key question on which so much else depends, in policy and practice, is the proper relation of formal to informal helping.

[CHAPTER 19]

From Charity to Justice?

It is our care of the helpless, our practice of loving kindness
that brands us in the eyes of many of our opponents.
'Only look,' they say, 'look how they love one another!'

—*Tertullian, Apology 39 [about 200], 1989*

And though I bestow all my goods to feed the poor,
and though I give my body to be burned,
and have not charity, it profiteth me nothing.

—*1 Cor 13:3 [KJV]*

TOLSTOY, WHO NOTWITHSTANDING HIS OWN WEIGHTY NOVELS
came to believe that the essence of art was the parable, calls one of his
later short stories "Where Love Is, God Is."[1] Written in 1885, the story
tells of Martin, an old cobbler who only recently and with the help of a
pilgrim and daily study of the gospel, had emerged from the despair and
self-preoccupation into which years of grief and loss had plunged him. He
works out of his small basement home, from the window of which he is
able to look out only on the feet of passersby, most of whom he recognizes
by their shoes. One night in his sleep, he hears a voice of a man telling him
to watch out for him the next day, as he will come by that window.

The next day, Martin works away while keeping an eye out for an unfa-
miliar pair of boots in the street above. In the course of the day he sees,

out in the snow-covered street, a hungry, broken-down old man, a mother in worn summer clothes struggling to keep her baby warm, and an old woman scolding her grandson who had stolen an apple. He invites each of them in to his modest room and gives them "food and comfort both for soul and body."[2]

I will not give away the conclusion—if only because the reader will already have figured it out—but suffice it to say that when Martin reaches for his gospel to continue reading where he had left off, the book opens at a different page, which he reads instead:

> "I was a hungered, and ye gave me meat: I was thirsty, and ye gave me drink: I was a stranger and ye took me in."
> And at the bottom of the page he read:
> "Inasmuch as ye did it unto one of these my brethren even these least, ye did it unto me."
> And Martin understood that his dream had come true; and that the Savior had really come to him that day, and he had welcomed him.[3]

Tolstoy here expresses his Christian understanding of charity, the understanding that nineteenth-century critics regarded either as sentimental and disorganized, or, like Scrooge at the start of *A Christmas Carol*, as a practice made redundant by tax-supported government programs. For professional social work, which grew out of the first critique and has come in more recent times to embrace something more like the second, the Christian virtue of charity has been something of an embarrassment. Today the core documents of the main professional bodies of social work or social-work education mention nothing of charity, but all accredited schools must account for social justice as a core value. Here I examine these developments in an attempt to clarify the relation between social justice and charity more widely. I do this with particular reference to social work, but similar considerations apply to other helping professions and voluntary activities.

Defining Charity

Social work is in principle a virtue-driven profession. It is a social practice that requires and develops certain virtues.[4] The character of a social worker is formed by the choices she makes—choices that form habits of the heart and mind,[5] and that constitute her as the person making each subsequent choice.[6] For Christians, the highest of these moral excellences is the theological or grace-dependent virtue of charity (*agape, caritas, love*), the Holy Spirit's greatest gift.[7]

Charity is a source of ambivalence for social workers, however. It is the very definition of God (1 Jn 4:8). It is generally regarded as the greatest virtue,[8] and it is at the heart of the Church's mission to the poor and oppressed, an organized social activity of the Church from the beginning. Yet it is something of an embarrassment for professional social work, which arose out of an attempt (mostly by Christians) to "organize" charity and replace its sentimentality by scientific practice. Unlike justice, charity appeals neither to social work's professional nor to its activist tendencies. And love, as charity is usually rendered in its theological context, does no better. Both its overtones of Hallmark-card sentiment and its religious roots make it something of an embarrassment to clinicians and activists alike. Moreover, in contrast to the virtue of justice, charity or love does not seem the kind of virtue that can be acquired and developed through secular professional education and practice. We see the difficulty if we consider how Christians have thought of charity as a virtue.

Charity as Queen of the Virtues

Charity also gets short shrift in the academic field of virtue ethics.[9] Yet for any understanding of the place of the virtues in social work, or especially in the formation of the Christian social worker, it cannot help but be central. Charity as *caritas* is inescapably a theological virtue. Like faith and hope, it is not part of the classical, pre-Christian understanding of the virtues. Christians from Paul on have understood it as a special gift of God's grace rather than as a natural process that can be understood in Aristotelian terms simply as a matter of training and habituation. Although love, charity, and *caritas* are used interchangeably among various New Testament translations, to avoid confusion and to be consistent with Michael Novak's discussion of *caritas* above, I will use *caritas* for the theological virtue (faith, hope, and *caritas*) and "charity" for the related but distinct practice and virtue of eleemosynary giving of time, treasure, or talent to those in need, traditionally called works of mercy.

Caritas has a special place among the virtues, even the theological ones. As Geach points out, following Aristotle, it would be vulgar to praise God as if he had certain human virtues. What would it mean, for example, to ascribe to the Divine Nature cardinal virtues such as temperance and courage or, for that matter, the theological virtues of faith and hope? But Love or *Caritas* is just what God is. God as Love is prior to and independent of any of his creations, and he does not need them to be Love. "God is Love," Geach argues, "because, and only because, the Three Persons eternally love each other."[10] As Michael Novak puts it above, in chapter five, in describing the principles of Catholic social teaching, "*Caritas* is the propelling drive in which Catholic social doctrine begins, toward which it aims, and under whose searing judgment it falls short or, at times, does well."

The Christian understanding of *caritas* as a human virtue stems from the complete self-giving of God as man and for humanity, and from Christ's call to us as creatures in his image to love him with all our hearts, souls, and minds . . . and, in consequence, our neighbors as ourselves (Mt 22:36). As Benedict XVI exhorts the Church's own charity workers: "The consciousness that, in Christ, God has given himself for us, even unto death, must inspire us to live no longer for ourselves but for him, and, with him, for others."[11]

Caritas, thus, is about self-giving, a love that, like God's, is superabundant rather than calculating. It is a matter of will, not simply emotion— for I can choose to love someone despite my emotions, for the love of God. But intensity and self-sacrifice are not enough to define the virtue of *caritas*. Intense commitment, as in the case of the most dedicated Nazis, may involve great self-sacrifice in the cause of evil. "Love can be thought of as a commitment of the will to the true good of another," suggests Deirdre McCloskey.[12] The word "true" implies that *caritas*, though superabundant, cannot be blind. *Caritas* is first and foremost the friendship of human beings for God, to which God invites us. The "love for God above all and love for neighbor because of God is the most important virtue of the Christian life."[13]

Origins of Christian Charity

Caritas, like justice, is not just a quality or abiding state of the individual character; it also finds expression in social activities and arrangements. *Caritas* as a virtue, and still more as definition of God, cannot be reduced to the altruistic practice, which we currently describe by the term "charity" and which is too readily associated, not with poor cobblers but with upper-middle-class women and clergy in the nineteenth century. Charity is the practice of providing relief for those in poverty. The focus on those in need distinguishes charity from the wider practice of philanthropy that includes giving to scientific research, universities, opera and symphony organizations, and museums. Still, charity as activity focused on the poor and vulnerable may or may not be infused with the Christian virtue of *caritas*, as selfless self-giving out of friendship for God and neighbor.

Nevertheless, charity was from the Church's beginnings an organized ecclesial activity. Christians' giving of their own time, treasure, and talent to aid those who were sick, in prison, poor, homeless, and strangers or outcasts rested on a new social ethic that sharply differentiated the Christian revolution's norms from those of the prevailing pagan world.[14] Charity as a Christian practice therefore took on a different form and rested on different relations of love among providers, recipients, and God.[15]

The historical sociologist Rodney Stark has shown how different the Christian response to the great plagues of the late Roman Empire in the second and third centuries was from that of the pagans.[16] That difference, he argues, was of immense importance for the rapid growth of the Church. Like David Bentley Hart in *Atheist Delusions*, Stark emphasizes the revolutionary impact of Christian doctrine in the ancient pagan world in which it took root.[17] He shows the importance of that doctrine, and especially the centrality of a God of Love who held individuals accountable for their love, in enabling Christianity to thrive and grow rapidly at the expense of traditional pagan religion.

In both theological and practical terms, the second- and third-century plagues overwhelmed the resources of the pagan tradition. The pagan gods required placatory sacrifices but did not love humanity or expect humans to love one another. The pagan response, as described by both pagan and Christian writers, was to flee for the hills, to avoid all contact with families where a member had been infected. The sick and dying were abandoned without nursing care—even food and water—or religious consolation, and they died at an enormously high rate. Something like a third of the empire's population and two-thirds of the population of the city of Alexandria were wiped out in the first plague, which broke out in 165 A.D.[18] The great pagan physician Galen abandoned Rome for a country estate in Asia Minor until the epidemic was over.

The Christian response was different. As Dionysius, bishop of Alexandria, and Cyprian, bishop of Carthage, explained, the plague was a time of terror for the pagans, who had no loving God and no hope of eternal life with God. Christianity offered explanation, comfort, and a prescription for action. The Christians did not abandon their sick, and they nursed pagans too as they could. Many sacrificed their own lives to care for others.

This contrast between pagan and Christian charity was clear even to those most hostile to Christianity, like the apostate emperor Julian, who wrote, "The impious Galileans [i.e., Christians] support not only their poor, but ours as well, everyone can see that our people lack aid from us."[19] Julian made energetic efforts to organize the pagan priests to emulate the Christians and develop their own charitable activities.[20]

All this points to the revolutionary character and depth of the Christian commitment to a new social ethic. Today it takes an effort of historical imagination to appreciate the power of this new morality in those first centuries of the Church's history. Christ's teaching of the equal worth and dignity of the human person as *imago Dei*—eventually to be adopted in secular form as a core social-work value—had a force not yet moderated by centuries of familiarity. Both pagan and Christian writers recognized that love and organized charity were central duties of Christian faith, not only in its scriptures but also in the everyday practice of the Church and its members.

The Christian understanding of the relation of religion to the virtues was fundamentally different from that of the pagan world. In emulating Christian charitable work, which he saw as the religion's one admirable feature, Julian tried to root his new pagan charity in Hellenistic rather than Judeo-Christian tradition. But that pagan culture lacked the moral resources for the social ethic of love that was, by contrast, so central to the Christian faith.[21]

In the context of what Gibbon, himself no admirer of the Christians, described as a pagan "religion which was destitute of theological principles, of moral precepts, and of ecclesiastical discipline," Julian achieved what could only be a superficial and ineffectual imitation of Christian charity.[22] Christianity, however, was rooted in a very different Jewish tradition in which, because God loves humanity, we cannot please God unless we love one another. This thought was—with the possible, partial exception of *xenia*, the Greek concept of hospitality toward strangers—alien to pagan ideas of the relations between human and divine.[23] Mercy—and so works of mercy like helping widows, orphans, the impoverished and downtrodden—was, in the eyes of the Greek philosophers and their Roman followers, not a virtue but a character defect.[24] Some moderns, like Nietzsche or Ayn Rand, who were nostalgic for paganism and contemptuous of the Christian social ethic, revived this ancient view.

Christian and Secular Charity Today

Christian charity was important to the growth of the Church and continues to be at its heart. Christians have not always behaved as well in subsequent plagues as they did in those first centuries. But we find in every century examples of heroic self-giving, such as that exemplified by Saint Damien of Molokai in nineteenth-century Hawaii.[25] A missionary from Belgium, Father Damien de Veuster (1840–89) asked his bishop in Honolulu for permission to serve the leper colony to which many of his parishioners were being sent. Men, women, and children who had contracted the disfiguring and debilitating disease of leprosy (Hansen's disease) were quarantined on a remote, isolated part of the island of Molokai. Like those third-century Christians who nursed the plague-stricken, Father Damien tended and ministered to the sick, heedless of the danger to himself, until eventually he contracted and died of the disease.

Or consider in our own day the men and women of Christian religious communities who serve the people of South Sudan, at great risk to themselves.[26] Much charitable activity is organized through dioceses and parishes—AIDS apostolates, prison ministries, food pantries, and the like, as well as in the form of contributions to larger efforts like Catholic Charities, Catholic Relief Services, Mother Teresa's Missionaries of Charity, and other charitable activities of all kinds of Christian communions across the globe.

From its earliest days, the Church understood charity as one of its essential organized activities, along with administering the sacraments and proclaiming the Word.[27] Charity was the responsibility of each individual member and of the entire ecclesial community at every level. From the original group of seven deacons, the *diakonia*, the well-ordered love of neighbor has been understood as involving both concrete and spiritual service, corporal and spiritual works of mercy.[28] Through its institutions and individuals, saints and sinners alike, the Church has been engaged in helping the poor and downtrodden. It is a record that extends through the work of deacons, monasteries, dioceses, and parishes, to the social-service organizations of the nineteenth and twentieth centuries and the development of modern social work.

Professionalizing Charity

Social work emerged as a profession out of the Charity Organization Societies (COS) in the late nineteenth and early twentieth centuries. It was an effort to adopt "scientific charity" in place of the disorganized efforts of the "sentimental" givers of alms. Social workers, like scientists in the same period, became professionals, and also like them, distanced themselves from amateurs and from their long historical association with the Church.[29] The COS movement aimed to replace "sentimental" with scientific, organized charity and to bring back personal concern and friendship to the relation of giver and receiver in charity. In a world where charity had become either a formal, impersonal, and demoralizing system of public poor relief supported by taxation, or else casual and random handouts, the COS aimed to bring the ordered love that Christian charity entails, charity infused with *caritas*.

The various existing societies for giving aid to the poor were uncoordinated, readily abused, and lacked ongoing help based on a real understanding of the specific needs of the poor families involved. It was disorganized charity. The COS offered individualized assistance to the poor "client" (COS leader and social-work pioneer Mary Richmond's term). They provided clinical assessment or social diagnosis, case conferencing, and intervention in the form of "friendly visiting" (later "social casework"). They conducted research and coordinated charitable giving in the community (from which the community chest and eventually the United Way evolved).

How did professionalization change approaches to helping those who were poor and downtrodden? Scientific charity required a more thoughtful, data-based, organized approach to helping. It recognized the Christian duty of charity, personal caring, and neighborly concern for the person and family, including subjective as well as material needs.[30]

But in growing industrial cities of the late nineteenth and early twentieth centuries, neighborliness of the affluent and the poor could not arise organically as part of a network of relationships in a shared neighborhood. The large social and, increasingly, physical distance between friendly visitor and client prevented ordinary neighborliness and rendered their relationship awkward and uncomfortable. The friendly visitors, forerunners of the professional social worker, were typically women of the business and professional classes seeking, as volunteers under auspices of the Charity Organization Societies, to help the poor by offering them, in the slogan of the COS, "not alms but a friend." It was not the friendship of an actual neighbor whom you could ask for a cup of sugar without fear of being refused and being offered instead—as the COS's "friendly visitors" were wont to do—advice on managing the family budget.[31]

Charity means friendship, but friendship implies a degree of equality between the friends.[32] Love between God and humans is possible only because of God's "condescension," but condescension among humans is not the stuff of friendship and so is incompatible with the virtue of *caritas* or Christian charity.

This is a paradox in that condescension in its sublunary form is precisely what charitable activity came to involve. It was the gratuitous, arbitrary activity of the business and professional classes and the clergy, often marked by motives other than self-giving love and commitment to the true good of the other—motives involving social status or display or the complacent self-satisfaction of the giver. Such activity by definition is not Christian charity or *caritas*, though called by the same name. Rather, it is the kind of activity of which Paul speaks when he says that without charity, the giver neither counts as nor gains anything.[33]

Professionalism offered a solution to this awkwardness, a way of understanding the helping relationship as more akin to that of lawyer and client than that of Good Samaritan and person in need of help.[34] Professionalism required a body of knowledge, formal organization, and a code of ethics. It was a path to ensuring quality of service. If not yet an evidence-based practice, at least it offered the informed and educated judgment of a competent professional. It was also a path to the legal recognition, improved status, and funding of professional social workers.

No one would belittle the importance of knowledge and competence on the part of those whose noble aim, in the words of the social-work code of ethics, is to "enhance human well-being and help meet the basic human needs of all people, with particular attention to the needs and empowerment of people who are vulnerable, oppressed, and living in poverty."[35] The point, rather, is that the striving for a more scientific, professional approach to helping carried with it the potential failure of the challenge of Christian charity, out of which the effort arose in the first place. The full impact of secularization in social work would not be felt for decades, when the more education a social worker had, the greater the distance between her beliefs and those of her clients, not least in matters of faith. The gap is probably most apparent in social-work education, where in public or other secular universities and colleges, students who share the evangelical Christian beliefs of the profession's founders report feeling isolation and the scorn of their professors.[36]

Professionalization of charity in the form of social work required a specific body of knowledge, skills, and values, a code of ethics, and the quest for licensure by the state. All of this required a distancing from the very word "charity," whether meaning poor-relief, sentimental giving, or even organized charity.

If the new professionals came to cringe at the term "charity," charity's reputation also suffered precisely from the attempt to organize it and make it more scientific and professional. As the poet John Boyle O'Reilly put it in 1886:

> The organized charity, scrimp'd and iced,
> In the name of a cautious, statistical Christ.[37]

Charity thus came under fire from all sides. Socialists criticized it for promoting an alternative to their own class struggle for a different order. The settlement houses were seen as competitors with the Socialist Party in Chicago and elsewhere. Social casework claimed, in the words of the London COS, to be "the only real antidote to Bolshevism,"[38] and Marxists criticized it accordingly. The supporters of "sentimental charity" criticized the organized kind for going cold and scientific. And as social workers became professionalized, they distanced themselves from the very term "charity," viewing it as an embarrassment. As they became activists for social change, they absorbed, in varying degrees, the socialist and Marxist critiques.

Charity and Justice

One of the challenges to charity as an organized activity of the Church has come from those, especially Marxists and Rawlsian liberals, who object to charity precisely as the gratuitous self-giving for the benefit of another in need of help. Works of charity, whether as almsgiving or personal service, are seen as intrinsically arbitrary, being free gifts to which the recipient has no specific or legal claim.

Among Christian writers, there is a range of approaches to the question. In *Rerum Novarum*, Leo XIII emphasizes almsgiving as charity not justice, while also describing it as a Christian duty. He says of almsgiving,

It is a duty, not of justice (save in extreme cases), but of Christian charity—a duty not enforced by human law. But the laws and judgments of men must yield place to the laws and judgments of Christ the true God, who in many ways urges on His followers the practice of almsgiving—"It is more blessed to give than to receive"; and who will count a kindness done or refused to the poor as done or refused to Himself—"As long as you did it to one of My least brethren you did it to Me." To sum up, then, what has been said: Whoever has received from the divine bounty a large share of temporal blessings, whether they be external and material, or gifts of the mind, has received them for the purpose of using them for the perfecting of his own nature, and, at the same time, that he may employ them, as the steward of God's providence, for the benefit of others.[39]

Nicholas Wolterstorff, on the other hand, offers a strong biblical argument for an emphasis on justice—and hence, he concludes, on individual rights as claims on the state—precisely at the expense of charity as Christians have traditionally understood it.[40] His work increasingly takes on the Christian tradition of the virtues in the name of rights and justice.[41] He thus provides a scholarly and biblical defense of a social-democratic theory of rights and social welfare, a theory that in practice may tend to crowd out charitable giving with government programs.[42]

In "Justice, Not Charity," Wolterstorff criticizes charity for its focus on the giver rather than the receiver: "If I see myself as treating you with love, charity, benevolence, rather than with justice, it is not unlikely that I will also think of myself as morally superior, and will expect gratitude for my generosity. It happens all the time."[43] From this "justice, not charity" perspective, charity is intrinsically demeaning. The need to which charity responds, at the same time, exists because society is unjustly ordered. The social-work task, then, is one of justice, not charity. It is to work for a justly ordered society that ensures that all citizens, especially the most vulnerable, receive adequate shelter, clothing, food, and income as a matter of right, not charity.

This approach treats justice and charity as mutually exclusive. Wolterstorff dispenses with the virtue as well as the practice of charity by substituting, in the name of justice, a focus on provision by the state. Rights-based claims on the state are more just and obviate the arbitrariness and condescension of charity.

When we see the world in terms of "justice, not charity," it is easy to reduce both terms to their material expressions, the provision of cash or services. The issue then becomes one of whether every citizen has the right to a minimum standard of economic security, education, health, or housing assured to him or her by the state as a matter of right, not charity. The welfare state is framed in just such terms. But the more holistic approach to alleviating poverty advanced by many international development experts such as Muhammad Yunus or Hernando de Soto sees that those in dire poverty do not need material resources alone. Transfers of resources—as in protection and subsidy of agriculture in Europe or North America, and the dumping of resulting surpluses in the form of aid on the poor of less-developed countries—can destroy local initiative and markets, create dependency, and trap whole communities in mean poverty. Justice for the poor involves not so much large-scale redistribution of resources from the affluent to the poor, but the removal of obstacles that prevent the poor from deploying their own God-given creative energy.

The poor of the Third World offer abundant evidence of their capacity for imaginative initiative, entrepreneurial spirit, and absorbing productive knowledge—yet are still blocked from access to wider markets and growth. The poor in most of the world are trapped in poverty because they are deprived of two essential rights that justice requires: private property and the rule of law. Without secure property rights and enforceable contracts, they remain at the mercy of the rich and powerful. Witness cities like Buenos Aires and Nairobi, where the wealthy live close to the desperately poor while excluding them from full participation in a free society.

Rodney Stark points to the extraordinary creativity and economic initiative of mere "commoners" in northern China in the late tenth century.[44] They built a thriving iron industry, producing as much as 35,000 tons a year by 1018, and developed markets and uses for the iron to improve agriculture and raise living standards. What happened, Stark explains, is that the Mandarins at the imperial court concluded that the new industrial wealth undermined Confucian values such as social harmony and stability. How? Because it implicitly challenged the view that commoners should be content with their state and not seek after riches. "So, they declared a state monopoly on iron and seized everything."[45]

Justice for the poor requires more than the removal of government red tape and onerous restrictions that create insurmountable barriers to building small businesses. It also requires secure private property rights and the rule of law for the poor. Only if the poor are free from fear of the loss of land, property, and the fruits of their enterprise will the initiative, creativity, and risk taking through which families and communities raise themselves out of poverty seem like a more fruitful option than that of the servant who was afraid and buried his talent in the ground (Mt 25:25).

Are the days of charity, loving personal concern, and direct voluntary helping now over? Does social justice supersede charity and render it obsolete? In the following chapter, drawing on Benedict XVI's encyclical on *caritas* and the role of the Church's own charitable workers, I show why these questions must receive a negative answer, and why *caritas* as love and its expression in charity remain indispensable to each other and to all of us.

CHAPTER 20

Charity Needs *Caritas*—
So Does Social Justice

WHETHER AS CASUAL ALMSGIVING, TAX-SUPPORTED POOR relief, or proto–social work, charity is itself often uncharitable. Karl Jaspers captured this oxymoronic paradox in the phrase "charity without love,"[1] which points to a recognizable reality and problem. Such charity clearly is not an expression of *caritas*, the Christian theological virtue, which is not self-regarding or morally superior in attitude, but involves a commitment of the will to the true good of another.

Efforts to help those who are poor and downtrodden may fall short of the virtue of *caritas* in several ways. One involves precisely an overemphasis on the giver—on good intentions and spiritual, social, or psychological benefits rather than on the outcomes for those helped.[2] *Caritas* requires by definition willing the true good of the other as other and so also requires, in helping activities, a focus on what actually helps. It requires the cardinal virtue of practical judgment or prudence to discipline and direct the good intentions. This is the legitimate concern raised by the proponents of "scientific charity" in the nineteenth century, as well as today, by advocates of a more empowering, partnership-oriented approach to charity, such as the asset-based approach to community development.[3]

Charity and Social Justice

What, then, is the relation of charity as love (*caritas*), the highest of all the virtues, to the practice of charity as works of mercy and to the virtue of social justice? In the tradition of Christian ethics, both charity and justice are virtues and, as such, are mutually reinforcing if not necessary to each other. They are virtues of the individual in community, and both find expression in social activities and arrangements. Justice is the virtue or habit of giving others their due, which requires judgments about what is due and what social arrangements can best secure it. Charity was from the Church's beginnings both the central virtue of the faith and expressed in an organized ministry to the poor and downtrodden, one involving both material and spiritual assistance.

When one considers it formally, as Aquinas does, justice is the highest of the moral virtues because it is ordered to the common good. But *caritas* is the highest of all the virtues, that without which the others are worthless. This is because *caritas* is the friendship based on God's communication of his own happiness to us.[4] "The soul lives through *caritas*, which lives through God, who is the life of the soul."[5]

Charity (as distinct from *caritas*) and social justice are best understood as forms or subvirtues of the cardinal virtue of justice. Both deal with what we owe others. Christian charity, though gratuitous and superabundant, unlike a legal claim, is nevertheless an absolute obligation on the giver. Jesus makes this clear, for example, in the Great Assize in which the sheep and goats are judged and separated, or in the parable of the rich man and the beggar Lazarus at his gate.[6] In both cases, failing in one's charitable duty has the direst possible consequences. Though not a legal obligation, charity is what we owe others in need and is thus a matter of justice.

Social justice is more obviously a kind of justice. It directs the virtues to giving others their due, inclining individuals to join with others to achieve a purpose that serves the common good. We practice and promote it in working to overcome social injustices inherent in the legal code, cultural institutions, the tenor of public life, or elsewhere in the structures of society that frustrate our ability to fulfill our moral obligations.[7]

The virtues touch and talk to each other. This aspect of social justice has been neglected in modern use. In contrast, Aquinas understood legal or general justice as directing all the virtues to the common good as *caritas* directs all the virtues to the Divine good. This is partly a matter of order in the soul. That is, acting with social justice requires acting with knowledge, skill, and such virtues as prudence, self-mastery or temperance, and courage.

When a virtue becomes isolated from other virtues and overdeveloped or specialized in an extreme way, it is no longer a virtue but a vice. This is clear enough in a case like courage, which in the absence of prudence, temperance, or justice, becomes recklessness that devalues life. Such distortion makes "charity without love" a possibility, when it becomes routinized, over-professionalized, or lacking in personal concern. It is what made the COS insist on the need for friendship—friendly visiting, not alms but a friend—but made it prone to deformation when *caritas* seemed to dissipate so that the COS itself was accused of charity without *caritas*. Social justice also may become separated from the other virtues, especially *caritas*, and thus eventually cease to be a virtue at all. When it becomes a utopian ideal to be enforced and regulated by the state, it also becomes deformed and unjust, nourished by the vices of envy and resentment.

Taking up the justice-based argument against charity, Benedict XVI acknowledges its force as put forward by Marxism, but emphasizes the intimate relations among justice, charity, and love.[8] He rejects the notion that any political order, no matter how just, will ever eliminate the need for charity. "Love—caritas—will always prove necessary even in the most just society," he writes. "There is no ordering of the State so just that it will eliminate the need for the service of love."[9] Such a utopian program of rendering charity unnecessary leads in practice to the hypertrophy of the bureaucratic state, stifling those charitable impulses that find their natural expression in the structures—of family, neighborhood, church, and voluntary association—that mediate between individual and state.[10] As Benedict puts it, "The state which would provide everything, absorbing everything into itself, would ultimately become a mere bureaucracy incapable of guaranteeing the very thing the suffering person—any person— needs: namely, loving personal concern."[11]

Benedict argues that for those who work in the Church's charitable agencies, professional competence and effectiveness are necessary, but not sufficient. "Charity workers need a 'formation of the heart': They need to be led to that encounter with God in Christ which awakens their love and opens their spirits to others."[12] He has a particular concern that the Church's own professional social workers may be infected with ideologies that deride charity as a stopgap, a substitute for justice that serves the status quo. This tendency is strong even among social workers whose own jobs depend on charitable support of their agency. "What we have" in such ideologies, Benedict states, "is really an inhuman philosophy. People of the present are sacrificed to the moloch of the future.... One does not make the world more human by refusing to act humanely here and now."[13] Such refusal is neither charitable nor just.

Love requires equanimity, restraint in the face of the temptation to take control of the lives of others. Benedict makes this point in noting the limits of the changes professionals themselves can effect. Social workers have a professional tendency toward what Thomas Sowell calls an unconstrained vision of what they can achieve, whether through counseling or social policy. They suffer from, in Roger Scruton's term, "unscrupulous optimism."[14] They tend to assume responsibility for solving social problems in a way that reflects an exaggerated sense of the power they can or should have over the lives of others. Benedict, however, points out that we "are only instruments in the Lord's hands; and this knowledge frees us from the presumption of thinking that we alone are responsible for building a better world. In all humility we will entrust the rest to the Lord."[15]

Benedict addresses himself specifically to the "charity workers" who carry out professionally the Church's ministry of *diakonia*. He assumes a shared purpose between the Church's "ecclesial charity," which is integral to its very being, and the professionals employed in carrying it out. He warns rightly (not least in light of the experience of liberation theology) of the dangers of activism in the name of parties and ideologies that are alien to that shared purpose.

How does all this relate to the profession of social work, the secular inheritor of scientific charity? The profession includes many who have chosen this field of relatively low pay and prestige precisely because of their Christian understanding and commitment to serving the needs of the poor and downtrodden. It also includes many who are nonreligious and perhaps even hostile to the Church.

Love among the Ruins: A Romance of the Near Future

This final heading draws from the evocative title of Evelyn Waugh's 1953 dystopian novella of the welfare state, which itself prompts consideration of what it means to be both a good helper and a faithful Christian. Where does this tension between the theological virtue of love (*caritas*, *agape*) and the language of justice, individual rights, and the state leave the professional social or charitable worker who is also a faithful Christian? These issues touch on the central question for social work and social welfare, the relation of formal to informal care and control. How does professional caring relate to personal caring on the one hand, and on the other to the caring capacities within families and communities?[16]

Ideological, political, and fiscal developments challenge professional social workers of faith as well as religious authorities. Archbishop Charles Chaput, for example, has described the archdiocese of Denver, of which he was then leader, as being under strong secularist threat.[17] Similar developments are occurring across the country, leading to the closing of high-quality Catholic adoption and foster-care services in Illinois, for example. Religious leaders are being pushed to define the limits of accommodation beyond which a Christian charity loses its soul and may as well drop its religious affiliation and become an offshoot of the bureaucratic-professional state.[18]

"Government cannot love," as Chaput says. "It has no soul and no heart. The greatest danger of the modern secularist state is this: In the name of humanity, under the banner of serving human needs and easing human suffering, it ultimately, ironically—and too often tragically—lacks humanity."[19] The secularist direction of law and policy is leading to a hypertrophy of the state and its bureaucratic-professional rigidities, all increasingly inhospitable to the Christian virtue of charity (*caritas*) as a total self-giving aimed at the good of the other.

Although "government cannot love," Saint Vincent de Paul in the seventeenth century, Damien in the nineteenth, Mother Teresa in the twentieth, and the early Christians in the plagues of the second and third centuries could and did. They offer models of love as a virtue of the Christian social worker. The question arises, then, of how best to preserve and cultivate in social workers the virtues of charity and *caritas*; and how to do this where the professionalizing, bureaucratizing, and secularizing of such work seem to render it all but impossible?

In his 2005 encyclical, *Deus Caritas Est—God is Love*, Pope Benedict offered some guidance for workers in the Church's own charitable agencies that applies to social workers in any setting. His remarks offer the necessary theological starting point of this all-important virtue.

As we talk of love, we recognize knowledge and competence as the sine qua non of professional social workers. Knowledge and competence are necessary, indeed, but not sufficient. Social workers also "need a 'formation of the heart.'"[20] The two—one a matter of knowledge and skill, the other of character—do not stand in opposition. As recent empirical research has reemphasized, the quality of the client-practitioner relationship, and so the character of the social worker, as distinct from the specific theories or methods she employs, is a key aspect of professional competence and effectiveness.[21] Speaking to the personnel who carry out the Church's charitable activity, and warning them against being diverted into a radical utopian activism in the name of justice, Benedict sees that, more than anything, they "must be persons moved by Christ's love, persons whose hearts Christ has conquered with his love, awakening in them a love of neighbor."[22]

The social worker whose character is formed in Christian love has, as a deep part of her character, a radical humility—which is necessary both to the virtue of love and to professional competence:

> My deep personal sharing in the needs and sufferings of others becomes a sharing of my very self with them: if my gift is not to prove a source of humiliation, I must give to others not only something that is my own, but my very self; I must be personally present in my gift.[23]

Benedict invokes here the radical humility of Christ on the Cross, which in Christian understanding redeemed us and constantly comes to our aid. In helping we also receive help, Benedict says—being able to help is no merit or achievement of our own. "This duty is a grace."[24]

Finally, we should highlight Benedict's emphasis on the importance of prayer "in the face of the activism and the growing secularism of many Christians engaged in charitable work."[25] The significance of prayer does not lie in Christian social workers' hope of changing God's mind about particular situations or the belief that prayer is more efficacious than, or a substitute for, legislative advocacy. Rather, a personal relation with God in a Christian's prayer life sustains love of neighbor and helps keep her from being drawn into ideologies and practices that replace love with hate, whether class or religious or ethnic hate. It also protects against burnout. Hope involves the virtue of patience, and faith leads practitioners to understand charity as participation through divine grace in God's love of the human person. In this way, hope and faith, the other theological virtues, give rise to and sustain the queen of virtues. All are central to the formation of Christians who seek to help the vulnerable, needy, and oppressed.

Social engagement is not an alternative or in opposition to a life committed to prayer, participation in the liturgical life of the Church, and love of God. As the experience of exemplars of charity like Mother Teresa, Dorothy Day, Saint Damien of Molokai, or the religious sisters of South Sudan indicates, love and service of God powers and sustains love and service of those most in need of care, "even these least."[26]

These saintly people committed themselves to the true good of the other as other, without sentimentalizing or romanticizing their work among the most poor and oppressed members of society. Mother Teresa and Dorothy Day both warned their enthusiastic young helpers that, as Day put it, the poor are ungrateful and they smell.[27] Their love was unconditional, expecting no return or personal gratification, and concrete in its practical expression. At the same time, they made no separation between their sacramental and spiritual lives on one hand and their practical work among the poor on the other. On the contrary, their spirituality and participation in the liturgical life of the Church powered and sustained their social engagement.

Day's diaries, *The Duty of Delight*, instructive as well as inspiring, are invaluable for social workers.[28] The book chronicles and reflects on a life of selfless love and commitment to social justice and is at the same time a great spiritual classic. It offers an incomparable account of how to integrate deep faith and the Christian virtue of love or charity into day-to-day practice. The diaries show that in the midst of the extraordinary challenges of leading and sustaining the Catholic Worker movement, Day herself was sustained by daily worship at Mass, the sacraments, and the Divine Office or liturgy of the hours (the Church's cycle of prayers, psalms, gospel readings, and meditations for each part of each day).

Day also drew nourishment for her work by reading and following the practice of great spiritual masters. Among these were two Jesuit priests, the order's founder, Saint Ignatius of Loyola (1491–1556), and Jean-Pierre de Cassaude (1675–1751), with their emphasis on the spirituality of the present moment and on equanimity—doing our part and leaving the rest to God.[29]

As Day drew consolation, energy, and encouragement from such spiritual sources, modern social workers also draw on Day's own diaries and other writings. Most social workers, of course, practice in agencies very different from the settings in which Day and the rest exercised the virtue of charity. Secularism, bureaucracy, and state funding do not conduce to a practice that is both professional and also rooted in a Christian charity that Tertullian, Bishops Cyprian and Dionysius, Saint Damien, or Mother Teresa might recognize. But as the Church reminds us, the call to be saints, the call to love God and neighbor, is for all, not only those recognized for their heroic virtue or martyrdom.[30] The "beacons of many generations" discussed here, like exemplars of the other virtues, help us understand what charity is and what it requires of us.[31] They show how loving, personal concern and effective helping require and build the other virtues of justice (especially social justice), prudence, and courage. They offer inspiration and guidance for growth in the virtue of charity as they challenge us to apply it consistently, in our personal and professional lives.

Social Justice: In the Vast Social Space between the Person and the State

IN THIS WHOLE INQUIRY WE HAVE COME ROUND AGAIN AND again to this thesis: *Social justice is first of all a virtue,* that is, *a habit* or *disposition* making it easier to perform certain social actions well, as if by second nature. In fact, Aristotle notes that a good test of how well a habit has become second nature is how one reacts when surprised and when an immediate response is called for. For there are times, not least in battle, when instantaneous action is essential, when a warrior has no time for hesitation. In a contemporary example, an enemy hurls a live grenade into a foxhole and one man instantly throws his body over it to protect his buddies. Such a man has been honing himself for bravery, to a keen edge.

Usually, we have seen, such a habit is learned through dogged repetition, in order to get control of one's passions. Sometimes one must practice again and again, with sheer determination, to get certain actions right, so that when summoned they are done quickly as well as right, and done so habitually—that is, done in the right way, at the right time, in the right spirit, reliably, and on the ready. Football players run through plays again and again, for months, to ready themselves for spontaneous action under varied circumstances. And George Washington, as we mentioned above in chapter two, took years to master his temper. When he at first failed to control it, he kept trying to do better. In these struggles, he often needed patience with himself—and persistence—until he got it right.

But some lucky humans seem to be born with gifts of social leadership, with an ability to inspire and direct others. Still others are born quite willing to follow good leaders and to cooperate easily with teammates, each one seeing what needs to be done and each adjusting without command to common purposes. Persons of such gifts help groups get things done quickly and effectively. They are precious collaborators.

Some people are born with certain social virtues, even social graces. They are natural team players. These are a joy to work with. A few others seem born to be, in all sorts of situations, a pain in the neck. Often such players need to be tolerated, and a shrewd leader looks for a special role, out of the way from others, to assign them. Every talent is useful somewhere.

Now, in social justice, the specific actions one needs to have a habit of doing well have two characteristics. The first is calling into being free associations and giving them direction, purpose, scope, and inner drive. The second is acting with others to improve the *common good* of families, a local neighborhood, a city, a whole nation, the whole world. Usually, this means "to improve the common good" in some *particular* aspect. It is rare to be able to improve the common good *in toto*, even in one small department of society. Yet even a little improvement often goes a long way. It gives hope for further improvements, one step at a time.

Social justice, then, is a *virtue*. It is a qualitative improvement in the character of a person. It adds to that person's social capital. It widens that person's range of action. It infuses a new energy into the social mass.

Moreover, social justice is the preeminent virtue of free societies. It is the inner energy that engenders free societies. It puts in place an alternative to statism and to "excessive" individualism (the two greatest worries of Popes Leo XIII and Pius XI).[1]

Some societies already have the social capital from which citizens know how to organize themselves for a multitude of social purposes. That social capital is constituted by good habits and dispositions already interiorized by many of its citizens. Where this social capital is missing, societies are demoralized, unable to stir themselves. Where it is present, societies show common will, drive, and adaptability to one another. People see what to do and start organizing right away to do it.

One favorite example of this is the response of Johnstown, Pennsylvania, within hours of the dam burst in 1889 that hit the trapped city with a cascading wall of water and debris higher than its homes. Some 600 more lives were lost in Johnstown during four hours that day than in all of Mississippi and Louisiana combined during Hurricane Katrina in 2005.

The next morning, Johnstown's leading citizens and crews of workmen got together at the flood's edge, elected an emergency government, designated certain standing structures as morgues, and sent all willing hands to dig dead bodies out of the wreckage. They also sent out word to others—not only in Johnstown but in the whole geographical area—to work feverishly to ship in 2,000 coffins. They fought off despair by beginning immediately to put up the most necessary shops, stores, and homes. The rubble piled up everywhere included train locomotives, giant trees, and smashed wooden houses, and lay thirty feet deep in the streets. The widespread habits of self-organization, insight into what to do next and in what order, and agreeable cooperation in dire need—such social capital, such a fund of social virtues—helped Johnstown to come back from three major floods: in 1889, 1936, and 1977.

Social justice, then, is the virtue that empowers individual persons (and whole peoples) to act for themselves, to exercise their inborn social creativity. This habit of building free associations is "the first law of democracy," according to Tocqueville. It is the social habit rooted in individuals and demanded by the "new things" (the *rerum novarum*) of the nineteenth and twentieth centuries. It is no wonder that this virtue could arise only late in human history, in the age of democracies, freely formed enterprises, free and independent unions, cooperatives, and social initiatives of all sorts (from town and village concerts to the worldwide Red Cross). In order for it to appear, there needed to be developed whole legions of joiners, organizers, and teams of willing volunteers to work together to achieve the social good—first in their own local, regional, and national communities, and then in the world as a whole.

Through the leadership of the popes, social justice slowly became a Christian alternative to atheist socialism and secular statism. The popes have insisted (while relying on the thinking of devoted public intellectuals of many faiths) that there is a humanism that rejects collectivism. The popes also remind intellectuals that there is a humanism which rejects a vicious form of individualism.

The vicious form of individualism, often enough visible both on the right and the left, loves the idea that there is no objective standard, only subjective truth, based upon the relativism of individual feelings and appetites. Some praise the denial of any truth except "my truth," that is, the subjective desires of each individual. They seem not to see how this vision atomizes them, and renders them naked against tyranny. They do not recognize that their relativism robs them of any intellectual defense against thugs and torturers. Any protest they might make is simply an expression of their own tastes. If there is no truth, there can be no injustice. If there is no truth, there can be no speaking truth to power. That is why tyrants and totalitarians are relativists, love relativism, and engorge themselves on it so rapidly and without resistance.

Relativism is an invisible gas that seeps into the soul's hunger for truth and its longing for justice, and renders them inert.

Some humans seem so terrified of being held accountable to anything beyond themselves that they cannot stomach the idea of God or truth or more-than-subjective reason. They do not want to be judged in any way, shape, or form. They do not grasp that to be human is to have the ability to judge—to judge true from false, good from evil, noble from ignoble. They expend huge efforts trying to convince themselves that to be a human is to be no more than a chimp or wolf or other animal. They boast of having ancestors who swung in trees. One can understand why some would convince themselves of this. But, as Alice von Hildebrand asked, why would anyone *boast* of it?

The fact is, no other species of animal but ours has banded together to build laboratories, universities, international institutions, worldwide commercial enterprises, bureaus of patents and copyrights, hospitals, orphanages, and schools for the poor. No other species seems to have social workers with high moral standards. In a word, the virtue of social justice teaches each generation to form associations, to be inventive, to be proactive, to move their society forward. That special virtue seems to be a main component of what gives humans special advantages over any other animal. Each human is personally responsible. Each is part of many communities.

We are lucky to live in an age when the virtue of social justice has captured the attention of the world. It is a virtue that was not well recognized in any age before our own. As an alternative to the immensely destructive, wasteful, anti-ecological collectivisms of the twentieth century, it is today the indispensable virtue. No society can be a free society without the widespread practice of social justice.

Bound professionally to work on the front lines, as it were, in places where social justice is barely or not at all practiced, social workers have come to recognize all too well, in the population at large, whole areas in which the lack of basic social virtues is apparent. Although social workers may not usually use the word "virtue," they do diagnose speedily enough its many absences.

The Power of Virtues in Social Work

A virtuous doctor is one who applies her knowledge and skills with such virtues as prudence, compassion and caring, courage, intellectual honesty, humility, and trustworthiness. Pellegrino and Thomasma have proposed such a list for the medical profession, and a similar list could be developed for the virtuous social worker, a list that would add equanimity and social justice as well as charity.[2] Social work, in MacIntyre's term, is a virtue-driven profession.[3] Its practice requires and develops such virtues.

Like medicine and law, social work as a profession serves many other goods important for human flourishing.[4] For social work, social justice is a key virtue. Viewing persons in their social environment, social workers practice and promote the virtue of joining with others to improve life. They further the common good at several levels from family to community, to nation, and beyond.

Nonetheless, as we found in the discussion of patch and Family Group Conferencing in chapter eighteen, even those practices most requiring and promoting the virtue of social justice are seldom discussed in terms of that virtue, or any virtue at all. Yet social work has been a virtue-based profession from its beginnings, and social justice from its beginnings has been a key virtue of its practitioners. There is certainly a temptation in social work to see the world either in individualist or in collectivist terms, emphasizing individual psychotherapy in isolation from family and community, on the one hand, or making ever larger demands on the state in the name of "social justice" on the other hand. Or both, as in demands for state-enforced claims against civil society.

At its best, though, social work is neither individualist nor collectivist. Never subordinating the individual to the collective (or vice versa), it emphasizes the scope for working with others involved in a social situation as often the best way to resolve or ameliorate it. Social justice is one of the most important of these social-work virtues, and it is essential for good practice. It informs and directs the other virtues to enable people to work with others to further the common good. One of the first questions a practitioner asks is "who else is involved?" Social workers do so explicitly in the patch approach to community-centered practice, in practices like Family Group Conferencing (FGC) that find their rationale in restorative justice, and in asset-based community development. Social workers commonly understand the practitioner-client relationship as *one* part of a larger ecosystem of relationships, involving family, neighbors, and key local helping figures, voluntary associations, churches, schools, as well as other formal and informal agencies of care and control. In poor and disorganized neighborhoods like the one in which the Iowa patch team worked, the informal helping systems may be weak and the formal intervention of state agents, police, and professional helpers, correspondingly strong. In the Iowa patch area in Cedar Rapids, there was little housing stability (residents came and went rather than putting down roots), many single mothers and small children, few fathers or men of any kind, few churches that had stayed in place as their parishioners had moved away, low employment and low work-force participation, and few voluntary associations or informal networks. It was a neighborhood with little social capital.

The social-work task in such circumstances is not to substitute professional expertise for the care and control missing from a community that lacks in norms, networks, and relations. It is both to work with those involved to address the immediate issue in a particular family (such as child neglect) and, in the very process of doing so, to find and strengthen the caring and self-regulating capacity of the family and community. It is to address those structures and systems, formal and informal, that frustrate the ability of those involved to fulfill their moral obligations and live virtuous lives. Society will not be just until individuals are virtuous—that is, until they habitually, reliably act well toward one another. Social, legal, and cultural structures and patterns may make it harder or easier to achieve that end. Social work at its best is particularly attuned to these connections between individual and social life.

Social-work intervention, then, aims to reverse the pattern that elicited it. It aims to leave the family and community stronger, more capable of caring for, protecting, and regulating their own. In exercising the virtue of social justice, practitioners build and develop that one virtue in particular in those with whom they work: the virtue of joining with them and helping them to develop the skills and habits required to join with others to achieve common purposes.

Such a virtue-based understanding of professional helping more commonly occurs, it is true, in implicit knowledge than in formal theory or method. For reasons we explored in chapter nineteen on charity and justice, social work became uncomfortable with its origins in charity. From its early efforts to render charitable practice better organized and more scientific, social work came to professionalize practice and emphasize psychotherapy, rather than religious views of life or even the Athenian virtues of Aristotle.

In the 1960s, in reaction to this clinical emphasis and in response to the movements of the times, an activist tendency came to the fore, focusing on social change and "social justice" (understood in partisan and utopian terms). In more recent times, there has been an emphasis on what actually works in achieving the aimed-for results, on evidence-based practice and specific interventions (for example, cognitive-behavioral therapy) that are effective, brief, and inexpensive. In all these developments, the virtues had no explicit place, so talk of them became exiguous to the point of nullity. Nevertheless, the virtue of social justice did not disappear; it found expression in concepts like empowerment, partnership practice, asset-based community development, restorative justice, and social capital.

It is not surprising, then, that other professions and disciplines such as medicine and law, philosophy and psychology, were drawn to the recovery of virtue-based ethics while social work ignored it.[5] On the other hand, social work has had from its beginnings a focus on human flourishing and the well-being of individuals and communities. That is, it always has been concerned with suffering in individuals, families, and communities, and conversely, with happiness as understood in Christianity (and Greek philosophy)—something inseparable from the virtues which are both necessary for and partly constitutive of human flourishing.

Jane Addams and the Settlement House residents, for example, both exercised and promoted the virtue of social justice. They built the capacity of working-class urban immigrants to fulfill their moral obligations by tapping into their own cultural resources in the new environment. (One enduring result was *The Settlement House Cookbook*.) They also worked as social reformers to remove obstacles to virtuous life in the cities, for example, opposing or promoting alternatives to the saloon, the spoils system, and the oppression of workers. They sought to join with others in the neighborhood to further the common good. Their work included political reform efforts, but the primary aim of their effort was to strengthen families and the associations, the intermediary groups of civil society—and not the state.

An important theme in social work, sometimes explicit, sometimes submerged, has been the particular virtues required for and developed by social-work practice. In a profession where the character of the agent has long been understood as inseparable from the professional intervention, the virtues focus attention on the character of the practitioner and the professional use of self. Recovery of the virtues, and of social justice in particular, accords well with the growing body of research suggesting the importance of the client-practitioner relationship as distinct from the specific theories or methods the practitioner utilizes. Social workers practice the virtue of social justice and hold it up as an ideal without yet avowing it or internalizing it as virtue in their own self-consciousness. For the moment, practice runs ahead of theory. Both authors of the present inquiry see this theory as putting into words what many others already practice.

The social-work example carries important lessons for how we frame social justice, the state, and civil society. In the cases of FGC and patch, we see that a too rigid dichotomy of state and civil society limits our thinking about how we can address social needs and problems. So, too, do hard dichotomies of professional and natural helping systems, of traditional prestate ways of repairing harm and those of the modern bureaucratic-professional state.

In the case of FGC, we see how informal and traditional ways of repairing harm and protecting children, such as the Maori *whanau hui* or the Hawaiian *ho'oponopono*, can inform child welfare or youth justice without substituting state for civil society or vice versa. It can build the capacity of families and communities to care for their own without the state's abdicating its responsibility to protect children or to protect the rights of due process. The strengths of formal and informal systems can be maximized while each constrains the weaknesses and potential abuses of the other.

It is not only that a severe dichotomy between individualism and collectivism is inadequate—ignoring how they feed each other and together compress the space of civil society. It is also a mistake to dichotomize the state and civil society, as both liberals and conservatives are wont to do. We can see this if we shift scale and consider for a moment our largest social program in the United States, Social Security.

Interpreting the demographic changes since 1935, when the program became law and when the full retirement age corresponded to the life expectancy of those who reached adulthood, lies beyond the scope of this book. But it is indisputable that the informal social security derived in earlier times from rearing children to productive adulthood and instilling in them a sense of filial obligation could not today adequately provide for all. For instance, those whose incomes cannot sustain them in old age, in disability, or in the death of the family breadwinner. It may be that Social Security itself plays a role in discouraging fertility, for it delinks fertility and economic security by diminishing the need for childrearing. Social Security leads each of us to depend on the childrearing of others. Meanwhile, the tax-equivalent contribution in kind that parents make to the system is not only unrecognized, but even penalized in the allocation of benefits, which now depends on one's earnings, not one's parenting.[6]

There is much debate about the sources of major demographic changes in recent times, and about other economic and cultural changes that have made reliance on the federal tax system (and one's own private pension and savings) more prudent than rearing one's own children and depending on their filial piety.

The important point here is that, while the enormous program of formal Social Security managed by the federal government has supplanted to a great extent the informal social security that preceded it, neither the family nor other institutions of civil society are up to the task of taking it back. Social justice can no longer get away without great government programs *or* without inspiring more self-helping and associating efforts. Social justice today requires not a substitution of civil society for the state (or vice versa), but more creative ways to marry the two, in order to escape the mistakes of the past. Social invention did not end in 1936. We should be able to do some of our own.

Social work at its best has always understood that one does little good to clients—and perhaps great harm—by making them more dependent, less motivated, and less able to think through their own problems than they already were. This is as true for families and neighborhoods as for individuals. It is crucial to have great respect for their own subjectivity, to use John Paul II's description of the singular and yet threefold capacities of the human person: to see into the failures in one's own *past*, to see new alternatives in the *future*, and to determine to take control over one's own *identity*. Helpers must respect with some delicacy those inner capacities that transform a person, a family, a community living as an "object," merely acted upon by outside forces, into a "subject," an active agent creating its own future.

Social-work professionals now realize not just that they do harm by doing to or for others in ways that reduce them to passivity or dependency. They also see that their professional task requires a different relationship of helper and helped. It requires restraining the tendency to control, rescue, impose solutions, and instead enabling those involved in the problematic situation to tap into their own wisdom, knowledge, and resources, to build and support the intermediary groups that occupy the vast and vital space between the bureaucratic-professional state and the individual.

In theological language, this inner transformation is a matter of grasping what it means to be "made as an image of God, the Creator." It is to begin at last to become a creator of one's own life story. A person, Karol Wojtyła wrote before he became John Paul II, is the creative agent (the *subject*) of his own decisions. A person is one who is responsible for who he or she becomes. But the same goes for the "subjectivity" of social groups, who through their own history develop their own resources, methods, and styles for assuming more and more responsibility over their own destiny. Think of the distinctive methods and styles brought into being in the Civil Rights movement of the 1960s, led so creatively by Martin Luther King, Jr. Or compare it to the equally distinctive methods and styles brought into being by the energy of *Solidarność*, the Polish labor union led so creatively by Lech Walesa and guided by the ideas of Pope John Paul II.

There is a different language in social work and in psychology for describing this same transformation from object to subject. The transformation occurs when human beings at last begin to appropriate their personal responsibility for how they live and who they are. For many years after birth, children and adolescents are more "thrown" into life in the trajectory imparted to them by their parents. As they mature, each is expected to become self-directed, not merely set on a path determined for them by others. They may in fact choose to appropriate the greatest of the strengths imparted to them by good parents. They may choose to correct inadequacies and weaknesses they come to recognize in their own growing body of social experience. More and more, they become the responsible ones, the ones responsible for making themselves what their native talents and acquired virtues now allow them to be.

As we mature, we learn that our growth toward relative (and temporary) independence entails taking responsibility for others in our family, community, and nation. We do so in the full realization that "no man is an island." We help others because we know how dependent on them we were when we were young. And we have now visited many hospital beds and assisted-living centers. We see ourselves as social creatures, almost totally dependent for some years after infancy, and soon enough to be dependent on others as we age and just plumb wear out. We are social beings. We are all—and not only the saintly exemplars of heroic virtue described by Brandon Vogt or the paid helpers discussed here who define their profession in terms of a principle of social justice—members of one body, members of each other. We are part of a chain of "reciprocal indebtedness," as MacIntyre would say.

————

In our adolescence some accustomed habits—of dependency, passivity, simply being taken care of by others—need to be outgrown. New inner resources need to be nurtured and brought to efficacy in daily living. The boy needs to become a man; the girl, a woman. These new inner resources are what the ancients called virtues, acquired habits ready to be drawn upon when needed in daily living.

Social justice is one of these virtues. Its development and practice occur *in between* the unformed, unencumbered, and naked individual and the political state—a truly vast space. That space, in all the liberty it affords, allows for the growth of different cultures and sets of historical institutions. In modern history, the coming of a new age of democratic republics, an age dependent on voluntary, creative leadership, has called loudly for the virtue of social justice.

A free society needs majorities with the habit of forming effective associations to accomplish tasks that improve the common good. This common good may be very modest and local (together digging a new well in a village), or it may be international (as in contributing microloans that might launch millions of new enterprises around the world, each of them employing five to ten persons). By these sorts of manifestations of social justice, world poverty has been cut in half in the last twenty-five years.

Yet there is not only material poverty. Our natural human rights are not defended by parchment barriers, James Madison wrote, but by the habits and institutions of the American people. Think of it. The civil rights of formerly enslaved black Americans were written on parchment in the Declaration of Independence. But they were not fully defended, not even by the Emancipation Proclamation, until the rise of free associations that brought into being the new institutions of the Civil Rights movement. Thousands, then millions, learned the habit of noticing a social need, loathing the gap between rhetoric and reality, and joining together to change things. Habits and institutions, conceived of and directed by a people longing to achieve liberty—longing to be "Free at last! Free at last!"—achieved a great victory in the 1960s. It was a victory for the human conscience, for a new institutional order, for social justice.

Social justice is an energy surging in humans everywhere, an energy that must not be allowed to freeze into a partisan ideology. Humans in all their factions and all their parties have different visions of how justice ought to be institutionalized. The more who compete for social justice in the public square, openly, honestly, and with respect for others, the more likely it will be that a nation will prosper in tolerable amity and friendship.

Such amity is the worldly form of that ultimate, freely chosen City of God, that "City on the Hill" which so many diverse peoples have sought to establish. It is that concrete reality, however imperfect, properly called *Caritapolis*—the City of a special kind of love, proper only to the inner life of God. *Caritas* is diffusive of itself, outgoing, creative, generous, forgiving (and yet demanding). Above all, *caritas* gives us our knowledge that we are all one. Even atheists as different as Bertrand Russell and Richard Rorty have asserted that their own form of humanism is not like that of the pagans of old (who called those not of their city "barbarians"). Rather, Russell and Rorty, as they themselves openly confessed, adopted from Judaism and Christianity the vision of humanity as one, bound together by mutual duties of compassion.

God shows us that the essence of our existence, and the inner existence of himself, is suffering love. Quite directly, the Lord tells us that we must also suffer—take up our cross, follow him, die to ourselves. This is how God made the world. To be like God, to be close to God, is to love even in suffering.

Thus, in showing us all this, God shows that he too plays by the same rules. He too submits in his Son to die the death of suffering love, surrounded by insults, held in contempt, scorned. In short, all this is God explaining to us: "My children this is what *caritas* is. You will all live through it. Embrace it. Let me pass this *caritas* through you, continuing to show it to all humans, and to live now through you. If you will allow me."

Now, this is where Catholic social, political, and economic thought begins. In *caritas*—in giving us a symbol and moving narrative of what a Civilization of Love is, what the *Caritapolis* of the future is to be like: Love until death for one another. One human family of brothers and sisters, willing to give their lives for each other.

Yet packed into this story are four important propositions. First, all human creatures form one family, each made in the image of God, each a unique image of God. Thus, "Go teach all nations" sends us far beyond boundaries of family, nation, language, race, or religion. It signifies a global, a universal, a *catholic* community (one that is worldwide, concrete, visible, as well as in its deepest part invisible).

Second, this community is not yet. It is real, in its fallenness and failures; it is concrete and can be seen with one's eyes. Yet there is also an inner war going on, in soul after soul in the invisible filament that girdles the earth, an intensely fought battle for the enduring commitment of each to each other, and thus to God. A battle between good and evil or, more exactly, between the living God and the not-god, between friendship with God and the turning away from God. This battle in the inalienable freedom of each soul is the ground of the Christian idea of progress. This epic battle is unending. It gives history its shape and its meaning. It distinguishes progress from decline.

Third, God offers friendship, but it must be freely accepted or freely rejected. If friendship is to burn like a fire, freedom is its oxygen. As the Society of Friends put it: "If friendship, then liberty." The Liberty Bell rings out that God does not want the coerced friendship of slaves. The deepest root of the idea of liberty lies here, in the freedom of free women and free men before God.

Fourth, our Creator and Redeemer is a straight talker, not a deceiver. He does not promise us a rose garden. He promises us the cross. He sees that all the inner beauty of freedom and suffering love flares out only when we see the burnt-out ember "fall, gall itself, gash gold-vermillion."[7] Only in dying to their earlier life do all beauty, all bravery, all heroism, all true love "gash gold-vermillion." That is the way the world was made. Therefore, beware of merely romantic love, beware of false promises, beware of utopias. Keep your eye on the points of suffering at the heart of things. Watch for concrete results, not sweet talk. *Caritas* is a teacher of realism, not soft-headedness; of fact, not sentiment; of suffering love, not illusory bliss. To think in a utopian way is a sin against *Caritapolis*.

Truly, the full end of the pursuit to dwell in a city of friendship, free conversation, and mutual respect is never quite achieved on earth, but it is widely aspired to. Each generation has a great many evils to fight against, many motes in the eyes of each of our parties, and immense amounts to learn, if we are to answer the great question put before humans everywhere:

Who are we, under these stars, with the wind upon our faces? Who are we, and what may we hope to become?

Seeing so much evil around us—even smelling its stench—it is easy to become afraid. Therefore the most important word of social justice may be: *Do not be afraid.* Humans are called upon to hope. To trust that our longings for justice and mercy are not in vain. To draw strength from the example of so many heroines and heroes who have gone before us, winning small victory after small victory, even in the spiritually darkest of times.

Examining where we have come from in history, it would be foolhardy to deny that *by our nature*, humans aspire upward.

Social justice certainly does.

NOTES

Introduction

1. Friedrich Hayek, *The Mirage of Social Justice*, vol. 2 of *Law, Legislation & Liberty* (Chicago: University of Chicago Press, 1976).

2. Cf. Thomas Sowell, *A Conflict of Visions: Ideological Origins of Political Struggles*, rev. ed. (New York: Basic Books, 2007); Jonah Goldberg, *The Tyranny of Clichés: How Liberals Cheat in the War of Ideas* (New York: Sentinel, 2012).

3. Daniel Patrick Moynihan, *Maximum Feasible Misunderstanding: Community Action in the War on Poverty* (New York: Free Press, 1969).

4. For example, there are many "social justice Catholics" for whom the term's papal pedigree provides convenient cover for narrowly partisan politics. This tendency was evident in the attacks on Senator Paul Ryan during the 2012 election campaign. See Robert P. George's response, "The Catholic Left's Unfair Attack on Paul Ryan," *First Things* (October 12, 2012), available at: http://www .firstthings.com/onthesquare/2012/10/the-catholic-leftrsquos-unfair-attack -on-paul-ryan. Too late for discussion in this book, Anthony Esolen, *Reclaiming Catholic Social Teaching* (Manchester, N.H.: Sophia Institute Press, 2014), analyzes all Leo XIII's social teaching and refutes modern distortions of Church doctrine about marriage, family, and state. We agree wholeheartedly with this brilliant work.

5. Brandon Vogt, *Saints and Social Justice: A Guide to Changing the World* (Huntington, Ind.: Our Sunday Visitor, 2014).

6. Council on Social Work Education, "Educational Policy and Accreditation Standards," accessed March 18, 2014: http://www.cswe.org/File.aspx?id=13780.

7. Ibid.

8. See Michael Novak, *Writing from Left to Right: My Journey From Liberal to Conservative* (New York: Image, 2013).

9. Andrew M. Haines, "Catholic Social Teaching: Why We Fight," *Ethica Politika* (February 6, 2014), accessed March 18, 2014: http://ethikapolitika.org/2014/ 02/06/catholic-social-teaching-why-we-fight/.

10. *Gaudium et Spes*, §24.

11. Cf. Edmund Phelps, *Mass Flourishing: How Grassroots Innovation Created Jobs, Challenge, and Change* (Princeton, N.J.: Princeton University Press, 2013).

12. John Paul II, *Centesimus Annus*, §42.

13. Patrick J. Deneen, "Would Someone Just Shut That Pope Up?" *The American Conservative* (December 5, 2013), available at: http://www.theamericanconservative .com/would-someone-just-shut-that-pope-up/.

14. Robert D. Putnam, *Bowling Alone: The Collapse and Revival of American Community* (New York: Simon & Schuster, 2000).

15. Cf. Putnam, *Bowling Alone*; Paul Collier, *The Bottom Billion: Why the Poorest Countries Are Failing and What Can Be Done about It* (New York: Oxford University Press, 2007); Hernando de Soto, *The Mystery of Capital: Why Capitalism Triumphs in the West and Fails Everywhere Else* (New York: Basic Books, 2000).

16. Thomas Patrick Burke, *The Concept of Justice: Is Social Justice Just?* (London and New York: Continuum, 2011).

17. Cf. Pius XI, *Quadragesimo Anno*, §78.

Chapter 1. Social Justice Isn't What You Think It Is

1. Matthew 25:44–46.

2. Irving Howe and Lewis Coser, "Images of Socialism," *Dissent* 1, no. 2 (April 1964): 122–38, at 122.

3. Alexis de Tocqueville, *Democracy in America*, ed. Eduardo Nolla, trans. James T. Schleifer (Indianapolis: Liberty Fund, Inc., 2012), 69–70.

4. Oswald von Nell-Breuning, *Reorganization of Social Economy: The Social Encyclical Developed and Explained* (New York: Bruce Publishing, 1939), 5.

5. See chapter 9, "'Social' or Distributive Justice," in *The Mirage of Social Justice*.

6. John Paul II, *Centesimus Annus*, §13.

7. Alexis de Tocqueville, *Democracy in America*, ed. Phillips Bradley (New York: Vintage Books, 1945), 189.

8. Cf. Jerry Muller, *Adam Smith in His Time and Ours: Designing the Decent Society* (New York: Free Press, 1993), 60, 68, 72, 148, 160.

9. See "No. 10" of Alexander Hamilton, James Madison, and John Jay, *The Federalist Papers*, ed. Clinton Rossiter (New York: Signet, 2003), 71–79, at 76ff.

10. See "No. 14" of *Federalist Papers*, 94–100, at 100.

11. See Pius XII, *Democracy and a Lasting Peace: 1944 Christmas* Message, §47: "A sound democracy, based on the immutable principles of the natural law and revealed truth, will resolutely turn its back on such corruption as gives to the state legislature in unchecked and unlimited power, and moreover, makes of the democratic regime, notwithstanding an outward show to the contrary, purely and simply a form of absolutism."

12. See, for example, "John Paul II on the American Experiment" (December 16, 1997), accessed March 18, 2014: http://www.firstthings.com/article/2008/11/ 005-john-paul-ii-on-the-american-experiment.

13. Cf. Richard W. Garnett, "Positive Secularism and the American Model of

Religious Liberty," *Engage* 11, no. 1 (March 2010): 126–27, available at: www
.fed-soc.org/aboutus/DownloadLibrary?id=2408.

Chapter 2. Six Secular Uses of "Social Justice"

1. G. J. Papageorgiou, "Social Values and Social Justice," *Economic Geography* 56,
   no. 2 (April 1980): 110–19, at 110.
2. *Gaudium et Spes*, §26.
3. C. S. Lewis, *God in the Dock* (Grand Rapids, Mich.: Wm. B. Eerdmans Publishing Co., 2001), 292.
4. See Maggie Haberman, "Gay Donor: Gay Rights Not Inevitable," *Politico* (May 2,
   2014), available at: http://www.politico.com/story/2014/05/tim-gill-a-top-gay-
   donor-talks-strategy-106265.html; Jay Mandle, "Funding Environmentalism,"
   Huffington Post (February 25, 2014), available at: http://www.huffingtonpost.
   com/jay-mandle/funding-environmentalism__b__4853710.html; and "Largest
   Anonymous ACLU Donor Reveals Identity and Reaffirms Support for Organization," available at: https://www.aclu.org/organization-news-and-highlights/
   largest-anonymous-aclu-donor-reveals-identity-and-reaffirms-support.
5. Randy Sly, "A Catholic College and Abortion Advocates: Here We Go Again,"
   Catholic Online (May 22, 2009), accessed November 21, 2013: http://www
   .catholic.org/college/story.php?id=33617.
6. "Gay Minister Claims Discrimination," *Waikato Times*, accessed November 23,
   2013: http://www.stuff.co.nz/waikato-times/news/509074/Gay-minister-
   claims-discrimination.
7. Cf. *The New Consensus on Family and Welfare*, ed. Michael Novak et al. (Washington, D.C.: American Enterprise Institute, 1987).

Chapter 3. A Mirage?

1. As even the titles of some of his work indicate: Friedrich A. Hayek, *Law, Legislation & Liberty* (as in Introduction note 1 above); and *The Constitution of Liberty*
   (Chicago: University of Chicago Press, 1978).
2. See Hayek, *The Mirage of Social Justice*, 62–100.
3. Samuel Gregg and Wolfgang Kasper, "No Third Way: Hayek and the Recovery of
   Freedom," in *Policy* (Winter 1999): 11: "Hayek's economic propositions are rather
   simple: that human knowledge is far from perfect; that this is at the root of scarcity; and that the finding and testing of useful skills and knowledge is central to
   economic prosperity. *No* human being, Hayek stresses, can know everything. In
   this regard, Hayek's greatness as an economist rests on the fact that he restored
   real human beings to the discipline [of economics], and has raised real questions
   about economists basing their propositions in the theoretical assumption of
   perfect knowledge and the fiction that people are anodyne, reactive, automatons
   who simply maximize and minimize. Hence, the basic supposition of economic
   planning—that government can know everything required to make correct
   decisions—is revealed as yet another example of human hubris."

4. Hayek notes expressly that the Roman Catholic Church especially has made the aim of "social justice" part of its official doctrine, while "the ministers of most Christian denominations appear to vie with each other with such offers of more mundane aims" (*The Mirage of Social Justice*, 66).

5. Ibid., 96–97.

6. Ibid., 66: "Even though until recently one would have vainly sought in the extensive literature for an intelligible definition of the term, there still seems to exist little doubt, either among ordinary people or among the learned, that the expression has a definite well understood sense."

7. "The main point of my argument is, then, that the conflict between, on the one hand, advocates of the spontaneous extended human order created by a competitive market, and on the other hand those who demand a deliberate arrangement of human interaction by central authority based on collective command over available resources is due to a factual error by the latter about how knowledge of these resources is and can be generated and utilized. As a question of fact, this conflict must be settled by scientific study. Such study shows that, by following the spontaneously generated moral traditions underlying the competitive market order (traditions which do not satisfy the canons or norms of rationality embraced by most socialists), we generate and garner greater knowledge and wealth than would ever be obtained or utilized in a centrally-directed economy whose adherents claim to proceed strictly in accordance with 'reason.' Thus socialist aims and programmes are factually impossible to achieve or execute; and they also happen, into the bargain as it were, to be logically impossible." Friedrich A. Hayek, *The Fatal Conceit* (Chicago: University of Chicago Press, 1988), 7.

8. Hayek writes scathingly in *Mirage* of "that anthropomorphism or personification by which naive thinking tries to account for all self-ordering processes. It is a sign of the immaturity of our minds that we have not yet outgrown these primitive concepts and still demand from an impersonal process which brings about a greater satisfaction of human desires than any deliberate human organization could achieve, that it conform to the moral precepts men have evolved for the guidance of their individual actions" (62–63).

9. Leo W. Shields, *The History and Meaning of the Term Social Justice* (Notre Dame, Ind.: University of Notre Dame Press, 1941).

10. John Stuart Mill, *Utilitarianism*, in *The English Utilitarians*, ed. H. Plamenplatz (Oxford: Oxford University Press, 1949), 225 (emphasis added).

11. Hume's entire text reads: "Most obvious thought would be to assign the largest possessions to the most extensive virtue, and give every one the power of doing proportioned to his inclination.... But were mankind to execute such a law, so great is the uncertainty of merit, both from its natural obscurity; and from the self-conceit of each individual that no determinate rule of conduct would ever follow from it; and the total dissolution of society must be the immediate consequence." *An Enquiry Concerning the Principles of Morals*, sect. III, part II,

Works IV, p. 187. Kant's text reads as follows: "Welfare, however, has no principle, neither for him who receives it, nor for him who distributes it (one will place it here and another there); because it depends on the material content of the will, which is dependent upon particular facts and therefore capable of a general rule." Immanuel Kant, *Der Streit der Fakultäten*, sec. 2, par. 6, n. 2.

12. "Individual man may be moral in the sense that they are able to consider interests other than their own in determining problems of conduct, and are capable on occasion, of preferring the advantages of others to their own. They are endowed by nature with a measure of sympathy and consideration for their kind.... Their rational faculty prompts them to a sense of justice which educational discipline may refine.... But all these achievements are more difficult, if not impossible, for human societies and social groups. In every human group there is less reason to guide and to check impulse, less capacity for self-transcendence, less ability to comprehend the need of others.... In part it is merely the revelation of a collective egoism, compounded of the egoistic impulses of individuals, which achieve a more vivid expression and a more cumulative effect when they are united in a common impulse than when they express themselves separately and discreetly." Reinhold Niebuhr, *Moral Man and Immoral Society* (New York: Charles Scribner's Sons, 1960), xi, and also chapter 1, "Man and Society."

13. Hayek, *The Fatal Conceit.*

14. Hayek, *The Mirage of Social Justice*, 68–69.

15. Hayek continues: "... and any particular conception of 'social justice' could be realized only in such a centrally directed system. It presupposes that people are guided by specific directions and not by rules of just individual conduct. Indeed, no system of rules of just individual conduct, and therefore no free action of the individuals, could produce results satisfying any principle of distributive justice" (ibid., 69).

16. *Main Currents of Marxism*, trans. P. S. Falla (Oxford: Clarendon Press, 1978), vol. 3, *The Breakdown*, 526 ff.

17. Hayek, *The Mirage of Social Justice*, 70. Also: "Yet we do cry out against the injustice when a succession of calamities befalls one family while another steadily prospers, when a meritorious effort is frustrated by some unforeseeable accident, and particularly if of many people whose endeavours seem equally great, some succeed brilliantly while others fail. It is certainly tragic to see the failure of the most meritorious effort of parents to bring up their children, of young men to build a career, or of an explorer or scientist pursuing a brilliant idea. And we will protest against such a fate although we do not know anyone who is to blame for it, or any way in which such disappointments can be prevented" (ibid., 68–69).

18. Ibid., 73: "It has been argued persuasively that people will tolerate major inequalities of the material positions only if they believe that the different individuals get on the whole what they deserve, that they did in fact support the market order

only because (and so long as) they thought that the differences of renumeration corresponded roughly to differences of merit, and that in consequence the maintenance of a free society presupposes the belief that some sort of 'social justice' is being done. The market order, however, does not in fact owe its origin to such beliefs, nor was it originally justified in this manner. This order could develop, after its earlier beginnings had decayed during the middle ages and to some extent been destroyed by the restrictions imposed by authority, when a thousand years of vain efforts to discover substantively just prices or wages were abandoned and the late schoolmen recognized them to be empty formulae and taught instead that the prices determined by just conduct of the parties in the market."

19. See Gregg and Kasper, "No Third Way," 12. They summarize four propositions that characterize Hayek's thought: (1) The institutions that coordinate society arise largely from human experience, but not human design; hence attempts to design society are fatal to its goodness. (2) In a free society, law is essentially found and not made. Law is normally derived not from the mere will of the rulers, be they kings or Rousseau's "General Will," but from the interaction and learning of all citizens. (3) The Rule of Law not only is the first and foremost principle of the free society, but is also dependent on the two previous propositions. (4) The Rule of Law requires all people to be treated equally (i.e., with procedural justice), but does not require them to be made equal, and indeed is undermined by attempts to engineer equal outcomes (i.e., "social" justice).

20. Hayek, *The Mirage of Social Justice*, 69–70.

21. Ibid., 73–74: "It certainly is important in the market order (or free enterprise society, misleadingly called 'capitalism') that the individuals believe that their well-being depends primarily on their own efforts and decisions. Indeed, few circumstances will do more to make a person energetic and efficient than the belief that it depends chiefly on him whether he will reach the goals he has set himself. For this reason this belief is often encouraged by education and governing opinion—it seems to me, generally much to the benefit of most members of the society in which it prevails, who will owe many important material and moral improvements to persons guided by it. But it leads no doubt also to an exaggerated confidence in the truth of this generalization which to those who regard themselves (and perhaps are) equally able but have failed must appear as a bitter irony and severe provocation."

22. Ibid., 70–71.

23. Ibid., 73–74: "The competitive prices arrived at without fraud, monopoly and violence, was all that justice required. It was from this tradition that John Locke and his contemporaries derived the classical liberal conception of justice for which, as has been rightly said, it was only 'the way in which competition was carried on, not the results,' that could be just or unjust."

24. Ibid., 79: "But from . . . an appeal to the conscience of the public to concern themselves with the unfortunate ones and recognize them as members of the same society, the conception gradually came to mean that 'society' ought to hold

itself responsible for the particular material position of all its members, and for assuring that each received what was 'due' to him. It implied that the processes of society should be deliberately directed to particular results and, by personifying society, represented it as a subject endowed with a conscious mind, capable of being guided in its operation by moral principles. 'Social' became more and more the description of the pre-eminent virtue, the attribute in which the good man excelled and the ideal by which communal action was to be guided."

25. In *The Fatal Conceit*, Hayek notes that the word "society" in present parlance not only refers to phenomena "produced by the various modes of cooperation among man," but it has "increasingly been turned into an exhortation, a sort of guide-word for rationalist morals intended to displace traditional morals, and now supplants the word 'good' as a designation of what is morally right. Because of this factual and normative meanings of the word 'social' constantly alternate, and what first seems a description imperceptibly turns into a prescription" (114). To illustrate his point he sums up "an instructive list of over one hundred and sixty nouns qualified by the adjective 'social' he had encountered" (115).

26. Hayek, *The Mirage of Social Justice*, 69: "'Social Justice' can be given a meaning only in a directed or 'command economy' (such as an army) in which the individuals are ordered what to do; and any particular conception of 'social justice' could be realized only in such a centrally directed system. It presupposes that people are guided by specific directions and not by rules of just individual conduct, and therefore no free action of the individuals, could produce results satisfying any principle of distributive justice."

27. *Antonio Gramsci: Selections from Political Writings, 1910–1920*, trans. John Matthews (Ann Arbor, Mich.: Books on Demand, UMI, 1976).

28. See Hayek, *The Mirage of Social Justice*, 97.

Chapter 4. Friedrich Hayek, Practitioner of Social Justice

1. See *The New Consensus on Family and Welfare*, 43–52.

2. See ibid., 71–89.

3. Charles Murray, "The Coming White Underclass," *The Wall Street Journal* (October 29, 1993).

4. See, for example, the data from the Centers for Disease Control: http://www.cdc.gov/nchs/data/databriefs/db18.pdf.

5. Cf. a somewhat less vivid account in Edwin J. Feulner, Jr., *Intellectual Pilgrims: The Fiftieth Anniversary of the Mont Pelerin Society* (Washington, D.C.: Heritage Foundation, 1999), 11.

6. Alexis de Tocqueville, *Democracy in America* (New York: Doubleday & Co., 1969), 517.

7. Hayek, *The Mirage of Social Justice*, 151.

8. Novak, *The Catholic Ethic and the Spirit of Capitalism* (New York: The Free Press, 1993), 62–88.

Chapter 5. Sixteen Principles of Catholic Social Thought: The Five Cs

1. The term "principle" tends to be understood as a rule or a law or an axiom. What needs stressing is its action as a source of energy, an inner drive and impulse.

2. Samuel P. Huntington, "Democracy's Third Wave," *Journal of Democracy* 2, no. 2 (Spring 1991): 13.

3. Etymologists suggest that *caritas* derives from *carus* or *cara*, meaning expensive, dear. But I suspect that theologians were following a different etymological path, linking *caritas* to the Greek *charis* meaning gratuitous, gifted, grace (think *charism* and *charisma*). In that line of thinking, *caritas* is a gratuitous gift of God—a participation by us in God's own form of love, beyond our natural capacities to love. Thus, to love one's enemies is not natural, but a gift of God.

4. Aristotle, *Physics* 2.8, in *The Basic Works*, ed. Richard McKeon (New York: Modern Library, 2001): 213–394, at 251.

5. "The god who gave us life gave us liberty at the same time: the hand of force may destroy, but cannot disjoin them." In Thomas Jefferson, "A Summary View of the Rights of British America," Document 10 in vol. 1 of *The Founders Constitution* (Chicago: University of Chicago Press, 2000), accessed March 13, 2014: http://press-pubs.uchicago.edu/founders/documents/v1ch14s10.html.

6. Jacques Maritain, *The Person and the Common Good*, trans. John J. Fitzgerald (1946; Notre Dame: University of Notre Dame Press, 1966), 20.

7. Thomas Aquinas, "On Charity," in *Disputed Questions on Virtue*, trans. Jeffery Hause and Claudia E. Murphy (Indianapolis: Hackett Publishing, 2010), 113.

8. John Locke, *Second Treatise of Government*, chapter 5, "Of Property." Nowadays, of course, there is a lively debate about the most recent forms of genetically modified seeds. Down through history there has always been ardent opposition to new discoveries and new procedures. Sometimes these debates have had merit, often not. In our day, it is good that such debates proceed and that evidence be patiently examined. It is not necessary to pronounce on these particular inquiries to recognize the principle that new wealth has often been created through the acquisition of new know-how and new knowledge.

9. John Paul II, *Centesimus Annus*, §32.

Chapter 6. The Five Rs

1. James Madison, "Memorial and Remonstrance against Religious Assessments" (1785).

2. Albert Einstein, "Why Socialism?" *Monthly Review* (May 1949).

3. John Paul II, *Centesimus Annus*, §13.

4. Ibid., §34.

Chapter 7. The Six Ss

1. My own extended study of what I call a philosophy of self-discovery or intelligent, critical subjectivity is in Michael Novak, *Belief & Unbelief: A Philosophy of Self-Knowledge* (1965; New Brunswick, N.J.: Transaction, 1994). Cf. Elizabeth

Shaw, "Intelligent Subjectivity: Into the Presence of God," in *Theologian & Philosopher of Liberty: Essays of Evaluation & Criticism in Honor of Michael Novak*, ed. Samuel Gregg (Grand Rapids, Mich.: Acton Institute, 2014), 1–9.

2. John Paul II, *Centesimus Annus*, §48.

3. See Hedrick Smith, *The Russians* (London: Sphere Books, 1976).

Chapter 8. Leo's XIII's Rerum Novarum

1. *Sacramentum Mundi*, ed. Karl Rahner et al., vol. 4 (New York: Herder & Herder, 1969), 204.

2. Rodger Charles, *The Christian Social Conscience* (Hales Corners: Clergy Book Services, 1970), 25.

3. Johannes Messner, *Social Ethics* (St. Louis: Herder Books, 1965), 320–21.

4. William Ferree, *Introduction to Social Justice* (Dayton, Ohio: Marianist Publications, 1948).

5. Thomas Patrick Burke, *The Concept of Social Justice*.

6. Ernest Fortin, "Natural Law and Social Justice," *American Journal of Jurisprudence* 30, no. 1 (1985): 1–20.

7. See Antonio Rosmini, *The Constitution under Social Justice*, trans. Alberto Mingardi (Lanham, Md.: Rowman & Littlefield, 2007).

8. Anyone interested in further discussion of these details would do well to consult Burke's text. He closely documents the main point, that at its origins the term social justice was nothing more than an extension of the ordinary understanding of justice—namely, as a quality of human actions, not of states of affairs—to society as a whole. In addition to Taparelli's conservative usage and Rosmini's liberal one, Burke notes a third: that of the Christian Socialists. Summarizing these three, he writes: "For the conservative Taparelli . . . social justice demanded acceptance of the existing constitutional arrangements of society, the inherited and established rights, and powers of the existing authorities, including the church; and injustice consisted in the forcible rejection of those rights and powers by persons who attempted to set up alternative forms of government. . . . For Rosmini, social justice was a quality of the constitutional arrangements of society in so far as they governed the distribution of the common good. . . . The great test of social justice for Rosmini was the inviolability of property, the protection given by the laws to individual ownership, such that no political majority could use its power to dispossess the minority. In other words, social justice was a quality of the laws, which of course are actions of persons, for which they can be held accountable, even if they act collectively. For the Christian Socialists, again, social justice consisted in "a fair day's wages for a fair day's work." . . . The original concept of social justice, therefore, was simply an extension of ordinary justice into the new arena of society as a whole." See Thomas Patrick Burke, *The Concept of Social Justice*, chapter 3.

9. Messner, *Social Ethics*, 320–21 (emphasis added).

10. Joseph Cardinal Höffner, *Christian Social Teaching* (Cologne: Ordo Socialis, 1983), 71.

11. Jean-Yves Calvez and J. Perrin, *The Church and Social Justice: Social Teaching of the Popes From Leo XIII to Pius XII*, trans. J. R. Kirwan (London: Burns and Oates, 1961), 153.

12. Normand Joseph Paulhus, "The Theological and Political Ideals of the Fribourg Union," Ph.D. dissertation, Boston College, 1983.

13. Alexis de Tocqueville, *Democracy in America*, trans. Henry Reeve, accessed March 20, 2014: http://xroads.virginia.edu/~Hyper/DETOC/ch4__06.htm.

14. Leo XIII, *Rerum Novarum*, §§4–19.

15. Ibid., §34.

16. Ibid.

17. Ibid., §15.

18. Ibid., §5.

19. Ibid., §6.

20. Ibid., §7.

21. Ibid., §10.

22. Ibid., §14.

23. Ibid., §18.

24. Ibid., §38.

25. Ibid., §17.

26. Ibid., §19.

27. Ibid., §21.

28. Ibid., §34.

29. See Peter L. Berger, *The Capitalist Revolution: Fifty Propositions about Prosperity, Equality, and Liberty* (New York: Basic Books, 1986).

30. "You know ... that the Encyclical of Our Predecessor of happy memory had in view chiefly that economic system, wherein, generally, some provide capital while others provide labor for a joint economic activity.... With all his energy Leo XIII sought to adjust this economic system according to the norms of right order; hence, it is evident that this system is not to be condemned in itself. And surely it is not of its own nature vicious. But it does violate right order when capital hires workers, that is, the non-owning working class, with a view to and under such terms that it directs business and even the whole economic system according to its own will and advantage, scorning the human dignity of the workers, the social character of economic activity and social justice itself, and the common good" (Pius XI, *Quadragesimo Anno*, §§100–101); Nell-Breuning, *Reorganization*, 251.

Chapter 9. Forty Years Later: Pius XI

1. Nell-Breuning, *Reorganization*, 251.

2. Pius XI, *Mit Brennender Sorge*, §42.

3. "Discourse of 15 May 1926," as quoted in William J. Ferree, *Introduction to Social Justice*, 3.

4. Cited in Ferree, *Introduction to Social Justice*, 7.
5. Pius XI, *Quadragesimo Anno*, §§57, 58, 71, 88, 101, 110, and 126. Social justice is referred to, but not named, in §§74 and 88.
6. Ibid., §71.
7. Nell-Breuning, *Reorganization*, 250.
8. Ibid., 250–51.
9. John XXIII, *Mater et Magistra*, §34.
10. Nell-Breuning, *Reorganization*, 250.
11. Ibid.
12. Ibid.
13. Ibid., 247–48.
14. As found ibid., 248. Nell-Breuning is quoting Pius XI: "Therefore, it is most necessary that economic life be again subjected to and governed by a true and effective directing principle" (*Quadragesimo Anno*, §88).
15. Ibid., 248–50.
16. See Pius XI, *Quadragesimo Anno*, §25.
17. Nell-Breuning refers to Lincoln in "Social Movements: Subsidiarity," *Sacramentum Mundi*, ed. Karl Rahner (New York: Herder & Herder, 1968–70), 6:115.
18. Nell-Breuning, *Reorganization*, 251.
19. The Sherman Act set limits, restrictions, and necessary conditions on business corporations, bringing them under the rule of law.
20. Cf. Heinrich Pesch, *Teaching Guide to Economics*, 5 vols., ed. and trans. Rupert J. Ederer (1905–23; Lewiston, N.Y.: Edwin Mellen Press, 2002); Franz Herman Mueller, *The Church and the Social Question* (Washington, D.C.: AEI Press, 1984); Normand Joseph Paulhus, "The Theological and Political Ideals of the Fribourg Union."
21. This did have repercussions on FDR's New Deal through Msgr. John A. Ryan, who earned the nickname "The Right Reverend New Dealer." On this nexus, see also Jonah Goldberg, *Liberal Fascism: The Secret History of the American Left, from Mussolini to the Politics of Meaning* (New York: Doubleday, 2008).

Chapter 10. American Realities and Catholic Social Thought

1. Cited above at chapter 9, n. 17.
2. Abraham Lincoln, "Lecture on Discoveries and Inventions," Jacksonville, Illinois (February 11, 1859), in *Speeches and Writings: 1859–1865* (Washington, D.C.: Library of America, 1989). Cited in Michael Novak, *The Fire of Invention: Civil Society and the Future of the Corporation* (Lanham, Md.: Rowman & Littlefield, 1997), 54.
3. Cited in Novak, *The Fire of Invention*, 54.
4. Ibid.
5. Ibid., 55.
6. Ibid.
7. Ibid., 56.
8. Ibid., 57.

9. Ibid.

10. Ibid., 58.

11. Lincoln, "Address at Gettysburg, Pennsylvania" (November 19, 1863) in
    Speeches, 405.

12. John Paul II, *Centesimus Annus*, §32.

13. Ibid.

14. Ibid.

15. Ibid., §31.

16. Fred Warshofsky, *The Patent Wars: The Battle to Own the World's Technology* (New
    York: Wiley & Sons, 1994), 3.

17. Ibid.

18. John Paul II, *Sollicitudo Rei Socialis*, §42.

19. John Paul II, *Centesimus Annus*, §49.

20. Ibid., §51.

21. Ibid., §60.

22. Ibid.

23. Ibid., §53.

24. John Paul II, *Sollicitudo Rei Socialis*, §15.

25. John Paul II, *Centesimus Annus*, §13.

26. Ibid., §54.

27. Ibid., §25.

28. Ibid.

29. Ibid.

30. Ibid.

Chapter 11. Centesimus Annus: *Capitalism, No and Yes*

1. John Paul II, *Centesimus Annus*, §48.

2. Ibid., §42.

3. Ibid., §32.

4. Ibid., §37.

5. Ibid., §43.

6. Ibid.

7. John Paul II, *Laborem Exercens*, §15.

8. Lincoln, "Annual Message to Congress" (December 3, 1861) in *Speeches*, 320–27,
   at 325–26.

9. John Paul II, *Centesimus Annus*, §31.

10. Ibid.

11. Ibid., §32 (emphasis added).

12. Ibid.

13. Ibid.

14. Ibid.

15. Ibid.

16. Ibid., §35.

17. Ibid.

18. Ibid.

19. Ibid.

20. Ibid. §33.

21. Ibid.

22. Ibid.

23. Ibid., §34.

24. Ibid., §33.

25. Ibid.

26. Ibid., §35.

27. Ibid.

28. Ibid.

29. Ibid.

30. Ibid.

31. Ibid., §42.

32. Ibid., §40.

33. "At the root of the senseless destruction of the natural environment lies an anthropological error, which unfortunately is widespread in our day. Man, who discovers his capacity to transform and in a certain sense create the world through his own work, forgets that this is always based on God's prior and original gift of the things that are" (ibid., §37).

34. Richard P. McBrien, *The Progress* (June 30, 1991).

35. "After Communism," *Commonweal* 118 (June 1, 1991): 355.

36. Jim Hug, "*Centesimus Annus*: Rescuing the Challenge, Probing the Vision," *Center Focus*, no. 102 (August 1991): 1 ff.

37. Ibid., 3.

38. John Paul II, *Centesimus Annus*, §33.

39. Ibid., §42.

40. David Hollenbach, S.J., "Christian Social Ethics after the Cold War," *Theological Studies* 53, no. 1 (March 1992): 95.

41. Ibid., 83.

42. John Paul II, *Centesimus Annus*, §33.

43. United States Catholic Conference/National Conference of Catholic Bishops, *Economic Justice for All: Catholic Social Teaching and the U.S. Economy* (November 13, 1986), §77.

44. John Paul II, *Centesimus Annus*, §33.

45. Ibid.

46. Michael Ignatieff, "Suburbia's Revenge," *The New Republic* (May 4, 1992): 11.

47. John Paul II, *Centesimus Annus*, §43.

48. Thomas L. Pangle, "The Liberal Paradox," *Crisis* (May 1992): 18–25.

Chapter 12. Benedict XVI and Caritas in Veritate

1. Benedict XVI, *Caritas in Veritate*, §57.

2. Ibid., §60.

3. Ibid., §67.

Chapter 13. Pope Francis on Unreformed Capitalism

1. John Paul II, *Centesimus Annus*, §58.
2. Ibid., §33.
3. Cf. Friedrich Hayek, *The Counterrevolution of Science: Studies in the Abuse of Reason* (Indianapolis: Liberty Press, 1952).
4. Francis, *Evangelii Gaudium*, §51.
5. See, for example, this report of the UN Millennium Project, accessed March 20, 2014: http://www.unmillenniumproject.org/resources/fastfacts__e.htm.
6. John Paul II, *Centesimus Annus*, §42.

Chapter 14. A New Theological Specialty: The Scout

1. Bernard Lonergan, *Method in Theology* (London: Darton, Longman & Todd, 1972). The eight specializations are research, interpretation, history, dialectic, foundations, doctrines, systematics, and communications.
2. Jacques Maritain, *Christianity and Democracy: The Rights of Man and Natural Law* (1942; San Francisco: Ignatius Press, 2011).
3. John Paul II, *Centesimus Annus*, §§5–11.
4. Letter to the Officers of the First Brigade of the Third Division of the Militia of Massachusetts (October 11, 1798, in *Revolutionary Services and Civil Life of General William Hull* (New York, 1848), 265–66.
5. John Paul II, *Centesimus Annus*, §§31–32.

Chapter 15. Needed: A Sharper Sense of Sin

1. Quoted in Austin Ruse, "The Gaying of America," *Crisis Magazine* (May 9, 2014), available at: http://www.crisismagazine.com/2014/the-gaying-of -america/reilly-cover-graphic-2.
2. Robert R. Reilly, *Making Gay Okay: How Rationalizing Homosexual Behavior is Changing Everything* (San Francisco: Ignatius Press, 2014).
3. Mary Eberstadt, *Adam and Eve after the Pill* (San Francisco: Ignatius Press, 2012), 12.
4. John Paul II, *Veritatis Splendor*, §101.
5. See, for example, *The Federalist* 6: "A man must be far gone in Utopian speculations who can seriously doubt that, if these States should either be wholly disunited, or only united in partial confederacies, the subdivisions into which they might be thrown would have frequent and violent contests with each other. To presume a want of motives for such contests as an argument against their existence, would be to forget that men are ambitious, vindictive, and rapacious. To look for a continuation of harmony between a number of independent, unconnected sovereignties in the same neighborhood, would be to disregard the uniform course of human events, and to set at defiance the accumulated experience of ages." And *The Federalist* 51: "But the great security against a gradual concentration of the several powers in the same department, consists in giving

to those who administer each department the necessary constitutional means and personal motives to resist encroachments of the others. The provision for defense must in this, as in all other cases, be made commensurate to the danger of attack. Ambition must be made to counteract ambition. The interest of the man must be connected with the constitutional rights of the place. It may be a reflection on human nature, that such devices should be necessary to control the abuses of government. But what is government itself, but the greatest of all reflections on human nature? If men were angels, no government would be necessary. If angels were to govern men, neither external nor internal controls on government would be necessary."

6. See, for example, Xiang Yan, "A Two-Prong Approach to Spike Entrepreneurship in Latin America," *South American Business Forum*, accessed March 20, 2014: http://www.sabf.org.ar/assets/files/essays/A%20Two-Prong%20 Approach%20to%20Spike%20Entrepreneurship%20in%20Latin%20 America2.pdf; Gabriel Zinny and James McBride, "Reshaping Education in Latin America through Innovation," Brookings Institution, September 27, 2013, accessed March 20, 2014: http://www.brookings.edu/blogs/education-plus-development/posts/2013/09/27-reshaping-edu-innovation-latin-america-zinny.

7. See Hernando de Soto, *The Mystery of Capital* (New York: Basic Books, 2000); and Nancy Truitt, "Peru's Hidden Resources," *The Tarrytown Letter* (September 1985): 8–9.

8. *Instruction on Christian Freedom and Liberation*, §75.

9. *Instruction on Certain Aspects of the "Theology of Liberation*," §IV.15.

10. This section draws from Angela Winkels, "The Structures of Sin" (unpublished paper, Ave Maria University, 2013).

11. John Paul II, *Reconciliation and Penance*, §16.

12. Ibid.

13. Ibid.

14. Ibid.

15. Ibid.

16. *Instruction on Christian Freedom and Liberation*, §74.

17. John Paul II, *Reconciliation and Penance*, §16.

Introduction to Part Two

1. See Charles Murray, *Coming Apart: The State of White America, 1960–2010* (New York: Crown, 2012).

Chapter 16. Conscience and Social Justice

1. See Robert P. George, *The Clash of Orthodoxies: Law, Religion, and Morality in Crisis* (Wilmington, Del.: ISI Books, 2002); and *Conscience and Its Enemies: Confronting the Dogmas of Liberal Secularism* (Wilmington, Del.: ISI Books, 2013).

2. See, for example, the blog site *Medicine and Social Justice*: http://medicinesocial justice.blogspot.com/2012/10/conscience-clauses-have-become.html.

3. See Stephen L. Darwall, *The Second-Person Standpoint: Morality, Respect, and Accountability* (Cambridge, Mass.: Harvard University Press, 2006); Joseph Ratzinger, *On Conscience* (San Francisco: Ignatius Press, 2007); Charles Taylor, *Sources of the Self* (Cambridge: Cambridge University Press, 1989); Robert K. Vischer, *Conscience and the Common Good: Reclaiming the Space between Person and State* (New York: Cambridge University Press, 2009).

4. Robert K. Vischer, "The Progressive Case for Conscience Protection," *Public Discourse* (March 9, 2011), accessed March 18, 2014: http://www.thepublic discourse.com/2011/03/2915/.

5. Ibid.

6. See, for example, E. Clark, "Spring, and Danger, in the Air," *NASW News* 57, no. 5 (May 2012); NASW Legal Defense Fund, *Social Workers and Conscience Clauses* (Washington, D.C.: National Association of Social Workers, 2010).

7. George, *The Clash of Orthodoxies*.

8. *Ward v. Polite et al.* See http://www.ca6.uscourts.gov/opinions.pdf/12a0024 p-06.pdf.

9. National Association of Scholars, "The Scandal of Social Work Education" (2007), accessed March 18, 2014: http://www.nas.org/articles/The_Scandal_ of_Social_Work_Education.

10. George Cardinal Pell, "Intolerant Tolerance," *First Things* (August/September 2009), accessed March 18, 2014: http://www.firstthings.com/article/2009/08/ intolerant-tolerance.

11. World Medical Association, *Declaration of Geneva Physician's Oath* (1948), accessed March 18, 2014: http://www.cirp.org/library/ethics/geneva/.

12. R. Joseph, *Human Rights and the Unborn Child* (Boston: Martinus Nijhoff, 2009).

13. P. A. Tozzi, "Vatican Tells United Nations to Quit Pressuring Countries to Legalize Abortion," *LifeNews* (November 28, 2008), accessed March 18, 2014: http://www.lifenews.com/int1003.html.

14. American College of Obstetricians and Gynecologists [ACOG], "The Limits of Conscientious Refusal in Reproductive Medicine," ACOG Committee Opinion, no. 385 (November 2007); Christopher Kaczor, *Thomas Aquinas on Faith, Hope, and Love: Edited and Explained for Everyone* (Ave Maria, Fla.: Sapientia Press, 2008).

15. Helen Alvaré, "The White House and Sexualityism," *Public Discourse* (July 16, 2012), accessed March 18, 2014: http://www.thepublicdiscourse.com/2012/ 07/5757/.

16. Ibid.

17. Francis Cardinal George, "What Are You Going to Give up This Lent?" *Catholic New World* (February 26, 2012), accessed March 18, 2014: http://www.catholic newworld.com/cnwonline/2012/0226/cardinal.aspx.

18. See George, *The Clash of Orthodoxies*.

19. J. Sweifach, "Conscientious Objection in Social Work: Rights vs. Responsibilities," *Journal of Social Work Values & Ethics* 8, no. 2 (2011).

20. American Pharmacists Association, "Code of Ethics for Pharmacists" (1994), accessed March 18, 2014: http://www.pharmacist.com/code-ethics.

21. American Medical Association, "Code of Medical Ethics" (2012), accessed March 18, 2014: http://www.ama-assn.org/ama/pub/physician-resources/medical-ethics/code-medical-ethics.page?.

22. American Nurses Association, "Code of Ethics for Nurses with Interpretive Statements (Silver Spring, Md.: American Nurses Publishing, 2001), accessed March 18, 2014: http://www.nursingworld.org/MainMenuCategories/Ethics Standards/CodeofEthicsforNurses/Code-of-Ethics.pdf.

23. L. Harpaz, "Compelled Lawyer Representation and the Free Speech Rights of Attorneys," *Western New England Law Review* 20, no. 20 (1998): 49–72, accessed March 18, 2014: http://digitalcommons.law.wne.edu/cgi/viewcontent.cgi?article=1247&context=lawreview.

24. Sweifach, "Conscientious Objection in Social Work."

25. Ibid.

26. N. Linzer, *Resolving Ethical Dilemmas in Social Work Practice* (Boston: Allyn & Bacon, 1999), 28.

27. Clark, "Spring, and Danger, in the Air."

28. NASW Legal Defense Fund, "Social Workers and Conscience Clauses."

29. M. P. Moreland, "Practical Reason and Subsidiarity: Response to Robert K. Vischer, Conscience and the Common Good," *Journal of Catholic Legal Studies* 49, no. 2 (2011): 320, accessed March 18, 2014: http://www.stjohns.edu/academics/graduate/law/journals_activities/catholiclegalstudies/issue/49_2.

30. Herbert McCabe, "Aquinas on Good Sense," *New Blackfriars* 67, no. 798 (October 1986), quoted in Moreland, "Practical Reason and Subsidiarity," 322.

31. Moreland, "Practical Reason and Subsidiarity," 322.

32. Elizabeth Anscombe, "Modern Moral Philosophy," in *Human Life, Action and Ethics: Essays by G. E. M. Anscombe*, ed. Mary Geach and Luke Gormally (Exeter, U.K.: Imprint Academic, 2005), 170.

33. See M. Pakaluk and M. Cheffers, *Accounting Ethics ... and the Near Collapse of the World's Financial System* (Sutton, Mass.: Allen David Press, 2011).

34. Elizabeth Anscombe, *Human Life, Action and Ethics: Essays by G.E.M. Anscombe*, 241.

35. See Brian Barry, *Culture and Equality: An Egalitarian Critique of Multiculturalism* (Cambridge, Mass.: Harvard University Press, 2001).

36. Melissa Moschella, "Taking (Conscience) Rights Seriously," *Public Discourse* (June 11, 2012), accessed March 18, 2014: http://www.thepublicdiscourse.com/2012/06/5603/.

37. Ibid.

38. Ibid.

39. 4 Maccabees 5:3.

40. Michael Stokes Paulsen, "Obama's Contraception Cram-down: The Pork Prec-edent," *Public Discourse* (February 21, 2012), accessed March 18, 2014: http://www.thepublicdiscourse.com/2012/02/4777/#sthash.gbY3yEUM.dpuf.

41. "Last-Minute Conscience Rule Grants Protection to Abortion Objectors," *Bioedge* (January 2, 2009), accessed March 18, 2014: http://www.bioedge.org/index.php/bioethics/bioethics_article/8433. Here I leave aside the tendentious way in which advocates of abortion, contraception, and sterilization—where these are not medically indicated—describe these interventions as part of "reproductive health care," although they are antireproductive, seldom have anything to do with the health of either mother or child, and in the case of abortion involve by definition not care but killing one of the patients.

42. I say "supposed" because it is not clear how the legal right to have an abortion, for example, in itself gives anyone a legal right to demand its provision, let alone legally obliging anyone else to carry it out or pay for it.

43. See Hadley Arkes, *Natural Rights and the Right to Choose* (Cambridge: Cambridge University Press, 2002).

44. Council on Social Work Education, "Educational Policy and Accreditation Standards."

45. Edmund Pellegrino, *The Philosophy of Medicine Reborn: A Pellegrino Reader*, ed. H. T. Engelhardt, Jr., and F. Jotterand (Notre Dame, Ind.: University of Notre Dame Press, 2008), 299.

46. Harpaz, "Compelled Lawyer Representation and the Free Speech Rights of Attorneys."

47. Robert K. Vischer, *Conscience and the Common Good*, 3.

48. Ibid., 4.

49. Moreland, "Practical Reason and Subsidiarity," 325.

50. Vischer, *Conscience and the Common Good*, 4.

51. N. Gilbert and P. Terrell, *Dimensions of Social Welfare Policy*, 8th ed. (Upper Saddle River, N.J.: Pearson, 2012).

52. Pius XI, *Quadragesimo Anno*, §78.

Chapter 17. Marriage as a Social Justice Issue

1. See Jason DeParle, "Two Classes, Divided by 'I Do'," *New York Times* (July 14, 2012), accessed December 5, 2013: http://www.nytimes.com/2012/07/15/us/two-classes-in-america-divided-by-i-do.html?pagewanted=all&_r=2&utm_source=RTA+Lu+marriage&utm_campaign=winstorg&utm_medium=email&; Kay S. Hymowitz, *Marriage and Caste in America: Separate and Unequal Families in a Post-Marital Age* (Chicago: Ivan R. Dee, 2006); Charles Murray, *Coming Apart: The State of White America, 1960–2010*; Robert Putnam, *Our Kids: The American Dream in Crisis* (New York: Simon & Schuster, 2015).

2. Paul R. Amato, "The Impact of Family Formation Change on the Cognitive, Social, and Emotional Well-Being of the Next Generation," *The Future of Children* 15, no. 2 (Fall 2005): 75–96.

3. Paula Fomby and Stacey J. Bosick, "Family Instability and the Transition to Adulthood," *Journal of Marriage and Family* 75, no. 5 (October 2013): 1266–87.

4. Michael Gähler and Anna Garriga, "Has the Association between Parental Divorce and Young Adults' Psychological Problems Changed Over Time? Evidence from Sweden, 1968–2000," *Journal of Family Issues* 34 (June 2013): 784–808. First published on June 14, 2012.

5. See George A. Akerlof, "Men Without Children," *Economic Journal, Royal Economic Society* 108, no. 447 (March 1998): 287–309; Alexandra Killewald, "Reconsiderations of the Fatherhood Premium: Marriage, Coresidence, Biology, and Fathers' Wages," *American Sociological Review* 78, no. 1 (February 2013): 96–116; Alexandra Killewald and Margaret Gough, "Does Specialization Explain Marriage Penalties and Premiums?" *American Sociological Review* 78, no. 3 (June 2013): 447–502; and also Nicholas W. Townsend, *The Package Deal: Marriage, Work, and Fatherhood in Men's Lives* (Philadelphia: Temple University Press, 2002).

6. Linda J. Waite and Maggie Gallagher, *The Case for Marriage: Why Married People are Happier, Healthier, and Better Off Financially* (New York: Doubleday, 2000).

7. Norval Glenn, *Closed Hearts, Closed Minds: The Textbook Story of Marriage* (New York: Institute for American Values, 1997).

8. Ibid., 4.

9. Mary Eberstadt, *Adam and Eve after the Pill* (San Francisco: Ignatius Press, 2012).

10. See Kathryn Edin and Maria Kefalas, *Promises I Can Keep: Why Poor Women Put Motherhood before Marriage* (Berkeley: University of California Press, 2011).

11. J. Brian Benestad, *Church, State, and Society: An Introduction to Catholic Social Doctrine* (Washington, D.C.: Catholic University of America Press, 2011), 151.

12. Alasdair MacIntyre, *Dependent Rational Animals: Why Human Beings Need the Virtues* (Chicago: Open Court, 1999).

13. Edward Feser, "Social Justice Reconsidered: Austrian Economics and Catholic Social Teaching" (Hayek Memorial Lecture delivered at the 2005 Austrian Scholars Conference, Auburn, Alabama), accessed December 5, 2013: http://www.edwardfeser.com/unpublishedpapers/socialjustice.html.

14. Thomas Aquinas, *Summa theologiae* II-II, q. 58, a. 1.

15. Feser, "Social Justice Reconsidered."

16. See chapter 2 of this work; also, Michael Novak, "Defining Social Justice," *First Things* (December 2000).

17. Michael Pakaluk, "What's Next for Marriage? After the Supreme Court," *National Review Online* (June 27, 2013), accessed December 5, 2013: http://www.nationalreview.com/article/352158/whats-next-marriage-nro-symposium/page/0/5.

18. *Gaudium et Spes*, §24.3.

19. Michael Pakaluk, "What's Next for Marriage? After the Supreme Court."

20. Anthony Esolen, "The Moral Structure of Pedophilia," *Public Discourse*

(September 30, 2013), accessed December 5, 2013: http://www.thepublic
discourse.com/2013/09/10295/.

21. For a social-scientific account of the phenomenon, see Elizabeth Marquardt, *The Revolution in Parenthood: The Emerging Global Clash between Adult Rights and Children's Needs* (New York: Institute for American Values, 2006).

22. Feser, "Social Justice Reconsidered."

23. Pakaluk, "What's Next for Marriage?"

24. Sherif Girgis, Ryan T. Anderson, and Robert P. George, "The Supreme Court, You and Me, and the Future of Marriage," *Public Discourse* (June 27, 2013), accessed December 5, 2013: http://www.thepublicdiscourse.com/2013/06/10455/.

25. Maggie Gallagher, *Can Government Strengthen Marriage? Evidence from the Social Sciences* (New York: Institute for American Values, 2004).

26. See Alvaré, "The White House and Sexualityism."

27. Alasdair MacIntyre, *After Virtue*, 3rd ed. (Notre Dame: Notre Dame University Press, 2007).

28. Ibid., 263.

29. Ibid., 34.

30. See Eberstadt, *Adam and Eve*, and *How the West Really Lost God: A New Theory of Secularization* (West Conshohocken, Penn.: Templeton Press, 2013).

31. Michael Novak, "A Humble and Rousing Shakespeare," *Gyrene Gazette* (June 11, 2013).

32. See Robert P. George, *Clash of Orthodoxies*.

33. See "What Does a Faith and Action Circle Meeting Look Like?" *Catholics for the Common Good*, accessed December 7, 2013: http://ccgaction.org/swc/faithand action/themeeting; Juan Puigbó and Hilary Towers, "Protecting Marriage: Part 1 of 2: Common Myths About Wedlock and Divorce," *National Catholic Register* (June 25, 2013), accessed December 7, 2013: http://www.ncregister.com/site/ article/protecting-marriage/%23ixzz2ZA4SiDIW; and also Puigbó and Towers, "Creating Communities Centered on Marriage: Last of a Two-Part Series on Protecting the Institution of Marriage," *National Catholic Register* (July 14, 2013), accessed December 7, 2013: http://www.ncregister.com/site/article/ creating-communities-centered-on-marriage/.

34. Nicole M. King, "Norway Rethinks Its Acceptance of Divorce," *MercatorNet* (November 6, 2013), accessed December 9, 2013: http://www.mercatornet.com/ family__edge/view/13055.

35. Benestad, *Church, State, and Society*, 151.

Chapter 18. Practicing Social Justice

1. Brandon Vogt, *Saints and Social Justice*

2. Benjamin Feigenberg, Erica M. Field, and Rohini Pande, "Building Social Capital through Microfinance," Harvard Kennedy School Faculty Research Working Paper Series (May 2010), NBER Working Paper No. 16018 (Cambridge, Mass.: National Bureau of Economic Research, 2010).

3. Lisa Y. Larance, "Fostering Social Capital through NGO Design: Grameen Bank Membership in Bangladesh," *International Social Work* 44, no. 1 (January 2001): 7–18.

4. Hernando de Soto, *The Mystery of Capital*.

5. Michael Matheson Miller, *The PovertyCure DVD Series* (2012), http://www .povertycure.org/dvd-series/.

6. Paul Adams and Karin Krauth, "Working with Families and Communities: The Patch Approach," in *Reinventing Human Services: Community- and Family-Centered Practice*, ed. Paul Adams and Karin Krauth (New York: Aldine de Gruyter, 1995); Paul Adams et al., *Strengthening Families and Neighborhoods: A Community-Centered Approach: Final Report on the Iowa Patch Project to U.S. Department of Health and Human Services, Administration for Children and Families* (Iowa City, Iowa: University of Iowa School of Social Work, 1995); Paul Adams, "Bringing the Community Back In: Patch and Group Decision-Making" in *Family Group Conferencing: New Directions in Community-Centered Child & Family Practice*, ed. Gale Burford and Joe Hudson (New York: Aldine de Gruyter: 2000), 105–19.

7. Adams, "Bringing the Community Back In."

8. John Braithwaite, *Restorative Justice and Responsive Regulation* (New York: Oxford University Press, 2002).

9. Braithwaite, *Restorative Justice*; Paul Adams and Susan M. Chandler, "Responsive Regulation in Child Welfare: Systematic Challenges to Mainstreaming the Family Group Conference," *Journal of Sociology and Social Welfare* 31, no. 1 (2004): 93–116.

10. *Family Group Conferencing: New Directions in Community-Centered Child & Family Practice*, ed. Gale Burford and Joe Hudson (New York: Aldine de Gruyter, 2000), xxiii.

11. See Robert D. Putnam, *Making Democracy Work: Civic Traditions in Modern Italy* (Princeton, N.J.: Princeton University Press, 1993).

12. See Feigenberg, Field, and Pande, "Building Social Capital."

13. Pius XI, *Quadragesimo Anno*.

14. John McKnight, *The Careless Society: Community and Its Counterfeits* (New York: Basic Books, 1995).

15. Paul Adams, "Ethics with Character: Virtues and the Ethical Social Worker," *Journal of Sociology and Social Welfare* 36, no. 3 (September, 2009): 83–105; James W. Drisko, "Common Factors in Psychotherapy Outcome: Meta-analytic Findings and Their Implications for Practice and Research," *Families in Society* 85, no. 1 (2004): 81–90; Clay T. Graybeal, "Evidence of the Art of Social Work," *Families in Society* 88, no. 4 (2007): 513–23; Bruce E. Wampold, *The Great Psychotherapy Debate: Models, Methods, and Findings* (Mahwah, N.J.: Erlbaum, 2007).

16. See Benestad, *Church, State, and Society*, 151.

17. Alasdair MacIntyre, *Three Rival Versions of Moral Enquiry: Encyclopaedia, Genealogy, and Tradition* (Notre Dame: University of Notre Dame Press, 1990); Adams, "Ethics with Character."

18. Braithwaite, *Restorative Justice*, 32.
19. Ibid., 33; see also Rob Neff, "Achieving Justice in Child Protection," *Journal of Sociology and Social Welfare* 31, no. 1 (March 2004): 137–54.
20. Braithwaite, *Restorative Justice*, 11.
21. Ibid.
22. John Braithwaite, "Families and the Republic," *Journal of Sociology and Social Welfare* 31, no. 1 (March 2004): 199–215, at 204–5.

Chapter 19. From Charity to Justice?

1. Leo Tolstoy, "Where Love Is, There God Is," in *Walk in the Light and Twenty-Three Tales*, trans. Louis and Aylmer Maude (Maryknoll, N.Y.: Orbis, 2003), 188–204. On art as a parable, see Leo Tolstoy, *What is Art?*, ed. W. Gareth Jones (London: Bristol Classical Press, 2011).
2. Tolstoy, "Where Love Is," 195.
3. Ibid., 201.
4. Adams, "Ethics with Character"; MacIntyre, *After Virtue*.
5. Alexis de Tocqueville, *Democracy in America*, ed. Isaac Kramnick (New York: Penguin, 2003).
6. John Finnis, *Fundamentals of Ethics* (Washington, D.C.: Georgetown University Press, 1983).
7. Servais Pinckaers, *The Sources of Christian Ethics*, trans. M. T. Noble (Washington, D.C.: Catholic University of America Press, 1995). See also Michael Novak's discussion of the "first C"—*caritas*—in chapter 5 above.
8. Timothy P. Jackson, *The Priority of Love: Christian Charity and Social Justice* (Princeton, N.J.: Princeton University Press, 2003).
9. With some notable exceptions, it is little discussed. For exceptions, see Peter T. Geach, *The Virtues* (Cambridge: Cambridge University Press, 1977); Deirdre N. McCloskey, *Bourgeois Virtues: Ethics for an Age of Commerce* (Chicago: Chicago University Press, 2006).
10. Geach, *The Virtues*, 80.
11. Benedict XVI, *God is Love: Deus Caritas Est* (San Francisco: Ignatius Press, 2006), 86.
12. McCloskey, *Bourgeois Virtues*, 91.
13. Christopher Kaczor, *Thomas Aquinas on Faith, Hope, and Love*; see also Geach, *The Virtues*.
14. David Bentley Hart, *Atheist Delusions: The Christian Revolution and Its Fashionable Enemies* (New Haven, Conn.: Yale University Press, 2009); Rodney Stark, *The Rise of Christianity: How the Obscure Marginal Jesus Movement Became the Dominant Religious Force in the Western World in a Few Centuries* (Princeton, N.J.: Princeton University Press, 1996); Rodney Stark, *The Triumph of Christianity: How the Jesus Movement Became the World's Largest Religion* (New York: Harper One, 2011).
15. Thomas C. Oden, *The Good Works Reader* (Grand Rapids, Mich.: Wm. B. Eerdmans, 2007).

16. See Stark's works cited in n. 14, above.
17. David Bentley Hart, *Atheist Delusions*.
18. Ibid.
19. As quoted in Stark, *The Rise of Christianity*, 84.
20. Benedict XVI, *God Is Love*; Hart, *Atheist Delusions*; Stark, *The Rise of Christianity*, and also *The Triumph of Christianity*.
21. Hart, *Atheist Delusions*.
22. As found ibid., 192.
23. See Ramsay MacMullen, *Paganism in the Roman Empire* (New Haven, Conn.: Yale University Press, 1981); and Louis Markos, *From Achilles to Christ: Why Christians Should Read the Pagan Classics* (Downer Grove, Ill.: IVP Academic, 2007).
24. See Edwin A. Judge, "The Quest for Mercy in Late Antiquity," in *God Who is Rich in Mercy: Essays Presented to D. B. Knox*, ed. Peter T. O'Brien and David G. Peterson (Sydney: MacQuarie University Press, 1986), 107–21; and Stark, *The Triumph of Christianity*.
25. See Gavan Daws, *Holy Man* (New York: Harper & Row, 1989); and Matthew Bunson and Margaret Bunson, *St. Damien of Molokai: Apostle of the Exiled* (Huntington, Ind.: Our Sunday Visitor, 2009).
26. "Solidarity with South Sudan," accessed December 10, 2013: http://www .solidarityssudan.org; and Nicholas D. Kristof, "A Church Mary Can Love," *New York Times* (April 17, 2010), accessed July 10, 2010: http://www.nytimes .com/2010/04/18/opinion/18kristof.html?hp; and also, Nicholas D. Kristof, "Who Can Mock this Church?" *New York Times* (May 1, 2010), accessed July 10, 2010: http://www.nytimes.com/2010/05/02/opinion/02kristof.html.
27. Benedict XVI, *God Is Love*.
28. Ibid.
29. For discussion of the contemporaneous shift in scientific work from clerical avocation—e.g., Copernicus, Mendel—to freestanding secular profession in the late nineteenth century, see James Hannam, "Modern Science's Christian Sources," *First Things* (October 2011): 47–51.
30. James Leiby, *A History of Social Welfare and Social Work in the United States* (New York: Columbia University Press, 1978).
31. Ibid.
32. Bernard Bro, *Saint Therese of Lisieux: Her Family, Her God, Her Message* (San Francisco: Ignatius Press, 2003).
33. 1 Corinthians 13:2–3.
34. Leiby, *A History of Social Welfare*.
35. National Association of Social Workers, *NASW Code of Ethics* (1999; Washington, D.C.: National Association of Social Workers, 2008). Available online at: http:/www.socialworkers.org/pubs/code/code.asp.
36. David Hodge, "Value Differences between Social Workers and Members of the Working and Middle Classes," *Social Work* 48, no. 1 (2003): 107–19.

37. John Boyle O'Reilly, "In Bohemia," in *In Bohemia* (Boston: The Pilot Publishing Co., 1886), 14–15.

38. As found in Kathleen Woodroofe, *From Charity to Social Work: In England and the United States* (London: Routledge & Kegan Paul, 1974), 55.

39. Leo XIII, *Rerum Novarum*, §22.

40. Nicholas Wolterstorff, "Justice, Not Charity: Social Work through the Eyes of Faith," *Social Work and Christianity* 33, no. 2 (2006): 123–40.

41. Nicholas Wolterstorff, *Justice: Rights and Wrongs* (Princeton, N.J.: Princeton University Press, 2010); and *Justice in Love*, Emory University Studies in Law and Religion (Grand Rapids, Mich.: Wm. B. Eerdmans Publishing, 2011).

42. Jonathan Gruber and Daniel M. Hungerman, "Faith-Based Charity and Crows out during the Great Depression," National Bureau of Economic Research, Working Paper 11332, Cambridge, Mass.

43. Wolterstorff, "Justice, Not Charity," 135.

44. Rodney Stark, *The Victory of Reason: How Christianity Led to Freedom, Capitalism, and Western Success* (New York: Random House, 2005).

45. Ibid., 72.

Chapter 20. Charity Needs Caritas—So Does Social Justice

1. Cited by Josef Pieper, *Faith, Hope, Love* (San Francisco: Ignatius Press, 1997), 151.

2. Robert D. Lupton, *Toxic Charity: How Churches and Charities Hurt Those They Help (And How to Reverse It)* (New York: Harper One, 2011).

3. See McKnight, *The Careless Society*; Lupton, *Toxic Charity*; Steve Corbett and Brian Fikkert, *When Helping Hurts: How to Alleviate Poverty without Hurting the Poor... and Yourself* (Chicago: Moody Publishers, 2012).

4. Aquinas, *Summa theologiae* II-II, q. 23, a. 6.

5. Aquinas, *Commentary on 1 Corinthians* 13, n. 760.

6. See Matthew 25; Luke 16:19–31.

7. Feser, "Social Justice Reconsidered."

8. Benedict XVI, *God Is Love.*

9. Ibid., §69.

10. Peter L. Berger and Richard John Neuhaus, *To Empower People: From State to Civil Society*, 2nd ed., ed. Michael Novak (Washington, D.C.: American Enterprise Institute Press, 1996).

11. Benedict XVI, *God Is Love*, §69.

12. Ibid., §79.

13. Ibid., §81.

14. Roger Scruton, *The Uses of Pessimism: And the Danger of False Hope* (New York: Oxford University Press, 2010).

15. Benedict XVI, *God Is Love*, §88.

16. Paul Adams and Kristine Nelson, *Reinventing Human Services: Community- and Family-centered Practice* (Hawthorne, N.Y.: Aldine de Gruyter, 1995); Gale

Burford and Paul Adams, "Restorative Justice, Responsive Regulation and Social Work," *Journal of Sociology and Social Welfare* 31, no. 1 (2004): 7–26; McKnight, *The Careless Society.*

17. Charles J. Chaput, "Protecting the Church's Freedom in Colorado," *First Things* (February 6, 2008), accessed February 7, 2008: http://www.firstthings.com/onthesquare/?p=966; Charles J. Chaput, "A Charitable Endeavor," *First Things* no. 197 (November 2009): 25–29.

18. Brian C. Anderson, "How Catholic Charities Lost Its Soul," *City Journal* (Winter 2000), accessed September 10, 2009: http://www.city-journal.org/printable.php?id=566; Chaput, "A Charitable Endeavor."

19. Chaput, "A Charitable Endeavor," 29.

20. Benedict XVI, *God Is Love*, §79.

21. See Adams, "Ethics with Character"; Drisko, "Common Factors in Psychotherapy Outcomes"; Wampold, *The Great Psychotherapy Debate.*

22. Benedict XVI, *God Is Love*, §85.

23. Ibid., §87.

24. Ibid., §88.

25. Ibid., §90.

26. Matthew 25:40.

27. Robert Barron, *The Strangest Way: Walking the Christian Path* (Maryknoll, N.Y.: Orbis, 2002).

28. Dorothy Day, *The Duty of Delight: The Diaries of Dorothy Day*, ed. Robert Ellsberg (New York: Image, 2011).

29. Jean Pierre De Cassaude, S.J., *Abandonment to Divine Providence* (San Francisco: Ignatius Press, 2011).

30. Matthew 5:48.

31. Benedict XVI, "On Everyone's Call to be a Saint," General Audience in Saint Peter's Square (April 4, 2011), accessed November 21, 2011: http://www.zenit.org/article-32316?1=english.

Epilogue. Social Justice: In the Vast Social Space between the Person and the State

1. The term "excessive individualism" indicates that there is a bad form of individualism, as well as a good form. Tocqueville called attention to the latter under the term "self-interest rightly understood," as when one person takes responsibility for doing his duty, and another shows initiative and creativity in helping a society find its way out of distress. No one should attack individualism in an undifferentiated way. See *Democracy in America*, vol. 2, part 2, chapter 8: "The American moralists do not profess that men ought to sacrifice themselves for their fellow-creatures because it is noble to make such sacrifices; but they boldly aver that such sacrifices are as necessary to him who imposes them upon himself as to him for whose sake they are made. They have found out that in their country and their age man is brought home to himself by an irresistible force; and losing all hope of stopping that force, they turn all their thoughts to

the direction of it. They therefore do not deny that every man may follow his own interest; but they endeavor to prove that it is the interest of every man to be virtuous."

2. Edmund Pellegrino and D. C. Thomasma, *The Virtues in Medical Practice* (New York: Oxford University Press, 1993); see also Edmund Pellegrino, *The Philosophy of Medicine Reborn: A Pellegrino Reader*.

3. Alasdair MacIntyre, *Three Rival Versions of Moral Enquiry*.

4. Justin Oakley and Dean Cocking, *Virtue Ethics and Professional Roles* (Cambridge: Cambridge University Press, 2001).

5. Paul Adams, "Ethics with Character." This 2009 article was the first in many decades in the American social-work literature to offer a serious discussion of the virtues and virtue ethics. Elizabeth Anscombe's devastating critique of Kantian and utilitarian ethics had been published in 1957, and Alasdair MacIntyre's path-breaking and influential study, *After Virtue*, in 1981. See G. E. M. Anscombe, "Modern Moral Philosophy."

6. Paul Adams, "Children as Contributions in Kind: Social Security and Family Policy," *Social Work* 35, no. 6 (1990): 492–98.

7. The image is from Gerard Manley Hopkins's poem "The Windhover."

INDEX

abortion, 36, 158, 205, 206, 231, 238, 304n41, 304n42; as matter of conscience, 208–9, 215; Progressives and, 33, 35. *See also* birth control; rights: reproductive

Acton, Lord, 53, 69

Adams, John, 68, 176

Adams, Paul, 16, 28, 93, 154, 156, 197, 199, 233

Aeterni Patris (Leo XIII, 1879), 93

agriculture, 18, 19, 22, 60, 75, 85, 97; agrarianism and, 95, 97, 174; economics and, 166, 263; progress in, 106, 263

Aid for Families with Dependent Children (AFDC), 51–52

almsgiving, 175, 259, 260, 261–62, 265, 267. *See also* charity

Alvaré, Helen, 206, 231

America, Americans, 18, 20, 31, 51, 72, 76, 84, 128, 147, 173, 206, 214, 224; associations and, 119; capitalism and, 165, 166, 168; Catholic social thought and, 121–38, 151; *Centesimus Annus* and, 149; civil rights and, 34, 35, 284; communitarianism in, 175, 176; democracy and, 3, 26, 28, 216; economics and, 114, 141, 263; as experiment, 4, 20, 176; founding of, 10, 22, 26, 27; freedom and, 18, 67, 141; immigrants to, 22, 23; individualism and, 113, 117, 311n1; liberalism and, 104, 151; poverty in, 24, 36,

75, 97, 169; Progressive elites in, 33, 34; religion and, 18, 67, 104; welfare in, 33, 52, 240. *See also* United States

Anderson, Ryan, 230

Andreotti, Giulio, 173

Antiochus IV Epiphanes, 212, 218

Argentina, Argentines, 161, 163, 166, 167, 168, 171, 239

Aristotle, 7, 20, 30, 108, 118, 119, 183, 184, 224, 235, 254, 273, 279; on common good, 31; on man as political, 43, 92, 93; on natural beings, 56; on private property, 71; on roots of social justice, 19, 39; on virtue, 137

associationism, associations: Aquinas on, 69, 70; democracy and, 27, 53–54; John Paul II and, 28, 71; right of, 69–71; voluntary, 175; virtue of, 21–24, 25, 50

atheism, atheists, 2, 29, 37, 67, 80, 256, 275, 284

Atlas Foundation, 52–53

Augustine, Saint, 85, 157, 187, 190, 224

Ave Maria, Florida, 4, 232–34

Ave Maria University, 4, 232

Bangladesh, 116, 160, 238–39

Beatitudes, 2, 16

Benedict XVI, 9, 28, 66, 88, 264; on *caritas*, 56, 255, 267; *Caritas in Veritate*, 156–60, 264; *Deus Caritas Est*, 56, 169. *See also* Ratzinger, Joseph Aloisius

Benestad, J. Brian, 223, 235, 246
Bentham, Jeremy, 95, 165
Berlin Wall, 138, 173
birth control, 35, 206. *See also* abortion;
  rights: reproductive
blacks, 34–35, 52, 76, 220, 284
Braithwaite, John, 242, 244, 247–48,
  250
Brazil, 123, 144, 153, 164, 167
bureaucracy, government, 24, 39, 192,
  239, 267, 272. *See also* government;
  state, the
Burke, Thomas Patrick, 9, 90, 91,
  288n16, 295n8

Cain and Abel, 57
Calvez, Jean-Yves, 89, 90, 92
Camus, Albert, 57, 179
Canada, 203, 217
capitalism, capitalists, 8, 22, 26, 34, 105,
  166; *Centesimus Annus* and, 62, 139–55;
  democratic, 2, 3, 4, 129; as economic
  system, 8–9, 47, 97, 107, 134, 160, 174,
  292n21; Francis on, 161–71; John Paul
  II and, 129, 132–35, 173
Caritapolis, 178–79, 284–86
caritas, 56–58, 169, 178–79, 201, 255–56,
  259, 260, 267, 284–86, 294n3;
  Benedict XVI and, 156–60, 264, 269;
  as greatest gift of Holy Spirit, 254;
  solidarity and, 71, 84; as theological
  virtue, 10, 254, 265–66, 269. *See also*
  charity
Caritas in Veritate (Benedict XVI, 2009),
  156–60
Carter, Jimmy, 75–76
Catholic Charities, 216, 258
Catholic Relief Services, 258
Catholic social teaching, 2, 4, 8, 31, 58,
  160, 179, 195, 217, 246; collectivism
  and, 201, 245; concern for poor in,
  6–7; individualism and, 201, 245;
  John Paul II and, 122, 171; principles
  of, 54, 55–88, 255; rights in, 55–77;

social justice in, 9, 31, 55, 87–88; 219;
  as theological specialization, 172–73;
  as work in progress, 5, 6
Catholic tradition, 3, 9, 31, 88, 139, 209,
  210
Cedar Rapids, Iowa, 240, 278
Centesimus Annus (John Paul II, 1991),
  28, 83, 85, 127, 129, 132, 156, 157, 173;
  on capitalism, 139–55; on dignity of
  labor, 62–63, 76, 87; *Gaudium et Spes*
  in, 7–8; on human capital, 40, 62–63,
  142, 152, 153, 178; inner logic of, 134;
  on marginalization, 161–62; outline
  of, 133–34; quoted, 62, 63–64, 80,
  83, 85, 87, 135, 136, 140, 143, 144, 145,
  147, 152, 153, 162; *Rerum Novarum* and,
  5, 80, 133; on socialism, 135–36; on
  solidarity, 83, 138
character, 246, 255; imperfection of, 246,
  257; inner, 31, 71; social justice and,
  24, 274; of social worker, 246, 253,
  270, 280; unique personal, 177, 235;
  virtue and, 20–21, 90
charity, 134, 259, 268, 279; as *caritas*, 10,
  58, 160, 265–72; justice and, 200,
  201, 252–64; social, 2, 10, 15, 87, 107,
  114; as theological virtue, 10, 16, 160,
  277. *See also* almsgiving; *caritas*
Charity Organization Societies (COS),
  230, 259–61, 267
Charles, Rodger, S.J., 89, 92
checks and balances, 26, 28
child protection, 228, 280; Child Protective Services (CPS) and, 241, 246,
  248; patch and, 240–41; state and, 10,
  243, 244; welfare and, 10, 249
Chile, 64, 73, 147, 164
China, 61, 73, 123, 164, 168, 263
Christian Democratic party, 120, 173
Christianity, Christians, 16, 51, 175; care
  for pagans during plagues, 256–57,
  258; concern for poor, 6–7; conscience
  and worship and, 68–69; human
  story in, 56, 57, 62

citizenship, citizens, 20, 23, 30, 32, 41, 50, 103; subjects vs., 3, 22

City of God, 58, 85, 155, 158, 284

City of Man (Human City), 50, 52, 155, 158

civil rights, 34–35, 282, 284

civil society, 50, 82, 93, 95, 101, 102, 107, 118, 120, 146, 159, 216, 234, 236; associations and, 23, 156, 225, 230, 237; *Centesimus Annus* and, 151, 154; collectivism and, 245, 281; conscience and, 200–203, 216; economy and, 27, 239; empowerment and, 154; Family Group Conferencing and, 250, 277, 280; government vs., 139, 146, 239, 280, 281; individuals and, 175, 245, 281; marriage and, 228, 230–31, 236; as mediating structure, 219, 228, 280; professionals and, 214, 245, 251; social justice required for, 2, 237, 281

collectivism, 9, 275, 276; individualism vs., 200–203, 218, 245, 281

colleges and universities, 23, 70, 176, 204, 221–22, 260–61; Catholic, 4, 16, 109, 130, 172, 206, 232–33

Colombia, 153, 164

command economy, 43, 293n26. *See also* state, the

common good, 9, 31–34, 74, 103, 117, 151, 157, 159, 167, 178, 188, 216, 234; associations and, 50, 70, 283; Beatitudes and, 2–3; conscience and, 211, 218; contributions to, 74, 79, 103; economic systems and, 116, 296n30; John Paul II and, 136, 137, 142; justice and, 235, 266; personal responsibility and property and, 73, 74, 79, 196; as principle of Catholic social teaching, 58–60, 85, 160; socialism and, 102, 120; social justice and, 36, 92, 95, 116, 196, 197, 219, 225, 237, 238, 246, 266, 295n8; societies and, 22, 23, 82, 83, 149, 170, 228, 274; social work professionals and, 235, 245, 277, 278, 280

Communism, Communists, 32, 38, 86, 104, 120, 140, 175; European, 4, 164; John Paul II and, 5, 185; Leo XIII and, 105, 108; Pius XI and, 113, 114; Poland and, 84, 130; revolution of, 173; Russian, 5, 155; social justice and, 19, 87

compassion, 25, 29, 35–36, 51, 59, 77, 184, 277, 284

conscience, 68, 69, 80, 176, 203, 204, 209–12, 217–18; coercion and, 67, 202, 205, 211, 214, 216; easing of, 7, 33; exemptions for, 202, 207–9, 213–16; Health and Human Services (HHS) mandate and, 206, 211; liberty of, 130, 131, 170; right of, 10, 66–69, 200; sin and, 181, 195; social justice and, 200–18; trivialization of, 203–8, 211

creation theology, 177–79

creativity, 61–63

cultural capital, 138

Cyprian, Bishop of Carthage, 256, 272

Damien of Molokai, Saint, 258, 269, 271, 272

Day, Dorothy, 271–72

Declaration of Independence, 284

democracy, 26–27, 32, 53, 87, 92, 173; associations and, 27, 53–54; democratic capitalism and, 2–4; democratic socialism and, 96; Pius XII on, 28; religion and, 17–18; in republics, 22, 27

de Soto, Hernando, 146, 191, 239, 263

Deus Caritas Est (Benedict XVI, 2005): church independent of state in, 66; God's love in, 56, 169; guidance to social workers in, 269

Deuteronomy, 68

developing nations, 4, 61. *See also* Third World

Dignitatis Humanae (Vatican II, 1965), 122

Dionysius, Bishop of Alexandria, 256, 272

distribution and redistribution, 21, 30, 41, 93, 263

divorce, 51, 207, 215, 220, 221–23, 227, 229–31, 234. *See also* marriage

Doctors Without Borders, 196

Dzielski, Mirosław, 62

earth, 59, 85

Eberstadt, Mary, 184, 222, 232

Ecclesiastes, 69

égalité, 17

Einstein, Albert, 73

elderly, 36, 145, 158

Emancipation Proclamation, 284

empowerment, 214, 242, 243; regulatory process and, 246–51; social justice and, 244, 279; social work and, 154, 219, 230, 234, 260

encyclicals, 3, 5, 6, 7. *See also titles of encyclicals*

Engels, Friedrich, 71, 95

Enlightenment, the, 51, 90

equality, 31, 29–30, 102–4. *See also* inequality

Esolen, Anthony, 228–29, 287n4

ethics, 151, 254; Aristotle on, 119; Christian social, 258, 266; codes of, 207–9, 213–14, 260–61; of individuals, 19, 40, 41, 42; social work and, 200, 204–5, 279; society and, 54

Europe, 5, 18, 28, 36, 61, 92, 95; American experiment and, 27, 173

euthanasia, 205

Evangelii Gaudium (Francis, 2014), 169; economic themes of, 167–69; Francis and, 161, 171

family, families, 2, 3, 22, 31, 70, 119, 137, 175, 217, 227, 230, 247–51; in agricultural societies, 18, 75; blended, 220, 223; as community, 70, 187–88; failure of, 36, 176; human race as, 58, 59, 84, 85; individuals and, 7, 8; in industrial societies, 8, 18, 95, 97;

living wage and, 111, 146, 149, 225, 238; poor, 24, 222, 259; religion and, 96, 97, 232; sex and, 185, 220, 234, 235; under socialism, 101, 113; state and, 51, 183–84, 231, 232, 244–47. *See also* marriage

Family Group Conference, Conferencing (FGC), 241–42, 277, 278, 280; as part of restorative justice, 243, 249; regulatory pyramid and, 246, 247, 249, 250; use of, 242, 250–51, 280

Fanfani, Amintore, 165, 173

Fascism, Fascists, 4, 108; in Italy, 5, 173; Pius XI and, 112, 113

federalism, 82, 122, 136–37, 186, 187. *See also* subsidiarity

Federalist, The, 186

Ferree, William, 89–90, 118

Feser, Edward, 224, 226, 230

Fisher, Antony, 52

Fortin, Ernest, 89, 90–91

France, French, 17, 23, 67, 96, 97, 130, 165, 169, 172, 176

Francis, 9, 88; *Evangelii Gaudium* (2013), 161, 171; as self-described sinner, 181; on unreformed capitalism, 161–71. *See also Evangelii Gaudium*

Franciscans, 70, 157, 238

freedom: big government and, 25; of choice, 45; in human nature, 57, 59; moral responsibility and, 47; of religion, 66–67. *See also* liberty, liberties; rights

free economy, 25, 26, 140; Hayek and, 37, 45–46, 53; John Paul II and, 129, 147, 151

friendship: charity and, 259–60; of God, 56–59, 66, 178–79, 185–86, 192, 255–56, 266, 285; marriage and, 228

Gaudium et Spes (Vatican II, 1965), 8, 58

Gaulle, Charles de, 173

gays, 33, 35

Geach, Peter, 254, 255

general justice, 19, 92, 108, 111, 266

Genesis, 57, 85, 131

George, Francis Cardinal, 206–7

George, Robert P., 204, 207, 230

Germany, 73, 92, 117, 165, 179; Hitler's rise in, 17, 108, 109; Nazism in, 5, 173; post–World War I, 106, 108; post–World War II, 140; Weimar, 118

Gibbon, Edward, 257

globalization, 64, 71, 84, 86, 153, 159, 174; solidarity and, 85; subsidiarity and, 158–59

God, 42, 103; *caritas* and, 56, 57, 58; condescension of, 260; as Creator, 18, 31, 55–60, 62, 66, 78, 85, 132, 178–79; death of, 43; as Father, 58; humans as image of, 257

Goethe, Johann Wolfgang von, 30

Gonzalez, Felipé, 129

Grameen Bank, 238–40, 243

Gramsci, Antonio, 47, 168

Great Depression, 17, 106, 108

Greece, Greeks, 20–21, 30, 257

Habermas, Jürgen, 29

Haines, Andrew M., 6

Hamilton, Alexander, 136

Hart, David Bentley, 256

Havel, Vaclav, 175

Hawaii, 242, 258, 280

Hayek, Friedrich, 1, 21, 115, 116, 141, 143, 165, 289n3, 290n4, 290n7, 290n8, 291n15, 291n17, 292n19, 293n25, 293n26; *The Fatal Conceit*, 41, 42–43; mirage of social justice and, 37–54; *The Mirage of Social Justice*, 45, 291n17; as Nobel prizewinner, 28, 37; as social justice practitioner, 49–54; on use of term "social justice," 17, 48

Hippocratic Oath, 205, 214

Hispanics, 76

Hitler, Adolf, 17, 39, 108, 109, 110, 186

Hobbes, Thomas, 93, 217

Höffner, Joseph Cardinal, 92

Hollywood, 176

Holy Spirit, 120, 254

Homestead Act (1862), 51, 122, 126

Hong Kong, 61, 164, 191, 239

human capital, 28, 88, 122, 239; John Paul II on, 40, 62–63, 142, 152, 153, 178; wealth and, 61, 86, 122, 143, 174

human nature, 22, 37, 57, 80, 98, 136, 138, 182, 301n5

human rights, 2, 18, 34, 65, 179, 192, 205, 213, 284; Church and, 55–56; democracy and, 28, 120, 173; John Paul II and, 28, 132–33, 140, 142; Leo XIII on, 99

human spirit, 59, 60, 66, 71

Hume, David, 41, 44, 183, 290n11

hypocrisy, hypocrites, 180–83

Ignatius of Loyola, Saint, 271

immigration, immigrants, 4, 18, 22, 33, 76, 166, 168, 206, 279

India, 34, 61, 73, 164, 168

individualism, individuals, 7, 23, 25, 27, 44–45, 95, 117, 275–76, 311n1; Anglo-American, 104, 113, 117, 156; collectivism and, 9, 200, 201, 203, 218, 245, 281; common good and, 32, 33; Leo XIII on, 96, 104, 274; Pius XI on, 218, 274; in United States, 175, 176

industrial development, Leo XIII on, 8, 18, 97

inequality, 20, 21, 30, 31, 32, 102, 104

Iron Curtain, 122, 130, 138

Israel, 59

Italy, Italians, 47, 90, 117, 119, 122, 172; capitalism in, 165, 168; Marxism in, 168; Mussolini and Fascism in, 5, 17, 108, 109, 113, 173

Japan, 108, 143, 164

Jaspers, Karl, 210, 265

Jefferson, Thomas, 56, 67, 126, 202, 203, 294n5

Jesuits, 19, 89, 90, 107, 271

Jesus Christ, 6, 29, 51, 58, 81, 261, 270; in Gospel of Matthew, 16, 65, 170, 262; parables of, 103, 264, 266; as Redeemer, 55, 103, 178

Job, 42

John, Saint, 170

John XXIII, 159; *Mater et Magistra* (1961), 74; *Pacem in Terris* (1963), 67; Vatican II and, 34

John Paul II, 9, 88, 121, 132–34, 178; *The Acting Person*, 129; anthropology of, 131; on associations, 71, 138; attempted assassination of, 131; on capitalism, 8, 129, 161–62; on Catholic social thought, 156; common good and, 136, 137; communism and, 5, 185; conscience and, 130; democracy and, 120, 129, 139; *Dignitatis Humanae* and, 122; economic liberty and, 122, 132; on historical change, 173; on human capital, 62, 63, 127, 128; human subjectivity and, 131; on labor, 87; ordered liberty and, 121; as philosopher of creativity, 131–32; in Poland, 84; *Reconciliation and Penance* (1984), 193; religious liberty and, 122, 132; *Rerum Novarum* and, 133; on shared work, 63–64; social doctrine of, 4; socialism and, 21–22, 73–74, 135, 136; on solidarity, 83, 129, 138, 148, 151, 156; *Sollicitudo Rei Socialis* (1987), 79, 135, 177; *Theology of the Body*, 7–8; *Veritas Splendor* (1993), 210; on wages, 74, 76; on wealth, 131. See also *Centesimus Annus*; *Laborem Exercens*; Wojtyła, Karol

Johnstown Flood (Pennsylvania), 275

Judaism, Jews, 51, 69, 81, 131, 175, 284; conscience and worship of, 68–69, 204; human story in, 56, 57, 62; John Paul II and, 132

Julea Ward Freedom of Conscience Act (Michigan, 2012), 204

Julian (Roman emperor), 257

Julius Caesar, 65, 66, 73, 109

justice, 19; charity and, 200, 201, 252–64. *See also* general justice; social justice

Kant, Immanuel, 41, 44, 291n11, 312n5

Kennedy, John F., 34

Kierkegaard, Søren, 66

King, Martin Luther, Jr., 282

Kinnock, Neil, 129

know-how, 28, 61, 86, 122, 126, 127, 144, 153, 178 191, 294n8. *See also* human capital

Kołakowski, Leszek, 43, 177

Komorowski, Bronisław, 84–85

labor, 18; creativity and, 62–63; unions and, 23, 71, 83; socialism and, 80, 100–101

Laborem Exercens (John Paul II, 1982), 74, 131, 142; capital and, 62, 132, 142

Last Judgment, 16

Latin America, 147, 165; capitalism in, 167; left in, 149, 151; liberation theology in, 149, 191; poor and poverty in, 146, 152, 164, 191–92

law, legislation: criminal courts and, 44; Hayek and, 37, 41, 48; rule of law, 42, 59, 264

left, 148, 150, 188; Catholic, 151, 154; *Centesimus Annus* and, 149, 151, 157; Leo XIII and, 91; on social justice, 7, 23. *See also* Communism, Communists; Socialism, Socialists

Lenin, Vladimir, 39, 47

Leo XIII, 3, 9, 18, 21, 86, 88, 95, 108, 173; *Aeterni Patris* (1879), 93; associations and, 118, 156, 196; on cause of wealth, 60; charity and, 261–62; civil society and, 118, 156; first social encyclical and, 5; individualism and, 274; influences on, 90; on liberalism, 31; on natural rights, 69; on private property, 72; socialism and, 73, 96, 98–102, 155, 196, 296n30; on social justice

as new virtue, 2, 15, 16, 110, 120; on
state's power, 71, 91, 112; studies U.S.
Constitution, 27–28; on wages, 74.
See also *Rerum Novarum*
Lewis, C. S., 32–33
liberalism, liberals, 7, 9, 10, 51, 281;
Catholic social thought and, 156, 201;
Hayek and, 53; Leo XIII on, 3, 104;
Mill and, 96; Pius XI on, 110, 118;
Rawlsian, 261
liberation theology, theologians, 149, 191,
192, 193, 195, 268; creation theology
vs., 177–79
Liberatore, Matteo, S.J., 91
libertarianism, 9, 147
liberty, liberties, 27, 37–38, 69, 71, 96,
122, 125, 138, 196, 285; civil, 18, 284;
of conscience, 130, 203–4; God-given,
56–57, 60, 67, 126, 136, 294n5; Hayek
and, 37, 48, 53, 54; John Paul II and,
8, 121, 129–31, 195; law and, 20, 48,
130; ordered, 121–22, 130; political,
140, 178; religious, 18, 28, 69, 122,
130, 142; socialism and, 7, 99. *See also*
freedom
Lincoln, Abraham, 83; on freedom,
126–27; on invention, 63, 123–27,
143; John Paul II's echo of, 127–28,
142; "Lecture on Discoveries and
Inventions," 122–26; on patents and
copyrights, 122–23, 126, 143, 166; on
subsidiarity, 82, 114, 122
living wage, 38, 111, 146, 149, 225, 238;
right to, 74–77
Locke, John, 63, 292n23, 294n8
Lonergan, Bernard, S.J., 172

Machiavelli, Niccolò, 92, 93
MacIntyre, Alisdair, 231–32, 246, 277,
283
Madison, James, 67–68, 128, 136, 187,
284
Magisterium, 5, 167
Maritain, Jacques, 57, 173

market, markets, 40, 45, 54, 116, 117, 150,
151, 167, 263; capitalism and, 140,
147, 148, 150, 160; *Centesimus Annus*
and, 150, 151; forces of, 42, 147, 170;
free, 26, 87, 97, 128, 148; global, 64,
133, 152, 153; information from, 116,
152; order of, 291–92n18, 292n21;
regulation of, 114, 117; social economy
and, 107, 146; systems of, 45, 87, 115,
116, 117, 137, 146, 149, 171, 174
marriage, 10, 226, 234; collapse of, 201;
gay, 33, 205, 216; social justice and,
10, 220–36; state and, 185. *See also*
divorce; family, families
Marx, Karl, 47, 62, 71, 92, 95, 97
Marxism, Marxists, 47, 132, 134–35, 168,
170, 177, 195, 261, 267
Mason, George, 67–68
Massachusetts Commission Against
Discrimination (MCAD), 215
Matthew, Saint, 264; Gospel of, 15–16
McCabe, Herbert, 209
McCloskey, Deirdre, 255
McKnight, John, 245
media elites, 176
mercy, 2, 52, 201, 254, 257–58, 266, 286;
in Bible, 175; of God, 201, 236
merit, 41, 44, 90, 103, 270, 290n11,
292n18
Messner, Johannes, 89, 91–92
microcredit, 239, 243
Middle East, 59
Mill, John Stuart, 41–42, 47, 72, 85, 95,
96, 165
missionaries, 15, 168, 173, 258
Mont Pelerin Society, 53
morality, 37, 111, 113, 183, 185, 190, 214,
217, 257; moral capital and, 176–77;
moral imperative and, 61, 91, 96–98;
moral man and, 42, 57
Moreland, Michael P., 209–10
Moschella, Melissa, 211–12
Moses, 51
Mother Teresa, 258, 269, 271, 272

Mussolini, Benito, 17, 39, 107, 108, 109; Pius XI and, 113, 118, 173. *See also* Fascism, Fascists

Napoleon III, 165
National Association of Social Workers (NASW), 203, 208; Code of Ethics of, 204, 207
National Longitudinal Study of Adolescent Health, 221
natural laws, 56, 128
natural rights, 90, 99, 126, 224; protection of, 69, 169
Nazism, National Socialism, 5, 47, 81, 129
Nietzsche, Friedrich, 184, 209, 257–58
Nell-Breuning, Oswald von, 93, 114, 118; *Quadragesimo Anno* and, 19, 91, 107; on Pius XI, 113, 114, 117; social justice and, 89, 107, 108, 112, 114, 115, 118
New Zealand, 35, 242
Niebuhr, Reinhold, 41, 42, 185–90, 291n12
nonhistorical orthodoxy, 4–5, 6
nonpartisanship, 3
North Korea, 73
Norway, 34, 234
Novak, Michael, 4, 6, 7, 9, 11, 233; on *caritas*, 254, 255; social justice and, 3, 200, 225
Novus Ordo Seclorum, 27, 105
nuns, 15

Obama, Barack, 203, 212
Obamacare, 25
O'Reilly, John Boyle, 261

paganism, pagans, 184, 256–57, 258, 284
Paine, Thomas, 67
Pakaluk, Michael, 225–27, 231, 232, 233, 236
patch approach, 240, 241, 243, 277, 278, 280
Paul, Saint, 260
Paul VI, 67, 85, 120

Paulhus, Normand Joseph, 92
Pellegrino, Edmund, 215, 277
Perrin, Jacques, 89, 90, 92
Peru, 239
Phillips, Trevor, 212
Pilsudsky, Josef, 109
Pius XI, 3, 4, 9, 19, 88, 91, 173, 218; encyclicals of, 91, 93, 105, 106, 107; individualism and, 218, 274; liberalism and, 110, 114; Mussolini and, 112–13; peace and, 109, 110; social justice and, 3, 15, 16, 87, 106–20. See also *Quadragesimo Anno*; Ratti, Achille
Pius XII, 28, 120, 173
Planned Parenthood, 33
Plato, 30, 184
Plotinus, 184
Poland, Poles, 81, 109, 127,164; Communism in, 130, 140; John Paul II and, 129, 130; martial law in, 84–85, 131; *Polonia* and, 81, 177–78; solidarity in, 71, 83–85, 130, 138. *See also* John Paul II; *Solidarnosc*; Wojtyła, Karol
political economy, 22, 27, 192; *Caritas in Veritate* on, 157, 160; *Centesimus Annus* and, 129, 139; *Evangelii Gaudium* and, 167
poor, 174, 259; Catholic duty to help, 8; Christian concern for, 6–7; creative energy of, 263, 264; daily practice of helping, 10–11; government programs to help, 24; as Hugo's *les misérables*, 47; inevitability of, 96; Progressives and, 33; relief of, 174; reproductive rights of, 35; secular humanists and, 51; working, 75–76. *See also* poverty
popes, 3, 5, 17, 28; Holy See, 27, 28. See *also* encyclicals; *and names of individual popes*
Populorum Progressio (Paul VI, 1967), 156, 157
poverty, 240, 260, 263; American War on, 36; capitalism and, 8; causes of, 60; as disgrace, 97; federal level of, 24;

Leo XIII and, 98; living wage and, 75; as natural, 178; oppression and, 177; reduction of, 86; removal of, 61, 104; socialism as cure of, 72. *See also* poor

private property, 8, 17, 85, 140, 171, 263; right to, 71–74, 91, 240, 263; socialists and, 98, 99, 113–14

privilege, privileged, 35, 165, 166

professionalization of charity, 259, 260–61

Progressives, progressives, 17, 19, 32, 53, 153; agenda of, 33–35, Catholics as, 82, 149, 150; conscience and, 10, 203; modern, 21, 72, 190

Protestantism, Protestants, 132, 157, 165, 175, 186

Proverbs, 69

Puritans, 34, 176

Putnam, Robert, 9

Quadragesimo Anno (Pius XI, 1931), 5; canonization of social justice in, 17, 19, 86, 91, 93, 111, 112, 218; Nell-Breuning drafts, 107, 108; *Rerum Novarum* and, 5, 105

Quakers (Society of Friends), 186, 285

Rand, Ayn, 7, 257–58

Ratti, Achille, 109. *See also* Pius XI

Ratzinger, Joseph Aloisius, 157, 193. *See also* Benedict XVI

Reagan, Ronald, 75, 76, 84–85

reason, 41, 43, 68, 72, 93, 99, 100, 130, 184

Red Cross, 196, 275

regulatory pyramid, 246–49

relativism, 183, 185, 276

religion, 17–18, 37, 38, 104, 212

republics, 20–21, 22, 27, 172–73

Rerum Novarum (Leo XIII, 1891), 21, 86, 89–105; Catholic teachings and, 5; on cause of wealth, 60; charity in, 261–62; European social economy in, 18; as first social encyclical, 5, 80; John

Paul II on, 22, 80, 133, 145; on natural rights, 69; on private property, 72; socialism and, 73, 79; on wages, 74

responsive regulation, 242, 244

Richmond, Mary, 259

rights, 19, 24; of association, 69–71; in Catholic social teaching, 55–77; to intellectual property, 125; to living wage, 74–77; new civil, 34–35; to private property, 71–74, 85; reproductive, 34–35; to worship, 67–69. *See also* freedom; liberty, liberties

Röpke, Wilhelm, 173

Rorty, Richard, 29, 51, 179, 284

Rosmini, Antonio, 91, 295n8

Rousseau, Jean-Jacques, 90–91, 183, 184, 292

Russell, Bertrand, 29, 51, 179, 284

Russia, 5, 101–2, 188. *See also* Soviet Union

Sacramentum Mundi, 81, 89, 122

saints, 2, 16, 181, 197, 227, 237, 258, 272

Saint-Simon, Henri de, 165

Sandusky, Jerry, 229

Scalia, Antonin, 234

Schumann, Robert, 173

science, scientists, 43, 57, 62, 63, 66, 125; charity and, 259–60, 261, 265, 268, 279; laws of nature and, 56; social, 47, 54, 114, 118–19, 128, 139, 190, 206, 221–22, 230, 254. *See also* know-how; reason

scouts, 9, 173, 179

Second Vatican Council. *See* Vatican II

secular humanists, 51, 57, 170

self, 62, 79, 202, 217, 219; control of, 20, 193; giving of, 255, 256, 258, 260, 261, 269, 270; government by, 20, 43, 46, 50, 120, 196; in marriage, 226, 227, 233, 235, 236; professional use of, 246, 280; self-interest, 30, 50, 93, 136, 137, 311n1; in social encyclicals, 7

separation of church and state, 65–67

separation of powers, 26, 28

Settlement House movement, 230, 261, 279–80

sexual expressionism (sexualityism), 206, 231, 233

sexual revolution, 183, 201, 223, 233; family structure and, 220, 234; Mary Eberstadt and, 185, 222, 232; government and, 231, 234. *See also* abortion; birth control; rights: reproductive; sexual expressionism

Shakespeare, William, 226, 233, 236

Sherman Antitrust Act (United States), 118, 297n19

sin, 9, 20, 88, 179, 180–97, 228, 236; sinful structures and, 191–95

slavery, slaves, 20, 98, 122, 125, 284

Slovakia, Slovaks, 4, 16, 22, 121

Smith, Adam, 26, 27, 97

social capital, 9, 243, 275, 278; social justice and, 244, 274, 279

social charity, 2, 15, 87, 107, 114

social clubs, 23. *See also* associationism, associations

Social Democratic party, 38, 107, 120, 148

social destination of goods, 79, 85–86, 133

social encyclicals, 3, 5, 7

Socialism, Socialists, 16, 19, 39, 43, 80, 86, 95, 96, 154, 261; *Centesimus Annus* and, 139, 140, 151; Eastern European, 150, 173; as economic system, 38, 72, 174, 290n7; failures of, 115–16, 129, 133, 155; forced equality and, 102–4; John Paul II and, 21–22, 73, 79–81, 129, 132, 134–36, 146; Leo XIII and, 73, 79, 96, 98–102, 105, 196; Pius XI and, 5, 112–14, 118; poverty and, 72, 175; social justice vs., 2, 91, 113, 118, 275, 295n8

social justice, 7, 17, 115; definitions of, 22; functional vagueness of, 1, 15, 39; as habit of heart, 24–28; history of, 17–21, 93; intellectual disrepute of,

38–39; as mirage (Hayek), 37–48; Pius XI and, 15, 91; rightly understood, 3, 9, 26–27, 28, 49, 50, 54; in social work education, 3, 10; striving toward, 16; as term, 1–2, 17, 29; as virtue, 2, 16, 20, 22, 38, 51, 54, 79, 90, 91, 107, 111, 112, 115, 119, 120, 196, 200, 219, 223–25, 228, 233, 235, 237, 244, 245, 266, 273–77, 283, 290n11; wrongly understood, 40–48

Social Security, 36, 281

social work, workers: accreditation standards of, 3, 22, 244, 246, 248; challenges of, 235–36, 269, 270; charity and, 253, 254, 258, 259, 261, 267, 268; conscience and, 102–3, 204, 207–10, 213–14; dichotomies in, 200; education for, 3, 10, 260, 271; empowerment and, 154, 219, 224; Family Group Conference and, 242, 247; marriage and, 222, 223, 225, 230, 236; moral agency of, 214–16; patch and, 240; practice of, 200, 237, 238, 246, 246, 251, 268; professionalism and, 259, 260, 267; secular world of, 233, 234, 257, 260; social justice and, 3, 201, 224, 228, 235, 237, 238, 262, 276; theory of, 200; threats to conscience of, 204–7; virtue and, 200, 201, 231, 23–36, 246, 253, 269–70, 277–83, 312n5

Socrates, 30, 51, 184

soft despotism, 94–95, 139

solidarity, 51, 55, 78, 83–85, 194, 201; associations and, 71, 130, 138; Benedict XVI and, 159; *caritas* and, 71, 134; *Centesimus Annus* and, 129, 151; John Paul II and, 138, 148, 156

Solidarnosc (Solidarity), 71, 84–85, 130, 138, 282

Sollicitudo Rei Socialis (John Paul II, 1987): initiative in, 132, 135, 142; subjectivity in, 79, 177

Sorel, Georges, 95

soul, 20, 64, 68, 90, 178, 179, 190, 229, 235, 276, 285; *caritas* and, 57, 58, 255, 266, 269; conscience and, 68, 208; government and, 66, 81, 269; John Paul II and, 84; labor and, 62, 80; social justice and, 90; virtues and, 246, 267. *See also* spirit

South Korea, 61, 73

Soviet Union, 32, 60, 81, 85, 98, 102, 155, 173. *See also* Russia

spirit, 59, 60, 68; life of, 17, 66, 71; work and, 62–63. *See also* Holy Spirit; soul

Stalin, Joseph, 39, 109, 120; Ukrainians murdered by, 17, 102, 108

Stand With Children, 234

Stark, Rodney, 256, 263

state, the, 34, 40, 82, 100, 175; big government and, 24, 25, 34, 55, 66; bureaucratic, 11, 39; charity and, 262; as Leviathan, 23, 94, 196, 200, 217, 237. *See also* welfare state

Sturzo, Don Luigi, 119, 173

subjectivity, 62, 132, 282, 294n1; creative, 79, 122, 129, 131, 132, 135, 142, 144, 151; human, 79, 157; of individual, 22, 62, 79–80, 120, 129, 131, 132, 134, 142, 144, 177; John Paul II and, 22, 177, 282; of society, 22, 78, 80–81, 131, 136, 151, 177

subjects vs. citizens, 3, 22

subsidiarity, 71, 78, 81–83, 159, 201, 230; as antidote to welfare state, 158, 159; Benedict XVI and, 159, 160; conscience and, 216–18; families and, 230, 245; John Paul II and, 82, 83; Pius XI and, 114; *Sacramentum Mundi* and, 81–82, 122; state and, 55, 119, 216–18

suffering, 15, 42, 43, 51, 101, 269, 285

suicide, 205, 221

Sunday school, 20

Swedish Level of Living Survey, 221

Sweifach, Jay, 207, 208

Taiwan, 164

Taliban, 188

Tammany Hall, 35–36

Taparelli d'Azeglio, Luigi, S.J., 90, 91, 122, 295n8

Temporary Assistance for Needy Families (TANF), 51, 52

Ten Commandments, 68

Tertullian, 272

theology of economics, 173–74

Third World, 161–62, 168, 263; John Paul II and, 122, 129, 133, 140, 146, 148–49, 151–53, 170

Thomas Aquinas, Saint, 7, 101, 224; on charity, 58, 160; conscience and, 209–10; general justice and, 108, 224, 235, 266–67; on right of association, 69–70; Thomistic revival and, 93, 157

Thomas More, Saint, 187

Thoreau, Henry David, 203

Tocqueville, Alexis de: associations and, 23, 27, 53, 104, 120, 176, 275; democracy and, 27, 53, 120; *Democracy in America*, 104, 155; on individualism, 311n1; on religion and democracy, 17–18; on soft despotism, 94–95, 139

Tolstoy, Leo, 252–53

torture, 173, 179, 183

totalitarianism, 80, 88, 94, 110, 114, 130, 174, 276; anti-totalitarianism, 66; Communist, 32, 218; compassion and, 36; democracy and, 185; soft, 218

Ukraine, Ukrainians, 17, 85, 102, 108, 188

United Nations Declaration of Human Rights, 205

United Nations Declaration of the Rights of the Child, 205

United Nations Human Rights Commission, 34

United States: Catholic bishops of, 82; common good in, 32; communitarianism in, 175, 176; elderly in, 36; as first developing nation, 4, 92; religion and liberty in, 18, 28. *See also* America, Americans

U.S. Congress, 24, 25, 68, 125, 142

U.S. Constitution, 143, 176; conscience and, 202; First Amendment to, 67–68; Leo XIII and, 27–28; natural right of authors and inventors, 123, 125; Preamble of, 115, 175; social justice and, 295n8, 300–301n5

U.S. Department of Health and Human Services (HHS) Mandate, 203, 204, 206, 211, 212, 231

U.S. Supreme Court, 133, 227; on marriage, 230, 234

universities. *See* colleges and universities

utopia, utopian, utopianism, 38, 111, 179, 187, 224, 225–26; *caritas* and, 267, 286; marriage and, 225–26; social, 47, 300n5; social justice and, 267, 279; social work and, 270

Vatican II, 173; common good and, 31, 32; *Dignitatis Humanae* and, 122; *Gaudium et Spes* and, 8; John Paul II and, 5–6; John XXIII and, 34; *Sacramentum Mundi* and, 81–82

Veritas Splendor (John Paul II, 1993), 210

virtue, 60, 63, 105, 119, 132, 140, 145, 182, 183, 196, 267, 270; charity as, 58, 134, 253, 254–58, 260, 262, 265, 266, 269–72; common good and, 137, 228, 234, 266; democracy as, 54, 186, 275; ethics and, 279, 312n5; faith and, 270, 271; hypocrisy and, 181, 182; justice as, 52, 92, 118, 235, 254, 262, 266, 272; Leo XIII and, 197; marriage and, 223, 225, 231, 235, 236; moral character and, 90, 93, 96, 97, 103, 110, 115, 141, 151, 189, 210, 235; as practice, 52, 182, 193, 219; professional helpers and, 238–46, 269; regulatory pyramid and, 249, 250; social, 274, 275, 293;

social justice as, 51, 54, 79, 90, 91, 107, 111, 112, 115, 119, 120, 196, 200, 219, 223–25, 228, 233, 235, 237, 244, 245, 266, 273–77, 283, 290n11; social work and, 200, 201, 231, 235, 236, 246, 253, 269–70, 277–83, 312n5; solidarity and, 83–85, 194

Vischer, Robert K., 203, 217

Vogt, Brandon, 2, 237, 283

Walesa, Lech, 83–84, 138, 282

Ward, Julea, 204

War on Poverty, 1, 36

Washington, George, 21, 67, 128, 273

wealth, cause of, 60–61, 86, 131, 174, 178, 191

welfare state, 7, 24, 33, 51–52, 133, 151, 158, 263, 268. *See also* state, the

Wojtyła, Karol, 62, 79, 81, 120, 130–32, 134–35, 157, 282. *See also* John Paul II

Wolterstorff, Nicholas, 262

women: abandoned, 97; associations and, 118, 119, 239; charity and, 255, 258, 259; employment of, 76; empowerment of, 239; free, 191, 285; as head of households, 75; liberation of, 47; marriage and, 222, 227, 236; mortality of, 160; poor, 238, 239; religion and, 185, 207; sexuality of, 206, 213; social organizations for, 23; solidarity and, 84; as unmarried mothers, 36, 52; virtue and, 181; welfare programs and, 51–52

work, community of, 63–64

World War I, 22, 37, 53, 106, 173

World War II, 53, 140, 149, 164, 167, 173; horrors of, 179; Poland in, 81

YMCA, 20

Yunus, Muhammad, 238, 240, 263